the FILM EDITING ROOM HANDBOOK

Second Edition

the FILM EDITING ROOM HANDBOOK

Coláiste Oideachais Mhuire Gan Smal Luimneach

Second Edition

Norman Hollyn

LONE
EAGLE

THE FILM EDITING ROOM HANDBOOK
Or, How To Manage The Near Chaos of the Cutting Room

Lone Eagle Publishing Company
2337 Roscomare Road, Suite Nine
Los Angeles, CA 90077-1815
310/471-8066 • 1/800-FILMBKS

Printed in the United States of America

First Lone Eagle Printing—April 1990

Cover and book designed by Heidi Frieder

Photo of author by Janet Conn

Library of Congress Cataloging in Publication Data
Hollyn, Norman
    The Film Editng Room Handbook/Norman Hollyn—2nd Ed.
       p. c.m.
    Includes bibliographical references
    ISBN 0-943728-33-9
       1. Motion Pictures—Editing. I. Title
    TR899.H64 1990   89-77252
    778.5'35—dc20   CIP

10 9 8 7 6 5 4 3
96 95 94 93 92

iv

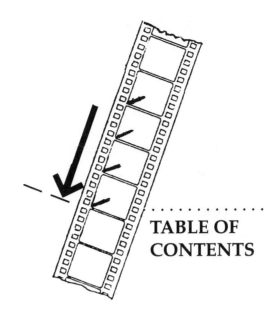

TABLE OF
CONTENTS

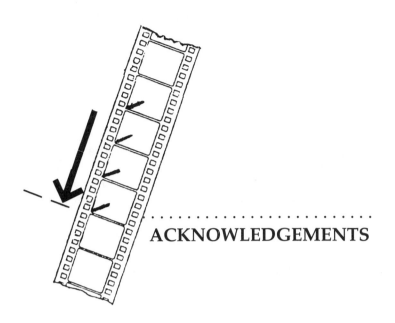

ACKNOWLEDGEMENTS

I have yet to have an editing room job in which I did not learn something about editing, filmmaking, or people. Many of the people I've worked with don't even know how much I've been able to learn from them. Maybe now they will. I want to thank them all for those experiences. I would also like to thank the rooting section for this book, in both its original and present editions — Bob, for kind words and sage advice (he's getting sager all the time), Lou, for putting us all together the first time, Joan, for getting behind me this second time (and pushing), Andy, Adam and everyone else who offered corrections and criticism on ways to improve this new edition, Irwin Simon and Suzana Peric for a speedy and efficient loan of editing equipment and photography space, Rick Roberts, Lori Ingle and a very tired Mark Speer for emergency Ediflex guidance, and my Mom and Dad for their continued support.

There is also no way that I can properly express enough thanks to my wife, Janet (who also took most of the photographs in the book). She did most everything that everyone mentioned above did for me, but she did it continuously, selflessly, and in quantities far greater than I deserved. I can never thank her enough.

And a final thank you to a person who wasn't even around to be thanked when the first edition of this book was published—my daughter Elizabeth. She's given me more opportunity to re-examine what is important in my own life than anyone else ever could.

Believe me, the result of all of these people's help is a better and richer book than I could ever have written by myself. Thank you everyone.

Norman Hollyn
Los Angeles, California

INTRODUCTION
TO THE
NEW EDITION

In the five years since this book was first published (and the seven years since it was first written) many changes have raced through the film editing world. Electronic/video editing has, in a few cases, begun to take over from film-based techniques, though the real change in this regard is that it is now possible to see the day when editors and directors will be able to make the choice as to whether they would like to cut on film or video. The number of film school graduates entering the editing room has increased dramatically, though the knowledge they bring with them ranges from spotty to adequate. The number of films produced in the United States and Great Britain has actually decreased, crowding the already swollen job market. The types of films produced have also changed—an entire sub–industry of smaller, independent feature films has come and gone in the interim, and documentaries are, sadly, becoming an endangered species.

Editing, like the rest of the film business, has had to adapt to these changes, though it is doing so very slowly. Editors have had to learn some new technology. Assistant editors have had to learn new techniques to go with this technology. But, when all is said and done, the basic skills needed to make an assistant editor a good assistant editor have changed very little. There is still the need for organization, planning and a pleasant personality.

As a result, much of this book remains the same as its first edition. I've made some changes throughout the book — correcting a few errors, making the approach to the systems discussed in it more applicable to work on either coast of the United States as well as in the United Kingdom, and taking the opportunity presented to me by my new publisher to expand on some points that I had to over simplify in the original. But, at its core, film editing is still film editing. And all of the skills and systems which have been developed over many decades to make the putting together of thousands of little pieces of celluloid go smoothly, are just as applicable as they were five years ago. On second thought, make that "twenty-five years ago." On third thought, make that "when assistant editors first started assistant editing."

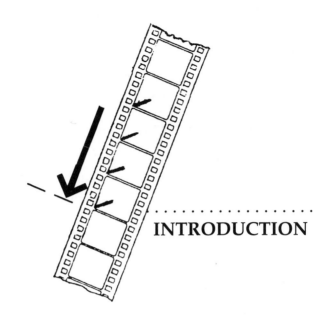

INTRODUCTION

At the end of my first week working on my first feature film I rushed out to the producer's bank to cash my very first paycheck. Though I saw long lines there I was not dismayed. I had in my hands a check from United Artists/ Marvin Worth Productions that proclaimed in bold letters: *Lenny*. I was working on a film with Dustin Hoffman! Surely the bank officers would usher me to the front of the line and give me my money without so much as a glance at my identification.

Of course, it didn't work out that way. Not only did I have to wait in line with everyone else, but when it finally was my turn, the teller refused to give me any money because I didn't have an account with the bank.

Thus I learned my first and perhaps most valuable lesson about working in the film business: film editing is a job —make no mistake about that. After all of the mumbo–jumbo that we read about the movies and their glamour, it is a bit of a shock to learn that people working in moviemaking are judged by the same criteria as the rest of the world: how well they get the job done. Film work, for the majority of those in it, promises no more "perks" than any other job. Your standing comes from how well you do the job, not just from the fact that you are doing it.

The second lesson to be learned about film editing is that there are a lot of ways to get the job done. Line up twenty different editors or assistant editors and you'll probably get twenty different ways of organizing a cutting room. Many ways work, some do not, but the worst thing that you can do is attempt to impose the system that worked on film 'A' onto the very different film 'B'. One of the tests of a good editing crew member is flexibility.

That leads to lesson number three — it takes a certain type of person to be comfortable in the field of editing. Flexible working habits are just the first necessity. You have to be able to work long days, long weeks, and long months in a small, dark, crowded room with the same small group of people. You have to be able to concentrate on the tiniest detail and never give up until it is right. Editing can be an obsession, good editing almost certainly is. The editing of any film usually requires large amounts of energy, not all of it well or gratifyingly spent. To work under these conditions takes real dedication.

Anyone interested in a career in film editing would be well advised to internalize these rules before stepping foot into a cutting room. For, while I try to talk in this book about film editing rooms and the nuts–and–bolts techniques used in running them, I could never write about how to *be* a film editor. You either are or you're not — or you learn how to be, by living in an editing room day after long day, month after long month.

If you are interested in editing as a way to meet people and become a director or a producer, forget about working there. Some editors eventually make those transitions but that comes after years of editing and being good at it. And the only way to do both of those things is to love what you are doing.

If you are a person who gets bored by details and constant repetition, you can also forget editing as a profession. Eventually, editors get past the most mundane details, but until they reach that point these details are their life, and it helps to be able to deal with that.

If you are a person who needs a separate, private life, you might as well forget most forms of editing. Fourteen–hour days and six– or seven–day weeks leave very little time for life as others know it. Unless our friends and loved ones are as flexible as you are, film editing's hours will leave you (and them) very unhappy.

But, all of that having been said, I can tell you this — once you do it, it is all worth it.

And let that be lesson number four.

This book is written primarily for those who have an active interest in how a professional cutting room operates. To help those who are thinking of making it their career, I will often be quite detailed, though this may give more information than the normal film student would like. But there is an additional purpose to this. Editing room procedures have been developed over many years to expedite the editing process. There are, therefore, many techniques which could be of help to *all* filmmakers, regardless of their budget or the type of film that they are doing. However, since few film teachers or professors are also professional film editors these techniques are rarely taught. This book will, I hope, give film students, independent filmmakers, and others enough knowledge about editing room procedures that they can decide for themselves just how they can best organize *their* editing process to conserve the time and money that is usually in short supply

Film buffs will probably be both fascinated and overwhelmed by the sheer mass of technical data here. To them, my apologies. But I believe that to truly understand the art of film, the *modus operandi* of the film editor must be understood as well. In the years to come, as increasing sophistication opens the film audience up to an awareness of film editing, those film buffs who know *how* it is done will be in a much better position to say *why* it was done.

A friend of mine describes the assistant's job as "primarily cataloguing work."

An assistant editor is defined, under the IATSE Local 771 (East Coast) contract as "a person who is directly assigned to assist the Editor(s) and a person who, among other duties, may be engaged in: synchronizing dailies, taking notes at screenings, obtaining cutting room facilities, breaking down daily takes, pulling out and assembling selected takes, making trims, ordering opticals, and performing other preparatory work in editing rooms."

The IATSE Local 776 (West Coast) contract defines the assistant as "... a person who is assigned to assist an Editor. His duties shall be such as are assigned to him and performed under the immediate direction, supervision and responsibility of the editor to who he is assigned to assist."

Frankly, though I dislike all of these definitions, I much prefer the last one (despite its innate sexism). The assistant's main task, as I see it, is to make sure that the cutting room runs smoothly for the editor. Period.

The implications of that statement are what this book is all about. Assistant editing always seems to boil down to this one question: "How can I make this run better?"

Keeping the editing room functioning depends upon many things. One of the most important is controlling the film. An average film prints about twenty miles of film. A good assistant should be able to locate, almost immediately, pieces as short as one–sixteenth of an inch long (one frame in 35mm). To this end, editing staffs have, over the years, developed a number of methods for logging, storing, and retrieving footage. As anyone who has ever looked for editing room work and been denied it can tell you, this is what is called "the system". As a rule, I (and almost every other editor I know of) would rather hire someone who knows this system than someone who doesn't, all other things being equal. As we shall soon see, however, there is no real mystery to this system; it is all rather logical and straightforward.

So why would people rather hire someone who knows the system? Simply put, the real test of an assistant editor comes when the editor is cutting fast and furiously. There is rarely time for the assistant to step back and *think* about how to handle new situations. The more that you have internalized this system (and the more you have internalized the exceptions to the system) the more that you will be able to serve the editor well during these constant crisis situations. This is where the experienced (and good) editing staff earns its salary.

Network, for example, was nearly a textbook case in proper editing room procedure. Everything seemed so easy to me. It was a dialogue film, for starters. The director, Sidney Lumet, shot in a straightforward style using only a single camera (except in some of the television studio/control room scenes). There were no complicated effects or opticals. Lumet shot very little footage; usually no more than 3000 feet (about twenty-seven minutes) were printed per day. The script supervisor, Kay Chapin, was a model of efficiency; her notes were explicit, fast, and accurate. I cannot remember a day when the picture and sound crews forgot to get slates for syncing purposes, or when their reports were inaccurate or misleading. There was only one editor on the film, Alan Heim, and he was wonderfully efficient. He worked on an upright Moviola, cutting primarily in the order that the scenes had been shot. Dailies were shown every evening after the day's shoot so we had plenty of time to prepare for them and still go about the business of cutting the picture.

Less than one week after the completion of shooting there was a first cut of the film for Lumet to look at. And no wonder. The wheels of the entire process had worked exceedingly smoothly, helping us in the editing room do our jobs very fast and just as effortlessly.

But *Network* was a rarity. Other films, with equally fine crews, can be very problematic.

Hair, for instance, was an organizational task of immense proportions. First, it was a musical, and that complicated the task. Then, the director, Milos Forman, was shooting with multiple cameras (most often with two, but on some days there were as many as seven) and shooting a lot of footage. Days where we had to sync 10,000 feet of film were very common; there were several days when we had 25,000 feet. Because of the subject matter of the film as well as Forman's personal style, much of the footage was neither as predictable nor as easily categorized as that from *Network*. Despite a superb script supervisor (Nancy Hopton), keeping up with the film was a herculean task. Not surprisingly, there were days when her notes, the camera and sound reports, and the processed footage and sound transfers, bore little resemblance to each other. There was one, then two, and then three editors on the film, all working on KEM flatbeds. Flatbeds, as we shall see, are more difficult to organize in general, but the fact that three editors were cutting at once added to the assistant's tasks. Dailies were often shown in the mid-afternoon on the set, and when the film was shooting out on location, the footage would not arrive in the cutting room until the afternoon. In both of these cases this gave the editing staff no more than a few hours to sync the dailies.

In short, *Hair* tested the organization of its editing crew to the utmost. The fact that we kept everything moving, accessible, and pleasant is a testament to what good, experienced crews can do with a good, workable system.

But organizing and accessing footage is only one part of an assistant's mandate to "keep things moving". He or she must be the editing crew's link to the outside world, interacting with the suppliers, laboratories, job seekers, and the general chaos that arrives at the editing room door every day.

Much of the assistant's day is spent on the phone making things happen. Equipment always seems to be breaking down; labs never seem to give you exactly what you've asked for; supplies always seem to be used up too fast; job seekers always seem to show up with their resumes just as the director walks in the door; and the editor *always* seems to need the piece of film that you just so happen to be working on for another purpose. The assistant editor must be able to cope with it all, sort it out, and make it all work on top of that. As we say in the business: "That's what they pay us the teeny–tiny bucks for."

The task of organizing an editing room is generally assigned to an assistant editor. For that reason, we will examine editing from the assistant's point of view in this book. There are three types of editors in feature filmmaking: picture, sound (which is further divided into several sub-categories), and music. Each of the three assistants perform some tasks that are similar to the others', and some which are very different. Because the first assistant picture editor is usually on the film before any other assistant, it is he or she who often has the information and the experience that the other assistants need. For this reason, there is an unwritten chain of command in the editing room. Both the sound and music departments maintain their own semi–autonomous crews, with apprentices taking direction from assistants who take direction from editors. The picture department has a similar chain of command, but it is the responsibility of the picture department to provide the sound and music people with all the help and information that they can give and, in exchange, the sound and music departments report to the picture department. Thus, the supervising picture editor is regarded as the ultimate editorial arbiter (though, of course, that editor is responsible to higher powers, like the producer and director).

Regardless of what kind of film you work on, you will

find that the tasks of these three departments have to get done one way or another. In many documentaries and low–budget films, one person does the work of all three departments. In still other situations, the editor functions as his or her own assistant. But, no matter who is doing the work, those tasks always exist in roughly the same chronological order as in the high-budget feature film.

You will find this book organized, more or less, in this chronological order — the order that the assistant will normally have to deal with the problems. As you read about how to make a cutting room work, therefore, you will also get a tour of the filmmaking process itself, as seen through the editor's eyes.

What you will not find in this book is a discussion of the aesthetics of film editing except as they influence the assistant's job. There are already several books and articles that talk about that subject (for a list of some of these works, see the bibliography). But what I hope becomes apparent from this book is that there is also an "aesthetics of assistant editing". There are good and bad ways to organize, there are smart and stupid ways to try to keep things moving. And when everything is working properly, the organization has a beauty all its own.

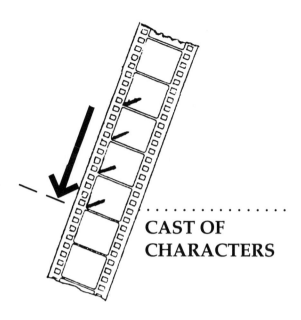

CAST OF CHARACTERS

Throughout this book, I refer to a core group of people who work in the editing rooms of our fictional film, *Silent Night, Silent Cowboy*. For your convenience, here is a list of who they are and what their functions on the film are.

DIRECTOR ....ADAM FREE

EDITOR.. WENDY LIBRE

ASSISTANT EDITOR ....YOU

APPRENTICE EDITOR ....PHILIP SPRING

MUSIC EDITOR ....NATE HIGH

ASSISTANT MUSIC EDITOR ....BETTY BOUND

SUPERVISING SOUND EDITOR ....CHARLES "CHUCK" LONE

ASSISTANT SOUND EDITOR ....LIZ CLEAR

1

EDITING WITHIN THE FILMMAKING PROCESS

Making a movie is often compared to running a war. It is a huge, complicated process, involving hundreds of people who must all be in the right place at the right time. They are all involved in their own chains of command with one or two leaders at the very top who determine, for right or for wrong, the course of their work. It is an exhausting process that is not often very fulfilling until the film is complete and viewable.

Editing is just one part of the movie–making battle-field but it is for me one of the most important parts, since it is where all of the disparate elements come together. Whoever controls the editing process (and this can be the direc-tor, the producer, the distributor, or, in a few cases, the editor) controls how the film is presented to the public. That person can, with the changes that can be made through editing, save or ruin a film. If the shooting process is one of creating, the editing process is one of *re*creating.

The overall filmmaking process is divided into three handy categories—pre-production, production, and post-production. Much has been written about the general process, and I won't attempt to delve very deeply into it, but here is a brief description of the tortuous road that a film must take to get to your neighborhood theatre.

Pre-production

The very earliest stage of moviemaking begins with an idea. Either a writer, producer, director or studio executive gets an idea for a film which is then sold to a movie company. As soon as the money is exchanged, the writer begins writing and the other facets of the production begin to come together. A director must be chosen, if none is already involved. A cast and crew are hired. Chief among these is the production manager, who will supervise the day-to-day operations for the producer. It is this production manager (sometimes called the line producer) who determines the actual budget and shooting schedule, supervises the obtaining of locations and equipment, makes most of the deals with the crew members (cast salaries and some heads of departments are handled by the producer) and, in general, makes sure that everything will be in place for the first day of shooting.

Production

When that day arrives, a battery of people descend on the set. On *Four Friends*, there were days when over 120 cast and crew were working. On *Cotton Club* there were often days when we had that many crew members alone (not to mention the dozens of cast, extras, and dancers; for a total over 250). There are departments to handle every conceivable job—from lighting the set to providing the cigarette lighters that the actors will use, from supplying bushes and shrubs to training the cats, dogs, sheep and cattle that may be used, and from driving the cars that transport the crew members to managing the special effects that will make it seem to rain or snow on cue.

While all of this chaos is occurring on the set, the editor and staff are quietly working away in another location, perhaps even another city. They are working so that the people on the set can see the results of the previous day's work (called the *rushes* or *dailies*). At the same time, they are beginning to cut the film.

Requests flood in from the set. "We need to reshoot a scene, how was the lead character wearing his tie?" or "The sound on one take last night wasn't very good, do we need to get a wild line?" Each question is important, and the answer can't come too soon. And, all the while, the film is being edited together.

Post-production

When the film is finished shooting, the crew goes off to find other work and the director returns to the editing room and, after a week or so, screens the cut that the editor has been working on during the shooting. Afterwards, they begin recutting the film, attempting to bring out what is good in the film and trying to minimize what is not. There are screenings after each version (or *cut*) is completed and, slowly, a film emerges from the mass of raw material shot on the set.

Publicity people from the distributor begin to make plans for the publicity campaign—posters, trailers (those "coming attractions" you see in movie theatres), television spots, promotions, etc., etc.

Sound editors are hired to begin work on the sound effects and dialogue where the soundtrack needs to be cleaned up. If some of the lines need to be redone for clarity, members of the cast are brought into a recording studio to rerecord the lines. A composer is hired and a music editor assists in creating a score for the film.

Finally the film's sound is mixed together into one soundtrack for the film's release. The original negative is cut to match the editor's cuts and the color is corrected on every shot used. The picture and the soundtrack are then *married* onto one piece of film and the first full screening of the movie can take place!

After that, the film opens and (everyone hopes) is very successful. All of the editing crew members can then go off of some badly needed vacations or onto other work on other films.

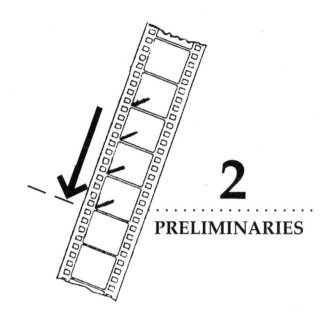

2

PRELIMINARIES

The first time I ever entered a feature film cutting room, I was looking for work. I had heard of a film called *The Taking of Pelham One Two Three* that needed an apprentice film editor. I had gone over the few film books that I could find trying to gather enough information so I wouldn't seem like a complete dunce when I went up for an interview. I called the editor, Jerry Greenberg, made an appointment, got reasonably well dressed—but not *too* dressed (mustn't look too green, I thought), and arrived about five minutes early on the appointed day.

I took only two steps into the cutting room before I realized just how useless all of my reading preparation had been. From ceiling to floor on several walls of the room were stacked hundreds of white boxes, each labeled with one of three or four colors of tape. Some boxes had red writing on them, some had black. On each of the editing tables was stacked an array of equipment and supplies that none of the books had mentioned. A stack of looseleaf notebooks lay open on a table and though I couldn't read anything in them,

I suspected that even if I could, I wouldn't be able to understand a thing.

No one had prepared me for the sheer awesome
complexity of the thing.

I still think of that day when I see job seekers visit the
cutting rooms where I work. What now seems simple and
logical to me must look frighteningly complex to anyone
seeing it for the first time.

How does a professional cutting room look? Depending on the film's budget, the cutting room may actually be
several rooms. Or it may be the back of someone's home or
office. But whatever the situation, every cutting room has
many things in common — they all have a place to store the
film, they all have a place to work on the film, and they all
must have the equipment to do both adequately. Figure 2.1
shows a typical editing room.

FIGURE 2.1 *A typical editing room using an upright Moviola (the usual
cutter Moviola is not shown.) The editor has attached a large velvet cloth
below the picture gate, on the right side of the Moviola, to protect the film
from rubbing against the Moviola and scratching.*

An average cutting room on a medium budget feature film begins with a place for the editor to do his or her work. The editor will need an editing machine or two, an editing table complete with all of his or her favorite supplies, the film logbooks, a series of trim barrels, and as much room as possible. Let's examine each of these in turn.

An Editing Machine Or Two

There are two types of editing machines common in today's cutting rooms: *uprights*, usually called *Moviolas®*; and *flatbeds*, called variously, *KEMs®*, *Steenbecks®*, *Moviola® flatbeds*, or by any number of other manufacturers' names.

The Moviola has been *the* editing machine for many years in the film business and, at least in 35mm, it is still a very popular choice. It retains this loyalty for several reasons: (1) most editors working today learned on these machines and old habits die hard; (2) it is much cheaper to buy and rent Moviolas than flatbeds, making them the preferred choice for filmed television and low-budget films; and (3) they make certain kinds of editing easier. (Sound and music editing is, in my experience, easier on uprights—they are easier to thread with short pieces and they stop on a dime.) In addition, as we shall see later, setting up a movie's logging system is easier for an upright than for a flatbed and, therefore, preferable when on a low budget or an abbreviated time frame.

Basically, a Moviola is an instrument which pulls the separate rolls of picture and soundtrack from reels on the bottom of the machine to the top, either independently or in synchronization. One of the first things an apprentice editor usually learns is how to thread a Moviola for the editor, and it's no wonder—next to his or her hands, the Moviola is the editor's most important physical tool. In fact, with the best editors, their hands actually become part of their Moviolas.

There are several types of Moviolas. Picture editors use two of them. The first is the kind shown in Figure 2.2, sometimes called a *takeup Moviola*. The second is often called

FIGURE 2.2 *An upright Moviola with reels for the takeup of film (on the right) and soundtrack (on the left). Note that the editor has placed strips of black tape at the top and bottom of the picture head in order to properly mask off the 1.85:1 screen ratio, even though the full–frame has a ratio of 1.33:1.*

FIGURE 2.3 A cutter Moviola has no gates above or below the picture head. This makes it softer on the film. The film and track are hand–held and fed through their proper heads off of the Moviola hand roll.

a *cutter Moviola* or, simply, a *cutter* (*see* Figure 2.3). It is much the same as the first except that is is designed to be softer on the film and faster to thread. The gentleness is a serious concern if you're going to be cutting a movie for six months or more—making, unmaking, and remaking splices constantly. The cutter has no take–up arms and no threading wheels above and below the picture gate and sound head. This means that it is simplicity itself to thread the machine — simply drop the picture in at the picture gate, the sound at the sound head and "let 'er rip" (figuratively, of course). This speed is of great help to the editor during the cutting process—the fewer physical encumbrances placed between the editor and the process of editing, the happier the editor will be.

Many editors like to cut with two Moviolas. This enables them to make their selections of good cutting points on one machine (usually the cutter) and then add them to the roll of already cut material on the other (either another cutter or a takeup Moviola). We'll see more about this later but, for now, it is only important to remember that these editors work best with two machines — one to keep the cut film on and one to select the next cut from.

The other type of machine now in use is the *flatbed*. Simply, a flatbed is an instrument which pulls the separate rolls of picture and soundtrack from left to right, either independently or in synchronization (*see* Figure 2.4). The flatbed has a few advantages over the upright. First, it is extremely gentle on film. As a result, it is my only choice for 16mm film — the upright can be so brutal that is a rare editor who can cut a complete film without damaging it at least once. Second, it has several fast-forward speeds. This makes it very easy to find one take or scene on large rolls of film, to rapidly compare two similar takes, or to make fine–cut corrections in an already cut film. A third advantage of the flatbed is its large screen size. Directors love this feature as it enables them to view the film without hunching over the

FIGURE 2.4 A flatbed editing machine, in this case a Steenbeck. The machine functions as the editor's editing table as well, with the editor making his or her cuts right at the machine rather than on a separate editing bench. Note the splicer and grease pencil on the front of the flatbed. A small rack for cores (and small rolls of film or fill on cores) is attached to the machine at the far left. (Photograph by the author)

editor's shoulder. Some editors, therefore, find this to be a bit of an encumbrance. Even these editors, however, will admit that a larger screen does help one to see things in a frame more clearly (though I find the focus sharper on an upright, precisely because of its smaller screen). Finally, compared to the upright, the flatbed is also very quiet, which makes it much nicer for screening. An editing room with more than one upright running can leave you wondering when the man with earplugs will be coming around.

Some editors, myself included, like to cut with a combination of uprights and a flatbed, either doing the first cut on uprights and changing to flatbeds for fine cutting or doing most of the cutting on the uprights and viewing and making fine trims on the flatbed.

The large flatbeds can run up to four separate rolls of film at one time (usually two picture/two sound, or, variously, three picture/one sound, or one picture/three sound). This enables the editor, on one machine, to run the equivalent of two uprights — leaving the cut footage on one pair of *gangs* (as each path is called) and the selecting of cut points on the other pair. In addition, more than one flatbed can be electronically linked together, giving the editor an almost overwhelming number of picture/track combinations.

Both of these types of editing machines have their own pluses and minuses and, therefore, their own set of supporters and detractors. The editor will make his or her own decision on what type of machine to cut on. The assistant editor is expected to be able to set up a system for any of them.

I have my own preferences, of course. I like to cut sound and music on upright Moviolas. I like to cut 16mm film and complicated 35mm films (musicals, action pictures, documentary-style films) on a flatbed. Dialogue pictures are no easier on one machine than on the other, so I let the demands of the individual film's schedule and budget, as well as the preference of the director, dictate what machine to use.

There are times when these uses overlap. What, you may ask, do you do then? Do the best you can.

An Editing Table With Supplies

In the United States, a normal editing table (or, editing bench; the two terms are interchangeable) looks very much like the one shown in Figure 2.5. (For a fairly thorough discussion of how an English editing table is set up, see Ernest Walter's *The Technique of the Cutting Room.*) The essentials on it are as follows:

Synchronizer: In much the same way that the Moviola or flatbed can pull the film and soundtrack along

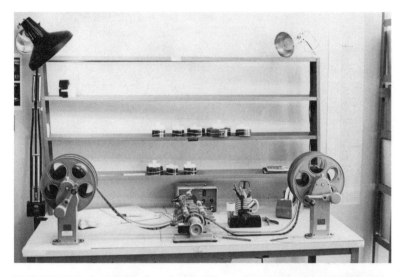

FIGURE 2.5 *An editing bench. The film and soundtrack are fed from the reels on the left rewind (picture first, and soundtrack behind it), through the synchronizer, and are taken up on the right rewind. Trims and outs for the scene which the editor is working on are sitting on the back rack. Note the other supplies and equipment on the table with the synchronizer: the sound amplifier (also called the sound box or squawk box) behind it, and the splicer and tape dispenser (with two rolls of white paper tape in it) to the right. Next to the splicer is a hole punch and at the front of the table, sitting next to the right rewind, is a Reddy-Eddy®, a time-to-footage converter.*

together in sync with each other, editors need to have a way of doing that on an editing table. The synchronizer (*see* Figure 2.6) does this so well that it is regarded as the ultimate sync setup (in fact, it is called a *sync block* by some). It is a passive mechanical device that usually has four identical wheels (called *gangs*) which are permanently locked together so that they spin with each other. Film locked into one of the four gangs will travel at exactly the same speed as film locked into any of the other gangs. Moviola and flatbed synchronization has been known to slip, but

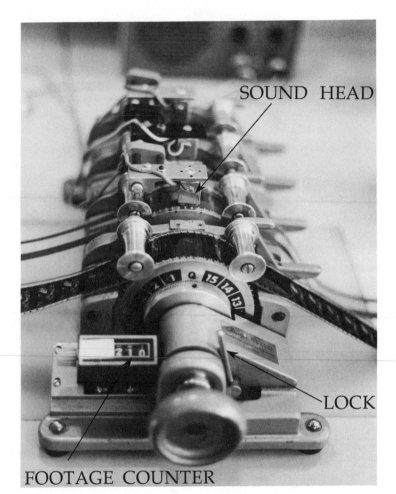

SOUND HEAD

LOCK

FOOTAGE COUNTER

FIGURE 2.6 A synchronizer. It is made up of (usually) four wheels called gangs which are all locked together. Each wheel has sprockets on it so that it can transport film or track. In this case, the first gang is running picture and the second gang is running sound. On the front of the first wheel is the frame counter which is marked from zero to fifteen frames. Notice from the frame counter on the synchronizer that the frame of picture on the white zero frame mark is at 210 feet and zero frames exactly (210'00). The lock on the right side of the synchronizer can be engaged to freeze the wheels at a particular frame. Normally, the wheels turn freely.

there is no way that film locked into the synchronizer can slip. Everyone in the editing room will have their own synchronizer, though flatbed editors will have less need of one than their upright Moviola counterparts.

Sound Reader: Some way of hearing the soundtrack which is running through the synchronizer must be provided. This is accomplished by placing a little sound head on at least one of the gangs (the first gang is usually not used, being reserved for picture) and connecting that up to an amplifier with a built-in speaker. This amplifier/speaker combination is known variously as the *sound reader*, *squawk box*, or "that damned box". Sound reproduction is *never* as good as it should be through a system like this, which is why many sound editors rent better amplifiers and separate speakers. On *Hair* we rented a good speaker and installed a good amplifier in our KEM flatbed as well.

Rewinds: These are two stands at either end of the editing bench. The reels containing the picture and sound film are slipped onto the protruding shafts of the rewinds. Clamped together, they can then be moved in forward or reverse by turning the handles. These handles can be pulled out part way from the rewind stand, disengaging the handle from the shaft. This does not mean, as I thought back in college, that you've broken the rewind. It is a particularly helpful way to wind film very fast. You turn the rewinds faster and faster, and when you've gotten up to a good speed simply pull the handle out and let the film coast along, virtually winding itself up.

FIGURE 2.7 A Rivas® splicer. The film is placed across the base of the splicer so that its sprocket holes fit into the pins. The tapper (A) is brought down lightly onto the film to smooth it out. The cutting blade (B) is then brought down to cut the film at the metal wedges (C). Soundtrack splices are made by placing each piece of track base up (oxide side down) on the pins so that the two butt up at the metal wedges. White splicing tape is then put on the base side of the track covering two sprockets on either side of the cut. The tapper is then brought down to smooth the tape over the cut and the tape is split using the blade built onto the side of the tapper. Picture is spliced differently. The piece of film on the right is placed so that two sprockets overlap past the pins on the right. The piece of film on the left is then butted up against it so no sprockets overlap. Clear tape is then placed over the cut, covering one sprocket on either side of the cut. These two -sprocket splices will barely be seen when projected in the 1.85 screen ratio. The same two sprockets are then spliced on the back of the film as well since film running through a Moviola needs to be spliced on both sides ('double–spliced') in order to go through smoothly. Film cut on a flatbed need only be spliced on one side, with the back side being spliced before screenings only.

FIGURE 2.8 *A Guillotine® splicer. The film is placed on the base of the splicer and cut with the blades at its right side (there are two — one is for a straight cut and the other is a diagonal blade). The cut portions are then moved to the center of the splicer, the sprocketless tape is pulled up over the cut and the top of the splicer is brought down on top of the film. This smooths the tape down as well as perforating the sprocket holes in the tape. (Photograph by the author)*

Splicer: There are a few types of splicers. The two most popular are the Rivas® (*see* Figure 2.7) and the Guillotine® (*see* Figure 2.8). Both do the same things: provide a cutting edge for cutting the film evenly on a frame line, and a setup block on which two pieces of cut film can be aligned and then taped together. This is the extent of the "cutting" part of film editing. Cut piece number one, cut piece number two, lay them side by side, and tape them together. It is ridiculously simple, which is why many editors (including myself) get touchy about being called "cutters". Cutting and splicing is easy, it's the editing that's difficult.

Both of these splicers use tape to fasten the pieces of film together. There is virtually no use for

17

cement splicers in a film editing room today unless you intend to cut your own camera original. If you don't, stick with the tape splicers.

There is one other type of splicer — the diagonal splicer. It is used for soundtrack only and it cuts on an angle, rather than straight up and down. This splicer is used primarily to finesse sound or music edits. A Guillotine splicer has a diagonal cutting surface mounted onto the splicer.

Supplies: First, the list, then the explanations.

> Splicing tape — clear and white
> Leader — white, yellow, and clear (some also use black)
> Fill leader (also called *slug film*)
> "Scene Missing" and "Shot Missing" leader
> Academy leader
> Stationery supplies
> Spring clamp
> Differential
> Loupe
> Rulers
> Architect's tape
> Reddy-Eddy® and/or calculator
> Trim tabs (also called *cinetabs*)
> Beep tone roll and virgin stock
> Spare take-up reels, split reels and cores
> Gloves
> Velvets
> Webril® wipes
> Cleaner (such as Ecco®)
> White boxes
> Differential
> Q-Tips®

Splicing tape — This is the tape that you use to splice the film together. Clear tape is used for picture splices, white tape is used for sound. On a guillotine splicer, many editors use clear tape for both picture and sound.

Leader — Solid white, yellow or black film, as well as clear. Its uses are myriad and we'll discuss each of them as we come on them in the text. For now, let's say that on the average feature you can expect to under-order this leader. Except for the black leader, which is pricier than the gold jewelry around the producer's neck, order accordingly.

Fill Leader — Fill is waste film. It is usually old movies or rejected lab prints which would have been discarded. It is spliced into the cut soundtrack when a length of silence is needed. Rather than hunting for a piece of general tone (with no dialogue or noises on it) to put in this place, the editor will quickly drop in a piece of fill of the proper length.

"Scene Missing" and "Shot Missing" Leader — As cut scenes are put together on reels for projection, scenes which belong in between two cut scenes but which have not yet been shot or cut are indicated with a short length (often, three feet) of leader which has the words "Scene Missing" printed on it. In addition, as the editor is cutting a scene which is missing some shots (usually an insert, that is, a close-up of some action, say a person's hand sliding a key into a lock), he or she will want to indicate where the shots should go and approximate lengths for them. They will cut in some leader which has the words "Shot Missing" on it. Both types of leader can be purchased from a film supply house. When you do, buy very little.

Academy Leader — The numbers that you sometimes see at the beginnings of films (you know, 8-7-6-5, etc.) are part of a standard used by projectionists as they set up the film for screening. The leaders count down in seconds from eight to two and then go to black before the picture begins (an alternate standard counts down in feet, from twelve to three, which is the same thing). Also imprinted on these standard leaders are all kinds of helpful information. There is a field for the projectionist to focus on, there are sometimes markings showing the borderline of the screen area (since, normally, only part of the full frame is meant to be projected, the rest has to be covered up by a plate in the projector). One Academy leader should be placed at the head of everything that is to be projected, so order a lot of it, either from your lab or a supply house.

On many films that I've worked on, *Heathers, Four Friends, Cotton Club*, the cinematographers shot their own head leader, which they felt more accurately gave them a sense of what their cameras were looking at as they screened dailies. The editing crew should cut this leader onto the head of every dailies reel. I find no real value in this after the first several days of shooting, but it does suggest an alternate, and cheaper, way of getting the scene and shot missing leaders — having the camera crew shoot them. A word of warning about using these leaders at the head of your picture. Industry standard is to have *exactly* twelve feet from a "picture start" mark to the end of leader (four feet and thirty-two frames in 16mm). You must keep this length constant in every leader that you make. (More on this in a later chapter)

Stationery Supplies — Editors use grease pencils (also called 'china markers') to write on film because the marks are easy to see and equally easy to erase. In addition, a healthy supply of regular pencils, pens, markers, various sizes of notepaper, rubber bands, and paper clips will keep the editing room humming along happily. It is the assistant's job to make sure that the editor never runs out of anything that he or she needs. Often, this job is delegated to an apprentice, if there is one on the job.

Spring clamp—Something has to hold the multiple reels on the rewind shafts together or they won't take up at the same rate. A clamp will do it. Make sure you get one with the table setup when you rent it.

Differential—A thick wheel-like gizmo which, when hooked up between a reel of picture and a reel of sound, forces them to take up at the same speed on your rewinds. A cheap, and less effective fix for this, is to separate the reels on your rewinds with 16mm cores and apply a little wrist action while winding the reels to make the soundtrack take up faster than the picture.

Loupe —This is a little magnifying glass that you can set on top of the film when you need to examine a single frame on the editing bench or flatbed. In the center of most editing tables there is a lamp set into the table and covered, at table level, with a sheet of frosted glass or plastic. You can turn on the light to provide back illumination for the film. Assistant editors will have a lot of need to see single frames as they sync up the dailies.

Rulers —There are a few times when it will be necessary to draw straight lines onto the film (to indicate fades, dissolves, or other types of opticals, for instance). A two-foot ruler will take care of most of these needs. Music and sound editors usually need three-foot rulers for their streamers. I find it helpful to have rulers in half, one, two, and three-foot lengths.

Architect's Tape — A niftier way of making these lines on the film is to set a length of thin architect's tape (usually 1/16") onto the film instead of drawing on it.

Reddy-Eddy® — This is a little wheel that converts footage to time. Calculators can do the same thing. In the appendix of this book there is a conversion chart. A copy of it might be handy to have around the editing room.

Trim tabs (also called *cinetabs*)—These are small pieces of cardboard onto which everything from code numbers to personal notes can be written. There are two main types of trim tabs in the United States (*see* Figure 2.9).

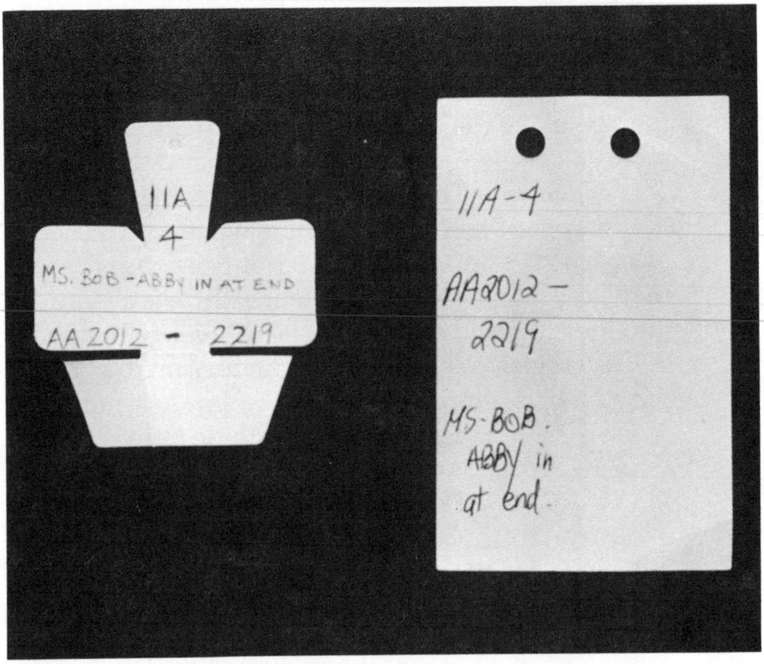

FIGURE 2.9 *Two types of trim tabs (also called cinetabs). Both are made of stiff cardboard. The version on the left is used primarily in New York. The one on the right is used largely on the West Coast (it is folded lengthwise down the center and inserted in between layers of the rolled–up film). Both types of tabs give the same information. In England, usually no trim tabs are used. A piece of tape is placed on the top of the rolled–up film instead.*

Beep tone —This is a roll of 35mm or 16mm soundtrack, depending on what gauge film you're cutting with, onto which a continuous tone (usually 1000 cycles, or Hertz) has been recorded. This has a lot of uses, which we shall discuss later, but the primary one is that you can cut single frames off of the roll and cut them into your leaders for the little beep (or 'pop') that occurs nine feet after the start mark. Some editors like to use little pieces of 1/4" tape with the tone recorded onto it which have had some glue put on the back so that they can be stuck directly onto the leader. I find this less accurate than cutting in exactly one frame of track. Besides, it's cheaper and easier to have someone in the transfer house knock off one minute of 1000 cycle tone than to be taping those messy pieces of tape onto the film.

Along with this beep tone roll, a small roll of track which has never been recorded onto (called *virgin stock* for all too obvious reasons) is useful. You can use it to check out the fidelity of all of the sound equipment.

Spare take-up reels, split reels and cores — On a Moviola, film is wound on reels, and a healthy supply of them is essential. Alternately, film can be wound on 3" plastic cores (also called *spools*) and placed into split reels (which are nothing more than take–up reels which can be split, or unscrewed, in two). A number of these reels (eight for each person in the editing room is not too many) along with a huge quantity of cores should be ordered. On flatbeds, film is always wound on cores, which are slotted onto the flatbed.

Other editing supplies — White editing gloves, film cleaner (like Ecco®), sound track cleaner, two-piece white boxes for storage, a few film cans for shipping, Q-Tips® for cleaning the machines, and whatever other effluvia the editor likes to have surrounding him or her. Some small black velvet cloths (usually sewn across the side) will work well for cleaning film without scratching it. Also, a phone list, placed prominently by the editing room phone, will save everyone a lot of time looking for the numbers of suppliers and contacts.

None of these supplies magically appear when you sign onto your job. It is the job of the assistant to rent what can be rented and to purchase the rest. In some situations, you can rent a cutting room complete with an editing machine, a table, synchronizer, sound reader, rewinds, splicer, and take-up reels for one flat price (on a daily, weekly, or monthly basis). More often, the room comes equipped with nothing other than a door and (rarely) a window or two. You will have to rent all of the equipment from a separate supply house. It is wise to order the equipment as far ahead of time as possible, since this equipment can get booked weeks in advance and you'll end up spending days of your time trying to find equipment for your editor.

Supplies, of course, can be purchased almost any time, so long as you've got the money.

If you are working on a studio lot some of the equipment and supplies might be provided for you by the post-production department or facilities manager of the studio. Let them know what it is you need and make sure that your editor's needs are taken care of.

The Film Logbooks

We will discuss the nature of the logbooks in several chapters but you should know that there will be a few types of logs. Some will be on clipboards hung on the walls and some will be in looseleaf notebooks near the editor or assistant. A small table will be helpful for these items. Editing tables get crowded almost immediately. They're no place for logbooks.

A Series of Trim Barrels

These are also usually rented as part of the editing room equipment package. There are two main types of barrels (or bins). One kind, popular on the East Coast, is a rectangular barrel, almost waist-high, lined with soft cotton material, and topped with either one or two parallel bars of metal (*see* Figure 2.10). The other kind (more popular on the West Coast) is a knee-high barrel, with a metal bar elevated above it (*see* Figure 2.11). In either case, out of these bars stick either a series of tiny pins or metal loops which fit neatly through the sprocket holes in the film. As the editor is cutting he or she will hang anything not used in the cut on one or another of these pins. This keeps the film hanging in an orderly manner near the Moviola. When the editor is done, it also keeps the pieces hanging in an orderly manner near the apprentice who spends hours splicing and wrapping them all back together.

Plenty of Room

Actually, this is the one thing that editors get all too little of. Editing rooms are usually small and dimly lit, with barely enough electricity to plug in the editing machines without blowing a fuse. This is the condition that you'll find in most New York editing rooms as well as in many independent houses in Los Angeles. Editing rooms at the major studios in Hollywood, range from the luxurious to the ludicrously closet-sized.

The assistant editor must also play the part of interior designer and come up with a comfortable and efficient layout for the room, whatever its size and wherever it is. Remember, you'll be living in it for the duration of the film.

For example, let's say that you have one editor, two Moviolas, one assistant, and one apprentice to fit into one room. Your first questions should always center around the editor's comforts. Does he/she like to work facing the windows or away from them? Near the door or far away from it?

25

FIGURE 2.10 *A tall trim bin of the kind normally used in New York. Film is hung beneath its trim tab so that the trims can be easily located by looking at the take and code numbers (see Figure 6.1 for a closer view). Note that very large trims are flanged up and hung by a rubber band run through the trim's center. In this photograph, rubber bands have been stretched across the pins over the tops of the trims to prevent them from falling off when the barrel is rolled from place to place.*

FIGURE 2.11 A short trim bin, common on the West Coast. Film is hung on the looped pins. The trim tabs are inserted into paper clips which have been taped on top of the single cross bar. (Photo by the author)

Near a phone or isolated from it? Some editors like to be insulated from the outside world; others like to be part of it.

Figure 2.12 shows one typically cramped arrangement that I've had to work in in the past. This layout is a good compromise between many bad elements. It insulates the editor somewhat from traffic, provides easy access for the

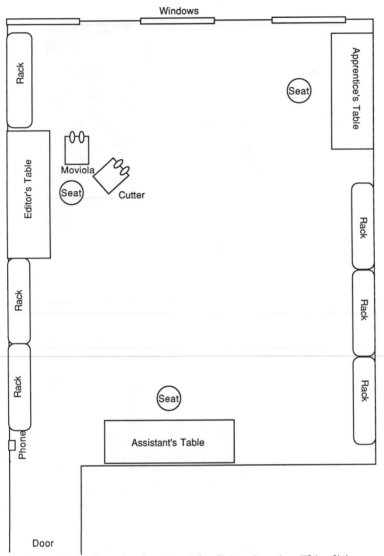

FIGURE 2.12 Floor plan for a Moviola editing situation. This editing room will be home for three people and four racks of film. If additional racks are needed they can be lined up against the windows. Note that in this position the editor works to his or her right and that the Moviola picture screens face away from the windows, avoiding glare.

assistant to the phone and the door (remember that an assistant spends much of his or her time dealing with the outside world), and it provides working space for the editor as well as some nearby rack space.

An alternative arrangement (for an editor who would like more isolation) would be to place him or her where the apprentice's table is. Note also that this revised arrangement works if the editor is right-handed and prefers to work with the Moviolas on the right side.

In the case where an editor wishes to work on a flatbed, I might arrange the room as shown in Figure 2.13. Most flatbed editors don't feel the need to have their own editing bench, as the space on the flatbed is designed to provide them with a cutting surface. A small table next to the flatbed would contain the logs and perhaps a small synchronizer (with no sound heads) for use in making precise footage counts. If the editor needs an editing bench, a small one might be set up nearby, out of the way. Often, a smaller flatbed is rented in addition to the larger one. This would be set up next to the first machine.

Frequently, on a feature film, you are able to rent two rooms, or one room with a smaller anteroom. In this case, I prefer to put the apprentice and the film library in the smaller room, and leave the editor and the assistant in the other. This is always preferable since apprentice work, by its very nature, is noisy and can often be distracting. Once again, it is the assistant's job to think of the editor's comfort. The fewer distractions, the faster and better the film can get edited. And, in the hierarchy of editing room personnel, if the assistant or the apprentice must be a little less comfortable in order to make the editor more so — so be it.

There are, of course, many other possible situations in editing rooms. Most non–features don't have apprentices at all. Some low–budget films can't even afford an assistant, leaving the editor to perform all of these tasks. Some high–budget films have more film than can fit in the same

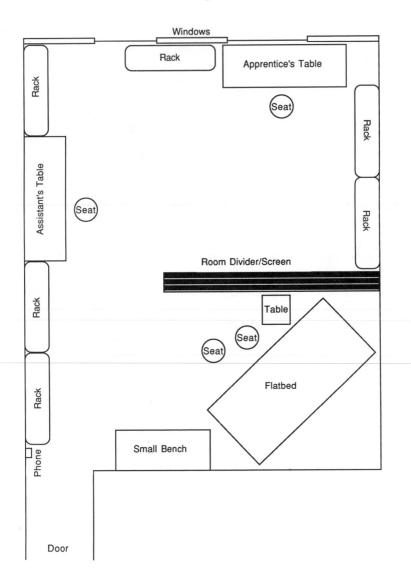

FIGURE 2.13 *Floor plan for a flatbed editing situation. Notice how much more room is needed here. There is no room for additional racks.*

room with the editors. On *Hair* we had one room stacked ceiling to floor with film. Some editing rooms are set up with videotape systems which everyone uses for reference. But the principle always remains the same — make sure that everyone can get their work done as efficiently and as humanely as possible. If that can happen, the job of making the best film out of the available material seems that much easier.

3

BEFORE
THE FILM
BEGINS

Before the Moviolas and the flatbeds move into the editing room there are things an assistant editor must do. The first, of course, is to get hired on the job, but let's assume you've already managed that (for an exploration of that topic, see Chapter 19: "The Hardest Job of All — Finding a Job.")

Let's say that you've just been hired onto the director Adam Free's new picture, entitled *Silent Night, Silent Cowboy*. Your editor is a woman named Wendy Libre (editing has traditionally had more women in it than almost any other film trade).

The first thing to do after Wendy hires you is to determine your salary, if this hasn't already been determined for you by Wendy or the film's production manager. Though some editors have agents or lawyers to talk money with the producer, assistants almost never do. I've found that the odious job of talking money is always better done as soon as you know that you've been hired, so that there are no problems which can crop up later. Be aware, if you negotiate your own salary, that people get paid in more ways than money. Working on a good film with good people, learning a lot about your craft, and making more contacts are all legitimate forms of payment on film. And while your landlord probably won't want to get paid with that kind of currency, all of these points should be taken into account when you are deciding how much you need in salary.

As soon as you've taken the job on *Silent Night* you should get a copy of the script. The script will tell you a lot about how you should set up the film. A musical will be organized differently than a straight dialogue film. On an action film, you will get different kinds of footage than on either of the above. You will see if there is much special effects work planned (*opticals, matte shots, stock footage, on-set projection,* et al). You will see if there are many short scenes, or if the film is made up primarily of longer ones. For the sake of complicating this example, let us assume the following about the movie you are about to do.

Silent Night, Silent Cowboy is a film about the shooting of a Western movie. It focuses on the scriptwriter's life, which is (naturally) falling apart just as the film is being made. There are going to be three weeks of shooting in a desertlike location (for the Western film–within–a–film), one week on various locations in the city, and four weeks in a studio. Because of the nature of the film, there will be scenes of people watching projected film, some opticals and some on–set music. Though there might be one or two scenes in the Western with fast action, most of the film appears to be dialogue oriented, with a lot of long scenes intercut with the Western.

This may be all that you can tell from a few readings of the script (and you should read it a few times so you know what everyone is talking about as they discuss the script with you), but this has already given you quite a bit of information. As you learn more and more of what different kinds of film demand of you in the editing room, you will be able to read scripts quite easily for these types of clues.

After you've read the script, you will discuss the job with Wendy. She will tell you how she wants things set up.

Some editors have more demands than others, but all of them have *some*. Most of their requests are reasonable ones that they have learned help them do their job better. In this case, Wendy wants to work on a Moviola. She tells you that she is not going to be on the location during the weeks when the company is shooting in the desert; instead, she will be cutting back in the city. She will also be able to tell you the results of any conversations she has had with the director — how much coverage he intends to shoot, any special requirements *he* has, what kind of cutting he wants done without him, when he wants to see the first cut, etc. etc.

The production manager will also be able to give you some valuable information. You'll want to know approximately how much printed footage he has budgeted for since you will have to organize the cutting room differently for 80,000 feet of film than for 500,000. He will probably also have decided what laboratory will be processing the dailies, what sound house will be transferring the sound dailies, and where you will be cutting. The production manager or the production office coordinator (often called the p.o.c.) can also give you some idea of where and how to obtain supplies, how you can obtain a supply of petty cash, and a current crew list. Get your name and Wendy's on the crew list immediately (as well as your apprentice's name, if you have one). Often, you will be working with people you already know. This can help you to see the strengths and weaknesses you will be faced with during the film.

The people you will need to know most directly are the director (of course), the sound recordist and whoever is taking the sound notes, the second assistant camera (this person takes the camera notes) and, most importantly, the script supervisor. The script supervisor's paperwork will be your most direct link with the set. If you have a good rapport with him or her, everything will run that much smoother.

Finally, you should do something that seems so obvious to me that I am always shocked by how many people never bother to do it. I make a point of meeting the people with whom I'll be dealing. I drop by the laboratory to introduce myself to the customer contact person and the shipping clerks. I say hello to the dailies projectionist (often this is at the lab where you'll be processing your dailies). I go by to see the person doing the sound transfers and the shipping clerks at the sound transfer house. In fact, I introduce myself to as many people as I can — at the editing rental house, in the production office, on the set. At each stop I'll try and iron out procedures. What time will I be getting my dailies? Should I pick them up or will you deliver? How reliable is that delivery service? When do you need the *negative* and *1/4" tapes*? Where can I reach you after–hours if there is any emergency (though editing staffs often work late and on weekends, many of your contacts will not)? I tell the projectionist all the details about the film (*aspect ratio*, whether the dailies will come on reel or cores, Moviola or flatbed wind, et al). I work out a system for the delivery of all paperwork to the editing room. I find out how to submit time cards and get paychecks.

The assistant's job is to keep things moving smoothly during the editing process. A little bit of advance work here will ease your path later in countless ways.

If you are lucky, you will have a production manager who will hire you early enough to do all of these things (two or three days is plenty). But one is rarely that lucky. On most films you will probably find yourself put on the payroll on the first day of shooting. The dailies will start arriving early the next morning and you will have your hands full making sure that all of the equipment and supplies arrive in the cutting on time and in one piece. With the general lethargy of suppliers you will find that one day isn't enough time to get all of this done properly. In that case, I usually spend a day or so during the preceding week making those contacts and ordering the supplies. This is not, of course, a completely satisfactory solution. There are always a thousand things that you must do in your personal life the week before you start a film (that dentist appointment really won't wait another ten months) but production managers seem to expect that you will give them this free time and, in order to avoid hassles later in the film, you should oblige them if there is no other alternative.

Meeting people before the film begins really *is* that important.

Another major task at this point is hiring the crew. On some films it is obvious at the outset that the complexity of the film will exceed the crew's capacity to get it done effectively, and the hiring of an extra assistant (or an additional apprentice) is permitted. In any case, if the crew of *Silent Night* is to exceed you and Wendy, the two of you will have to decide who to hire.

There are many ways of finding qualified editing crews. After having worked in the business for a while, you will probably know people with whom you're comfortable working. Actually, this is one of the assets that you bring to the editing crew — your contacts with potential apprentices. It is possible that Wendy might have someone that she wants to hire. You may have worked with an apprentice before who already knows how you work and could handle the job with a minimum of learning your system. The unions also keep lists of qualified people and you can call them for this "availability list" (though I have often found these lists to be quite out of date). In many cutting rooms, job seekers come by in a seemingly never-ending stream, leaving their resumes behind. I have sometimes hired from among these people after talking with them.

One word of warning on this last method. For union jobs on either coast, there is a rule that you must first give all out–of–work and qualified union members a chance at the job before hiring outside of the union. In practice, this means interviewing the people on the availability list first. In some cases it may be helpful to involve the production manager in your decision. The Los Angeles union is very strict about this rule and sometimes enforces it with crippling severity — so be careful before you hire.

However you've chosen to find additional crew, the one guiding factor in making that decision is to realize that this person must help to move things smoothly during the editing process. That is why many people prefer to hire someone they've already worked with and with whom they feel the most comfortable.

From reading the script, you and Wendy have decided that no additional assistant will be necessary on this film. This is often a budgetary constraint put on you rather than a well thought-out decision on your part. The crew will consist of the two of you and an apprentice. Let's say that Wendy and you have decided to hire Philip Spring, a young man who worked with the two of you on your last film. You've all settled on your salaries and read the script, you have already set up the cutting room with the Moviolas and supplies. Maybe you've even met the director to say hello.

The first day's shooting has been completed. It is now Tuesday morning. Your real work is about to begin.

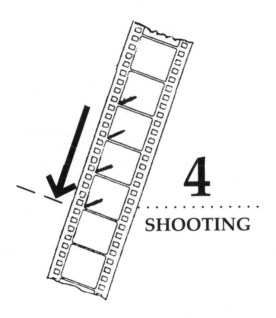

4
. . . .
SHOOTING

Dailies Preparation

If everything is moving smoothly, on Tuesday morning you will either pick up or get three different packages from three different locations. From the film laboratory, you will receive the picture dailies and their accompanying paperwork. The sound transfer house will get you the track dailies and their accompanying paperwork. And, from the production office, you will receive a copy of the script supervisor's notes (some supervisors supply you with a rough copy now and follow up a few days later with a typed-up final version). If you are lucky enough to be working at a studio in Los Angeles where everything is done on the lot (with the probable exception of the lab work) your apprentice can pick everything up in five minutes. On films with tight deadlines I often have the dailies picked up very early in the morning so the synching can be finished early. Every assistant starts at different times depending upon when the film and track comes to them but, during dailies, you can count on starting anywhere between 7:00 and 8:30 a.m.

The papers you should get with the picture dailies are

the *laboratory report* and the *camera report* (sometimes the camera reports come from the production office rather than the lab). You should also get at least a verbal report (a *negative report*) from the customer contact person if there is anything wrong *whatsoever* with the printed dailies. By the time you walk into the dailies screening later on in the day you should know everything there is to know about the footage that everyone else is going to look at for the first time. If something looks wrong, people will want to know immediately whether it is a problem with the print or on the camera original, and whether or not it is correctable. You, as the assistant, will probably be the only one who can know the answer and you'd better know it (it's also a good idea to tell the editor about it as soon as you find out; that way he or she can determine just how serious the problem is with regards to the rest of the coverage).

One note about lab contact people. I have only twice met anyone in this position who did not think that part of their job description was to protect their lab — even by lying, if necessary. This is why a good rapport with them is absolutely essential. You'll find out fast if you can trust them or not.

The camera report that you receive is written up by the second assistant cameraperson on the set (*see* Figure 4.1). It lists a lot of information that is helpful to the lab and a few useful tidbits for you. For starters, it shows you everything that was shot on Monday.

In the normal American system of shooting, each successive camera set-up (that is, each time that the camera or lens is reset to a different positions) is given a different and unique letter. In Scene 11, for instance, the first set-up would be called Scene 11. The next set-up would be Scene 11A, followed by 11B, 11C, etc. etc. Each time the camera is rolled on a set-up the set-up letter is followed by a sequential take number. Therefore, the first take of Scene 11A is called Scene 11A-1, followed by 11A-2, 11A-3, etc. After the last take of 11A

CAMERA REPORT

	Roll #	Sheet #
	/	/

Film: Silent Night	Director Adam Free	Cam# 2	Mag# A
Job #	D.P. M. Carne		
Date 9·10·90	Asst.		

Scene	TK	SD	Ftge	Remarks	Scene	TK	SD	Ftge	Remarks
10	1		70						
	2		105						
	3		178						
	4		250						
	(5)		320						
	(6)		390						
10A	1		410	MOS					
	(2)		435	"					
10B	1		485						
	(2)		535						
10C	(1)		585						
10D	1		625						
	(2)		676						
	(3)		755						
10E	1		775	TS					
	(2)		800	TS					

INSTRUCTIONS: **PRINT CIRCLED TAKES ONLY**

PRINT NORMAL
DAY - INT

TYPE of NEG 5247

FIGURE 4.1 A camera report. As this is the first roll shot on the first day of filming, it is labelled "Roll # 1". Note that both takes on setup 10A are MOS and that both takes on setup 10E were tail slated ("TS"). Only the circled takes will be printed. The processed takes from the rest of the negative (called the "B-negative") will be stored at the lab. The camerperson has instructed the lab to print the circled takes normally for a day interior scene.

is shot, the next take would be Scene 11B-1, followed by 11B-2, 11B-3, etc.

Takes which your director, Adam Free, wanted printed for editing are circled. Each camera roll is usually 1000 feet in 35mm or 400 feet in 16mm (approximately 11 minutes). As each take is shot, the second assistant marks the approximate ending footage of each take on the sheet. This continues until the camera roll is used up, or is used up enough so that the second assistant does not want to take a chance that it will roll out before the end of the next take.

On top of the camera report are two items of information that are also important — the shooting date (in this case September 10, 1990) and the camera roll number (this is the cumulative count of rolls shot over the entire movie shoot; since this is the first roll shot on the first day it is called camera roll number one). Each camera roll takes up one or two sheets, depending upon how many takes were shot on that roll. In no case does any camera report include data for more than one camera roll.

With the camera report and the picture dailies, it is common for most labs to send a *lab report* (*see* Figure 4.2). After processing the original negative, a *negative assembly* person at the lab pulls out the negative for the selected (circled) takes and strings them all together. The lab then prints only these selects (the remaining non-printed takes — called *B-negative* — are stored for possible later use). Since a lot of negative has been removed from the camera rolls, selected takes from several camera rolls usually end up on a single lab roll. The lab report is a list of all takes on that lab roll. Also listed will be the color timing lights (the amount of red, blue, and green used in the printing process to get the color image you see in the print, these numbers are sometimes given for their complementary colors—yellow, cyan and magenta, and the numbers are therefore sometimes known as *Y-C-M numbers*) for the takes on the lab roll, the date, and a few other pieces of information. In 16mm it is common practice to print all

41

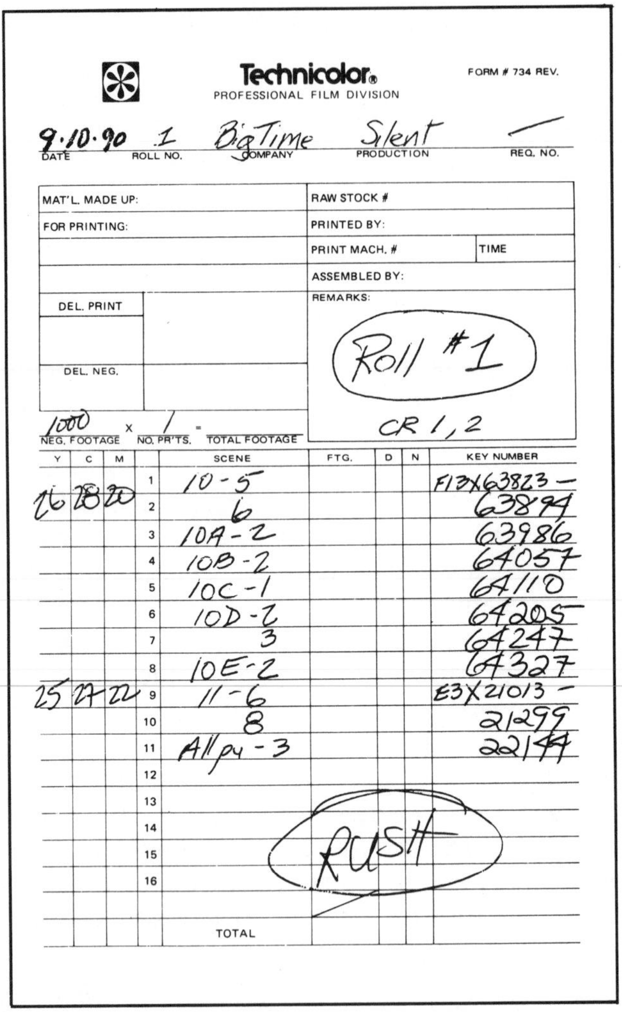

Technicolor®
PROFESSIONAL FILM DIVISION
FORM # 734 REV.

DATE	ROLL NO.	COMPANY	PRODUCTION	REQ. NO.
9·10·90	1	BigTime	Silent	—

MAT'L. MADE UP:	RAW STOCK #
FOR PRINTING:	PRINTED BY:
	PRINT MACH. # / TIME
	ASSEMBLED BY:
DEL. PRINT	REMARKS: Roll #1
DEL. NEG.	CR 1, 2

1000 x 1 =
NEG. FOOTAGE NO. PR'TS. TOTAL FOOTAGE

Y	C	M		SCENE	FTG.	D	N	KEY NUMBER
			1	10-5				F13X63823 —
26	28	20	2	6				63894
			3	10A-2				63986
			4	10B-2				64057
			5	10C-1				64110
			6	10D-2				64205
			7	3				64247
			8	10E-2				64327
25	27	22	9	11-6				E3X21013 —
			10	8				21299
			11	All pu-3				22144
			12					
			13					
			14					
			15					
			16					
				TOTAL				

RUSH

FIGURE 4.2 The lab report. Only the circled takes from the camera reports have been printed. This single lab roll contains takes from camera rolls one and two. The numbers listed on the left are the amounts of yellow, cyan, and magenta used in color balancing (timing) the dailies. When you get one-light dailies all takes will be printed at the same timing lights. The numbers at the right are the initial key numbers for each take. (Courtesy Technicolor, Inc.)

SOUND REPORT

COMPANY Big Time Films Inc. DATE 9/10/90
DIRECTOR Adam Free ROLL # 1 SHEET # 1 OF 1
TITLE Silent Night PROD. #
Recorder T.A. Edison Mic. Speed 7½ ips

SOUND ONE CORPORATION
1619 BROADWAY, NEW YORK, NY 10019 (212) 765-4757

SCENE	SOUND	REMARKS	SCENE	SOUND	REMARKS
		1K Tone	11	2	
				(3)	Print for sound only
10	1	Bad hum		4	
	2	" "		5	
	3	OK		(6)	
	4			7	
	(5)	Best for sound		(8)	
	(6)		All pu	1	
10B	1			2	
	(2)			(3)	
10C	(1)				
10D	1				
	(2)				
	(3)				
10E	1				
	2				
WT100	1	Room Tone			
11	1				

INSTRUCTIONS FOR TRANSFER

Nagra Stereo Sync
Combine tracks

FIGURE 4.3 A sound report. Since setup 10A was shot MOS there is no sound listed for those takes. Note the wild track taken and the printed take marked "Print for sound only." No picture will be printed for this take. Note its presence in the lined script and the log, then file this extra print along with the wild track. The instructions in the lower right–hand corner are for the transfer house. In this case they note that the sound has been recorded in stereo and that the monaural dailies track should be made up of a combination of both of the two stereo tracks rather than just one of the two. (Courtesy Sound One Corp.)

takes on every camera roll, since most labs won't take the chance of damaging the smaller negative by handling it to remove takes.

At some point, your sound dailies will arrive (often, this occurs before the picture dailies). And, like almost everything else involved in your job, they come with some paperwork. The *sound report* (*see* Figure 4.3) is analogous to the camera report — it lists all takes recorded and indicates (by circling the take number) which are the selected ones. It also lists the sound roll number (the cumulative roll number for the original quarter-inch tape reel that the sound has been recorded on), the date of recording, and any special transfer instructions. In addition, a report similar to the lab report often comes from the transfer house. This *transfer report* will list everything that was actually transferred along with any special things that were done to the sound dailies.

A final, but crucial, piece of paperwork you will receive is the *script supervisor's notes*, made up of two pieces of paper, the *script notes* (see Figure 4.4) and the *lined script*, so called because they are script pages onto which the supervisor has drawn lines denoting just what lines of dialogue are covered by which takes (*see* Figure 4.5). You will also often get a list of all the takes made during the day and which takes the director asked to be printed (often the script supervisor will add *why* the takes were good or not good). This paperwork is the only real link you have with the director. You will soon find that there are as many systems for script supervisors as there are for assistant editors. Every person seems to have his or her own paperwork form. Often you will get more paperwork than listed here (many script supervisors like to supply a list of all of the printed takes and their descriptions, a valuable list for the assistant who needs to assure that everything that he or she needs printed has indeed been printed) some of which will be useful and some of it completely superfluous to your job (script supervisors have to create a lot of paperwork for departments other than editorial). It is a good idea to familiarize yourself with the type of notes that the script supervisor will be sending to you *before* shooting begins since they are all interesting, but you won't have a lot of time to peruse them during the busy synching period.

Frequently, it is possible to get the camera, sound and script reports from the production office *before* the actual film and sound comes to you. In that case, you can do all of your organizing early, with just the paperwork in hand.

PICTURE __Silent Night, Silent Cowboy__   DIRECTOR __Adam Free__
                                              DATE __9·10·90__

Sc.	Tk	SR	CR	Comments	Description
10	1	1	1	0:40 "Horrid"	40MM - ABBY enters room screen r., x's to desk and throws mss. onto table. He reaches for cabinet, gets shocked, then pulls out liquor. He drinks, hears typewriter, then exits cam. r.
	2			0:20 INC	
	3			0:41	
	4			0:38 "Rushed"	
	⑤			0:45 "Good"	
	⑥			0:45 "Best"	
10A	1	MOS		0:10	40MM - ABBY's P.O.V. of the room.
	②			0:12	
10B	1	1		0:35	60MM - ABBY reaches for cabinet, gets shocked, hears noise, and exits cam. r.
	②			0:37	
10C	①			0:29	90MM - Closer of 10B
10D	1			0:21 "NG"	75MM - ABBY walks in from S.R. and throws mss. on table. He exits S.R.
	②			0:20 "Good"	
	③			0:30 "Best" (slated TK4)	
10E	1 TS			0:15	75MM - ABBY enters D.S.L., goes into bedroom hall, and exits.
	② TS			0:10 "Good"	

FIGURE 4.4 The script supervisor's notes. (See the caption for Figure 4.5.)

The first thing that you'll want to do is to compare all of the paperwork to make sure that everything that was supposed to be printed was actually printed. You may be surprised to find out how often things go wrong, either because the second assistant camera or assistant sound person

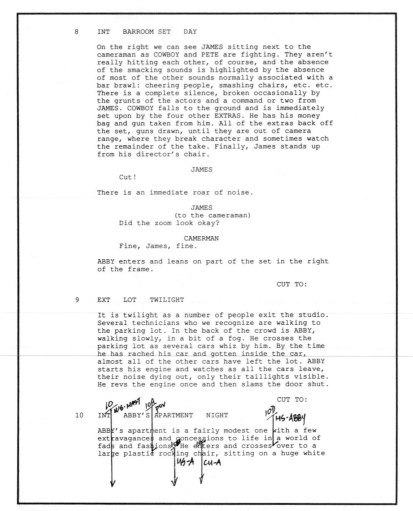

8   INT   BARROOM SET   DAY

On the right we can see JAMES sitting next to the
cameraman as COWBOY and PETE are fighting. They aren't
really hitting each other, of course, and the absence
of the smacking sounds is highlighted by the absence
of most of the other sounds normally associated with a
bar brawl: cheering people, smashing chairs, etc. etc.
There is a complete silence, broken occasionally by
the grunts of the actors and a command or two from
JAMES. COWBOY falls to the ground and is immediately
set upon by the four other EXTRAS. He has his money
bag and gun taken from him. All of the extras back off
the set, guns drawn, until they are out of camera
range, where they break character and sometimes watch
the remainder of the take. Finally, James stands up
from his director's chair.

                    JAMES
        Cut!

There is an immediate roar of noise.

                    JAMES
               (to the cameraman)
        Did the zoom look okay?

                    CAMERMAN
        Fine, James, fine.

ABBY enters and leans on part of the set in the right
of the frame.

                              CUT TO:

9   EXT   LOT   TWILIGHT

It is twilight as a number of people exit the studio.
Several technicians who we recognize are walking to
the parking lot. In the back of the crowd is ABBY,
walking slowly, in a bit of a fog. He crosses the
parking lot as several cars whiz by him. By the time
he has rached his car and gotten inside the car,
almost all of the other cars have left the lot. ABBY
starts his engine and watches as all the cars leave,
their noise dying out, only their taillights visible.
He revs the engine once and then slams the door shut.

                              CUT TO:

10   INT   ABBY'S APARTMENT   NIGHT

ABBY's apartment is a fairly modest one with a few
extravagances and concessions to life in a world of
fads and fashions. He enters and crosses over to a
large plastic rocking chair, sitting on a huge white

FIGURE 4.5 The lined script. The script notes (see Figure 4.4) and the
lined script are your best links with the set. Every take made is listed along
with comments on them. By looking at any given line of dialogue or action
on this lined script you can easily see the shots that were taken that cover
that line. For instance, for the last line on the second page of the script you
can see that there were eight shots made: a master and its pickup, three
shots of BOB (including a pickup) and three shots of ABBY. The squiggly
lines denote action or dialogue that is not performed on camera in that
particular setup.

46

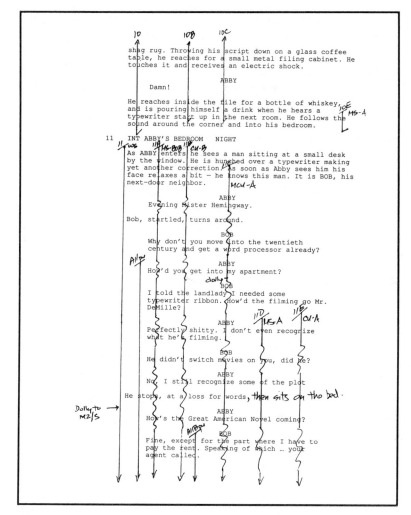

Figure 4.5 continued

didn't circle the proper takes, or because the lab or sound house made an error. If there is any discrepancy, you should call the lab or sound house and get it corrected immediately. If the dailies screening is not scheduled until the end of the day it is often possible to get an unprinted take sent to you in the afternoon, in time to get into the screening. Sound transfers are usually easier to get than picture reprints.

The ability to phone in for a quick print is why I prefer to have the original negative and 1/4" tapes stored at the lab and sound house, respectively. On some documentaries or low-budget films the sound tapes and sometimes even the negative are stored in the editing room. I don't like this idea because labs and sound houses are better equipped to store and handle this material than an editing staff. All you need is one friend stopping by to say hello carrying a big radio (or any other item with a large magnet in it) and stepping too close to the sound tapes and — presto! — instant blank tape. There is a scene in Brian DePalma's *Blow-Out* in which sound editor John Travolta returns to his editing room to find all of his sound tapes demagnetized. He plays roll after roll and hears no more than tape hiss on any of them. It is a sound editor's ultimate nightmare.

So I prefer to let the sound house store the tapes.

After you've checked all of the paperwork you can plan the dailies rolls. Based on the camera and lab reports you should know how long each printed take is. Based on the other paperwork you can now make a plan for how to lay out the dailies roll. Generally, it is a good idea to keep the rolls in the 800- to 900-foot range (not too big but also big enough to give the projectionist time to thread up the next reel). If possible, it is nice to leave the takes on the dailies rolls in the same order as the lab rolls. That way there is no cutting and pasting of the picture to do. This is very helpful if you are pressed for time. What this means, though, is that the crew will see the film projected in the order it was shot. However many directors and editors, myself included, prefer to see the dailies in the order that it will appear in the final film (that is, in scene number order).

There are other times when the lab rolls will have to be cut apart and respliced. When a director is shooting with more than one camera, he or she will usually want to see both cameras for each camera set-up (or take) one right after another. Since the takes will come in different camera rolls (since they've come from different cameras) they will almost never end up in the proper sequence in the lab rolls. You will then have to cut the takes apart and resplice them into the proper order.

Once you have determined the content and order of each dailies roll, make up one list for each reel. Tape them somewhere prominent.

Up until now you've done a lot of paper pushing and haven't even touched the film. Now you can do that (about time, huh?). Assuming that the last of the paperwork arrived by 8:30 a.m. (this almost never happens, but let's make believe), by 9:15 you should have had your morning coffee, chatted with the crew of the film down the hall from you, checked out all of the paperwork and are now ready to proceed.

So, let's sync the dailies already.

By this time, Philip, your apprentice, should have made up a complete set of leaders for each reel you're going to sync up today (I usually have the apprentice make up plenty of leaders before the job begins—about 20 is enough). Use white leader for both the picture and track leaders. Then put a long piece of 1" white tape on one end of the leader and write on it with black felt-tip pen or Sharpie® (*all* picture labeling should be in black) as shown in Figure 4.6. The soundtrack leader should be written in red as in Figure 4.7. All soundtrack labeling should be in red marker; this will help you to easily differentiate between reels of picture and track.

Before you even stick the white tape onto the leader make sure that you are taping it onto the correct side of the leader. Leader, as well as film, has two sides to it — a shiny side called the *base* and a slightly duller side called the *emulsion*. When 35mm picture is projected it reads correctly if the emulsion if "up", meaning up as it spins off the reel

(16mm reversal film, on the other hand, reads correctly "base–up"). But this emulsion can scrape off fairly easily when dragged across sound heads. For that reason, the soundtrack leader (as well as any fill you are going to insert into the sound rolls) should *never* be emulsion–up; it must always be base–up.

You can usually tell which side of a piece of film or leader is which by holding it near a light and moving it around. The emulsion side will appear more matted than the base side, which will seem quite shiny. If it is a piece of film, you might even be able to see some raised edges within the frame on the emulsion side (this is actually a colored layer of the picture image). If you still can't tell, a surefire test is to touch the film with your lips. If you've just 'kissed' the base side, the moisture left on the base side will wipe off very easily. One of the two disadvantages of this method is, of course, that if you've just 'kissed' the emulsion side of the film, it will leave little marks there. Try to test a portion of of the film that won't be needed (like the leader that is on the head and tail of the lab roll). The other disadvantage of this method is that you can look awful silly kissing a piece of film at 9:00 in the morning.

So, when you begin to prepare your leaders, make sure that the *picture* leaders have their tape stuck onto the emulsion side (since that is how you will wind them on the reels) and the *track* leaders have their tape stuck onto the base side (since you don't want the sound head to be running over the emulsion side of the leader).

After ten 35mm feet or so (this extra length is necessary so that the projectionist has some footage to thread–up on his projector before the start mark), splice the picture leader onto the Academy leader about one foot before the picture start mark as shown in Figure 4.8. Punch a hole in the middle of the start mark frame. From this frame, there are exactly twelve feet to the end of the Academy leader. If you put your start mark in at the zero frame on your synchronizer

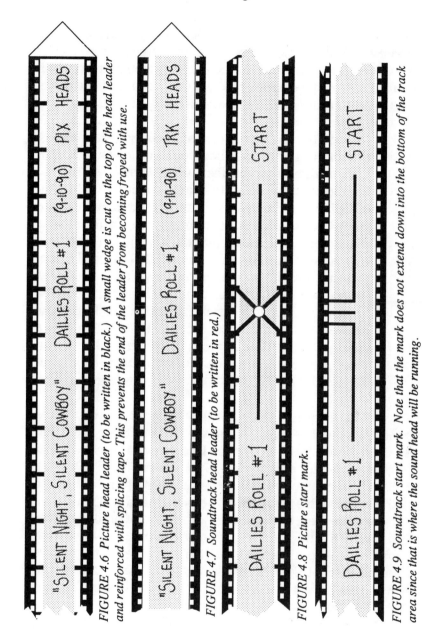

FIGURE 4.6 Picture head leader (to be written in black.) A small wedge is cut on the top of the head leader and reinforced with splicing tape. This prevents the end of the leader from becoming frayed with use.

FIGURE 4.7 Soundtrack head leader (to be written in red.)

FIGURE 4.8 Picture start mark.

FIGURE 4.9 Soundtrack start mark. Note that the mark does not extend down into the bottom of the track area since that is where the sound head will be running.

and set its counter to zero, you should cut your Academy leader off at the frame line between the fifteenth frame after the eleven-foot mark and the exact zero frame of the twelve-foot mark. You 'll be happy to know that actually *doing* this is much simpler than reading about it.

> [NOTE: To make our lives easier, we will standardize our method of talking about footage. If I want a length of film which is twelve feet long, I'll write 12'0 feet (12 feet, zero frames). By the same token, a footage of 370'07 means the seventh frame after the 370 foot zero frame mark. On a synchronizer, you would always place your first frame (which we will call the zero frame) on the white zero mark. 370'07 would therefore fall on the frame marked "seven". However, when I want to mark the frame that I am cutting on, I'll write 11'15/00, which means to cut on the frame line between 11'15 and 12'00. A cut at 370'07/08 means a cut on the frame line between 370'07 and 370'08. So, an Academy leader begins at 0'00 and cuts to footage at 11'15/00.]

The length of the soundtrack leader should be the same, but it will be made entirely out of white leader. After ten or so 35mm feet on the track leader, put a piece of white tape on the leader and mark it as shown in Figure 4.9. Mark it in red, of course (DO NOT write in the bottom half of the leader because this passes over the sound head and may leave some residue there that will degrade the sound quality). Once again, punch a hole in the start mark frame. Now, put that frame in the second gang of your synchronizer (your picture is in the first) at the 0'00 mark (the 'zero frame') and spin down to the 12 foot mark. Mark it at 11'15/00 and make a cut there. Your picture and track leader will now be the same length *from the start marks* (which is where it counts). All of your leaders should be made this length since it is the standard leader length and will guarantee that when you mix-and-match picture and sound leaders from different reels, they will all be the same length.

Tail leaders are much less complicated to set up. They are about ten feet long and end with the inscription shown in Figure 4.10 written on a piece of 1" tape (the example shown is for a *track* tail leader only).

At the tips of both the head and tail leaders I like to cover four to six sprockets with splicing tape cut into a wedge as shown in Figure 4.10. This wedge helps you to thread the film onto a reel and prevents the ends from being slowly shredded away by the constant wear and tear they will get.

Dailies Synching

You've already decided what is going into each dailies roll. You even have little pieces of paper listing them. For today's dailies you have decided to make the lab rolls the dailies rolls. You will notice that this means that one of the dailies rolls will be a little large (since lab roll one is 980 feet long), but this is not inordinately large (1025 feet or more is too large). I prefer to keep the rolls smaller, but in this case, it just isn't worth the extra work to begin splitting everything up into smaller rolls. This would involve splitting take 11pu–3 (the pick–up of set-up 11) off of lab roll number one and putting it onto the head of lab roll number two; and then splitting take 11D–5 off the end of lab roll number two and putting that onto the head of lab roll number three.

This illustrates one of the conflicts you will be getting into nearly every day on a film. No matter how many sensible rules you may have set up, they won't help the editing room run smoothly if you don't know when to bend them a little. You must have a sense of priorities. When there is time to do everything you want to do (this will happen once every ten years or so), you can do them the way you want to do them. But when things are moving slower than you would like, it is wise to sacrifice some things in order to make sure that there is a complete set of dailies for the crew to watch. You will have to use your judgment as to which things can be sacrificed and which cannot; this can only come from experience.

About now, the producer, the production manager and/or the director of photography will probably be calling you to find out "if everything looks alright". Naturally, everyone is nervous. Can the camera operator follow focus? Is the lighting too dark? Did the lab do the job they were supposed to do? If you have to tell them, "Hey, I'm not finished synching yet. I'm still moving the takes around on the lab rolls so I can have all the reels be under 900 feet" they're not going to be very happy or secure with you. So, let's bend the rules about reels being about 900 feet for now.

So, you now have several rolls of film and several rolls of soundtrack. Things move much faster if the film is already marked. Let's do that.

Take the first roll of film. The chances are that it is wound with the end of the roll at the top, called *tails out*. (If it isn't, don't worry; this system works just as well from the head of the roll as from the tail.) Attach a tail leader to the end of the roll, cutting off anything that is truly garbage. Generally, you will not want to remove anything from the picture roll in case someone needs to see it, but there are some things that are plainly not needed. Cut off portions of the picture before or after the takes which are completely clear or black. Cut off long pieces at the ends of takes where the assistant cameraperson has put his or her hand over the lens. Make sure you remove footage in increments of one frame (four sprockets in 35mm) so that the frame will stay in registration on either side of the splice. Do not cut out, unless asked, *color cards, grey scales,* or pauses at the end of takes where the actors are still visible. On *Fame*, one take was going badly for one of the actresses. She stopped in the middle of the take and waved for the director to cut. Later on, the editor, Gerry Hambling, was able to utilize that wave to make another story point altogether. Had I thrown away this "obviously

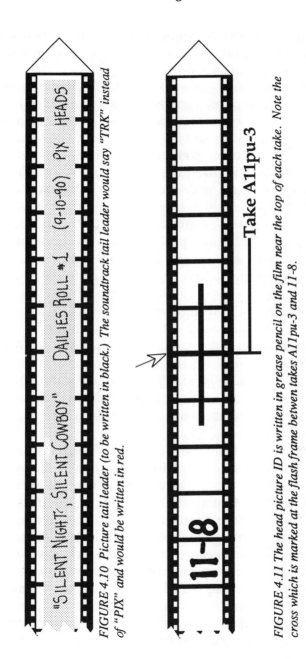

FIGURE 4.10 Picture tail leader (to be written in black.) The soundtrack tail leader would say "TRK" instead of "PIX" and would be written in red.

FIGURE 4.11 The head picture ID is written in grease pencil on the film near the top of each take. Note the cross which is marked at the flash frame between takes A11pu-3 and 11-8.

bad" part of the take, he never would have known that it existed on the negative and he would have lost the solution to the problem with this scene.

So, take the tail leader for the first dailies roll, attach it (on the frame line please) emulsion-up to the end of lab roll number one, and begin to rewind it until the beginning of the last take on the roll (take 11–8). In between takes there are usually one or two completely clear frames called *flash frames*. Even if you are rewinding quite fast, you should be able to see these easily. This gets quite simple to do with practice.

At the point where take 11pu–3 is cut together with 11–8, put a cross on the frame line and, just to the left of this cross (at the beginning of 11pu–3), write the take number very large in yellow or white grease pencil (*see* Figure 4.11). Then, using your loupe if you have to, find the first frame where the slate is completely closed. While you're looking at this frame, check the setup and take number to make sure that this really is 11pu–3. If it is, then mark that frame as indicated in Figure 4.12 — large and in grease pencil. On some takes you will see a frame where there is a slate which is completely closed but also has a blurry trail showing the top of the slate closing on the bottom of the slate (*see* Figure 4.13). If this is the case, mark that frame with a big zero and mark the next frame with the 'X'.

The theory behind this is very simple, but it requires a little sidetrack, while I explain how film projection works.

Film is a series of still pictures shown at the rate of twenty-four every second (the ability of the eye to blend all of these still pictures into one moving image is based on the fact that our eyes retain an image for a short period of time, a phenomenon called *persistence of vision*). The way in which this works in a projector is quite ingenious. One frame of film is shown for one forty–eighth of a second. A plate then drops down in front of the film, blacking out the image for another one forty-eighth of a second. During this time the next frame is pulled down in front of the lens. The plate moves out of the

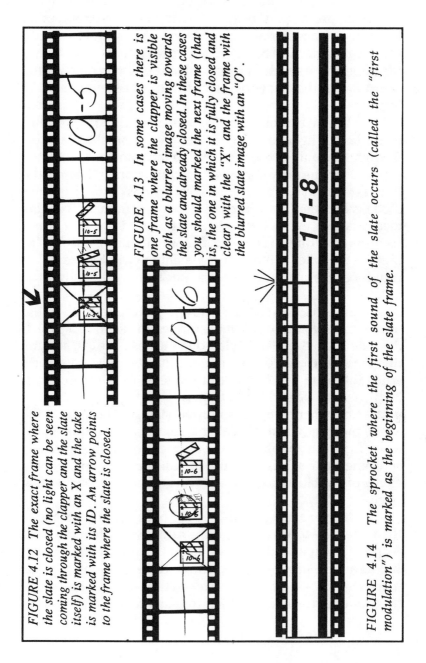

FIGURE 4.12 The exact frame where the slate is closed (no light can be seen coming through the clapper and the slate itself) is marked with an X and the take is marked with its ID. An arrow points to the frame where the slate is closed.

FIGURE 4.13 In some cases there is one frame where the clapper is visible both as a blurred image moving towards the slate and already closed. In these cases you should marked the next frame (that is, the one in which it is fully closed and clear) with the "X" and the frame with the blurred slate image with an "O".

FIGURE 4.14 The sprocket where the first sound of the slate occurs (called the "first modulation") is marked as the beginning of the slate frame.

way and this next frame is projected for one forty–eighth of a second before the plate drops down in front of the film again. If that plate were not dropping down we would actually see the image of the film being pulled down into view. But since the projector is synchronized so that the film is only pulled down while the image is blacked out, we never see that happen.

A similar thing happens when the film is shot. But, instead of the light going out to the screen from the projector, the light is coming from the set *into* the camera. The film is exposed for one forty–eighth of a second, during the time the film is steady in the camera. The plate drops down in front of the lens and the film is moved down one frame. What this means is that every forty–eighth of second the film is not recording anything. (This also means that during one–half of the time we watch a film, we are watching a blank screen. This could account for the quality of some of what gets distributed today.)

So... back to marking up the picture frames. In the normal case, you can look at the frames and see one in which the slate is open and see it closed in the next. We can assume that the slate closed during the one forty-eighth of a second when the plate was in front of the lens. In other words, it happened between the two frames — on the frame line. But in the case where there is a blurred slate, we know that the actual moment when the slate made contact was during the frame in which it is blurred as well as closed. To be precise in synching dailies, I like to note the difference. Thus, the big circles on the blurred frame. We will get back to them in a few pages.

After marking 11pu–3, move back to the next take in the reel — 11–8. Mark this in the same way. Then do 11–6. Normally, you would continue along the roll after this, doing 10E–2, and so on until you'd finished the roll. But 10E–2 is marked "T.S." (short for *tail slate*) on the reports. This means that, for one reason or another, the slate comes at the end of the take, rather than at the head. So, you should not spin back to the top of take 10E–2, but you will find it (and mark it in the same way as just described) at the tail of the take. Every time you write the take number (at the identification at the top of the take as well as on your paperwork) list this take as 10E–2ts.

After you've marked this slate then go to the head of the take and make your cross dividing 10E–2ts from 10D–2. Mark the head identification. Then continue on with the process until you get to the top of the roll.

When you get there, and have finished with 10–5, attach (at a frame line please) the end of your head leader onto the head of the roll, leaving out any of the garbage before take 10–5. When this is done, the very first frame of the roll will begin at 12'00, if the head leader is inserted into the synchronizer in our standard way — at 0'00. You have now completed marking up your first roll of picture dailies. When you complete the other two rolls you will have three rolls of picture dailies, all marked up, and all heads out. If the picture came to you heads out, and you marked it from the head rather than from the tail, you would have ended up tails out. In this case, all three rolls should be rewound so that they are heads out and ready for synching.

But before you are completely ready for synching you must similarly mark up the soundtrack dailies, a process known as "popping the tracks." The track will also, in all likelihood, come to you tails out, but very rarely will they come to arranged in rolls in the same manner as the picture dailies. To help you out of this, it is best to begin marking them up from the tail. That way, you can build them into the rolls that you've already determined as you go along (you can now see the advantage of figuring out the dailies reel breakdown ahead of time).

There is a slightly different procedure for marking the track dailies. For now, don't put any leaders on the rolls. Just spin them onto reels in the order you want them. Run them through the synchronizer on the gang with the sound head, so you can listen to them. At the beginning of every take the sound recordist will probably have put a beep on the track. At the end of the take they usually beep several times. Just as you look for the flash frames when you mark up the picture, you will be listening for these beeps as you pop the tracks. As you rewind and hear the beeps (which should be quite evident, even at high speed), stop and roll forward, listening to the track. You should hear the assistant cameraperson call out the take number (for 11F–7, for instance, it would sound something like "Scene 11, Frank. Take Seven. Marker!") Continue to roll forward until you hear the sticks of the slate close. Listen carefully since there are often noises on the set which you might confuse with the sticks.

When you have found the area with the sound of the sticks hitting, rock the track slowly back and forth under the sound head until you find the exact point where the sound begins (this is called the *first modulation*). Slate boards are designed to have very sharp sound attacks so there should be very little problem with this. Mark this with grease pencil as the first sprocket of your slate frame (*see* Figure 4.14) and then mark the entire frame much as you did the track start mark. Once again, be careful not to extend your mark down into the area where the sound is, as the grease pencil will rub off on the sound head it you do.

After you've marked and identified the slate, move back to the next one, continuing in this fashion until you've got to 11E–4. In between the point where there is a double beep signifying the end of the preceding take (11D–5) and the beep signifying the beginning of 11E–4, make a straight cut on your splicer. This will be, as you've already determined, the beginning of Dailies Roll Three. Put this up on the shelf next to the already marked picture reel for dailies roll three. Tape the little piece of paper that lists the takes on that reel to the front of the reels. You can now move along to the other takes.

After you've gotten to 11A–4, you'll break the reels

again (this does not mean that you will take an axe to them; it means that you will make a cut between 11A–4 and 11pu–3), and then continue back to the beginning of the roll.

A few words of warning. There are times when the sound recordist will take some wild sound (that is, sound for which there is no picture). These *wild tracks*, along with any sync sound takes that have no matching picture (either because of the director's request or because the recordist thought that there would be something valuable in them), should be cut out of the dailies roll and saved on a separate roll. There is often a need for them in the editing process and it will be good for the editor to have them available. There are also times when a take is shot *MOS*, without sound, take 10A-2 for instance. We will see how to deal with this in a few pages.

We now have three rolls of marked picture and three rolls of matching marked track. If there have been no terrible problems with paperwork or slating, it is now probably about 10:00 am. We are now ready to sync everything up.

Put the matching picture and track rolls up on your bench. Thread them up on the synchronizer so that the picture is in the first gang and the track is on the second, where the sound head is (these are the positions that you will most often load the film on your synchronizer). With this arrangement you will find that the track will not wind up (or 'take up') at the same rate as the picture. This is what the *differential* is for. Many editors use this to make sure that the picture and track both take up at the same rate; this will save them the embarrassment of having tons of track spilling out onto the floor while they are working with it. You put the differential in between the picture and sound reels on the right (take–up) side, after making sure that you've put the little washer that comes with it between the picture reel and the rewind. The two reels will now take up at the same rate. If you don't have a differential you can use 16mm cores to space the reels out (or use actual, rented, spacers) or, you might want to reverse the order of the picture and track by putting the track in gang two where there is a sound head and putting the picture in gang three where there is not (if there is a head there, you will obviously want to be *very* careful not to let the head slip onto the film as it will put an embarrassingly long colored gouge into the film).

Put the reels into the synchronizer so that the picture start mark is at 0'00 on the counter. Since you have no head leader yet on the track, put the track in randomly. Then wind the two of them down until you see the first picture slate — for take 10–5. The chances are infinitesimal that the sound slate will line up exactly with it. In fact, it's quite likely that you sound slate is many feet away. To correct this, remove the track from the synchronizer and, by hand and without running the synchronizer, pull the sound out of the feed reel (the left one) until you get to the marked-up slate. Put this slate into the second gang so that it lines up exactly with the picture slate. The picture and sound are now locked in sync with each other. Now, slowly roll backwards (you might want to rotate the wheel of the synchronizer with your thumb) until you see the cut point on the picture, which in this case is where the top of take 10–5 is cut to the head leader. Make a little mark on the track. Cut the track at this point and attach the head track leader to it (you'll probably want to put your splicer on the right side of the synchronizer to do this; one of the only times that you'll be making your cuts on that side of the synchronizer). When you run backwards to the picture start mark, the track start mark should line up perfectly with it, at the 0'00 mark. If this has happened, congratulations, you've just sunk up your first take ("sunk up" appears to be the past tense for sync up; I know it looks silly, but that's what everybody says).

At the head of the take on the track you can now write 10–5 (the scene and take number) in the position corresponding to the identification mark on the picture. Hang the excess track that you've chopped off on a pin in a trim bin that you've cleverly placed next to you, and you're ready to move onto the next take.

But, before we do, let's take a step back and examine what we've just done. The theory behind synching dailies is really quite simple. Because the recording of sound and picture is done on two different machines you will end up with materials of differing lengths. In order to sync the two, you leave the picture as is and adjust the length of the track to match the picture by adding or, more often, removing pieces of track as necessary.

Now, move down to the end of take 10–5. Where you have made the cross dividing the two picture takes, make a cross on the corresponding point on the track (once again, making sure not to write in the lower stripe where the sound is). This cross will be a sync point for you.

Roll down until you reach the next picture slate (10–6), lock the synchronizer at that point, then pull out the track from the feed reel until you get to the track slate. At this point there are two schools of thought on how to sync the rest of reel. Some assistants prefer to continue as they did for the first take on the reel, removing the track from synchronizer and pulling out the track so that the track slate lines up with the picture slate. Other assistants prefer never to remove the track from the synchronizer (thereby minimizing the danger of losing sync). That method is the one that I'll describe here.

After finding the track slate for 10–6 put it into the *third* gang on the synchronizer so that the slate lines up exactly with the picture slate. Then slowly roll back until you get to the cross between the two picture takes, mark the corresponding point on the track in the third gang (as well as on the second gang, if you haven't already done so — some assistants using this method prefer to make both of the marks at the same time). You have just marked the beginning of take 10-6 on the track in the third gang as well as the end of take 10–5 on the track in the second gang. All you have to do now is remove everything in between these two marks. To do this, roll backwards a bit and make cuts at both of these marks (with your splicer on the left side of the synchronizer). You will then have a long piece which you can remove from the splicer (this is the footage between the end of 10–5 and the start of 10–6). Hang the piece which you've just removed on top of the other piece of track in your bin, splice the pieces that are still in the synchronizer together and roll forward. You will now have sunk up 10–6, leaving the picture in the first gang and the track in the second. You should have nothing running in the third gang.

What you have done, essentially, is find the end of 10–5 and the beginning of 10–6, removed the excess between them, and then butted the two takes together so that the end of 10–5 comes at the same point as the beginning of 10–6 — at the cross.

If there had not been enough track at the end of 10–5 before 10–6 began you would have found the beginning of 10–6 and added as much fill onto the end of 10–5 as was necessary to butt it up against 10–6.

You can now move onto the next take. Spin down to the end of 10–6, and mark the cross on the track. However, you can see that the next take, 10A–2, was shot MOS, that is, without sound (this is why I write MOS after the take number on all of the identifications; i.e. 10A–2MOS). The next take on the sound roll will, therefore, be 10B–2, not 10A–2 (since no sound was taken during 10A–2). Make your track cut at the end of 10–6, at the cross as usual, but splice fill leader onto the end of the take. Then spin down to the end of 10A–2 and mark the cut point as you normally would, except you will put it on the fill. You can then proceed as normal, finding the slate for 10B–2, putting that in the third gang, rolling backwards, lining up the cross marks and splicing the fill to the head of 10B–2.

To simplify it, you do everything that you would normally do except you obviously don't have to listen for the sound slate on the MOS take and line it up.

Continue until the end of the roll. When you've finished, cut the track tail leader on at the last cut point and you are finished with your first roll of dailies. Continue onto the next two rolls and, by 11:00am or noon, you should be done with the day's dailies.

A word about those pieces of track which you've been accumulating in your trim bin (one dailies reel per pin). After you've sunk all of the dailies you or Wendy will be checking them for proper sync. If you find that you've made any mistakes in synching up the dailies, it will be relatively easy to go back to the pin where you've hung the excess track for the reel you've made the mistake in, find the piece of track for that take, and re–sync it all. If everything is all right (and it most often will be) you can throw all of those pieces away.

One final note. Remember those takes with blurred slates? Remember how I asked you to put a big circle on the blurred frame? Now I'll tell you why, and it involves a slight adaptation to your synching method. For these takes, we can assume that the actual first modulation occurs, on average, two sprockets before a normal slate. That is, instead of it happening on the frame line before the frame you've marked with an 'X', it is happening somewhere in the middle of the preceding frame. So, as you sync a take like this (and you'll know which takes they are because they'll be the ones with the circles on them), instead of making the first modulation fall on the first sprocket of the 'X' frame, you make it come two sprockets before that frame line, in the middle of the frame with 'O' on it. When you put the track in the synchronizer, you put it in two sprockets earlier than normal. You would then erase the old slate mark and correct it (*see* Figure 4.15). This enables you to get to within two sprockets of what the correct sync must be, and as that is one forty–eighth of a second, that should be close enough for everyone. Of course, in 16mm you won't have the option of sliding it a fraction of frame as there is only sprocket per frame. This is an inaccuracy that you'll have to live with. In this case, I usually put the 'X' of the slate on the first fully closed frame.

Now comes the time to check your work. It is essential

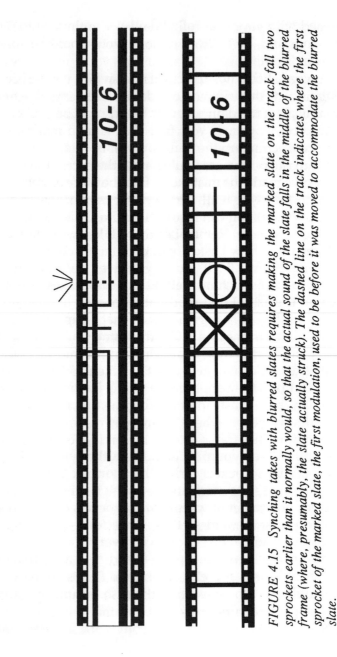

FIGURE 4.15 Synching takes with blurred slates requires making the marked slate on the track fall two sprockets earlier than it normally would, so that the actual sound of the slate falls in the middle of the blurred frame (where, presumably, the slate actually struck). The dashed line on the track indicates where the first sprocket of the marked slate, the first modulation, used to be before it was moved to accommodate the blurred slate.

for the assistant (with or without Wendy) to look at the dailies before anyone else, unless there is absolutely no time to do so. Not only can you check sync that way, but you can prepare all of the paperwork that will help the editor take notes at dailies. It also gives you the first real look at any problems inherent in the footage. If there is anything serious that hasn't come to your attention by now, a viewing (and, let us not forget, a listening) will bring them to your attention.

Thread the Moviola (*see* Figure 4.16). There is a special way to accurately thread the film at the picture and sound gates and it is tied in with how you've marked the slates. You've sunk the film up so that the sound of the slate hitting occurs in between two frames; you should line them up in the Moviola that way.

To do that, place the start marks for the reels in their gates. Then disengage the two heads so that you can move the picture independently of the track. First, frame up the picture so that it is positioned correctly in the gate (use the Academy leader for this, to make sure that the full frame can be seen in the Moviola, with no frame lines visible at either the top or bottom of the frame), then go back to the start mark and, rocking it with the connecting bar, position it so that with one more little turn of the bar it would begin to bring the picture into the frame. Then, position the track so that the first sprocket of the start mark line is under the sound head. Now you can lock the two of them together and know that they are in as close a sync as the machines can give you.

At this point, you should also set the *footage counter* on the Moviola to 0000'00. It is a good idea to get in the habit of *zeroing out* the counter before running any roll on the Moviola.

Often, you will have access to a flatbed for screening dailies. The threading of these machines varies, depending on their make, but I find it nearly impossible to get as accurate a line–up as I can on a Moviola. There is a point on most flatbeds where, by rocking the picture back and forth, you

FIGURE 4.16 The picture is threaded up from the feed reel (A), around two sets of rollers (B), through a gate (C), under the picture head (D), through another gate (E), a roller (F), and onto the take–up reel (G). Care must be taken to leave adequately sized loops on either side of the picture head, between each of the gates.

will be able to see two frames superimposed on one another. This is as close to the frameline position as you will be able to get. Line that up with the first modulation of track, lock the two together, and you'll be in sync.

Now you can run the dailies. Try to listen with headphones, especially if you are using a noisy stand–up Moviola. As you watch the dailies you should have the script supervisor's notes to refer to as well as your own lists of what is on each dailies roll.

You are now going to make the *Editor's Dailies Notes Sheets* for Wendy (*see* Figure 4.17). Some editors like these notes on looseleaf paper, some in spiral notebooks. Whatever their preference, the basic concept remains the same. At the top of the page is the *dailies roll number* and the *date of shooting*. Following each take on the roll is a short description of the shot. Leave some room for any notes that Wendy or Adam will want to make during the dailies screening. Your description should be fairly short and standardized. List the size of the shot (WS for wide shot, CU for close–up, etc.) and a description that will help identify it for the editor (master, dolly to CU of ABBY, etc.). You can decide what to write as you watch the shot (using the script supervisor's notes if necessary). And, as you watch the dailies, check that everything is in perfect sync.

When you've finished checking the dailies, Philip should clean the picture and track with a velvet while he rewinds it, making sure that no scratches are put on the film during this cleaning. Then the reels should be packed into some transporting device (the most common are fiber cases which hold six reels comfortably and have a handle on top for ease of carrying) along with notes and a little penlight for Wendy to see and write with in the darkened screening room.

When you're done with all of this, you're done with synching the dailies.

Date Shot _9·10·90_

DAILIES NOTES — REEL #_1_

10-5   WS - MASTER

-6

10A-2 MOS   WS - POV EMPTY ROOM

10B-2   MWS - ABBY to cabinet

EDITOR'S DAILIES NOTES

FIGURE 4.17. The Editor's Dailies Notes. Enough room is left so that the editor can write his or her (along with the director's) comments during dailies and cutting. Note also that when more than one take from a set up is printed only the take number of the second is listed, not the scene number. This provides a good visual clue to anyone looking at the list that those takes are from the same set up.

Dailies Screening

Later on that day, your film, Wendy, Philip, and much of the production crew will march into a screening room ready to watch the first day's dailies. Actually, you and your film had better arrive ten or fifteen minutes before the scheduled time to make sure that everything is going to flow as smoothly as it can. Philip should have rewound and cleaned each reel of dailies so that the picture and track are both wound correctly for projection and are free from dirt. Give Wendy all of your notes and check everything out with the projectionist (I usually tell him — and it still usually is a him — what reel numbers he is showing that day, what format the picture is in, and what wind) and then you will take your seat in the room.

Seating preferences vary from film to film. I've worked on movies where the director has opened the dailies to anyone who wanted to come, and I've worked on some where attendance was very restricted. Some directors prefer that everyone sit in the same places every day; and some don't really give a hoot. The most important thing for you, as the assistant, is to be near the sound level controls (if you're going to be working them) and the intercom to the projectionist so that you can relay the seemingly endless stream of instructions up to him.

Some directors like the assistant or the editor to call out the number of prints of each setup as they are screened (e.g., "Scene ten master, two takes"), some don't. Ask Wendy what Adam will want.

Once everyone has arrived and the doors have been closed, someone (guess who?) will signal to the projectionist to begin. Then you will notice several things beginning to happen. For one thing, every person in the room is going to be looking at the film for his or her own reasons. The camera crew is going to want to be sure that the film was shot and printed correctly. The sound crew is going to be listening for sound problems. Costume and makeup will dislike certain

71

takes because the star had his hair messed or his handkerchief wasn't folded properly, and the producer is going to want to be sure that the production is looking good and is also getting useable footage without wasting time and money. In fact, about the only people who will be looking at the film as a whole are the two people whose jobs depend on it — the director and the editor.

This is going to put you in a very interesting spot. For one thing, you are going to have to be noticing *all* of the things that the other people are noticing individually. It is important that the star's handkerchief matches from shot to shot. It will also be important to remember just which shots have lousy sound or focus problems (as these things are usually difficult to tell on the editing machine). It is also important to note which shots have the best performances in them, and which are the most consistent with each other.

All of these things are important to the editing of a film and Wendy should be taking careful note of all of them. Yet, very often, it is the assistant who must take note of things like technical problems so that he or she can mark it down on all of the paperwork as necessary. There's a good chance that at some point during the editing, Wendy will turn to you and say, "Remember the shot that had the bump in the middle of the dolly?" It helps if you take your own notes during dailies screenings so that you can remember all of these things. And since you'll never write it down if you don't notice it first, pay attention at dailies.

At the same time that you will be taking some of your notes, Wendy will probably be taking hers. She will most likely be seated next to Adam, who will be giving her feedback on what things he likes best and least in the dailies. Some directors prefer that their editor do no cutting until they are there with them, but the more normal practice is for the editor to be cutting day by day as the crew shoots. Adam's notes on what takes he liked and didn't like (and why) will be very helpful to Wendy as she cuts the footage.

As a result of these notes, Wendy may ask you for certain things. For instance, she may ask you to print up an unrequested take (the *B-negative*), or to reprint a take with a different color balance. Or she may ask that you listen to the original quarter-inch tape on a particular take to see if some annoying sounds can be gotten rid of. Write all of these requests down (it helps to buy a nice supply of flashlight pens or little flashlights) and act on them immediately after the screening or the first thing the following day.

After the screening is over, collect all of the paperwork and film and arrange to get it back to the editing room. That footage is too important to get misplaced by screening room personnel who don't really care about your troubles (they have three more films coming in after you anyway). Unless you feel 100 percent sure that your film will return to you safely, always move it yourself.

One final word about dailies screenings. Many production managers, in their desire to be thrifty, think that banning editorial assistants and apprentices from dailies (if they are in the evening overtime hours) is a good way to save money. The truth, however, is exactly the opposite. The more that you and Philip know the film, the more help you will be to Wendy in the editing. This will, in the long run, save a lot of time and money. There is no better way to examine the film than to see it on a large screen. In addition, there is also the very human side of things. You and Philip will be working for many more months (possibly a year or more) and there is no faster way to alienate people than to ban them from a screening of a project that they are working on. Besides, Philip can help you get all of the film back to the cutting room after the screening.

So, we will assume that you and Philip have gathered up Wendy's notes after the dailies. You have dutifully written down all of the instructions that have been given to you. Wendy is going out to dinner with Adam to discuss the footage with him (and, presumably, a dozen other depart-

ment heads, all of whom need to know some crucial information in order to plan for the next day's shooting). The two of
you, therefore, bring the film back to the editing room,
rewind it (many projectionists will not rewind your film for
you unless they're given something extra—like money), clean
it, and set it out on the film racks, ready for tomorrow's work.

Since we have been to an evening dailies screening, it
is probably about 8:00 or 9:00 pm before you've finished with
all of your work. What do you do now? If you ask me, you
should go home to your other life already.

5

PREPARING FOR EDITING

Coding and Logging

One of the greatest tasks of an assistant editor is making sure that the editor will always have any piece of film whenever it is needed. It is this vast librarian–like task that makes good assistants so valuable. If Wendy cannot find the three frame addition to a shot she knows that she needs to make an edit work, then she's not going to be able to edit the film, is she? There are assistant editors who always seem to work in a chaotic state of near-hysteria, in which the three frames are always misplaced, always madly searched for, and always belatedly found. A good system will enable anyone — be it the editor, assistant, or apprentice — to find anything within seconds. If Wendy wants to see a take, it should take no longer to get it than it takes to walk over to a box, lift it out, and bring it back to her. If I seem rather insistent on this point it is only because it is one which I see as the cornerstone of good assistant work. Unless everyone, including the director, editor, apprentice, and producer, works better in the midst of chaos, I see no reason to have chaos in the editing room. Personally relaxed but tightly organized editorial situations make for better filmmaking.

So it is important that every assistant get serious about the setting up of the system for a film. There are virtually as many systems as there are assistants organizing them. Yet nearly all are based on certain principles that make life easier for the editor(s).

The cornerstone of any film editing system is the code number. With over 100,000 feet of film printed on most features, finding individual frames could get very complicated if there were no way of identifying each frame. How, pray tell, does one differentiate between one take of a closeup of our hero Abby and another take from the same camera angle? There is no way to tell by looking at the picture. And how does one identify a piece from the soundtrack? There is nothing on it to see.

One thing you definitely DO NOT do with unidentifiable pieces is throw them out. That tiny little piece of film that you need today is almost always the one you threw away two weeks ago. *Nothing should ever be thrown away*. That's rule number one for a system.

So, how will you identify the film and track? Luckily, this is a problem solved long ago. Before any film gets cut you will have it *edge coded* (sometimes called *edge numbered*).

What this means is that your film (both picture and track) will be run through a machine which will print inked numbers on one edge of the film (*see* Figure 5.1). One number will be printed for every foot, which means that there will be one number every sixteen frames in 35mm and one every forty frames in 16mm (unless you ask for 16mm coding that is also coded once every sixteen frames). The coding machine that prints the numbers automatically increases the printed number by one every time it prints a new number. In that way every foot of the film will have a different code number assigned to it. In practice, this will be just as good as if you had coded every frame of the film. In fact, it will be better, since film with code numbers on every frame would make the

FIGURE 5.1 *Coded film. The frame with the design in it is coded AA1047. The frame with the single large arrow is AA1048. Thus, the frame with only the two small arrows is called AA1048+3. Note that the frame with the single small arrow in it can be called either AA1047+9 or AA1048-7. The arrows all point towards the tail of the film.*

work of editing much messier.

In many editing rooms, the apprentice editor will be the one coding the dailies on a rented coding machine. Renting these machines, though, can get expensive, so some companies send their film out to coding services to have it edge numbered.

The numbers that get printed on the film are almost completely up to you, within the limits of the printing blocks on the coding machines. One setup is to have two letters followed by four numbers (such as AB3456). Another common arrangement is to have seven or eight digits, of which only the last four need be numbers (e.g., 123C5678 or 1234567 or 1BCD5678,etc.). These machines have many different brand names but the two most common are Acmade® and Moy® coding machines.

Though using code numbers for identification is very important for the assistant editor, the editor has an even more important use for it. If matching rolls of already sunk-up picture and track (such as the pix and track rolls for dailies roll) are coded in the same way, then each code number will also serve as a point where the picture and track sync up in much the same way that the slate does. In this manner, the editor can instantaneously line up his picture and his track in the Moviola and run them in sync.

Don't worry if this sounds a little confusing in theory. It is actually much easier in practice, as we shall now see.

After the dailies have been returned from the dailies screening you can have them coded. For our system we will use the common New York system and code them sequentially by dailies roll numbers. In this way, dailies roll one will be assigned the code number AA1000 at its start mark. At the start mark, fasten a piece of paper tape which says exactly that ("Start Code AA1000") on both the picture and the track reels. Dailies roll two will be coded AA2000, roll three will be AA3000, up to roll 10 which will be AA0000. Then I would cycle to the codes BB1000, BB2000, etc. Generally, it is a good idea not to use *both* EE and FF, or VV and WW prefixes (since they look alike) or the letter OO codes (since it can get confused with the number zero).

There are many variations on this particular coding system. In one, some attempt is made to use code numbers on each take that will coincide with the setup and take numbers. Eight digit codes are particularly good for this as you can set up codes something like 010E2000 for Scene 10E, Take 2. Another variation is to cycle the code numbers in this manner AA1000, AA2000, ... , AA9000, AA0000, AB1000, AB2000, ..., AB0000, AC1000, and so on. This system is of most value when you expect a large amount of footage and you are worried about running out of numbers (26 letters of the alphabet with ten rolls used for each letter gives room for only 260 dailies rolls). In actual practice many coding machines don't have all of the letters of the alphabet. Some don't have the letter J or the letter O, for instance, and some only have the letters from AA through KK. In addition, many of the letters that you *do* have should be reserved for other uses, which we shall discuss later.

Practically speaking, if the director intends to print more than 120,000 feet of film I would choose the second method. If there is some doubt, I prefer the first method, always leaving open the option of cycling back to the letters AB, AC, etc., if I run out of prefix letter combinations before the end of dailies.

In the case of eight–digit systems, a common practice is to use the first three digits for either the dailies reel number or the scene number. Thus, our Dailies Reel One would be coded 001 0000 (note the space after the first three digits), or takes from scene ten would be coded 010 000. Be careful when you use this last system to make sure that when you code dailies reels with more than one scene number in them that you do not miscode any of the takes.

After the footage is coded it will be tails out and will have a lot of funny white, yellow or black numbers running down one edge of the film. Two things need to be done now — checking that the coding was done properly, and logging the numbers into a logbook for easy reference. Both of these things can be accomplished quite easily if we make one small adjustment to the synching procedure that we've already discussed. Before you send your dailies reels out for coding put them up on your table, run them through your synchronizer and log them in. This is how you do that.

Run the film through the synchronizer and put the start marks in at 0000'00. This is where the AA1000 code number will fall after the reel is coded. Take out a blank code book sheet. Gather all of your paperwork around you and then begin rolling down on the synchronizer until you get to the first take on the roll (in this case 10–5). Begin to fill out the sheets as shown in Figure 5.2. Enter the dailies roll number and the date the footage was shot at the top of the page. Then enter the information pertinent to this particular take — the lab roll number, scene and take number, camera and sound roll numbers, and the short description which you gave the take in the editor's dailies notes.

Now, look at the footage counter at the first frame of the take. It should read "0012." This means that, when this roll is coded, the code number AA1012 will be on that frame. Enter that number under the column "Code Numbers". Now look at the edge of the film which has a color band on it. Every 16 frames there is a number imprinted within that blue or black band. For 35mm film the number will usually look something like F32X12345. In 16mm the numbers are much smaller and less visible. They look something like $^{12}_{38}0938$. This is called the *latent edge number* or the *key number*. This is a number which Kodak (or whatever company manufactured the raw stock that your movie is being shot on) imprinted in the original stock. These numbers become visible after processing and printing. These are the *only* numbers on the original negative and therefore are the only numbers that your laboratory will know about. Enter this number in your

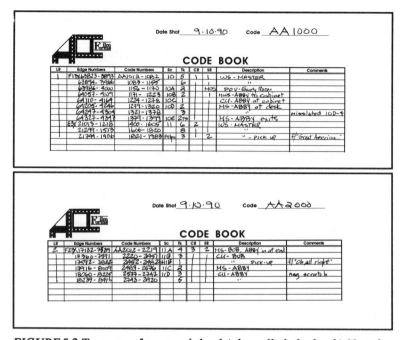

FIGURE 5.2 Two pages from a code book (also called a logbook). Note that this assistant is using a new page for each code number prefix (one page for AA1000 and another for AA2000 in this case). This makes codes somewhat easier to find than the alternative, which is to put as many dailies reels on one page as will fit without breaking up a dailies roll onto two pages. The comments column is for notations of misslates, negative damage, etc.

logbook under the "Edge Numbers" column. Don't worry if the first number is many frames down from the first frame of the take. Use the first number within the take.

Spin the film down (through the synchronizer of course) until the end of the take. Note the last code and edge numbers within the take and write them down. Now, on the next line, list the pertinent information for the next take (10–6, in this case). Continue until you have gotten to the end of the dailies roll. You should now have gotten the code numbers

81

for every take on that roll, along with the other information necessary to find any of them later.

At this point your tail leaders should be beginning to come into the synchronizer. At the first code number in the tail leader put a small piece of white tape on both the picture and track, mark the exact frame where that code number would fall, and write on that tape what the code number would be (in the case of Dailies Roll One, it would be AA1983).

Now you can code this reel (and the other dailies rolls when you have logged them in) and when they are done they will be tails out. All you need to do is to check that the first code number that falls on the tail leader falls on the exact frame that you marked on that small piece of white tape and that it is, indeed, the correct number. If all is well then the reels have been coded correctly and you have entered them in the logbook correctly.

Some assistants, given enough time, like to do this logging as they are synching the dailies since it means that they won't have to put the film up and run it through the synchronizer a second time. If you've got the time during the synching process as well as the ability to keep all of the synching and logging tasks straight in your head at one time, then by all means go ahead and do this. Just be extra careful about making mistakes.

Breaking Down The Footage

At this point you've got an awful lot of paperwork and some coded footage sitting tails out on your film rack. Wendy is probably dying to begin editing and to do this she will need that footage. After all, at this point in the film, there is nothing else for her to cut. Once you are further along into the film the chances are good that she will be cutting slower than the film crew is shooting so that there will be a bit less pressure to provide her with footage.

So, can you just give her the footage and paperwork

and let her cut? Of course not. There are still two more major pieces of paperwork to account for.

The first things are those *trim tabs* I mentioned back in the list of supplies. These tabs will eventually be stored with the film — one tab for each take (*see* Figure 5.3). Listed on them will be the shot (10–5, in this example), the code numbers (AA1012—1082), and the short description you gave the take (WS — MASTER). Now you can see why I encouraged you to be concise in these descriptions; there just isn't much room on these damned things. These trim tabs can be made up as soon as the logbook has been done since all of the necessary information is in it.

The final bit of necessary paperwork to be done is filling in the code numbers in the lined script. On the notes pages you should fill in, next to each printed take, its proper

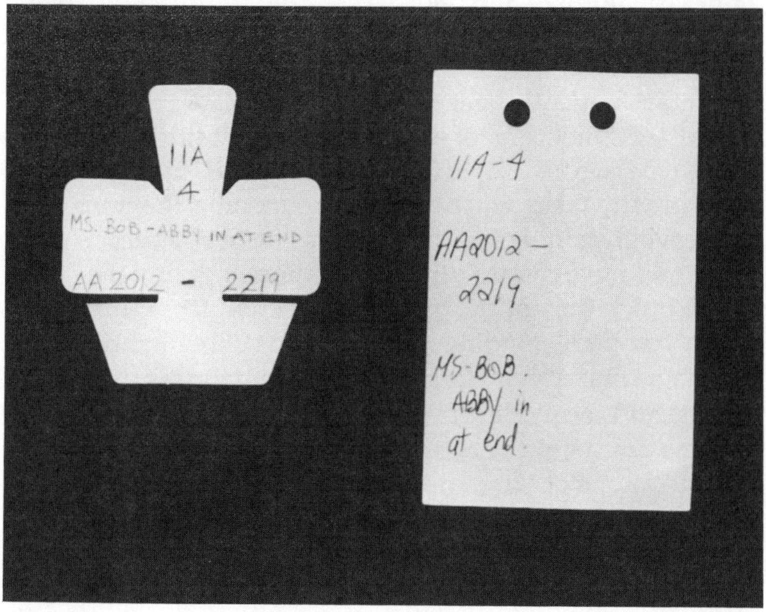

FIGURE 5.3 Note that the descriptions used on these tabs (the East Coast tab on the left, the West Coast tab on the left) are the ones used in both the dailies log and the code book.

83

code numbers (*see* Figure 5.4). The script pages should then be put in a three-ring binder. Every day, as the new script pages come in, you will add these new script pages into the binder in their proper scene number order.

Writing the codes into the script can save Wendy a lot of time when she's looking for takes. All she has to do is look at the script, find the setup she needs, and she knows the code number.

Once these things have been done, the individual takes can be flanged off and made ready for the Wendy. To do this, place the picture and track rolls on the rewind on the right side of your bench, tails out (this is how they ended up after they were coded anyway). Put them into the synchronizer, in sync. Take off the tail leaders and hang them up in a trim bin (you can reuse them by simply taping a different dailies roll number and date over the old information). Now, wind the take onto your flange (this is a piece of equipment which looks like half of a take-up reel with a one-inch hub at its center) until you get to the head of that take. Wind it *through* the synchronizer until it is on the left side of the table, and cut the two takes apart at the grease pencil mark you used to divide the takes when you were synching them up. This will leave the single take by itself on the flange, heads out.

Remove this take from the flange by giving the flange a little quick turn in the opposite direction from the way in which you were winding it up. Wrap a rubber hand around the take so that it won't flap loose, tuck the trim tab in between the first and second layers of film, and set it up on your table. It's now ready for the editor. Of course, one take isn't going to do her much good so continue this process until you've got all of the footage for one scene broken down (*see* Figure 5.5).

Now, and only now, can Wendy actually cut the scene.

PICTURE Silent Night, Silent Cowboy

DIRECTOR Adam Free

DATE 10·7·83

Sc.	Tk	SR	CR	Comments	Description
10	1	1	1	0:40 "Horrid"	40MM - ABBY enters room screen r., x's to desk and throws mss. onto table. He reaches for cabinet, gets shocked, then pulls out liquor. He drinks, hears typewriter, then exits cam. r.
	2			0:20 INC	
	3			0:41	
	4			0:38 "Rushed"	
AA1012-1082	⑤			0:45 "Good"	
AA1083-1155	⑥			0:45 "Best"	
10A AA1156-1170	1 ②	MOS		0:10 0:12	40MM - ABBY's P.O.V. of the room.
10B AA1171-1223	1 ②		1	0:35 0:37	60MM - ABBY reaches for cabinet, gets shocked, hears noise, and exits cam. r.
10C AA1224-1276	①			0:29	90MM - Closer of 10B
10D AA1277-1320 AA1321-1378	1 ② ③			0:21 "NG" 0:20 "Good" 0:30 "Best" (slated TK4)	75MM - ABBY walks in from S.R. and throws mss. on table. He exits S.R.
10E AA1379-1399	1 TS ② TS			0:15 0:10 "Good"	75MM - ABBY enters o.s.l., goes into bedroom hall, and exits.

FIGURE 5.4 *Marked-up script notes. The editor can find takes using the lined script and these notes without ever referring to the log book.*

Odds And Ends

You will notice that you've got some track left over from the synching of the dailies that you never used. This *wild track* or *wild sound* was sound taken on the set with no picture rolling. This is often done to get the ambiance of the room (helpful for the sound effects editors later on), specific effects peculiar to the location, or readings of lines that the director wanted to do on the set. (Off–camera lines, on the other end of a telephone for instance, voice-over speeches and the like are often done this way; they are often redone in a looping stage (see Chapter 13 for more details on this) near the end of the editing process but having temporary lines here can help the editor pace out the scene properly.

This soundtrack material may be very helpful to Wendy as she cuts. Then again, it may be of no use to her whatsoever, but give *her* the opportunity to make that decision. For that reason, it should also be coded and logged. The easiest way to do this is to build up a reel of wild sound as the dailies progress. Unless Wendy has an immediate need for the sound, let it build up until there are five or six hundred feet on the roll. (Always make sure, however, that all wild track for any scene is given to Wendy before she is ready to cut that scene.) Then get it coded and logged into your logbook on a separate page reserved for wild sound. Most assistants will code this wild track with the prefixes WS, WT, and WV (or 001W0000, 002W0000, etc.) so make sure not to use these codes for any of your dailies. When you or Philip write up the trim tabs, do them all in red (to indicate soundtrack, of course).

The way in which you divide the work described here between you and Philip depends entirely upon your work load and your confidence in him. At the beginning of any film the assistant normally syncs the dailies. As the shooting progresses it is not uncommon to hand this task over to the apprentice. It is a good way for your apprentice to learn as well as a good way to free you up for other tasks, especially if Wendy is the type of editor who wants you to stand next to her as she edits.

However, you should always be the one to screen the footage before dailies and prepare the editor's logs. In this way you will get familiar with the film. Also remember that, ultimately, it is your job to make sure that every task in the editing (whether you or Philip does it) is done correctly.

Different editors will ask for their film in different ways. I generally like all the takes for any given scene put in order into a series of white two-piece boxes. The assistant marks on the outside of the box what scene number is inside. Never put takes from different scenes in the same box. The box can then be put on a shelf reserved for material that the editor has not yet begun to cut.

Thus, when Wendy asks you for the footage to Scene

FIGURE 5.5 These three takes have been flanged up and wrapped up with a rubber band. With their trim tabs slipped between the first and second layers of film, they can now be given to the editor for cutting.

10 you can go to the boxes on the shelf marked Scene 10 (which includes all takes and wild tracks) and either give them to her in the boxes or set them out for her, as she wishes. When she asks you for Scene 11 it will also be ready for her. As you get more and more footage in, you should always check with her to see if she has a priority as to which scenes she would like to cut next. In that way, if you have four scenes to prepare you can know the order in which you should code and log them. Most of the time you will be able to keep up with the dailies on a day-to-day basis, so that you will never be more than a day behind in getting footage ready for Wendy. Sometimes, however, you will fall behind. On *Hair*, one scene took two and a half weeks to shoot and ran through nearly 80,000 feet of film. It took us nearly a week to get it all prepared. The bottom line, though, is to ensure that Wendy has the film she wants to cut when she wants to cut it.

6

THE
EDITOR
EDITS

At some point Wendy is going to want to begin editing the movie. On some films the producer or director may be in a mad rush to get the first few scenes cut to see whether a particular actor or actress can really act, if a director is getting the proper coverage, or if the editor can edit.

In any case, Wendy will begin editing. Her first step will probably be to screen all of the footage shot for the scene she is about to edit. In general, most directors like to shoot a master shot of all or most of the scene from the widest possible angle (so it shows as much of the action as possible). They will then go in to shoot *coverage*, which are the myriad of other camera set–ups which make up the film — close-ups, two-shots, panning shots, etc. etc. Anything which covers the action shot in the master is called coverage. Wendy will examine all of it.

If she has already cut the scene that comes immediately preceding or following it she may screen those scenes as well. All the while she will probably be taking notes as to what her preferences are and what the problems are with each take. She will integrate these notes with those that she took at the dailies screenings so that she has a thorough idea of what both she and Adam want to do with the scene. She will then make a little plan (either in her head or on paper) as to how she wants to cut the scene. She will decide what take she wants to begin the scene with. Placing that take in her Moviola she will run it until she gets to the point where she wants to cut to her second take. She will mark this frame with a grease pencil. Leaving the first take in the Moviola she will screen other takes on her cutter to remind herself of her options. When she finally decides on the correct take to cut to, she will find the frame she wants to cut into on the second take. She will mark this frame. She will then rewind the cut film (that is the piece that she is cutting out of) back out of the Moviola until she has the frame she marked over her splicer on the editing table. Then she will make the cut. She will then remove the second take's picture from the cutter, find that marked frame, and cut it. Some editors will immediately cut the sound as well. Others run the picture cut first to make sure that they have chosen the correct cut points and, if they decide that they have, then cut the soundtrack to match the picture.

If you think about it, this will leave several things around the editor's table. There will be the first part of the first take (from its very beginning, including the slate) cut onto the second part of the second take (all the way until its very end including the flash frames) all together on the Moviola. This piece, because it contains the cut (or cuts) that Wendy has already made, is known as the *cut*. There will be no film on the cutter. There will be two loose rolls — one of them will be the remainder of the first take and the other will be the first part of the second take. Pieces left over after a cut has been made are called *trims*. A trim that comes after a piece which is in the cut is called *tail trim*, and a trim that comes before a piece in the cut is called a *head trim*.

Let's assume that Wendy was cutting Scene 10. She has decided to start with the master shot and to use Take Six (i.e., Scene 10–6) for the opening of the scene. She wants to cut out of it after ABBY enters and stops to look around the room; then she will cut to a shot of ABBY looking (she will use 10D–3 for this).

After she has made this cut, you will have the following:

a) Head trim on 10D–3
b) Tail trim on 10-6
c) Cut-together pieces of 10-6 onto 10D-3 (the cut)

You will also have the master shot, Take Five, which she did not use. Takes which are not used at all are called *outs*. So, unless Wendy uses 10-5 later on in the scene you will have 10-5 as an out.

Some editors will leave the slate and excess material on the head of the take with which they started the scene (scene 10-6, in this case) until they have scenes to cut it onto. Others do not. Let's assume that Wendy does not want to keep the head piece on. She makes a decision as to where she will want the scene to begin and removes the very head piece. You will now have two trims from 10-6 — a head trim and a tail trim.

Well, what do you do with these trims? If Wendy is the kind of editor who works by herself you will have to do nothing — she will do it all. But some editors like to have their assistants standing by them, doing all of the filing work. In that case you would have a trim bin right next to you. When Wendy wants to use a take, you (or she) would take the trim tab from the take and hang it (and its rubber band) onto the top row of pins. If you are using a low bin you would place it onto the rack above the curled pins. You and she will then be able to see the code numbers, scene/take numbers, and description quite clearly.

When Wendy hands you the two pieces of 10–6 you hang them on the pin on the rack immediately below the matching trim tab. It is all right to spool off the film from a short roll so that it is all unwound in the barrel. If the trim,

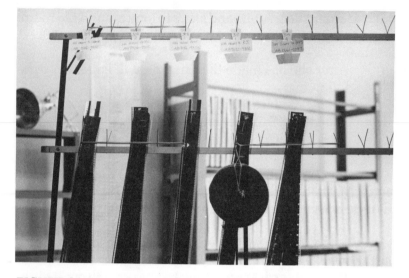

FIGURE 6.1 These trims are hung underneath their respective trim tabs. Note that very small trims which might get lost hanging with the long ones on the lower rack are hung underneath the trim tab on the first rack. This insures that they won't accidentally be dropped into the bin while the editor is looking through the trims on the lower rack.

however, is too big you can take the rubber band, thread it through the center of the roll, loop it back onto itself to make a sort of rubber band hook, and hang the trim (as a roll) from the proper pin. In this way, all trims from any particular take are located immediately below their identifying trim tab. They will be easy to find this way (*see* Figure 6.1.)

As Wendy gets further into Scene 10 you will have more takes to hang up and, undoubtedly more individual trims from any particular take. If you are standing right by Wendy and the barrel, it would be very helpful to you to make sure that the trims are hung in numerical order (I like to hang them with the lowest numbers on the bottom but some assistants hang them in the opposite order; it really makes no difference). Later on, when Philip puts away the trims they will have to be put away in numerical order so this will save time later on as well as making finding individual trims just a little bit faster while you are working with Wendy.

So, Wendy is going to have a cut on her Moviola. When she is finished cutting the scene it would be nice if she could look at it from the very beginning, but since she has cut it from the very first frame she (or you) won't be able to thread it up on her Moviola or flatbed (many editors like to view cut material on a flatbed, even if they've cut it on uprights). You deal with this problem by having Philip prepare a number of leaders that can be used for thread-up purposes. He can make them just like the dailies reel leaders except he should leave the identification section blank (the leader will list just the name of the film followed by a blank space, then the designation "Cut Pix" or "Cut Trk," and finally the word "Heads.") Tail leaders can also be made for this purpose. The cut scene number with a description will be inserted into the blank section (Sc.10 — ABBY arrives home).

Some editors, myself included, don't like to have all of that leader before their cut film. They prefer just four or five feet of blank white leader onto which they can write the scene number. They will use the first frame of picture and track to sync the footage up rather than a start mark.

You will find it extremely helpful to make a list giving all of the scene numbers in the film followed by a short four- or five-word description of the scene. This list is called a *continuity* (*see* Figure 6.2). As you get further into the editing of the film it will be easier to identify scenes by this description rather than by their scene numbers. If you make up the scene list everyone can get to know them faster. These descriptions can be merely a few words of memorable dialogue from the scene (Scene 11 might be called, "How'd the filming go Mister DeMille?" or just "Mr. DeMille"), a reminder of a particular shot in the scene, or a piece of scenery from the scene in question (on *Hair* we entitled three musical numbers shot together in a Central Park tunnel as "The Tunnel Suite.")

The idea of these descriptions is to give everyone in

"Silent Night, Silent Cowboy"

--Continuity--

September 3, 1990 script

Scene	Description	Scene	Description
1	Credit montage	A49	"The yellow zone is for
2	On the set		loading"
3	Abby and James	49	Abby's still empty room
4	Backstage	50	Sean and Bob talk
5	Driving home	51	Sean and Bob pick up Bob
6	Abby's empty room	52	The three musketeers party
7	Driving to work the next	54	Driving to work happy
	day	55	Redo the bar fight
8	"Did the zoom look okay?"	56	James is happy
9	Alone in the parking lot	57	The happy parking lot
10	Abby arrives home and gets	58	Bob and Abby at "La Bar"
	shocked	59	"La Bar" backstage
11	"Evening, Mr. DeMille"	60-61	Abby writes, day into night
12	The hot dog stand	62	Abby, Michael, Uri talk
13	Abby talks about Claire	63	"Great dailies!!"
14-16	Pinball hall montage	64	Abby & Sean's eat Mexican
17	Abby meets Sean	65	Abby writes/Sean writes
18	Abby and Sean back at	66	Sean tries to sleep
	Abby's	67	Drive to the baseball game
19	"Jimmy the Baby"	68	Outside Dodger Stadium
20	Cowboy and James fight	69	"Those Dodgers!"
22	Lunch with Genie	70	In the stands
23	"The rushes are a disaster"	71	In the Dodger bathroom
24	Parking lot rewrites	72	Return from the ballgame
25	Phone call from Genie	73	They watch the sports
26	"Have it out with him"		channel
27	Abby and James have it out.	74-75	Abby and Sean on the roof
28-30	Abby wanders about	76	"No dailies today"
31	Dream montage	77	"I've got a bad feeling"
32-33	Abby in the hills/L.A. at	78	"We've got a problem"
	night	79	Abby rewriting
34	"Can I make a nuisance of	80	Abby at Pink's
	myself?"	81	Abby at Musso's
35ptI	Abby/Sean at Sean's	82	Abby at City
36	"I can't get out of bed"	83	Abby writes into the dawn
37	Phone call home	84	Abby and J.B. - "A two base
39-42	Going home		hit"
44	Abby sits in front of his	85	"Puck him, it was a home
	home		run"
45	The family inside	86	Abby with Sean at Griffith
46	Abby Returns	87	Abby rewrites for a homer
47	Birthday party	88	Abby & J.B. - "You try
48	Abby flies back to L.A.		harder."
		90	Champagne corks don't pop

"Silent Night, Silent Cowboy" Continuity

Page 1

FIGURE 6.2 It is helpful to have some sort of list which shows all of the scripted scenes. Later on, as you build reels and drop scenes you can adapt this continuity to your changing cut film.

the editing room a handy set of short cuts to describe and remember the scenes in a film.

To return to the scene of the editing...Wendy is now cutting away. As she looks at the cut again, she realizes that she would like to add three more frames of the master shot 10-6 before she cuts to 10D-3. Those three frames are on the tail trim hanging in the barrel. She will look at the code numbers on the cut film, see that last code number before the cut is AA1032, and ask you for "the tail trim of AA1032" or for "the tail trim, AA1033." You can look across at the trim tabs and, at a glance, see in which take AA1033 falls, go to the take immediately underneath the tab and find the piece that she's asking for almost at once (since you've put the trims in numerical order on their proper pin). This additional piece that she is going to cut in (called an *extension*) will normally always be called for by code number since she has the code number of the piece staring up at her on her cut. Sometimes she may ask for the extension by its description — "the trim on that big wide master shot," for instance. You can determine which take she wants from the description on the cinetab or, if there are several "big wide master shots," you can ask her which one she means.

There is an alternative to asking Wendy for the code number and, as you get better at assistanting, you will get better at this method. If you are paying attention while she is editing, you will be following her progress as she cuts. By the time she asks you for a trim you should know the footage and the cut points almost as well as she does. All you have to do then is look at the point that she is examining on her Moviola and you can know what take she will need. It is this kind of shorthand that makes an observant assistant editor so valuable. There were times, when I was working on *Hair* or *Fame*, where I would try to guess ahead as to what my editors' needs were going to be and have the piece ready for them before they even asked for it. When they did, it was fun to have it ready for them.

Assistants get their kicks from strange things, don't they?

After The Editor Edits

When Wendy is finished with Scene 10 she will want two things to happen. First, she will want to go on to Scene 11 (assuming the footage for that scene has already been shot.) You should have everything ready so that she can begin cutting the next scene as soon as she is ready for it. You should try to stay at least two or three scenes ahead of Wendy, whenever possible. Once again, being ready means that all footage, wild sound, and paperwork are complete and ready for the editor's use.

The second thing that Wendy will want is to have the trims from Scene 10 taken away and to be given an empty barrel for Scene 11.

Once she is working on Scene 11, you should have Philip put away the trims from Scene 10. Trims must be put away in an orderly manner so that they may be retrieved rapidly, upon demand.

One system that I have seen for this is to file the trims in one set of two–piece white boxes, arranged by code numbers, and to file the outs separately by their scene numbers. This is handy, because if Wendy needs an extension, she will generally call for the needed trim by its code number (since she will have the adjacent code number on the film in the cut). But if she wants an out, she will normally ask for it by scene number or description (e.g., "Do we have alternate on Scene 10-6?")

I prefer a different system where all footage, whether trims or outs, is stored together. In this way, all of the footage is in one place. But, for now, let's assume that Wendy wants the trims and outs filed separately.

You will have three kinds of film to store away after a scene is cut — trims, outs, and wild track. Each will be handled differently and stored separately.

Filing the trims is the most tedious task of the three. The trims should be organized in the trim bin in numerical order with particular attention to two problems. The first concerns those pieces Wendy cut apart but which actually belong together. Splice them back together, checking to make sure that the sequential code numbers are sixteen frames apart (or forty frames, in 16mm). The second problem concerns those pieces that don't belong together but which have been spliced together by Wendy. These trims must be separated and hung on their own pins.

Once all of the trims have been set into order, remove them from the pin while still holding them together in the proper order. Wrap a rubber band around the top of all of the trims about an inch or so down from their ends (*see* Figure 6.3). Wrap it around them two or three times to get them to hold together, then flange up the trims starting from the end with the rubber band. When you get to the other end the trims

FIGURE 6.3 After the trims have been put together in numerical order a rubber band is wrapped around them at the head (top). They are then flanged up from their head.

will be tails out. Wrap a rubber band around the entire roll, slip the trim tab back in as you did originally and go on to the next trim (*see* Figure 6.4).

If Wendy has cut into the wild track, splice the roll back together in order even where pieces have been removed. Differentiate these splices from continuous ones with a red grease pencilled "X" across the cut.

When you are done you should have a set of trims wound tails out, a number of outs wound heads out, and the wild track. Now you should box them up for easy access.

To do this, take a white box, run a strip of white tape

FIGURE 6.4 After the take has been flanged up, a rubber band is put around it and its tab is removed from the trim bin and put into the trim. Note that this tab has been put into the center hole rather than slid between a few wraps of the film at the trim's edge. This has been done to show you the rubber band in the center. Normally you would wind trims as shown in Figure 5.5.

horizontally down one of its sides, and write on it as shown in Figure 6.5. Then put all of the trims pertaining to those code numbers in the box. In this way you will have one box for AA1000, one for AA2000, and so on. At times you may find that you will need more than one box for a set of code numbers (this often happens when there are long takes). In that case mark the second box with the starting number of the numerical first take within it (AA1606, for instance, if 11–6 were to start this box). Try to leave enough room (but not too much) for additional takes which may be added to the boxes later.

The outs will be handled differently. I like to write

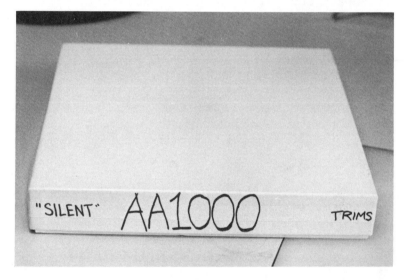

FIGURE 6.5 *A trim box used in a system where trims and outs are filed separately. If there were too many AA1000 trims to fit into one box this box would also list the last code number inside (such as AA1000—1605) and a second box would begin with the first code number of the next trim (AA1606).*

vertically on the box, rather than horizontally (*see* Figure 6.6). Each take inside the box should be listed on the outside. In that way, when Wendy asks if there is an out for a particular setup you can look at the outside of the box and tell her the answer. When you remove the take from the box, cover over its number with a piece of white tape; in that way if she decides not to use the trim you can just peel the tape off, exposing the number again.

Wild track is filed, as I've already said, wound up in individual takes and stored by code number. Since you are coding the wild track in the order that it is coming to you and since wild track numbers increase in the order in which they are shot (WT1001, WT1002, WT1003, etc.) the code numbers will be in the same ascending order as the wild track number.

As scene after scene is completed and the trims and outs are done, you will find yourself building up quite a number of shelves of trims and outs. In order to keep them

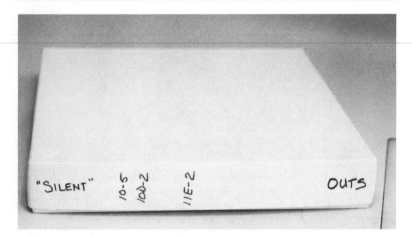

FIGURE 6.6 An outs box used in a system where trims and outs are filed separately. Note that one take, which had been an out, has been removed from the box and, presumably, used in the film. Its number has been covered over with tape. If it is ever returned as an out it is a simple matter to remove the tape from the box.

orderly I would store the boxes for trims on a separate rack from the outs and leave one or two shelves for the wild track (you rarely need more than this). You should mark the front of the shelf crossbar with a long length of tape. You can write on the tape what kind of footage is on that rack (trims, outs, etc.). Right now, when all you have are trims, outs, and wild track this may seem like a silly idea. But later on, when you have opticals, dupes, scratch mixes, temp music transfers, temp sound effects, and more, these categories may he helpful to those trying to locate material in the cutting room.

If Wendy had decided *not* to file trims and outs separately you would box the footage up differently. All takes, whether trims (wound tails out) or outs (wound heads out) would go into the same box. On.the outside of the box, you would list all of the takes in the box (*see* Figure 6.7), once again being careful to leave room for takes which haven't been cut yet but which have the codes which will also go into the box. Wild track would be filed the same way as in the separate trims and out system.

All At The Same Time?

You may have noticed that a lot of things happen simultaneously during shooting. Dailies have to be sunk and screened, logs must be maintained, there's footage to be readied for the editor, scenes to be cut, and trims and outs to be stored. All of this happens *right now* and

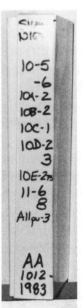

FIGURE 6.7 A trim box where trims and outs are filed together. All of the takes included in the box are listed on the side, with the code numbers included in the box printed large at the bottom of the box. Often there are several boxes needed for each code prefix (whether it be AA1000, in this case, or 001 0000, in an eight-digit coding system).(Photograph by the author).

this can be a problem. An assistant editor must be a good office manager in order to accomplish everything without forgetting anything.

Quite often there will be special requests from the producer, director, or other people on the set. On *Fame*, for instance, one rented lens was out of focus and ruined a day's shoot for us. In order to claim the insurance money due us, we had to ship the takes in question to Panavision out on the West Coast as well as screen them for our insurance company. This meant separating them out from the dailies (I got them coded first so that the coding process could go on uninterrupted) and shipping them from one place to another. It was my responsibility to make sure that I knew where the footage was at all times and that it got back to me safely.

On the same film we had to send selected takes out to Hollywood for screening by M-G-M executives every week or so. You can appreciate how that disrupted the normal flow of the film from screening to cutting. I had to keep logs of exactly what the executives had seen and what they hadn't. I had to keep a record of the status of the footage at every moment (some of the footage had been coded and some, unfortunately, couldn't be). I had to keep Gerry Hambling, the editor, informed of exactly what scenes were completely ready for him to cut and what scenes were partially in Los Angeles.

On *Hair* we were always sending clips of previously shot scenes out to the set so that they could check matches on hair, makeup, lighting, and set.

In short, there are always too many disruptions and never enough time. But, if the editing room system is set up efficiently, then everything can flow very smoothly anyway. Gerry never lacked scenes from *Fame* to cut, the *Hair* set people always got their clips, the M-G-M executives always got their takes to screen, and everyone seemed happy. Everything depends on creating a system that can function so smoothly that even when things mess up the works they can't stop the work.

Other Bits to Remember

There are a few other items which you can be doing during the editing process (as if you didn't already have enough to do). Once a week or so you or Philip should maintain Wendy's editing machines, and you should also be keeping and updating a calendar.

Running film through Moviolas or flatbed editing machines tends to get it dirty. Celluloid picks up a static charge as it is run and that, in turn, picks up dust. That dust is easily transferred to the Moviolas. Wendy will also constantly be making grease pencil marks on the film. She will also be inadvertently marking up the editing machines around the picture and track heads. In addition, the grease pencil marks tend to come off around the gates. Finally, editing machines are big mechanical beasts. They tend to get oily and will break down on an all-too-frequent basis.

It is essential, then, that you or Philip keep the machines in as fine a running order as possible. About once a week you should clean the machines. To do this, take a Q-Tip®, dip it in some alcohol or film cleaner and rub it along any surface with which the film comes in contact. Clean around the sprocket wheels. Clean the sound heads. Clean around the picture gate. Take a Webril and put a batch of film cleaner on *it*. Clean up any stray grease pencil marks on Wendy's Moviola and/or flatbed.

Keep a stock of extra Moviola or flatbed bulbs handy (there's a small well in the front of the Moviola that has a removable cover; it is a perfect place to store a few extra Moviola bulbs) since I can assure you that, machines being what they are, they will only blow bulbs late at night or on weekends when you can't easily get a fresh supply.

If Wendy is cutting on a English style bench dig into the bags hanging in it and fish out any loose pieces of fill, picture or track as she is finishing each scene. There are liable to be pieces that you need to file away down in those bags.

In short, no matter how sloppy Wendy is, try and keep her working area as clean as she will allow you.

Finally, you will want to keep a calendar hanging in the cutting room. Periodically, you will receive memos from the producer giving his or her latest version of the post-production schedule. Keep your calendar updated to reflect these changes. Write down on the calendar the date and time for any screenings, mixes, meetings, or shoots which need to be remembered. (The wall calendar is also a handy place to put people's birthdays.)

I have recently started using a computer program to print out the calendars that we use in the editing room. They are very flexible and there is no muss and fuss when dates are changed for the tenth time. The only problem is that you really need to have the computer in the editing room or changes are very inconvenient to make.

On some films that I've worked on, the assistant actually made a calendar on a large sheet of thick, clear plastic. Information was written in with grease pencil which made it easy to do those inevitable changes.

Whatever system you come up with, the calendar should be big, hung in a prominent place, and easily changed. Flexibility is, after all, the hallmark of a good editing system, isn't it?

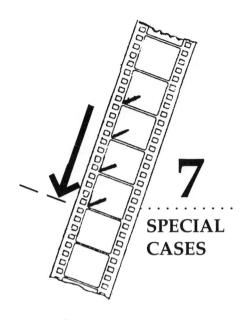

7

SPECIAL
CASES

The procedures I've already outlined apply primarily to straight dialogue movies being cut on an upright Moviola in the United States. There are a lot more types of movies and ways to edit them than that. We'll consider a few of them now.

Musical Systems

I mentioned earlier that *Silent Night, Silent Cowboy* had a few musical scenes in it. One of them takes place on a saloon set where the lead in our movie-within-a-movie, COWBOY, enters the town saloon for the first time and gets involved in a fixed poker game. As he enters, he walks around the room, amazed at the newness of everything. One of the sights he sees is two cowboys singing together, one of whom is playing a guitar.

This scene could be shot in several ways. One way would be to hire actors who could sing and actually have them play and sing live on the set. This, however, would create two problems. First, since the performers would rarely be singing at the exact same rhythm and pitch from take to take and from angle to angle it would be impossible for the editor to cut performances from different takes together and have them make musical sense. In addition, music recorded on the set wouldn't be as clean as if it were recorded in a music studio.

Many songs are recorded this way, however, to the chagrin of the director and editor when they see (and hear) it later on in the editing room. Often an absolutely clean wild track of the song to be sung is recorded and used as the main soundtrack against which the editor cuts his or her picture, hoping that the actor's lips will match the tune in all of the takes that are cut in (after some adjustments).

A better way, from the standpoint of lip sync, is to record to *playback*. One clean track is obtained, either through a recording in a music studio (this is the way musicals are done) or by recording a wild track on the set before the shooting of the scene. This sound track is then played back over loudspeakers to the actors on the set who sing and play back to it, attempting to copy it as exactly as possible. In this way there is only one musical track, and this would therefore be at the same rhythm and pitch in all takes. Later on, in the music editing, variations in the lip sync can be corrected so that any sync mistakes the actor or actress made during the shooting can be modified or eliminated.

The way a playback sequence is handled on the set of a major feature is to have two recording machines, such as Nagras. One of them is used to play back the 1/4" tape of the song to the actors. The output of this machine is also fed to another Nagra, which records it as well as the synching slate and any other sounds that the sound recordist is able to isolate from the din of the played-back song.

If this method is used, you can sync the dailies as you normally would. Each take will have a slate as recorded live on the set. The soundtrack will then segue into the direct feed of the song from the playback Nagra.

However, on lower-budget films, it often is not possible to rent two tape machines. As a result the tape machine is used for playback only and no live recording is done. This creates much extra bother in the synching. Since no sound was taken during the playback takes the dailies will either have to be looked at in silence or the sync tracks will have to be created by you in the editing room. To do this you would need a copy of the original playback 1/4" tape (you will need this tape anyway, even if you were supplied with dailies soundtrack from two Nagras; so you should make sure that your music editor or sound recordist gets you a copy).

From this tape, make as many transfers of the song as there were takes made on the set that used the song (you will need to have the script supervisor's daily notes to determine this). On a Moviola or flatbed, you must then match up by eye every take to its own transfer of the music. Be aware that the singers or guitar picker will rarely be exactly in sync for the entire length of the song. You should choose the sync position that puts most of the song in comfortable sync. Then mark a fake slate mark near the top of each take. This will help you to sync and Wendy to line up the takes on her Moviola later on. Then you can prepare the dailies rolls just as you normally would. Now, regardless of whether one or two Nagras were used, you will have sync dailies with sound for all takes.

When these dailies rolls come back to you after the dailies screening your coding complications will begin, for coding musical takes is a much different process than coding normal dailies. Once again, the problem stems from the fact that all of the sound has been generated from only one source — that original 1/4" tape. When Wendy cuts the picture it will be much easier for her to cut all of her picture takes to only one soundtrack. In that way, she will end up with a cut picture that will run in frame-to-frame sync with the original recording.

For Wendy to cut take after take to one soundtrack she must have *all* her picture takes coded in sync to that one track.

To do this you must *spot code* each of the takes individually. You will need a synchronizer with sound heads in both the second and third gangs in order to do this.

To start, you must have one copy of the complete song on 35mm sound film (called the *playback master*). Before you

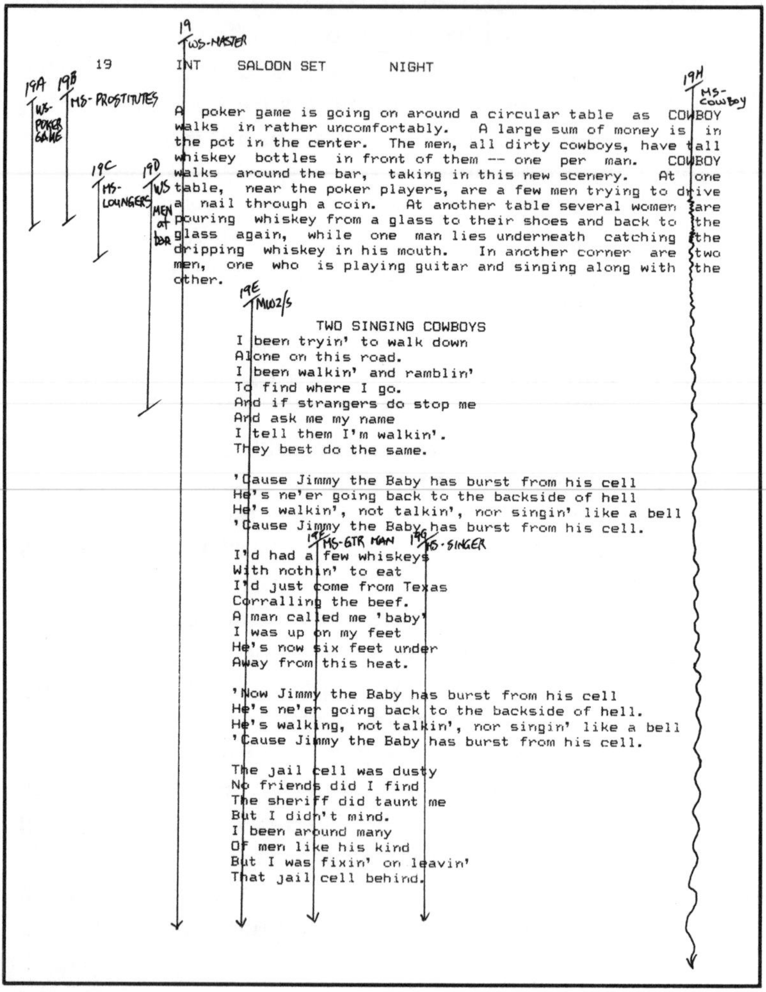
19 INT SALOON SET NIGHT

A poker game is going on around a circular table as COWBOY walks in rather uncomfortably. A large sum of money is in the pot in the center. The men, all dirty cowboys, have tall whiskey bottles in front of them -- one per man. COWBOY walks around the bar, taking in this new scenery. At one table, near the poker players, are a few men trying to drive a nail through a coin. At another table several women are pouring whiskey from a glass to their shoes and back to the glass again, while one man lies underneath catching the dripping whiskey in his mouth. In another corner are two men, one who is playing guitar and singing along with the other.

TWO SINGING COWBOYS

I been tryin' to walk down
Alone on this road.
I been walkin' and ramblin'
To find where I go.
And if strangers do stop me
And ask me my name
I tell them I'm walkin'.
They best do the same.

'Cause Jimmy the Baby has burst from his cell
He's ne'er going back to the backside of hell
He's walkin', not talkin', nor singin' like a bell
'Cause Jimmy the Baby has burst from his cell.

I'd had a few whiskeys
With nothin' to eat
I'd just come from Texas
Corralling the beef.
A man called me 'baby'
I was up on my feet
He's now six feet under
Away from this heat.

'Now Jimmy the Baby has burst from his cell
He's ne'er going back to the backside of hell.
He's walking, not talkin', nor singin' like a bell
'Cause Jimmy the Baby has burst from his cell.

The jail cell was dusty
No friends did I find
The sheriff did taunt me
But I didn't mind.
I been around many
Of men like his kind
But I was fixin' on leavin'
That jail cell behind.

FIGURE 7.1 Script pages for a musical scene.

code any of your dailies, this track must be coded. My suggestion for what to code it is to assign each musical number its own prefix code. For instance let's say that there are three musical numbers in our film. For convenience's sake we shall code the playback for our first song, "Jimmy the

```
         17      19E     19F          19G              19H

              'Now Jimmy the Baby has burst from his cell
              He's ne'er going back to the backside of hell.
              He's walkin', not talkin', nor singin' like a bell.
              'Cause Jimmy the Baby has burst from his cell.

         Eventually  COWBOY finds his way to the outside of the  poker
         table.  A round has just been completed.
           19H    19J
             MS-SAM-MS-JIM    JIM
           That's it for me.

                              SAM
           Chrissakes Jim.

                              JIM
           Naw,  that's  it.   I gotta save some money for  some
           more booze.

         He gets up and exits through the crowd,  past COWBOY who  is
         looking on nervously.  Unfortunately,  at that minute, SAM
         sees him.

                              SAM
           Well,  someone  new!  How'd  you  like  to  get  your
           official welcome to this friendly town.  My name's Sam
           Robson.

         He holds out his hand to COWBOY who,  startled, takes it.  He
         is  quite confused about the offer.  Of course he  wants  to
         play but, at the same time, he doesn't want anyone to see how
         green he is.  Still, he feels that he is being tested.

                              COWBOY
           Sure.   19K
                      MUS-POKER
                        GAME
         He sits down in JIM'S seat and looks about nervously.

                              SAM
           The kitty, son. 19P
                                19N
         It  is  a  few  seconds before COWBOY realizes what  SAM  is
         talking  about.   When  he does catch the  man's  meaning  he
         hurriedly pushes some money into the pot.  SAM deals out  the
         cards  and  a  game ensues in which COWBOY plays stupidly  and
         loses.   During  this game we see the SHERIFF enter and  watch
         from the  opposite end of the room.  He is just about the only
         person  in  the bar who is interested in the  game  including
         most of the players at it, besides COWBOY and SAM.  There are
         cuts  of  money being exchanged and pushed into the  pot  or
         various pockets.  Finally, we notice that after several games
         have gone on that COWBOY is winning.  At this point he  looks
         up,  sees SHERIFF and excitedly gets out of the game despite
         the  protests,  to catch the SHERIFF who has gotten up  and is
         exiting the saloon.  COWBOY exits in pursuit.
```

FIGURE 7.1 continued

Baby" (*see* Figure 7.1, script pages for this scene), with the prefix code 1. On this film we will use a seven-digit coding system for playback numbers, leaving the six-digit numbers for the straight dialogue scenes. This will make it immediately apparent to us whether a trim is from a musical playback take or from one with dialogue only. We will code this "Jimmy the Baby" master 35mm track with the code 1AA0000 (if we had only six digits to work with we might code it P10000; and reserve all codes with the prefix P for musical playback takes).

If you were using an eight-digit system, then you would try to find some way of differentiating each take from each other as well as from the non-musical takes (101M0000, 102M0000, 103M0000, for instance; the 'M' meaning 'music').

Actually, I usually don't code my musical playback masters beginning with the numbers 0000, I always start two or three hundred numbers in. For now, let's code this playback master 1AA0300. You will see the reason for this in a minute.

After the playback master is coded you will be ready to code each of the takes. Let's say that there were four set–ups involving our singers. They are as follows:

19, takes 4,6,8 — Master shot of the entire scene
19E, takes 2,4,7 — MWS of the two singers
19F, takes 2,3 — MCU of the singer/guitarist
19G, take 2 — MCU of the singer

All of the other setups involve portions of the scene where the musicians are not visible. These set–ups were, therefore, not shot to playback. Let us also assume that Adam, knowing that he would not begin the scene with the medium close–ups of the singers, only shot them singing from the second verse until the end, as shown in the line script.

Take the playback master and run it down on your synchronizer until you can hear the song from your sound-box. Now, choose a word of the song that has a definite *hit* to it. This means a sound that is as sharp and identifiable as the slate is. Good choices for this are words which begin with the letters b, a hard c, d, g, k, p, or t. In this song, a few good hits would be the beginnings of the words "been", "tryin'", or "down" in the first line. Listen to your playback master on your synchronizer and locate a few of these easily identifiable hits. You can find them by sliding the track back and forth under the sound head exactly as you did when you found the sound slates as you were synching the dailies. As you find each word mark the exact sprocket on the track and note the word that you've found as shown in Figure 7.2. Since you know that some of the takes don't begin until the second verse mark some sync points down there as well (the second syllable in the word "whiskey" might be a good choice as well as the word "Texas.")

Then temporarily take your playback master out of your synchronizer (you don't have to rewind it past the beginning of the song), and put the dailies roll with the playback takes up. Any takes without playback in them

FIGURE 7.2 *A section of a musical playback master track with three sync points marked on it. Each point is marked at its first modulation.*

111

should be separated so that all playback takes are on one reel and all non-playback reels on another (note that they will still all be entered in the logbook as from the same dailies rolls; they are being separated here for coding purposes only.) Run them down until you get to the first take (19–4). Run down even further until you get to the first word that you decided was your sync point ("been" in this case). When you find the first modulation of the word, mark it on your dailies track with a grease pencil. In the third gang place your playback master at the same point so that the two sync points line up sprocket for sprocket. If you roll down to the next word that you marked on the playback master you should find that it lines up exactly with the same word on the dailies take. Do this for a few more sync points so you know that the two tracks are running exactly in sync.

There is an additional way of verifying sync on these two music tracks, though it is very difficult to describe in words. If you listen to both tracks at the same time with both at the same volume you should hear the two sounds *phasing* with each other. This phasing sounds like a very slight echo; I've heard it described as a "tunnel" effect. If the tracks are one or two sprockets out of sync there wouldn't be any phasing but you would hear a very fast echo instead (the further out of sync they are the longer the echo delay will be.) If this happens, move the playback master one sprocket at a time and listen. When you no longer hear this echo but hear the sound take on an eerie, hollow quality then you know that the tracks are phasing and are therefore in as close a sync as possible.

It is sometimes difficult to hear this phasing, especially with poor quality sound equipment. Phasing occurs more easily on instruments like strings or on single vocals than it does on drums or brass instruments. As a result, don't count on using phasing as the only measure for whether you're in sync. Always use the individual sync point technique first, and use phasing as a final verification.

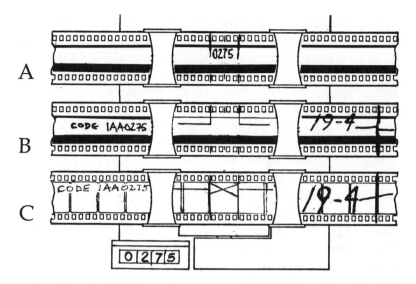

FIGURE 7.3 The playback master (A) is lined up in the synchronizer with the dailies track (B) and picture (C). The code number 0275 on the playback on the playback master would actually be edge coded on the side of the film. It is shown in the center here for legibility only.

After you are sure that the tracks are in sync with each other, roll backwards to the top of the picture take. Then look at the first code number on the playback master that lies within the take. The last four numbers are the code numbers that you are going to tell the coding service to begin coding this take at.

For an example, look at Figure 7.3. The first code number on the playback master that lies parallel to the beginning of 19–4 is 1AA0275. This number comes before 1AA0300 because there was some time when the camera was running *before* the men began to sing the song, perhaps because the characters had some dialogue before they started singing. This frequently occurs.

We can now see why it was better to start coding at 1AA0300 rather than at 1AA0000. This way you can have enough room before the song begins to accommodate these sorts of occasions. Always be careful that the starting number you assign a playback master is not so high that it gives the song an ending code number which is over 1000. A playback master which begins 1AA0300 should run no longer than 699 feet in length and thus have a code number no higher than 1AA0999

So, 1AA0275 is the first code number on the master. You will want to code each dailies take differently, of course, while still preserving the last three digits for Wendy's sync. I recommend coding this take 1AB0275. In this system you would code succeeding reels 1AB0..., 1AC0..., 1AD0..., etc. After you run out of letters (1AY0..., 1AZ0...) you would change to the next thousands number (1AB1..., 1AC1..., etc.). This method is very flexible. If Adam ever decides to go back and print up any B-negative or to reshoot the scene it gives you many more numbers to play with without changing your basic system.

Let us, therefore, code take 19-4 1AB0275. Put a small piece of white tape across the exact frame of the picture and track that this number will fall on. Write on it "Code 1AB0275" — black for picture and, of course, red for track.

Now comes the tricky part. Every coding machine or service has different requirements for spot-coding reels. Some want each take wound on its own individual reel (most coding services charge by the reel for their coding services). Others use electronic sensing equipment to stop and start their machines, so you either have to attach a piece of foil to the end of each take or cut out a little notch on one edge of the film. Other services prefer the takes strung together on one set of reels but with leader connecting each take so that it is easy for their operators to see where they should stop their machine and set up for a new take.

On *Fame* we had our own coding machine and an apprentice was hired to run it. This apprentice carefully watched the footage for flash frames or for the white tape splice on the track.

After you set up each take for coding you can enter their beginning numbers in your logbook. It is also possible to put end code tapes on each take so that you can check that each take has been coded properly. I find, however, that this requires so much extra time and effort that it is easier to check them after the reels have been coded by running them through the synchronizer.

The only other slight adaptation you will have to make in your system is in how you file your trims. I usually list the code numbers of several takes on the outside of the box (for instance, "1AB0275—1AE0216" or "1AB—1AE").

Unslated Takes

Sometimes, through problems on the set or some other exigency, you will get a take where you have no visible slate to mark for synching purposes. On *Hair* several shots during the song "Good Morning Starshine" were shot from a helicopter too far away from the action to have slates.

In this case there was nothing to do but to eye-sync each take on the Moviola or flatbed in much the way that I described for musicals where sound was taken with only one Nagra.

Sometimes, the camera operator will miss the slate either by being out of focus during it or by being pointed just slightly too far up or down. At other times the lab will cut off the head of the shot, losing the slate with it.

In these cases you will have some tricky eye matching to do. Once again, the trick is to find something that would have a definite *hit* to it. In many cases you can use door slams, an actor pounding on a table, or any number of other sharp sound effects to sync things up with (you can usually find the exact frame where these effects happen). Always be sure to check the footage in the Moviola to make sure that you really do have the proper sync.

Some times there are no visual clues (this often happens on actor's close-ups) and you must use dialogue to eye-sync. Here, you can use the same technique as in lining up takes with the playback music master. Look for the letters b, c, d, k, p, or t. These usually have fairly definite sounds as well as being reasonably identifiable by lip movements. If you need to, say the words of dialogue while you hold your fingers over your lips to feel them move to see what shape the lips of the actor on your Moviola should be making. And, as always, check your sync on the Moviola or flatbed before moving along to the next take.

KEM and Other Flatbed Systems

Until now we have discussed only upright Moviola systems. In these systems, takes are individually broken down before being given to the editor. Each take is treated as a separate entity.

But one of the advantages of a flatbed is its ability to high-speed from one take to another. This advantage would be lost if all of the takes were broken down individually as we do for a Moviola. Therefore, a flatbed system is set up with completely different parameters than a Moviola system.

To examine the basic reasoning behind a flatbed system let us re–examine the mode of cutting on a Moviola. On *Silent Night*, Wendy is cutting with two Moviolas — one to examine potential cutting points and another on which to make the cuts. On a flatbed she would do much the same thing. Let us say that she was using an eight-plate KEM. On four of these plates (for one reel of picture and one of track, each reel would have a feed and a take-up plate) she would have her picture and track for the cut and on the other four she would have the picture and track for takes she is going to examine.

One of the problems of a flatbed is that it is more difficult to thread and re-thread each roll of film than on an upright. One of the tasks of an efficient flatbed system, therefore, should be to minimize such setup time.

One way of doing this is to put as many takes on the same roll as are sensible. These cutting rolls are called KEM rolls. A KEM roll has no equivalent in a Moviola system since all takes are broken down individually before they are cut. But on a flatbed system takes are not broken down individually for the editor but are rearranged into more orderly cutting rolls.

There must be some intelligence put into the organization of these KEM rolls, however, otherwise Wendy will spend more time finding takes within a roll or changing them than she would save by using the flatbed.

To give an example, let's say that to save time you decided to take the dailies rolls that we've already discussed and use them as the KEM rolls for Wendy to cut from. You would then have all of the setups for Scene 10 on one roll. If Wendy needed to cut take 10A–2 onto take 10–6 she would have a problem. First she would roll down on the KEM roll until she found the frame on 10–6 that she would like to cut out on. Then she would have to roll further down on the same roll (losing her place on 10–6) to find the frame of 10A–2 that she would want to cut into.

This is far more difficult to do for an editor than having both frames visible simultaneously and it doesn't take advantage of the flatbed's other picture head.

An obvious solution, therefore, would be to make sure that shots 10–6 and 10A–2 were on different KEM rolls.

This, in fact, is the basis of the flatbed system. Any shot that the editor might want to cut *to* should be on a different KEM roll than the shot that the editor would be cutting away *from*.

There are times when this won't be possible to know in advance. In the music playback scene I described earlier in this chapter you would probably never know ahead of time in just what order all of the cutaway shots at the beginning of the scene (19A through 19D) would be used. In general, however, there are some rules which will work for your planning. First, keep all shots of the same person (no matter what their size—wide, medium, or close) on the same roll. In the scene in Abby's bedroom (Scene 11, Figure 4.5) I would keep all of the shots of Bob separate from Abby's shots. Next, keep the *master shots* on the same roll with the *insert shots*. Inserts are very close up shots of some action (an example would be an extreme close-up of Bob's fingers making a correction at the typewriter) which would be inserted, let us say, into a medium shot of him. Master shots will very rarely be intercut with insert shots, as the cut from very wide to very tight shot is usually not attractive. Insert shots are usually cut to medium close-up or to close-up shots. By the same token, wide shots are usually cut to medium-wide or medium shots. This rule obviously depends upon the footage that you get so it is imperative that you use your brains and your experience in making these kinds of choices. Lastly, in a montage-like sequence (which may be as complex as a car chase or as easy as all of those atmosphere shots at the beginning of our music playback scene) almost anything can be cut to anything else. In this case it is helpful to have all of the montage elements on the same KEM roll, as close to each other as possible. I would put all takes of scenes 19A through 19D one right after another on a KEM roll (though not the same KEM roll as the master shot). In this way, Wendy could roll down past each one rather rapidly and decide which one she wanted to cut into the master shot on the other roll. She would then make the cut, and then find another cutaway if she wanted one immediately afterwards. This is not a perfect solution but it is an acceptable one.

Obviously, if this method of cutting is to make any sense at all, all takes of any given camera setup should be on the same KEM roll. It would do the editor no good to have to put up two different KEM rolls to see two takes of the same setup. So, unless the lengths of the individual takes are too long to permit it, put all takes of the same setup together.

KEM rolls should be neither too short nor too long. If

the rolls are too long (over 800 feet) then it will take more time to fast-forward or rewind between setups than it would to put up a new roll. If they are too short (this minimum size will vary depending on the lengths of the takes involved but let us say, for an example only, less than 400 feet) then the assistant will spend more time threading up the KEM rolls than the editor will spend looking at them.

As you work more and more with editors, you will find out how they like to cut. As you pay attention to this you will learn better ways to organize KEM rolls for them. It is not an easy task to think ahead as to how the editor will probably cut, but it is an important one, and it is one which you will get experienced at with time.

What changes will this new system cause you to make in your paperwork and work-style? As you might expect, there will be many. The most obvious one is that rather than breaking the dailies rolls down into individual takes you will be breaking them apart only to have to build them back again into the KEM rolls. This also means that, if you coded the film when it was still in dailies roll form, all of the numbers would get jumbled up once the takes were rebuilt into the usually very different order of the KEM rolls.

For this reason, it would be wise to wait until after the KEM rolls are built before you code and log them. This will, inevitably, slow down the process by which the editor gets his or her film to cut but it is an unavoidable side effect of using a flatbed.

In some cases it might also be helpful to have an extra logbook which would be organized by scene numbers rather than by code number. In most Moviola systems, the arrangement by code number is the same thing as an arrangement by set–ups within the scene (19 is followed by 19A which is followed by 19B). But since this will rarely be the case in a flatbed system some assistants like to have a log organized by scene and setup. Frankly, in most cases, this is an indulgence as very similar information can be obtained from the numbers you insert into the lined script notes (which can include KEM roll number as well as the code number). However, if the lined script is badly organized or inaccurate then such an extra log might be a good idea.

As the film is being shot, this KEM system also creates more work in the editing room, resulting in a slightly different work flow for everyone involved there. In an average feature editing room the assistant editor would supervise the synching of dailies, determine the KEM roll breakdown, and supervise the building of the KEM rolls. The apprentice would then have to sync dailies, build KEM rolls, and put away trims. Unless there is going to be very little footage every day it would be wise to think about putting on a second assistant to sync the dailies, freeing the first assistant up to work with the editor and organize the editing room, and allowing the apprentice to do the work of trims and building KEM rolls (which is a very laborious task).

Building KEM rolls involves pulling the takes for each KEM roll from all of the dailies rolls that are involved. The best way to do this is to organize the paperwork first. You should determine exactly what takes would go on what KEM roll while, at the same time, noting from which dailies roll each take came.

You or Philip would then take all of those dailies rolls and spin down each one on a synchronizer until you found the necessary take which you would then built into your KEM roll on another synchronizer. In actuality, this process is far more time consuming than it would appear from this description, very often involving two synchronizers (and/or KEMs) and much running around with splicers and pieces of paper. And, all the while that you are building the KEM rolls, you should also be logging in the footage and setting it up for coding.

On some films, KEM roll building resembles an early Three Stooges film and requires one person's complete attention. It is an unfortunate fact of life, however, that most production managers do not realize the necessity of an extra assistant (or even an extra apprentice) and insist that everything be handled by a three-person crew. This works on easy dialogue films but is usually a disaster on larger projects. Editors should insist on a fourth person but they rarely do (or, if they do, can rarely get one). What this means is that you and your apprentice will be putting in a lot of overtime hours and that your editor will be getting less of your time and, ultimately, less work done.

There will be times, during recutting, when Wendy will not actually want to look at a whole roll for a trim but will call for it by the code number, much as she would on a Moviola film. In that case you will grab the KEM roll that contains the piece that she is asking for and either put it up on your synchronizer or on another flatbed in the editing room (most flatbed shows rent little four-plate or six-plate machines for just this purpose), sync up the reels at the start marks and then spin down to the code number that she's called for. Then you unsplice the picture and/or track at that point and either give her the entire roll that she needs (either the roll that contains the head trim or the tail trim, depending on what she has asked for) or, if she just wants a short piece, you would give her a short length of picture and/or track. As you can imagine, this is quite a bit more time consuming than finding a Moviola trim.

Another adjustment that you'll have to make in your system is dealing with trims and outs. As the editor removes varying amounts of picture and track from her KEM rolls she will generally be throwing these reels out of sync. When she is done cutting, Philip's major tasks will be to put all of the trims that are hanging in her barrel back into these reels and fill out either the picture (with white leader) or the track (with fill) so that the footage will always run in sync. In that way, when Wendy next puts up her KEM rolls to search for a piece of film she will see everything in sync — the way it was meant to be seen.

To do this, Philip will organize all of the trims in the barrel by KEM roll (this will hopefully also be the same number as the prefix on the code number), most often one pin for each roll. He will also organize the trims so that they are in numerical order on the pin, with the lowest on the top. He will then put up the KEM roll in his synchronizer, line the picture and track up at the start marks, and roll down until he gets to the number of the first trim that he has to put away or until he notices that the picture has gotten out of sync with the track (whichever comes first). He will then insert the trim that he has in his barrel, if necessary, and then add leader or fill to the picture or track to bring everything back into sync. He will then roll down to the next place where a trim belongs, or that is out of sync and do the same thing.

This, you may notice, is a much more time consuming process than filing Moviola trims, which is one reason why I prefer to work on the Moviola system on low-budget films with short schedules.

You can see that KEM systems, in general, create much more work for the assistant than Moviola systems do. But, for the editor, there are distinct advantages to working on flatbeds. You will learn about these as you do more films with them. Until then I can only reassure you that all of the extra work you will have to do is worth it.

On low budget films, 16mm films, and features with very short post-production schedules, it is often impossible to organize KEM rolls in the way that I've been describing. It would be impossible, for instance, to do all of the work necessary to organize and sync dailies, organize and build KEM rolls, put trims away, work with the editor *and* do all of the other assistant tasks, if there were only one assistant on the film. But sometimes the film's budget only allows for one assistant. In these cases, dailies rolls often become KEM rolls, much logging is skipped, and the assistant never works directly with the editor. Your job on a film like this is much akin to surviving a guerilla war. It is only your past experience that can guide you in deciding which parts of your system you can afford to omit and which you cannot.

Location Shooting

Two weeks of the shooting of *Silent Night* involve location shooting in a desert-like area. As mentioned, Wendy will not be going on location but will be staying back in town, continuing to cut as the footage comes in. But Adam and the rest of the crew will still need to see the film every day. This will inevitably complicate your life but it is necessary.

In order for the crew to see the film on location they will need three things — a projection system, a projectionist, and the sunk film. The first two should be arranged for by the production manager who will have already scouted the location. In a few cases, a local movie theatre can be outfitted with a *double–system projector* (a projector that can run separate film and soundtrack units in sync with each other, much as a Moviola or KEM can) so that the crew can see the dailies there. In most cases, however, a portable projector must be brought in to the location. In either case it will be important that you find out the projectionist's requirements before the first day of location dailies. Some projectors will not accept film on cores so the film must be shipped on reels. For others, the reverse is true. Some projectors can handle reels built over 1000 feet, others cannot. If there are any special requirements that you must meet, you need to know about them *before* you send the first day's footage or the dailies might not be able to be screened.

You, or the production office coordinator (the person who supervises the day-to-day details of the film), should determine the best way to ship the film to the location. Prompt delivery must be assured and it is for this reason that the film's production assistants are often utilized rather than messenger services which are doing runs for many other clients at the same time. Film can be shipped by air, train, or bus. If delivery is to be made out of the country, a customs broker should be hired to prepare all of the shipping papers that the various governments will require at the airports, both to get the film to the set as well as to get it back to you. In any case, the fastest, most reliable method should be chosen. (A side note — some editors are afraid of the security machines at airports, fearing that they will degauss (erase) the film's soundtrack; I have done several experiments with these machines and have never had a track damaged.)

The major change in your dailies schedule will obviously be one of time. If the dailies screening on location is at 7:00 p.m. and the film takes six hours to reach the location you will obviously have to be finished synching and checking the dailies in time for the film to make it to the airport by 1:00 p.m. If possible, try to leave yourself an hour or two of spare time for the inevitable delays.

A copy of the editor's notes should be sent out to the set so that someone can take down Adam's notes for the selected takes just as you or Wendy would if the dailies were in town.

Of course, arrangements should also be made to get the film back to you as fast as possible so that you can proceed with the coding, logging, and cutting. Often it is possible to ship the sunk dailies back with the unprocessed film and 1/4" tape. When film is shipped to location it is not uncommon to expect a one day delay in being able to code and log everything.

There are times when the editor will be asked to come onto location. In this case, it will be up to the assistant to create a completely functioning editing room there. Editing rooms have been set up in such diverse locations as Bora Bora, Morocco, and Norway. Once you are on location, you can't just get on the phone one morning to order a roll of splicing tape or a Moviola bulb and expect to have it that afternoon, so you will have to bring enough supplies to last you the length of time you will be on location.

I should also warn you that being in an editing room in Bora Bora is not as much fun as it sounds.

Film-Within-Film

In several scenes in *Silent Night* people watch projected film, dailies for instance. In order to set this up, you will have to provide the film for the shooting.

An example was the *Rocky Horror Show* sequence in *Fame*. In it, several of our characters were in a large audience watching the famous midnight show film. I had to prepare the film for that showing.

Several segments of the film were used. Each was cut from a new print of the movie supplied to us by Twentieth Century-Fox. Each segment was placed on its own reel (along with a backup copy on another reel in case the first one was damaged), each with its own Academy Leader so both the projectionist and the cameraman could quickly focus. In this case, since the film already had a sound track on it, the actual sound of the movie was used for playback to the extras who were playing the audience (in other cases, an interlocking 35mm magnetic soundtrack might have been used).

In addition to the married film I supplied the soundman, Chris Newman, with playback tapes of the soundtrack of the sections we were using. I did this so that when the camera was shooting at the audience (and the screen was not visible) only the playback tape needed to be run to give the audience the soundtrack to the movie to shout back to. This saved a lot of time and confusion on the set.

There are frequently times when characters in a film are shown watching television. Supplying the footage that they are looking at is often the editor's job. Once the footage has been selected, it needs to be put onto 3/4" videotape for playback. In addition, to avoid the annoying roll-bar effect, common when shooting directly off of a TV set, you should have this tape made at 24 frames per second, rather than the usual 30 frames per second. This will enable the camera operator and the video playback man to synchronize their two machines perfectly.

Foreign Systems

If you have been reading this book in sequential order you will have noticed that there are many times when the organization will be up to the assistant. As a result almost every assistant has a slightly different way of organizing an editing room. It should come as no surprise to you then that editing systems in other countries vary from those I've described. If you are ever called upon to assist an editor from a foreign country (as I did with Gerry Hambling on *Fame*) you will have to learn the differences. Always keep in mind, however, that film is film and that editing is editing. Though there are differences between the countries they are mostly surface ones. Film is still spliced together by a person concerned with the aesthetics of editing.

That said, I will also add that an editor from England works in a slightly different manner than an editor in the United States. First of all, their table setup looks different. Rather than working with a pair of rewinds on their table they have a rewind only on the right side of the table. On the left they have something called a *horse*, a rack onto which the editor can slip many rolls of film which can then feed into the synchronizer. On either side of the synchronizer large holes have been cut into the table into which bags (exactly like those in a trim barrel) are hung. The English editor does a lot more of his or her work at the synchronizer and, as a result, needs to have receptacles for the film on either side. As an assistant, you will find yourself continually searching the bottom of these bags for lost trims or rolls of film. Often, you will find something there.

Trims and outs are stored together, by code numbers. This is made easier by the eight-digit coding system in use there. As I mentioned briefly in the section of coding systems in Chapter 5, English editors use an eight-digit coding block on a *Moy* coding machine. The numbers look something like 123D5678. This is a particularly good coding system because of the way that takes are slated in England. Instead of using scene numbers and setup letters (such as Scene 12A, take 3), the English system begins with slate number one on the first day of shooting and continues sequentially each time a new set–up is done. Thus, if a film shoots twenty setups on the first day of shooting they would be Slates 1 through 20 (such as Slate 15, take 2). The next day, they would pick up with Slate 21. In this system there is no relationship between the slate number and the scene number, but that is always evident from the lined script.

Each take is spot coded, as were the musical play-backs. For Slate 35, take 3, A camera, the slate mark would be coded 035A3000. If the next printed take is Slate 36, take 1, A camera, the slate mark would be coded 036A1000. If there was also a second camera printed on that take (or a B camera, as it is called) it would be coded 036B1000. This requires special attention during the coding process since each take must be coded by itself. As I've mentioned, on *Fame*, we hired an apprentice who did very little else besides code the dailies and put away trims.

There is one big advantage to this process and that is that since the code number and the slate number are the same, one will immediately lead you to the other. If the editor wants to see another take on Slate 34 all you do is march to the place where Slate 34 is kept and you will immediately see what is there. There is no need to look in a log for a code number first. That is another reason why you do not store the trims and the outs separately, since the editor will be calling for both of them in the same way — by the slate number.

On the cinetab for a film shot in this manner I usually put the scene number that the scene is for (I also enter this information in the logbook). I put it up in the top part of the tab.

There are other differences in the English system. Trims and outs are not usually stored in white two-piece boxes but in 1000-foot film cans. A notation as to what is inside is put onto the outside of the can using paper tape. Often, there are no cinetabs. Instead, a square piece of tape is taped on the top of the roll of film as it sits in the can. This tape contains the information normally found on the cinetab. On *Fame*, I found this method to be less helpful to me than a cinetab so I decided to use tabs anyway. Once again, everyone adapts the systems to his or her own use.

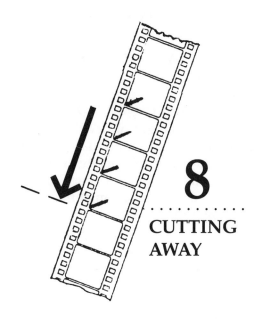

8
CUTTING
AWAY

At some point, usually just as you think that you won't be able to handle any more dailies, the shooting will stop. The producers will have a wrap party, the requests from the set for frame clips or special dailies screenings will end, the early morning laboratory delivery problems will cease and the focus of the film will shift to the editing room—right where you are.

It's a rather strange feeling to suddenly be in the spotlight. During the shooting you find that the editing room people are often the last to know about many things—changes in dailies screenings times, adjustments in the shooting schedule, and many other items. The director is, if not exactly a stranger, seen very rarely. It's just been you, Wendy, and Philip.

Now, everything is going to be different. Adam will be coming to the editing room a lot more often (some directors, like Milos Forman, are in the editing room all the time; others, like Alan Parker, rarely visit it) and this will change your routine. Dailies will stop and this will change your routine. The editing will get more intense and this will change your routine.

Balancing The Cut Reels

As Wendy has been cutting *Silent Night, Silent Cowboy* she has been accumulating individual cut scenes. After a while she will have accumulated enough consecutive scenes to build them together into a reel. Very often she will be building these reels as she cuts. Sometimes you will notice that, because of the order in which she has had to cut the scenes, there are now several consecutive cut scenes which have not yet been put together. She may want to cut them together herself or she may ask you to do it. As the scenes are put together onto the projection reels there are several things to keep in mind.

As usual, the head and the tail of each reel should be leadered. The leader should look something like Figure 8.1 (the example given here is for picture only). Once again, use red ink for track and black for picture.

The next thing to remember is the length limitation. Reels should, once again, not exceed 1000 feet by much more than 25 feet or so. However, they should be larger than 700 feet to give the projectionist enough time to thread up the next reel. I like to leave the reels at about 800 feet. As the film is recut, scenes may be rearranged or lengthened. Leaving 200 feet on each reel gives you room to add footage at a later date without totally reordering the reels.

This determination of reel length and content is called *balancing the reels* and it will become quite important later on in the editing process. For now, however, it is most important to balance the film in a way to help expedite the handling of it in the editing and projection rooms.

Another thing to know about when you balance the reels is something called *changeovers*. These are the circles that you sometimes see in the upper right-hand corner of the screen when you watch a film. They are cues for the projectionist so he'll know exactly when to make the changeover from the reel on one projector to the reel on the other (projection rooms have two projectors). There are two sets of circles that you will see on the screen. The first set (on screen the set actually appears as a single circle, but in order to make it visible to the human eye it is actually a single circle appearing in the same spot on four succeeding frames) cues the projectionist to begin running the other projector, though not to turn on its light and sound. It is called the *motor cue* since it cues the starting of the second projector's motor. The second set is called the *changeover cue* and signals the projectionist to turn the picture and sound off on the first projector at the exact same moment that he turns the picture and sound on on the second one—the projector containing the new reel.

Human reflexes being what they are, it would be impossible for the projectionist to make the changeover exactly from the last frame of one reel to the very first frame of the next. The adopted stan-

FIGURE 8.1 *Head leader (to be written in black.) The usual adjustments would be made for track leader.*

dard is to give the projectionist one second from the change-over cue to the end of the reel "just in case he misses it." Reaction time is supposed to be approximately two–thirds of a second. The extra time is for slower projectionists.

In reality, projectionists are often a careless lot and you will rarely have a screening with perfect changeovers, so it is wise to plan ahead for these eventualities. I try to put changeovers in places where a missed half second will not be so crucial—commonly, reel changes come in between scenes. I try to choose a place where the outgoing scene has a few seconds of pause at its end and the incoming scene has no dialogue in its first few seconds. It is also helpful if the incoming scene has a very different sound quality than the outgoing one (for instance, louder/softer, or interior/exterior).

Some editors like to add *changeover tails* to the end of the picture. These are 24 additional frames beyond the last frame where you would normally make the picture cut to the next scene. Often, the assistant editor will add these tails and be responsible for removing them from the scene if the reel balance should change so the scene no longer comes at the end of the reel. If you do have to put the changeover tails on, you should make sure that the piece of footage you add does not contain any movement of actors that would be distracting, and that the matching length of track that you add is comprised completely of tone. Sometimes it will be impossible to add 24 frames (some editors actually prefer to add 16 frames in all cases). In these cases you should add as many frames as you can up to the length you would ideally add.

Then, after the reel balance has been decided, you can mark the changeovers. Since the balance will be changing a lot before the reels are *locked* (that is, finished, with no more cutting to be done) it is important that these changeover marks be very... well... changeable. Some assistants use grease pencil to make a slash mark extending from the upper right-hand corner of the frame a short way into the frame

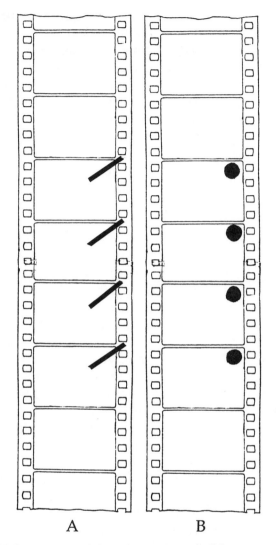

A   B

FIGURE 8.2 Two types of changeovers. In method A a grease pencil slash mark is drawn. In method B a small stick-on dot (often made from a piece of punched-out paper tape) is placed on the film. In either case you must make sure that the mark extends well past the 1.85 cutoff so that the projectionist will be able to see it during projection.

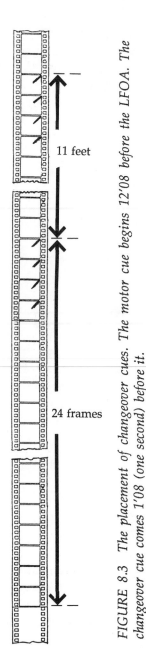

FIGURE 8.3 *The placement of changeover cues. The motor cue begins 12'08 before the LFOA. The changeover cue comes 1'08 (one second) before it.*

11 feet

24 frames

itself (*see* Figure 8.2). Others like to punch out little dots with a hole puncher from a roll of paper tape. These dots can then be stuck onto the frame, but easily removed when necessary. This method looks the neatest and has the advantage of looking more like the standard changeover marks (which are hollow circles scribed onto the film). If you ever go into a screening room with a projectionist who is only used to projecting finished films these circular changeovers will be more recognizable to him. This will lower the possibility of an embarrassing mistake during a screening. Always make sure that your marks extend far enough into the frame to be seen, even if you are projecting in a 1.85 screen ratio.

There is a standard for where the changeover marks (whatever kind you use) go on the film (*see* Figure 8.3).

You need only mark your picture for changeovers. Visible cue marks would make little sense on the track.

As more and more reels are built up Wendy and Adam will want to screen the film more often in a screening room than on an editing machine. It will be up to you, as the assistant, to book these screenings. For that reason it is very helpful if you know as many screening rooms in town as possible and the relative merits and demerits of each. Notice, for instance, which room have sharper focus, and check out the sound quality of each room (some rooms have more treble than others, some have more bass). All of this will be important as you analyze your movie.

In a studio situation in Hollywood, you will usually be assigned an available screening screen. Often you will have no choice in the matter. However, even here it is helpful to know which rooms and which projectionists are better than others.

Keeping Track

As the film begins to take shape you will want to keep a list of just what scenes are included on each screening reel. This list is called the reel *breakdown* or reel *continuity* (*see* Figure 8.4). On it you will list the sequential reel numbers, the scene numbers included on that reel, and the LFOA. These initials stand for "Last frame of action," which is the footage (from the 0'00 start mark) up to and including the last frame of picture before the tail leader begins. At the bottom of the sheet the total length of the film in both length and time is given. Note that, since the LFOA includes the Academy leader, in order to find out the length of the film you must subtract 11'15 from each reel. Sometimes, the LFOA is called the LFOP (Last Frame Of Picture) or the EOR (End Of Reel).

Some assistants also like to make a slightly more complicated reel continuity. An example of this one is shown in Figure 8.5 and we can see that it includes the short scene descriptions as well as the scene numbers. This makes the list rather difficult to refer to quickly but its comprehensiveness will often come in very handy.

On recent films, I've used a continuity like the one in Figure 8.6, printing it out on my Macintosh® computer.

CONTINUITY **1·8·91**
Date

Reel	Scenes	LFOA	Time
1	1 - 26	930 + 07	10:12.3
2	27 - 35PT	944 + 05	10:21.6
3	35PT - 52	904 + 03	9:54.8
4	54 - 72	994 + 02	10:54.8
5	73 - 85	934 + 15	10:15.3
6	86 - 102PT	993 + 09	10:54.4
7	102PT - 113	955 + 11	10:29.2
8	114 - 130	973 + 07	10:41.0
9	132 - 156	943 + 04	10:20.9
10	160 - 181	978 + 03	10:44.2
11			
12			
13			
14			
15			

Total Length 9432 + 12
Total Time 1:44:48.5

FIGURE 8.4 A reel breakdown. The length of each reel is often substituted for the LFOA (the length is 11' 15 less than the LFOA). The time is exclusive of the Academy leaders.

"Silent Night, Silent Cowboy"

--Continuity--

2nd Screening
January 8, 1991

Scene	Description	Scene	Description
	Reel One	48	Abby flies back to L.A.
1	Credit montage	A49	"The yellow zone is for loading"
2	On the set	49	Abby's still empty room
4	Backstage	50	Sean and Bob talk
5	Driving home	52	The three musketeers party
6	Abby's empty room		
7	Driving to work the next day		**Reel Four**
8	"Did the zoom look okay?"	54	Driving to work happy
9	Alone in the parking lot	55	Redo the bar fight
10	Abby arrives home and gets	56	James is happy
	shocked	57	The happy parking lot
11	"Evening, Mr. DeMille"	58	Bob and Abby at "La Bar"
12	The hot dog stand	59	"La Bar" backstage
17	Abby meets Sean	60-61	Abby writes, day into night
18	Abby and Sean back at Abby's	62	Abby, Michael, Uri talk
19	"Jimmy the Baby"	63	"Great dailies!!"
20	Cowboy and James fight	64	Abby & Sean's eat Mexican
22	Lunch with Genie	65	Abby writes/Sean writes
23	"The rushes are a disaster"	66	Sean tries to sleep
24	Parking lot rewrites	67	Drive to the baseball game
25	Phone call from Genie		
26	"Have it out with him"		**Reel Five**
		68	Outside Dodger Stadium
	Reel Two	69	"Those Dodgers!"
27	Abby and James have it out.	70	In the stands
28-30	Abby wanders about	72	Return from the ballgame
31	Dream montage	73	They watch the sports channel
32-33	Abby in the hills/L.A. at night	74-75	Abby and Sean on the roof
34	"Can I make a nuisance of	76	"No dailies today"
	myself?"	78	"We've got a problem"
35ptI	Abby/Sean at Sean's — pt I	79	Abby rewriting
		80	Abby at Pink's
	Reel Three	81	Abby at Musso's
35ptII	Abby/Sean at Sean's — pt II	82	Abby at City
36	"I can't get out of bed"	83	Abby writes into the dawn
37	Phone call home		
39-42	Going home		**Reel Six**
44	Abby sits in front of his home	84	Abby and J.B. - "A two base hit"
45	The family inside	85	"Fuck him, it was a home run"
46	Abby Returns	86	Abby with Sean at observatory
47	Birthday party	87	Abby rewrites for a homer

"Silent Night, Silent Cowboy" Continuity
January 8, 1991
Page 1

FIGURE 8.5   *A Reel Continuity (Breakdown). Those scene numbers missing from the list were either not shot or cut from the film during editing. Note how scenes which bridge two reels (such as scene 35) are handled.*

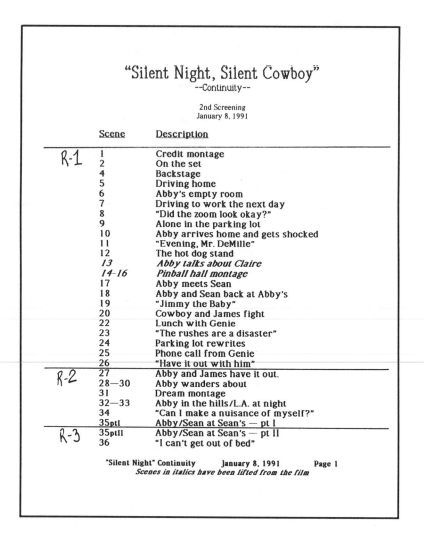

"Silent Night, Silent Cowboy"
--Continuity--

2nd Screening
January 8, 1991

	Scene	Description
R-1	1	Credit montage
	2	On the set
	4	Backstage
	5	Driving home
	6	Abby's empty room
	7	Driving to work the next day
	8	"Did the zoom look okay?"
	9	Alone in the parking lot
	10	Abby arrives home and gets shocked
	11	"Evening, Mr. DeMille"
	12	The hot dog stand
	13	*Abby talks about Claire*
	14-16	*Pinball hall montage*
	17	Abby meets Sean
	18	Abby and Sean back at Abby's
	19	"Jimmy the Baby"
	20	Cowboy and James fight
	22	Lunch with Genie
	23	"The rushes are a disaster"
	24	Parking lot rewrites
	25	Phone call from Genie
	26	"Have it out with him"
R-2	27	Abby and James have it out.
	28—30	Abby wanders about
	31	Dream montage
	32—33	Abby in the hills/L.A. at night
	34	"Can I make a nuisance of myself?"
	35ptI	Abby/Sean at Sean's — pt I
R-3	35ptII	Abby/Sean at Sean's — pt II
	36	"I can't get out of bed"

"Silent Night" Continuity   January 8, 1991   Page 1
Scenes in italics have been lifted from the film

FIGURE 8.6 Though this reel continuity will take up more pages than the one in Figure 8.5 if it is taped to the wall, it is easier to read from your editing bench. It also lists every scene shot, whether in the current version of the film or not, making it easier to discuss lifts. Notice how reel breaks are shown, as well as scenes which bridge reels (such as Scene 35). On the last page of the continuity I always list the running time.

Scenes which are removed from the film during the recutting are listed in italics. Reel breaks are noted by drawing thick lines between the scenes where the reel changes.

Once you've determined the footages of each reel you should determine the length of the complete film in minutes and seconds. Add up the lengths of all of the reels (picture lengths, not LFOAs) then use a footage/time chart (*see* Appendix I), a Reddy-Eddy, or a calculator to convert to time.

One of the uses for this kind of continuity comes after rough-cut screenings. After the film has been assembled into its first full cut it is customary (nay, it is necessary) to take it into a screening room and see just how well it plays "on the big silver" (as one director I've worked with used to call it). This first cut will often include everything that was shot and so it will seem overly long and quite boring to almost everyone.

First-cut screenings are always very tense moments for everyone involved in the film editing process. Directors often get very insecure or irritable. Editors begin to worry about minutiae (like the number of people who will be coming to the screening.) Usually, no one wants the producer around because this is where all of the film's worst faults will be all too visible. Studio personnel are almost never invited to these screenings (they usually see the film only after the director has completed his contractually guaranteed cut.)

As an assistant you can minimize some of the craziness by making sure that the film is in proper shape for projection. Be sure that the changeovers are on every reel (except, obviously, the last one) and in the proper places. Make sure that the head and tail leaders are properly labeled so that the reels are projected in their proper order. Before the screening you should check both the film and the track for splices. To do this, run the picture or track (do not do them together) slowly on your rewinds without going through the synchronizer. With your free hand, gently pinch the edges of the film so it bows slightly as it goes through your hand. Doing this, you will be able to feel whether a splice extends beyond the edges of the film (such spliceswil have to be sahved level with the film) or whether there are any broken sprocket holes which need to be repaired. As you are running the reel through your fingers, make a visible inspection of the splices to make sure that there is not a gap between the incoming and outgoing pieces of film or track.

In addition, if the film was cut on a KEM, the chances are good that the editor only spliced the film on one side (usually the emulsion side). Projectors, being the tough machines that they are, will often chew up film spliced only on one side. So, in addition to everything else that you and Philip will have to do to prepare for the screening, you will have to splice the base side of the film. This process is called *back-splicing*.

After you have checked the splices and changeovers, you should thoroughly clean the film with a film cleaner like *Ecco* (being careful not to wipe off any of Wendy's marks for optical effects, about which we will discuss more later). This is a rather painstaking and disagreeable task that involves soaking a *Webril wipe* with Ecco and running the film through it v-e-r-r-r-y slowly. Cleaning it slowly allows the Ecco enough time to evaporate off the film before it is wound up on the right rewind. If it is wound up too fast the Ecco will leave streak marks on the film that are almost worse than the dirt that it removed. When you are finished cleaning the film with Ecco, rewind it back to the head through a velvet to buff it up. Clean the track with a velvet (no Ecco, please, as it will dissolve the track).

You will probably find it helpful to have a screening check list (*see* Figure 8.7) posted nearby the assistant's table to keep you apprised of just what still needs to be done in the preparation.

Then pack up all of the reels in order into some sort of packing cartons and get them to the screening room. Bring along several copies of your reel breakdown with you as well as a paper listing the running time of the film (everyone will want to know the length of the picture).

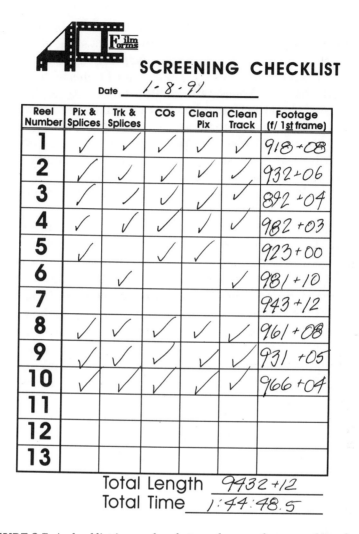

SCREENING CHECKLIST

Date *1-8-91*

Reel Number	Pix & Splices	Trk & Splices	COs	Clean Pix	Clean Track	Footage (f/ 1st frame)
1	✓	✓	✓	✓	✓	918 +08
2	✓	✓	✓	✓	✓	932 +06
3	✓	✓	✓	✓	✓	892 +04
4	✓	✓	✓	✓	✓	982 +03
5	✓		✓	✓		923 +00
6		✓			✓	981 +10
7						943 +12
8	✓	✓	✓	✓	✓	961 +08
9	✓	✓	✓	✓	✓	931 +05
10	✓	✓	✓	✓	✓	966 +04
11						
12						
13						

Total Length *9432 +12*
Total Time *1:44:48.5*

FIGURE 8.7 *A checklist is very handy to make sure that everything that needs to be prepared before a screening is done. Note that in this example all of the reels have been completely prepared except for reel five (picture only has been prepared), six (track only has been prepared), and seven (nothing has been prepared).*

After the screening there is bound to be a meeting between Adam and Wendy. During the meeting you should be listening to what everyone feels are the film's major strengths and weaknesses. Take careful notes as to the proposed changes. These will include what scenes should be dropped from the film, what alternate takes need to be used, what scenes need to be moved to different places in the film, what sequences need to have major recutting done on them, and a host of other suggestions. All of these points require work from you to prepare for the director and editor. Be sure that you know what it is they want done, and when they want it.

It is wise, at this point, if the film has the budget to do so, to strike what is called a *slop print* or a *black and white dupe* of the entire film. This is a black and white copy of the picture and a track copy of the soundtrack which will be stored as a reference. Some times, in recutting, a scene will get worse rather than better. It is helpful to have a record of the way the scene was before it was recut so that it will be easier to reconstruct properly. On *Four Friends* we struck a videocassette of the film rather than go to the expense of making a film dupe. Though it is not easy to take the videocassette and check exact cuts, we felt that all we needed to preserve was a record of the general approaches to the cut scenes. The video was all that was needed for this; it was merely a record of the film's continuity with all of its scenes rather than a record of the cutting of individual scenes.

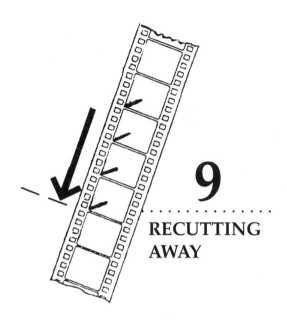

9

RECUTTING AWAY

After the first cut is screened, critiqued, and recritiqued it will then be time to begin recutting the film. There are some editors and directors who love this part of the film; there are others who despise it. For, at one time, it encapsulates everything that makes editing what it is — attention to the minutest detail while still paying attention to the whole film.

On *Four Friends*, the director and editors continually experimented with the order of different scenes. The editors would re–edit the film for a week and then screen for the director. Then they would return to the editing room, work for another week, and go back to the screening room for another screening. The process went on for months.

After every screening there would be intense discussions about the relative weight we were attaching to a given character, a given scene, or a given action. "It moved slowly in this part," someone would say, and if there was agreement to this then everyone would try to figure out why the sequence moved slowly and what could best be done to help the situation.

As an assistant editor you have to keep track of all of those suggestions and prepare to carry them out. I would keep a spiral notebook with each page a new date, listing everything to be done that day and everything that was done on that day (rarely the same). Meeting notes, special addresses, or other pertinent information were kept in it as well. This helped me to plan what it was I was going to have to do to prepare for the editor. It is also helpful to have an erasable calendar posted prominently on the wall.

Lifts

The first type of recut that you are liable to face is called a *lift*. A lift is, simply, a scene (or major portion of a scene) which is being dropped in its entirety from the film. Often a director will want to see how the film will play without a scene. You will then lift the scene from the film.

Lifts are never broken down and returned to the trims unless Wendy specifically requests it (in which case they really wouldn't be lifts at all, merely trims). They are stored and logged as lifts and saved for the time when the entire lift or pieces from it may need to be used again. In this way, if it is ever decided to put the scene back into the film, you won't have to reconstruct every one of the cuts from scratch.

This system is not as elegant as it may seem on the surface. For one thing, it means that there is now one more place where pieces of the picture or track may be found — in the lifts as well as the trims, outs, or in the cut. You will need a way of locating specific code numbers in the lifts, and this necessitates another log. This log, which we will (predictably enough) call the *lift log*, is not very difficult to maintain. It consists of large index cards on which all of the code numbers (both picture and track) included in the lift are written (*see* Figure 9.1.) These numbers (the head and tail codes of each cut in the lift) are taken directly from the film while it is in the synchronizer.

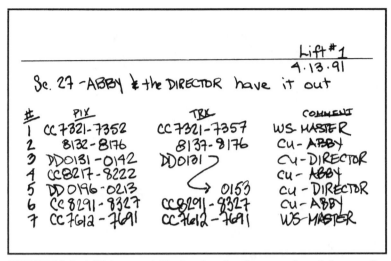

FIGURE 9.1 A lift log card. Notice that for shots numbered three to five only one piece of track (the DIRECTOR'S) was used.

In the example shown for Scene 27, "ABBY and the DIRECTOR have it out" (this is from your scene description chart), we can see that the lift is made up of seven picture cuts and five track cuts (two picture cuts, numbers four and five, have cheated track running under them — that is, track from another shot, in this case the shot used in cut number three of the lift). We can see what the scene is and what each of the picture cuts actually are. We label this lift 'Lift # 1'.

This card should be put in an index file reserved for lifts and filed in scene number order. During the cutting process some large scenes may have as many as three or four sections pulled from them, each filed as its own lift. If you cannot find a particular trim in its proper trim box, you should check the lift log to see if it might be in one of the lifts from that scene.

The lift itself should be put into a box reserved for lifts. You should make up a cinetab for it (*see* Figure 9.2). Then label the outside of the box "LIFTS 41–", leaving room for the number of the last lift in the box (eventually you will probably

FIGURE 9.2 A trim tab for a lift.

have to have several boxes of lifts).

Another, quicker, way to file lifts is to label each by its scene number and a description of the part of the scene that the lift is from, if it is not the entire scene ("Scene 27 — DIRECTOR and ABBY at desk during fight," for instance). A simple log is kept listing only these two items and the lift is filed in a lift box labelled with all the scene numbers of the lifts in that box. If there are three lifts from scene 27 in the box, then the number 27 would be written three times on the side of the box. Each number should be written on a small piece of white paper tape and taped to the side of the box. In that way, when you give Wendy a lift you can also peel the tape off the side of the box so that you will always be able to tell just how many lifts you have for any given scene. When Wendy needs a piece of film, and it is not in the trims, you will have to check the entire lift to see if it is within it, obviously a slower process than checking the lift log index card. However, you save so much time in compiling the lift log that it is generally worth the extra time later on.

146

Complete Recuts

In some cases, everyone is so depressed by the way a particular scene is cut that they feel that it is better to recut the scene from scratch. In this case, you will do exactly what you did not do in the case of the lifts — completely break down the scene, returning each piece to its virgin state as complete uncut takes (outs).

In cases like this I feel it is very important to have a black and white dupe of the cut that you will be destroying. There are always times when, after recutting the scene, someone feels that the old scene was better or that a combination of the two approaches would work better. At that stage it would be almost impossible to remember exactly how the original scene was cut. So I like to make a black and white dupe to preserve a record of the cut.

When you order the dupe you should tell the lab to print through both edges. In this way your dupe will have the edge and the key numbers copied onto it as well as the picture image.

But how does one match up the track? When you make a track copy there is no way to print code numbers onto the new track. How can you get back to the old cut on the track?

To do this you will have to hand–code the track with the numbers. The easiest way to do this is as follows. Before you send the track in for duping (or retransferring), put a one-frame long beep tone on its head leader (you will remember to put head and tail leaders on everything that you send out of the editing room, won't you?) There is a standard place for this — exactly three feet before the first frame. Then, when the dupe track comes back from the transfer house you can listen to it, find the beep tone, and from there find the first frame of action. You should also, just as a matter of practice, check the two tracks — original and dupe — against each other to make sure that they are the same. You do this by listening for phasing as described in Chapter 7 in the section on lining up playback music tracks.

Now you will have the original picture, the original track, and this dupe track all lined up in your synchronizer. Run them down together and every time that there is a picture or track cut mark it as shown in Figure 9.3 using black to mark picture cuts and red to mark track cuts. Where the picture and track are cut at the same spot, mark the cut point with both red and black marks. On either side of each cut, mark the closest code number. Where the picture and track cuts do not come at the same spot mark each of them separately, again marking the code numbers that appear on either side of the cut. If you are in a rush, or if the cuts are coming rather close together, you can leave out the code number preceding the cut. But always mark the one following it.

Some people do not mark down the picture code numbers since there is already a picture dupe that marks the cuts. I find it helpful to have all the information in the same place. But, if there is a lot of time pressure, you can do without the picture code numbers. Once again, you should always be aware of the priorities in running an editing room.

With this set of dupes it is relatively easy to get back to the original cut picture and track if necessary. Simply put the dupe picture and track in the back two gangs of your synchronizer and match the cuts and code numbers on both the picture and the track in the first two gangs. After you have finished doing that you should check the picture against its dupe visually, and run the two tracks together to check them (using phasing).

Normal Recutting

By far the largest part of your recutting work, however, will lie somewhere between the extremes of completely recutting a scene, and completely lifting it out of the picture.

Before Wendy begins recutting each scene you should know which reel it appears on and give her that reel. You

FIGURE 9.3 *Marking up dupe track. Black cut marks (shown with the letter A) are drawn wherever picture cuts were made on the cut work picture. Red cut marks are made where track cuts were made on the work track. Code numbers are listed where helpful. At point A the picture and track cut at the same time. The last code number on the outgoing shot, before the cut, is EE6328. But the incoming shot used track cheated from another take than the picture, so both code numbers are written down (picture codes in black, track codes in red)*

149

should also know the scene number so you can research the outs for it and let Wendy know, as she asks, just what other choices are available to her. You should make yourself aware of any lifts that have already been made on the scene, if any.

Wendy will begin recutting and will almost immediately ask you for some footage. She will ask for it in one of two ways. If she wants to extend a shot that is already in the film she will look at the take in the cut footage and ask for either the head trim (if she wants to extend the top of the cut) or the tail trim (if she wants to extend the end). In both cases she will look at the number in the cut and ask for "the head (or tail) trim of CC8141." Since the trims are filed by code number all you have to do is to walk over to the box with the CC8000 trims in them, open it, and look for the take which includes CC8141 in it. When you find it, you take it out of the box, remove the cinetab and the rubber band from the take and hang them above the footage pin on the trim barrel. You then unwind the take, remove the rubber band from around the top of the pieces of film (hanging it up with the rubber band already there), and put the trims on the pin directly below the cinetab and rubber bands. Since the trims are in numerical order it should take only a matter of seconds to find the proper trim and hand it to her. All of this should take about thirty seconds to accomplish if everything is moving right. In fact, some editors prefer to get their own trims if they know how everything is filed.

Obviously, the importance of making sure that every trim is filed properly cannot be stressed enough. Each time a trim is filed with the wrong take, or in the wrong box, or not put away at all (as sometimes happens if it falls into the bottom of a barrel) it takes up time while the editor sits around doing nothing except getting angry. The fewer mistakes the better. No mistakes is the ideal.

The other way that Wendy may ask for a piece of film is if she and Adam (or just Adam, let's be honest about who is calling the shots) feel that a take that she used for a piece of dialogue or a piece of action was not as good as it could have been. She may want to see other takes or angles shot for that part of the scene. In that case she will ask for "an alternate take to CC8141." Or, if she's already looked at the lined script and knows what setup she needs she may ask for "an alternate take to 42A–4." If she asks for it in the first way all you have to do is look in the logbook to ;see what take CC8141 comes from. "Aha," you'd say. "Take 42A–4." A look at the logbook will also tell you what other takes were shot for this setup. Write them down on a piece of paper or a piece of paper tape that you can stick to the back of your hand.

Then, check the outs boxes for Scene 42, if you are filing them separately. Written on the outside will be a list of the takes for Scene 42. If you see another 42A there, take it out and give it to Wendy. Make sure that you immediately cover over its take number on the outside of the box. If she decides not to use the out you can always remove the tape from the box, but if she does use it you will never have to go back and remove the number from the box at a later time (when you may have already forgotten just which take it was that you used from the outs). From that moment on, that take will be treated as a regular trim. Once cut, it will be filed as a trim, not as an out.

Sometimes, the alternate takes will not be in the out boxes but will be classified as trims because other parts of the take have been used in the film. In that case you will give those entire trims to Wendy so she can find the part that she needs (if you've been following her as she edits perhaps you can do it). One of the advantages to filing trims and outs together is that there is only one place to look for alternate takes.

The two other places that you might find a trim are the lifts and, in a few cases, in the cut itself. Sometimes the editor has used the exact part of a shot that she needs in another part of the scene (as a reaction shot, perhaps). What usually happens in this case is that you run around in a small panic for a bit because you can't find the trim in any of the places you've looked and you dread spending time going through all of the takes in the movie looking for a misfiled trim. Then you ask Wendy if she could have used it anywhere else in the film. She will either answer an embarrassed "yes" and go on editing or she will say "no" and go and check the footage and give you a doubly embarrassed "yes" a few moments later.

Unfortunately, there are times when the dreaded event does happen: the trim has been misplaced and you do have to look in all of the takes of the film to find it. Because the editor is going to be pacing around waiting for you to find the missing piece, the time you spend frantically looking for the trim will feel like a short visit to Hell. There are some common mistakes that people make that might save you some time in searching.

First, check all the other takes of that same setup. Then, if you still haven't found the take, look in takes with code numbers that are similar. Eights sometimes look like zeroes on inked code numbers, especially after a few months of wear and tear. The letter E looks like the letter F (which is why I never use both in any one coding system). The letter B might be confused with the letter R. Check for reversals of numbers — CC4253 might be filed as CC4523.

If the entire take is missing, the search becomes a little easier since all you have to do is to check other, nearby, boxes for the errant take. Also be aware that another person (another editor, if you have one, or a sound or music editor if you have one of them on) might also be working on that scene and have the take.

Questions! Questions! Questions!

All during the re–editing of the film you will be faced with questions you have to answer. Many of them will deal with organization — how should we code this print, how should we log in this scratch mix, how should we handle this optical? All these questions will have to be dealt with some degree of foresight. For in much the same way that you have attempted to create a system that will function all the way through the movie, you must learn how to deal with those exceptions to the system without ruining your system or creating even more work for you and your system.

Let's examine these exceptions one at a time.

During the course of editing, someone will most assuredly rip a piece of film or soundtrack, or put a gouge in the film to such a degree that the piece is no longer acceptable for viewing, either because it would be too distracting to look at or because it won't go through a projector without trouble.

You will need to order another print of that piece of film or track and be able to integrate it into the system. The best way to do that is to reprint the entire take from which the ripped piece came.

In your logbook (*see* Figure 5.2) you can see a list of all of the takes that were on the first dailies roll. Let's say that the piece that Wendy ripped had the code number AA1352. A quick look in the code book tells us that this comes from 10D–3. This will be the only piece with that code number since that's the way the system works (nice, isn't it?). The information in the log will also tell us that the take (1) was shot on September 10, 1990; (2) was from lab roll number one; (3) was from camera roll number one; (4) had the code numbers AA1321—1378; and (5) had the latent edge numbers F13X64247 through F13X64304.

This gives you all of the information that you need to reorder the take from the lab. Tell them that you want a reprint of take 10D–3, shot 9-10-90, lab roll number one, key numbers F13X64247—64304. Tell them you would like it at the same timing lights as before. That's all you have to do (except to make sure that they deliver it on time). If you were ordering the track reprint (sometimes called the *retransfer*) of this take you would tell the sound transfer house that you wanted a retransfer of take 10D–3, shot 9-10-90, from sound roll number one.

When you get the reprint back from the lab you have to code it exactly as you did the first print. The best way of doing this is to get the trims of that take out from the trim box and line up the new and the old prints in the synchronizer. Copy all the marks (slates, identifications, etc.) onto the new take. Add about ten feet of leader to the head of the reprint then find the first code number on the old take (it will be AA1321) and mark where it would fall on the reprint. Then set your footage counter to 0'00 at that frame and proceed to back up one full foot. This should put you into the leader you've just added. On the leader, in marker, mark that frame. Then, just as you set up your dailies reels for coding, mark that frame for spot coding with its first number being AA1320 (that is, one foot before the first code number that you want to print on the film).

There is a very good reason for backing up the one foot. Some coding machines do not print the first number or, if they do, it is smudged and difficult to read. In this way you will get readable numbers all the way through the take.

When you get the take back from coding you are going to completely replace the old print with the new one. Once again, get the trims from that take down from their box. In the synchronizer, line up the new and old prints. Then roll forward until you get to the first place where there is a piece of film missing on the old print. This is where there is either something in the cut work picture or in a lift. Make a cut in your new print in exactly the same spot and hang the two head trims (old and new) on separate pins in a barrel.

Then find the next trim and line it up against the new print in the synchronizer. Cut the reprint at exactly the same point that the old trim begins. The piece that you've just cut off will be a piece that is being used (either in the cut work picture or in a lift). For now, hold it aside on its own pin, clearly marked as "New Print—In Cut." This way you won't confuse it with any part of the old print.

Continue on in this manner, replacing all of the pieces

in the trims with the reprint. When you have finished you should have three pins of material—the first will be the trims from the old print, the second will be the matching trims from the new print, and the third will be those pieces destined for the cut. Make sure that each of the three is clearly marked.

Now take the cut work picture for the scene that you are replacing (in this case, you would take the reel that contained Scene 10 on it) and roll it down in the synchronizer until you get to a cut which comes from 10D-3 (you will be able to check this with the code numbers but you should have a very good idea of what it looks like and be able to spot it by eye). Choose the proper piece of reprint from the third pin and line it up against the cut work picture. The first frame of that piece of the reprint should exactly coincide with a piece of picture in the work picture (where the old print begins). If it does not, you have made a mistake somewhere along the line and you must go back and figure out where.

But, if all is well (and there is no reason to think that it won't be), you will find that the new reprint will exactly replace the old print frame to frame. In that case, carefully undo the splice in the cut work picture, remove the old print, and replace it exactly with the new reprint making sure that all code and key numbers still line up in exactly the same way that they used to.

When this is done, hang the old print up on a fourth pin and continue with the replacement process until all of your new reprint pieces are used up. If you finish your scene without using up all of the pieces, check to make sure that you haven't skipped a piece in the workprint. If you haven't then check to see if there is a lift from that scene and, if there is, replace the old print in the lift with the new reprint. If you have checked all the trims, all of the lifts and still have a piece left over then you have made a mistake somewhere or there is a missing piece of film.

In that case there is only one piece of advice I can give you — find the piece!!

155

When you have finished replacing all the pieces you will have ended up with three pins of film. The first holds the old reprint trims, the second the new trims, and the third is the old print which used to be in the cut or in the lifts. Wrap up the second pin, with its track as you normally would, and return it to the trims. Then combine the other two pins. You should find that all of the pieces of the old print should now cut together sequentially, forming one complete take. When you have done this you know that you have found every piece of old print that exists.

Then you throw away the entire old print. Make sure that there is no bit of the old take left in the cutting room to be confused with the new print.

The reason you go through this long involved process is rather simple, though not immediately apparent. Despite your request for a reprint at the same timing lights as the first print, differences in the temperature of the water at the laboratory, slight differences in the lengths of time that various parts of the printing process take place, and many other minute differences will make the new reprint look slightly different than the old print. If Wendy ever wanted to extend a shot and cut part of the old print onto a part of the reprint, the color would not match exactly. And this would be very distracting to look at. So, in order to have a consistent color balance throughout any one take you must make sure that all of the pieces of that take are from the same printing of that take.

The process for reprinting and replacing track is much the same as that for picture. After retransferring the needed take at your sound house in the same way as it was originally transferred, you will code it to match the original track. You will then replace all of the trims, then all of the pieces in the cut work track.

Scratch Mixes/Temp Dubs

When Wendy and Adam screen the film there may be sections where more than one sound is happening at the same time (there is dialogue between two characters while a scene is being shot in the background, for instance) or places where they would like to hear temporary music under dialogue. Because the work track is only a single strand of track they won't be able to hear both things at once.

Most of these things are left until the end of the movie, when a sound editor will correct everything in preparation for the final film mix (or dub). But sometimes there will be things that they want done for earlier screenings (either for themselves or for producers, distributors, etc.). Then you will have to *scratch mix* (also called *temp dub*) the movie.

Understanding the process of scratch mixing requires that you understand the process of film mixing, which is too large a subject for this book. But let me give a brief explanation that should suffice for now.

When a movie is being shot, the sound behind any given piece of dialogue will almost surely not match the sound behind any other piece of dialogue, even if that second piece is just the reverse angle on the same scene. If there is a scene of two people talking, and the director has covered it in a wide-shot master, a closer two shot, and close-ups on each of the people talking, the chances that all of these four camera set–ups will have the same background sound is very slim. This is not the fault of the sound recordist but is a simple function of differing microphone placements as well as (for films shot on location) the uncontrollability of the background sound outside of camera range.

Now, when Wendy cuts these angles together there is going to be a different background sound every time she changes the take she is using. Those kinds of changes aren't too bothersome when you are cutting a movie but in a movie theatre a regular audience would be distracted by them, since they are accustomed to smooth backgrounds. A dialogue editor is brought on to correct these *bumps* (as the points where the background changes are called).

This dialogue editor will *split* the dialogue tracks, which simply means that he or she will split apart the dialogue onto two or more synchronously running tracks so that each sound can be controlled separately, with a separate volume control and equalizer. In that way, when the tracks are combined back into one whole track at the film mix any disagreeable differences can be evened out by the dialogue mixer.

Now, of course, nothing is as easy as all that. The dialogue editor must do a lot of trickery with these tracks in order to prepare them properly for the dialogue mixer. But that is much too complicated a subject for us to deal with here and now. That must be left for another book (which, hopefully, someone else will write).

Another task of a sound editor is to add sound effects to the soundtrack. In order to have the utmost control of the dialogue sections in both the editing and the mixing, dialogue is shot with as few extra noises as possible. Phones ringing, radios playing, guns shooting, etc., are all left out during the shooting, to be added in the final mix. But it is just those kind of things that can help a story along. So, before some screenings, Wendy and Adam may want to add those sounds (along with some music) to give them some rough idea about how the film plays.

Usually there is no sound editor on the film at this time so it will fall to Wendy, you, and Philip to prepare for this mix. Since this will be a mix just to give everyone a rough idea of the film, the mix will be done very fast and without much finesse. For that reason it is often called a rough, scratch, slop, or temp mix. Dialogue is almost never split in these mixes. The usual purpose is to add a few sound effects to make the film more intelligible, and to try out some sample music.

Music is usually lifted from already recorded records, or CDs. Sound effects are available at many sound houses or from sound effects records. You will usually call up the effects house, or go there for an hour or two and audition some effects. You will tell them, "I need a very loud door slam, two different types of horse hoofbeats, a series of gunshots, and a few modern phone rings," and they will be able to give them all to you in a short period of time, transferred directly onto 35mm film (or 16mm, if that is your need). You should always make a note of the effects numbers of every effect (all reputable sound libraries have their effects catalogued in some manner) so that, in the likely event that Adam falls in love with one of the effects, the sound editor will later be able to go back and get additional prints of the same effect if needed.

Then, you should have all of the scratch effects and music coded. I like to code the effects with the prefix code FX1000 (or 001F0000) and up, and the music with the code MX1000 (or 001M0000) and up. Any effects which you are going to be using from the wild track will already be coded so you don't have to worry about coding them.

Start two new sections in your logbook — one for the temp effects and one for the temp music. List each effect by its code numbers, origin (effects house), catalogue number, date transferred, and description of effect. Make up cinetabs that list the code number and description on the front, and origin and catalogue number on the reverse. List each piece of music by its code numbers, origin, date, and title. Make up cinetabs that list the code numbers and title.

You then must do a little sound editing. Many editors like to do this themselves and many do not. In case they do, watch them closely to see how they do it. But in case they do not, I can offer only this brief explanation.

You will need a three-head (called a Moviola *console*, or a Moviola with an add–a–plate) or a flatbed with two sound heads and one picture head. Thread up the picture and sound at the start mark (on the Moviola you should put the cut work track on the outside sound head, leaving the center one free) and zero out the counter. Run down the film until

FIGURE 9.4 *This sound effect begins at 152'10. The first whole number is marked on the piece of track. An alternate way would be to write the footage 152'10 at the head of the effect. Some sound editors will put a mark on the picture at 153'00 to match the one on the track.*

you get to the place that you want to add the effect or music cue. Place the effect in the center sound head (or, on a flatbed, in the other sound head), disengage this head from the other ones, and run the effect or music cue until you get to the place in the sound that you want to line up against the picture point that you are at in the cut reel. Engage all three heads and run them together. You will be able to hear both tracks (dialogue and effect, or dialogue and music) at the same time and get some idea of how they line up. If you need to change the relationship between the cut reel and the new piece, move the effect or music cue only. Never move just the picture or just the dialogue track as that will throw them out of sync.

Once you have a relationship that you are happy with, go back to the beginning of the effect or music and find a zero frame (if the effect begins at 152'10, go to 153'00). Now, with grease pencil, mark that frame on the track (*see* Figure 9.4). On a piece of paper you should begin to make a cue sheet (*see* Figure 9.5). This cue sheet will list all of the elements for the temp dub for this reel.

For this example (a portion of the cue sheet for reel one) we can see that we have our work track running during the entire reel. At 152'10 we have the effect that we just selected — which happens to be the sound of a horse whinnying. We also have some gunshots later on, as well as two pieces of music. Let's analyze the cue sheet a little bit.

At the top of the cue sheet we have listed much of the same information as you put on the head leaders of reels — the name of the film and the reel number. We have also listed the date of the scratch mix.

Under that, we have listed the mix *units* (also called *elements*.) After we cut all of the effects they will all have footage numbers on them. We will then have to cut them into reels of fill at those exact numbers so that they can run on other machines in perfect sync with the dialogue track. Since only one effect can be on a reel at one time whenever we have more than one sound going on at a time, we will need more

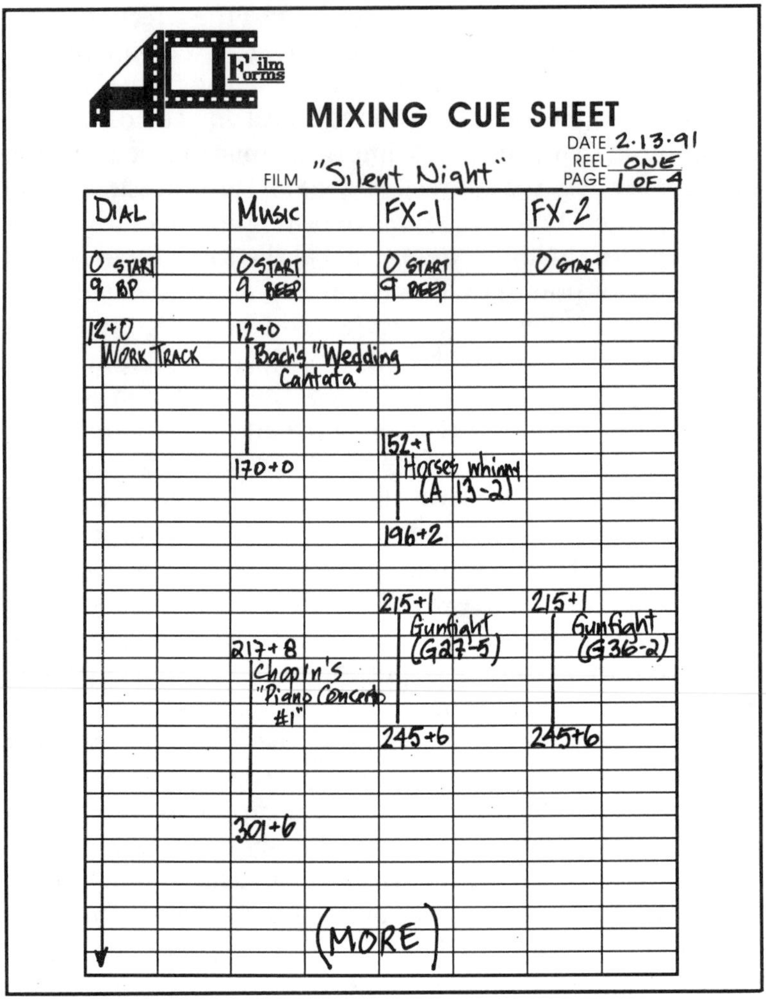

MIXING CUE SHEET

DATE 2·13·91
REEL ONE
FILM "Silent Night"
PAGE 1 OF 4

DIAL	MUSIC	FX-1	FX-2
O START	O START	O START	O START
9 BP	9 BEEP	9 BEEP	
12+0	12+0		
WORK TRACK	Bach's "Wedding Cantata"		
		152+1	
	170+0	Horses whinny (A 13-2)	
		196+2	
		215+1	215+1
		Gunfight (G27-5)	Gunfight (G36-2)
	217+8		
	Chopin's "Piano Concerto #1"		
		245+6	245+6
	301+6		
	(MORE)		

FIGURE 9.5 A cue sheet for a temp dub (also called a scratch mix). Note that the work track runs continuously from the first frame of action. Also note that beeps are put on the track at 9' 00 on the first unit of any set of units (i.e. dialogue, music, effects).

162

than one reel. In this case we are going to need four reels. One of these reels will be your work track reel, which contains the dialogue. Another reel contains the music. And the remaining two reels contain effects we will need including the horse whinnies. When all of the elements are run together, in sync, the dialogue, effects, and music will be combined — mixed together into one soundtrack for the screening.

On the first effects track (called FX–1, though it is sometimes called FX–A) we have put a beep at 9'00, the standard place for a beep (this is three feet before the first frame of action). This beep will transfer across during the mix and give you a way to line up the mix with the picture. Then, at 12 feet, a piece of music begins which lasts until 170 feet. The carat symbol (>) at the end of the line means that the music should be faded out. This is also noted by the initials F.O.

Apparently the music is fading out into the sound of horses whinnying. The horses come in at 152'10 and last until 196'02 (during this entire time, the dialogue track has still been running). Since the music, the horses, and the dialogue are all going on at the same time during the period from 152'10 to 170'00 we need three tracks to hold all of the elements.

Then, at 215'01, a gunfight breaks out and, in order to attain the proper frenzy, there will be two tracks of gunshots going at the same time. For that we need a second effects track. We might have put it on the music track but it is best to keep all the music on its own track. In any case, the music returns again before the end of the gunfight (at 217'08) so we would need all four tracks running at that time to handle every sound that we want.

You can see just from this simple explanation, that this process can get complicated very, very fast. In fact, for final mixes it is not uncommon to have eighty to ninety tracks running for the same reel. On one film that I worked on there were over one hundred tracks on one reel! But since this is just a scratch mix you are going to want to keep it as simple as possible while still getting the effects added that you need. On the average, five tracks is the most that you will need for these types of mixes.

When you go to the mix, all of these four tracks will be lined up at their start marks and then run together. If everything has been lined up properly, when you get to 152'10 you should hear the horse whinnying while the dialogue and music are going on. The mixer will then set the relative levels of everything and mix them together. This process will continue for all of the reels of the film that need to have things added to them.

At the completion of the mix what you will want to take back to the editing room with you is a 35mm stripe copy of the mix. This is also called the mixed mag. A stripe copy is, simply, the type of track that you are used to dealing with — a strip of oxide on 35mm film with a second, smaller stripe, called a balance stripe, on the other edge (*see* Figure 4.14). Some studios can mix directly onto 35mm stripe, others must mix onto a 35mm four–track (a piece of soundtrack which is completely covered with oxide and onto which four separate tracks can be recorded; because of this it is often called full–coat) and then make a transfer of that mix onto stripe. Regardless, when you are done you should end up with a 35mm stripe that you will code (I like to code it SA1000, or 001S0000, for "scratch mix" and then to move through SB, SC, etc., or 001S1000, 001S2000, etc., as the need arises). Log it in a section of your logbook devoted to scratch mixes. The mix can now be used instead of the dialogue/work track.

Some editors, in order to save money on 35mm stock, like to mix only that portion of the reel that needs mixing and then to cut that portion into the work track before the screening. I have never found this a particularly worthwhile way to save money since the amount of time needed to cut the mixes into the work track reels and remove them later (after the screening, when you will want the reels returned to normal) more than makes up for the increased cost in stock used. I like to mix the entire reel, even those sections which don't need mixing. For those areas, this "mix" amounts to nothing more than a straight transfer. But, after the mix is over, you end up with one complete track for the reel that will completely substitute for the unmixed reel. During subsequent scratch mixes, when you may not need to remix the horse whinny section but want to mix something else in the reel, I would simply use this mix as an element in the new mix.

After the mix is over, the elements should be saved in their own section of the cutting room, plainly labeled as to what date they were used and what reel they come from. If those effects are ever needed again a look at the filed cue sheets will automatically lead you back to those exact reels. If Adam liked those horse whinnies, the sound editor will be able to use those exact ones for the final mix. To this end, it would be helpful if there was a mark on the horse whinny track which listed not only the footage (153'00 as we have already written) but the closest picture code number of the shot around that 153-foot mark. In that way we will always be able to find the exact sync point of the effect even though the reel may have been recut and rebalanced so many times that the footage count may be meaningless. This is a wise thing to put on every effect as you cut them as it will save the sound editor the time-consuming task of syncing up the effect later on.

There are many more fine points in the process of scratch mixing which you will only learn by watching and doing. Every editor and assistant has his or her own method. What you have just learned are only the basics.

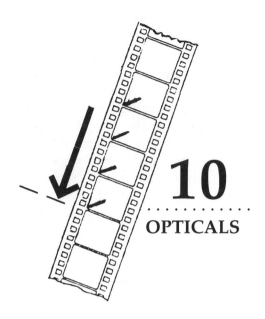

10

OPTICALS

The act of making the impossible possible is one of the things that makes movie–going so attractive. Watching the Red Sea part or spaceships fly through space is an experience hard to find anywhere other than in a movie theatre.

Creating these fantastic effects, as well as a host of much less spectacular ones, falls under the category of making *opticals*. An optical can be as simple an effect as a scene fading out or as complicated as the space battles in *Star Wars*. All opticals, however, involve the manipulation of the film negative to create a new negative with some change in the original's image.

Simple Opticals

The four simplest, and most common, opticals used in film editing are the *fade–in, fade–out, dissolve*, and *superimposition*. In addition, the creation of titles is an optical effect. In 16mm these effects are not created optically (even though they may still be referred to as "optical effects" or just "effects"), they are created in the lab through a process called

A and B roll printing (we will discuss this in more detail in a minute). In 35mm, however, these effects are almost always created optically, albeit in a very analogous manner.

Let's say that, at the end of one scene in *Silent Night, Silent Cowboy* we wanted the image to fade to black. This is called a fade–out and it is accomplished by darkening the image gradually until we can see nothing but black. One way to accomplish this, of course, would be to do it in the camera, while we were shooting the scene. We would simply close the camera's aperture slowly while the actors performed in front of us so that less and less light would be thrown on the negative. When we saw the dailies we would see the image get darker and darker until all we saw was black.

But if we changed our minds later on during the editing process and wanted the fade–out to come two seconds later than we had determined during the shooting, or if we wanted the fade to be a little slower or a little faster, there would be no way to do it since there would be no image on the negative to play around with. By creating optical effects in the camera we force ourselves to accept whatever comes out of the camera, no matter how bad or inappropriate it is.

One solution, then, would be to wait until we are making our release prints (i.e., the prints that we will use for showing in theatres) to do these effects. In that way we could have the lab *stop down* the printing camera's aperture (stopping down is the process of closing the camera aperture so that it throws less light onto the film). We could tell the lab exactly where we wanted the fade–out to start and how long we wanted the fade to go on for before the frame was completely dark. We would preserve our original negative as well as all of our options until the very end.

In fact, this is exactly what is done in most 16mm films. It is called A and B roll printing because the negative to be printed is made up in two reels (rather than one, which is the norm in 35 mm.) After the negative is prepared for the lab (and we will see how to do that in a later chapter) the lab does

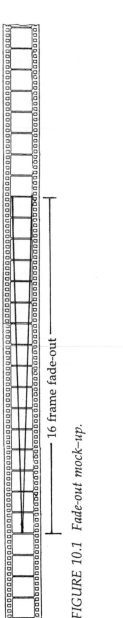

16 frame fade-out

FIGURE 10.1 Fade-out mock-up.

all of the optical work based upon certain marks that you put on the workprint. The accepted marking for a fade–out is a long 'V' whose length is the length of the desired fade–out; the open end is at the first frame of the fade and the point is at the last frame, as in Figure 10.1 (the open end is for *more* light, the closed end is for *no* light).

The marking for a fade–in, in which the image on the screen gradually emerges from complete black, is exactly the opposite — a 'V' that grows from a single point.

The optical dissolve is actually a combination of the fade–in and the fade–out: one image is fading in at the same time as the other is fading out. The effect on screen is of one image crossing into another, thus we say that one image "dissolves into" another (*see* Figure 10.2).

The fourth type of optical — the superimposition — is actually an extension of the dissolve. In it two images are run together at the same time. If one of the characters in our film is reading a letter from another character and we want to show

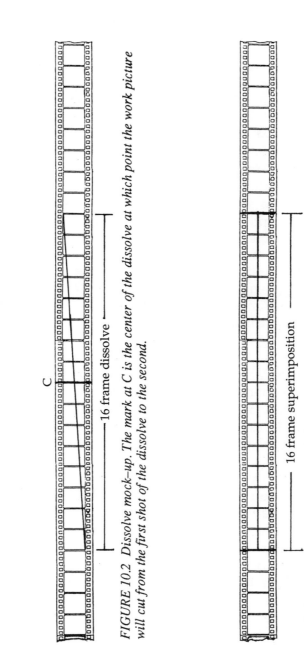

FIGURE 10.2 *Dissolve mock–up. The mark at C is the center of the dissolve at which point the work picture will cut from the first shot of the dissolve to the second.*

FIGURE 10.3 *Superimposition mock–up.*

him thinking of that person, we might show a picture of that other person superimposed over a close-up of our first character thinking. We would then run the close-up of him and the shot of the other character, exposing both at the same time. When projected, the end result would be that we would see both images — one right on top of the other (*see* Figure 10.3).

There are two major problems and restrictions in making opticals at the lab. The first is that it is extremely expensive. You may have to make many prints of your film so that it can play in many theatres. If someone from the lab has to turn the printing camera aperture up or down every time you want an optical effect on every print, printing your film will be very expensive.

The second problem is that in the lab it is necessary to restrict the lengths of your opticals to predetermined lengths and to keep them at certain distances from each other. This places certain limitations on the editing of a film since it will be impossible to make, for instance, several quick dissolves in a row.

You can solve these problems by not doing your opticals in the lab at all but in a place which is designed to do nothing but opticals — the optical house.

In general, all of your opticals will be done in an optical house, resulting in a piece of completely new negative with the optical effect incorporated into it. It is this negative, rather than the original negative that was shot on the set, that will be sent to the laboratory for making your release prints. In this way you will end up with one long strand of cut negative with all of your optical effects already incorporated into it. No one from the lab has to stand at the printing machine and create each effect. Each effect can be exactly the length and kind that you desire.

Let us follow one short scene from our movie through the optical house to see just how it works. In this scene we are watching a scene from the movie-within-the-movie when it freezes, and turns to black and white. We then find out that this frozen scene is actually a publicity photo that the director is looking at.

On the surface it sounds complicated. In fact, it is complicated. But this is how you would handle it.

In this case the editing room staff probably worked with the people on the set during the shooting. When the scene of the director looking at the photo was being prepared the art director may have asked for a frame clip of the already shot scene to make into the photo. Wendy would have cut that movie-within-the-movie scene and have already chosen the frame where the freeze would be. You would have sent a frame or two of that shot to the art director who would have made it into a black and white photo to be used as the prop in the shooting of the director's scene.

When that scene was shot it began with a close-up of the black and white photo. The photo was then pulled away from the camera and we were able to see that the director had been holding it. The idea, therefore, would be to take the shot of the movie-within-the-movie, freeze the proper frame, and dissolve into the beginning of the shot of the black and white photo. This complicated optical is actually three opticals. The first is the freeze frame. The second is the color turning into black and white, called *color desaturation*. The third is the dissolve from that into the live shot with the photo.

By the time all of the material has been shot and cut, Wendy will have determined the exact frame where the freeze frame should begin, the length of time before it begins to desaturate, the length of time it takes to desaturate, the length of time before this image begins dissolving into the black and white photo, and the length of the dissolve. These five items determine how you will lay out the optical.

Let's say that these are the details of the optical:

1. freeze frame marked with an X
2. length of time before desaturation —
    3 feet (2 seconds)
3. length of desaturation — 6 feet (4 seconds)

4. length before dissolve — 4.5 feet (3 seconds)
5. length of dissolve — 6 feet (4 seconds)

You should make a list of all of the pieces of film involved in the optical. In this case, it is only two — the movie scene and the director's scene. From your logbook find the information that you would normally give to the lab for a reprint order (that is, key and take numbers, lab roll number, date shot). Now, you will order an *interpositive* (or a *registration interpositive*, your optical house will tell you which one is needed; see below for details) from the lab for these two scenes.

To understand just what an interpositive is let's go over a bit of lab technology (don't worry, it's not too complicated or scary). When a copy of a negative is made the negative is run through a *contact printer*. This means that the negative is sandwiched with a new piece of film and some light is shot through it. As a result, any part of the frame which is black will appear white on the copy, and any part which was white will appear black. Colors are reversed in a similar fashion. Therefore, any copy off the negative will be a *positive* image. The work picture which you got every day in dailies was struck in just this manner. If you were to go back and look at the negative for any particular shot in the film you would see that the image's color was reversed (that is why camera original is called 'negative') and the actual film stock was a funny orange color.

When your film is all finished the negative will be cut together and contact printed to make a film which looks normal. Any opticals which we create for the film must also, therefore, be negative images so that when *they* are contact printed the print will also appear normal. But if we were to create our optical negative directly from our original negative image that optical negative would be a positive image (since it would be made by contact printing from a negative image). In order to remedy this situation we need to make an intermediate print off of the original negative and from this intermediate contact print our optical. Since the intermediate print will be reversed from our original negative, it will be a positive image. Then when we make our optical negative it will reverse color again, resulting in the negative image that we want.

This intermediate print with the positive image is called (oddly enough) an *interpositive*, or an IP. It is a *positive* image actually printed onto *negative* stock. If you were to look at it, the color would look more or less correct, but the image would have an orange tint since it is printed onto the orange negative stock.

For certain kinds of optical sequences where it is crucial that the image be rock steady (such as those that will appear behind titles) there is a special kind of interpositive, called a *registration IP*, that you should order. Your optical house will tell you what kind of IP you will need.

I should note here that some optical houses prefer to make their own interpositives rather than have you make them at your own lab. I've worked both ways, with mixed results. Sometimes, it is better to have the lab which did the original processing do the interpositive to maintain consistency. But, if the optical house's lab is very good, then it is sometimes better to go with them. That way, they can control the creation of the IP. If anything goes wrong, they will know best how to correct it.

After the IP is struck, you should remove the involved scenes from the workprint so that you can prepare them for the optical house. Remove the entire cut on either side of the optical even if, for instance, the shot in the director's office goes on for twenty-five feet before it cuts to another shot. Put head and tail leaders on the removed workprint. In the cut workprint reel where you removed the footage, replace the extracted footage with the exact same length of white leader so that the reel may be run in sync with the track. Mark on the white leader exactly who removed the footage, when it was removed, and why (this will help anyone else looking for

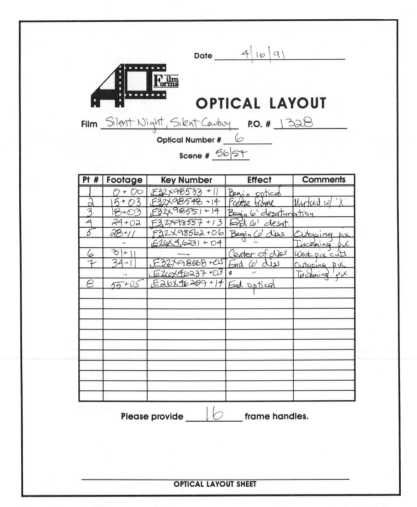

Date ___4/16/91___

OPTICAL LAYOUT

Film __Silent Night, Silent Cowboy__   P.O. # __1328__

Optical Number # __6__

Scene # __56/57__

Pt #	Footage	Key Number	Effect	Comments
1	0 + 00	F32X98533 +11	Begin optical	
2	15+03	F32X98548 +14	Freeze frame	Marked w/ "X"
3	18+03	F32X98551 +14	Begin 6' desaturation	
4	24+02	F32X98557 +13	End 6' desat.	
5	28+11	F32X98562 +06	Begin 6' diss	Outgoing pix
"		E26X4,6231 + 04	"	Incoming pix
6	31+11	—	Center of diss	Work pix cuts
7	34+11	F32X98568 +05	End 6' diss	Outgoing pix
"		E26X46237 +03	"	Incoming pix
8	55+05	E26X46259 +14	End optical	

Please provide ___16___ frame handles.

OPTICAL LAYOUT SHEET

FIGURE 10.4 An optical layout sheet for our sample optical. Note the box below certain of the numbers in the key numbers. This lets the optical layout person know just what part of the key number the zero frame was measured from. Note that this assistant requested one foot handles. Note also that the comment at point six indicates that the work picture cuts from one shot to the other at this point. There are two lines of information given at both ends of the dissolve. That is because there are two pieces of negative involved in the dissolve. The outgoing picture is often called the "A side" and the incoming piece is often referred to as the "B side".

information about that section of the film). Also mark code numbers of the individual pieces of film used in the optical (as you did when you marked up dupe track) on the leader so you know how the work picture had been cut in.

Now take the removed workprint and put it in the synchronizer. Let us say that our optical house wants the first frame of picture to be considered 0'00. Zero out your synchronizer at the first frame of picture and begin a sheet of paper which will be your optical layout sheet. The purpose of this log will be to communicate directly to the optical house how you want the optical to look. This paper will supplement the workprint which you will also show to the optical house.

Your optical layout sheet (*see* Figure 10.4) should contain columns for the footage, key number, effect wanted, and comments. I have also included a column at the beginning called "Point Number" which counts off the number of instructions I'm giving to the optical house. This will make it easier to talk to the optical house over the phone later on. All you will have to say is, "For point number three I want you to... etc." instead of, "You know, the point where the desaturation begins."

The information for the first cue point is rather simple. It is point number one, at 0'00. It is described as "Beginning of Optical." The key number can be found by locating the frame with the key number on it (if the number is spread between two frames choose the one in which the number begins) and count backward to the first frame of the optical. In this case it comes five frames before the key number F32X98534. Since there are sixteen frames to a foot this frame is also equivalent to being eleven frames after F32X98533. The key number is, therefore, F32X98533^{+11}. Key numbers are usually expressed as positive numbers, that is frames *after* a given number. In addition, I usually mark on the layout sheet exactly where the frame comes in the key number. In this case it comes between the three and the two of the prefix F32X.

It is also a good practice to ask for extra frames both

before and after the optical "just in case." This is called the *handle*. Lengths of handles differ from optical house to optical house, so make sure that you know what it will be. In this case, we've requested "sixteen frame handles" (sometimes you will be given the choice of handle length), that is one extra foot at the head and tail of the optical.

Then, run down on the synchronizer until you reach the next point of reference. This will be the frame that Wendy has marked for the beginning of the freeze frame. Note the footage and key number. On your layout sheet you will mark down this information for point number two. Also mark down that you want a freeze-frame optical. You might also want to note that the frame is marked on the workprint with an X.

Run down until you reach the next point. This will be the beginning of the desaturation. Note the footage and key number and mark these down on your layout sheet for point number three. Note on the sheet the length of the optical that you want, in this instance, "Begin six-foot desaturation."

Your next point should be the end of the desaturation optical, not the beginning of the dissolve. All points of reference should be noted, both on the film and on your layout sheet.

When you are done with all the optical reference points you should pick up the original negative or interpositive from whoever has your camera original and IPs and bring it (along with your workprint and layout sheets) to the optical house. There you should sit down with the person who will be supervising your optical and show him or her exactly what you want. Some opticals are simpler than others. Straight fades or dissolves are such common opticals that your optical house should be able to do them without much consultation. Always, however, explain the more complex opticals such as this one — optical number one.

After you've explained the optical to the supervisor you will leave all your materials at the optical house. Make sure that you have copies of all your layout sheets on file at the editing room. When they have completed the optical, which may take as few as two days or as long as one or two weeks depending upon the optical's complexity, you (or Philip) should pick up the materials from them. This will include the marked-up workprint that you supplied them along with an *optical print*, which is a viewable (positive) print of the optical that they have just made for you. This print is made from the optical negative, just as your workprint is made from a camera negative. If the optical turns out to be perfect then you can send the negative to your negative cutter or your lab to be stored along with the original camera negative. If the optical turns out to need more work, then you should mark the can that the bad optical was in "NG — DNU" (for "no good/do not use") and either keep it in the editing room or send it to the negative cutter or lab.

Once the completed optical is in the editing room, check to make sure that it looks all right. This involves screening it on the Moviola (and in a screening room if possible) as well as running it through the synchronizer along with the marked–up workprint. Since the optical is shot on its own negative it will have its own key numbers which will bear no relationship to the key numbers on the cut workprint. To give you a reference back to your workprint some optical houses scratch onto the negative, along the edge, a key number so that you may easily line up the completed optical with the cut workprint.

Some optical houses, however, do not provide this service. In this case there is no way to line up the optical against the workprint other than by eye matching. This is a tedious and often difficult process that involves finding at least one frame where you can get a precise match between the optical and the cut workprint. Good things to look for are frames where characters enter or exit, frames where two objects hit one another, frames where light bulbs go on or off (be careful about these however, since there are usually two or three frames where the light level is gradually increasing), and the like. Find three different sync points, then line one of them up and see if the other two points also line up. If they do, then you know that you have found proper sync.

Once you have the optical lined up and have marked where the first and last frames are then you should code the optical (unless you've coded it before you lined it up). I generally reserve the prefix code OP for opticals. Naturally, you should enter the complete information about the optical — optical number, codes, key numbers, scenes involved, description of optical, date made, et al, into a new section in your logbook reserved for opticals.

When the optical is lined up and coded you can cut it into the cut work picture reel where the original shot was (there should be white leader there now). Then, you, Wendy, and Adam (and Philip if he is invited to participate in such things) should screen the film to check for several items. The first is that the optical is correct. It is possible that, even though the optical house followed all your instructions correctly, the optical seems wrong when viewed on the screen. This can happen for several reasons. First, it is possible that Wendy miscalculated some of the footage. If this is the case you must completely remake the optical. Second, even with the materials available today, it is not always possible to control opticals precisely. Long fades or dissolves suffer the most from this, since the degree to which the optical negative will gradually fade in or out is not completely predictable over long lengths. For that reason, a long fade will not always seem gradual. There is virtually nothing that can be done about this problem except to try and avoid very long fades or to redo the optical and hope for better results.

Another thing you will be looking for, as a further check that you have lined up and cut the optical in correctly, is sync of the picture against the track. This will be the first time that you will have seen the optical with a soundtrack.

You will also want to check that the color of the optical

does not vary too much from the non-optical shots in the same scene. Do not worry too much about minor color shifts. Slight variations in color are always correctable in the laboratory at the end of the film. But major variations may not be correctable.

A final word about the quality of opticals. Since the optical print is made from a negative which has been made from an interpositive print which was made from the original negative its quality will be slightly worse than the quality of the surrounding non–optical material. You will notice an increase in the graininess of the image and the colors may be a bit more contrasty. Some shots degrade worse than other shots. This is an unavoidable by-product of making an optical. Care in making the optical can minimize this problem. Some films, such as *Body Heat* and *Modern Problems,* did their optical dissolves in the lab using A and B rolling rather than in an optical house, just as 16mm films do. If a scene is to contain many opticals intercut with original negative, many editors like to make the entire section (even those parts of the scene which would not normally be opticals) an optical. In that way, the entire scene will be of the same quality. Even though it is of a lesser quality than the original negative, it will be less noticeable than the intercutting of good and less good material.

If, after screening, the optical is not approved and must be redone, you might need to send the workprint back to the optical house. If the layout of the optical is to be changed you would give it a new optical number (or call it Optical Number 1R, for 'revised') and make a new layout sheet for it, then go over to the optical house and talk them through it again. However, if the optical is approved then you should have Philip bring the optical negative to your negative cutter or the lab so that it can be stored with the rest of the original negative.

The original cut workprint which you've replaced with the optical can be stored in a box marked "Workprint

Replaced By Opticals." The trims from the optical can be stored in a box for OP trims. I like to use different colored tape on the side of this box so that you can easily see which section of the trims is devoted to opticals. In fact, I like to use different colors for lifts, rough mixes, and scratch music as well. In this way it is faster to get to any one particular box that you might need and the chances of misfiling a box are less. One final note about these colors. Some people overdo the color system until it more complicated to remember what color is what than it would be to find the materials mixed in with other footage. Usually, a color for trims/outs (white tape), opticals (yellow), scratch mixes (red), and, if there is a lot of it, music (blue) are enough for any film.

Titles

A special kind of optical work is the creation of titles (or credits) for the beginning and end of the film. Though credits usually are not done until the very end of the cutting process (on some films, in fact, the credits are so late in coming that they arrive only days before the opening of the movie) we will consider them here with the other opticals.

Titles come in several forms — on a colored background, supered, or animated. The first kind (such as the kind seen in Woody Allen's films) involves lettering on a plain background. The background may be colored, black, or white, and the lettering may be any color at all. The second kind of titles are those which are superimposed over a scene from the film. There are combinations of the two, such as in *Heathers* where the first few titles came up on a plain background but the bulk of them were superimposed over action. Animated titles are an entirely different set of titles, involving someone who draws each frame of the titles, shoots them, and supplies you with a finished piece of negative to be dropped into your workprint.

There are several companies which design title sequences for movies. Sometimes they simply design the

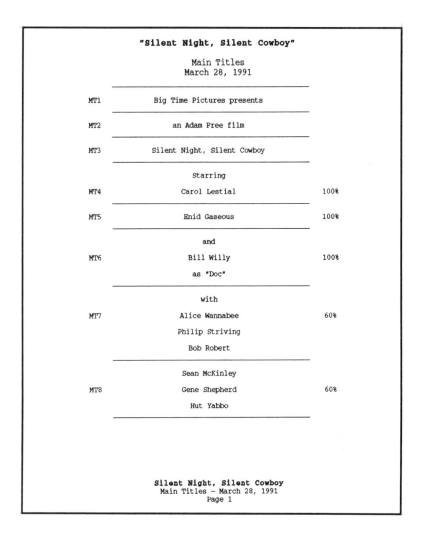

```
                    "Silent Night, Silent Cowboy"

                              Main Titles
                            March 28, 1991

        MT1          Big Time Pictures presents


        MT2             an Adam Free film


        MT3          Silent Night, Silent Cowboy


                               Starring
        MT4              Carol Lestial                    100%


        MT5               Enid Gaseous                    100%


                                  and
        MT6                Bill Willy                     100%

                              as "Doc"


                                 with
        MT7             Alice Wannabee                    60%

                        Philip Striving

                          Bob Robert


                        Sean McKinley
        MT8            Gene Shepherd                      60%

                          Hut Yabbo




                  Silent Night, Silent Cowboy
                   Main Titles — March 28, 1991
                            Page 1
```

FIGURE 10.5 *The first page of the Main Titles list supplied by the producer's office. The cards on the End Titles list (if the end titles used cards rather than a crawl) would be numbered ET1, ET2, ET3, etc. Note the numbers on the right hand side of the page. These refer to the size, expressed as a percentage of the main title ("Silent Night, Silent Cowboy"), that each card must be.*

typestyle (along with the advertising department of the company that is going to distribute the film). At other times they design elaborate title sequences which are almost little movies in themselves. The Pink Panther and James Bond title sequences are two of this type.

You should get an approved list of credits from the producer's office (*see* Figure 10.5). These will include a breakdown of all of the credits which will go at the beginning of the film and, on a separate list, the end. It will show which people will share space on the screen (or 'share a card' as it is called) and which get 'single card' credits. Many directors', writers', or stars' contracts require that their names be no smaller (or the same size) than a certain percentage of the title of the film so this list should also show the relative sizes of the credits.

Each card will be assigned a number. Thus, the first title would be MT1, meaning Main Title card number 1 ("An Adam Free Film.")

Wendy, the director, and the producer will also determine whether they wish the end titles to be a crawl, cards, or a combination of the two. These terms refer to the manner in which the mass of names at the end of the film will be displayed. Some films roll the credits up on the screen slowly (this is called a *crawl*), others present them as cards which fade in and out sequentially. Other films combine the two approaches. Once this approach has been decided on, you will be able to determine how the end titles will fall out on the screen. If the names are to be on cards then they will have to be divided up logically (usually by job category) without making the individual names so small as to be unreadable. Usually no more than seven or eight names are readable on any one card. If the names are to be on a crawl then it may be wise to separate job categories with an extra few lines of space to increase the readability. It also helps to be aware of the legal requirements which various actors and unions have in their contracts. Though the producer's office should have dealt with all of these questions before giving you the list, often someone just plain forgets to check. It is nice if you are aware enough of what credits normally look like, to spot anything that looks out of the ordinary.

Once all of these questions have been solved then you need to have the type prepared for the title cards. A typestyle will have to be selected. Adam should do this, with Wendy (or the title designer) making sure that he is selecting a typestyle that is readable.

Then you have to go to the typesetter with the titles list to have the type setup for shooting. If you have a title designer, then that person will take care of this. In most cases, your optical house will have an arrangement with a type house (or do it themselves) and so your optical house will be able to handle the technical details for you. But in some cases this will not be possible. Then you will have to go to the typesetter and go over the list of the names with him or her to make sure that it is all understandable. You should discuss with this person exactly how you would like the titles to appear on screen.

Once the typesetter has the list he will begin laying out the type and printing it. Typically, this will take several days. While he or she is doing that there is one other piece of title material which you will be needing that you can get now if you haven't already. That is the main title logo.

Every distribution company has its own logo. Twentieth Century Fox has the large letters with the meandering klieg lights. M-G-M has Leo the Lion. Columbia has the friendly torch lady. These are all opticals which have already been created by the individual company's advertising departments. You should get a print and a negative of that logo (and any soundtrack which will go with it) as early on in the cutting of the film as possible and cut it onto the head of reel one just as it will appear in the film. It is important to cut it on before the sound editor begins working because it will affect the length of the reel. When you get this print and negative, treat it as an optical, giving it an optical number and coding it with the OP prefix. Then, just as you would with an optical, keep the trims in an optical box and send the negative to the lab to be stored with the rest of your negative.

When the typesetter has finished his or her job you will receive a printed list of all of the titles in the way that they will look when shot. You and the producer should very carefully check each name and title to make sure that everything has been spelled correctly and that no names have been left out.

If everything is not perfect (and it rarely is on the first try) then the typesetter must redo the incorrect parts of the list. If you have any other changes in the titles list, now is the time to bring them up. When everything is perfect then you should have the typesetter send a clean copy of all of the titles to the optical house.

Like any other optical, the optical house will need a layout sheet and a workprint mock-up. The most common way of mocking up titles on the workprint is to put a piece of white paper tape on the film indicating which title card is going where on the film. Let me explain a little further.

If you are having plain head title cards then you would make the mock-up on a long piece of white leader. Assuming that the titles came directly after the distributor's logo you would cut a piece of white leader onto the end of the logo. Then you would roll down a pre-determined length until you wanted the first title to fade in. This predetermined length is a purely aesthetic decision and should he made by Wendy and Adam. Let's say that *Silent Night* is going to have ten seconds of black before the first title, MT1 (which will say "An Adam Free Film"), fades in. That is the equivalent of fifteen feet.

If the titles were to be supered onto an existing scene the process is very much the same with one exception. Instead of writing with magic marker on white leader you would be making your optical marks with grease pencil. You would also be making your identification notations with magic marker on a piece of white paper tape which you would attach to the film at the proper place.

Once all this has been determined, the optical house makes a *hi–con* of the titles. The term hi-con is short for *high contrast* and it is a very sharp black and white negative that will be used in the superimposition of the titles onto the picture (background) negative. Certain decisions must be made now as to how you want the titles to appear. These involve the color of the lettering, the type of lettering (in order to increase readability many titles are made with a *drop shadow* which is merely an extension of the letters at the bottom and to the right of each letter), and the color and treatment of the background. In *Four Friends*, when the background scene faded up behind the already running credits it came in first out of focus and then sharpened up. All of this was created at the optical house. Once again, these are artistic decisions which Adam and Wendy will make together.

All of these instructions must be communicated to the people at the optical house in as clear a manner as possible. Title creation is a costly process and any mistakes that necessitate a redoing of the credits will be very expensive and unwelcome.

Special Opticals

Another kind of optical which is very popular nowadays really deserves an entire book all to itself — the *special effects optical*. These occur quite frequently in science-fiction movies or historical films where scenes must be recreated in the optical house that would have cost too much to shoot live (if they could have been shot at all). The complexity of these types of opticals is so great that it makes the examples that I gave at the beginning of this chapter seem as easy as breathing. Some of the opticals in the *Star Wars* movies combine as many as eight or nine separate pieces of film and in *Return of the Jedi* there were almost nine hundred complete opticals. On such jobs the assistant editor rarely supervises opticals. The job is given to an *optical effects supervisor*. The assistant is involved in communicating the editor's needs to the optical people and vice versa.

But even with all of those complexities one fact about opticals still remains — optical creation is a process of manipulating the original negative (or negatives) to create a new one. All opticals require laying out of the effects. There is no mystery to the process, though there is great artistry. The idea is not to be intimidated, but to realize that it is all "playing with film" and understandable.

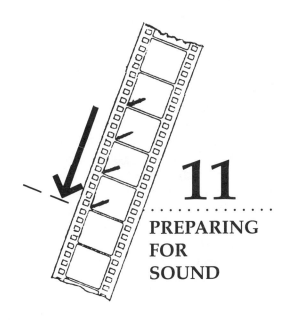

11

PREPARING
FOR
SOUND

After many months of cutting and recutting the day will come when the film is nearly finished. Now, the movie should be turned over to a sound crew who will prepare the film's soundtrack for the final film mix (or dub).

Things never seem to work out this smoothly, however. Mixing studio time is usually booked many months before the film is ready to be handed over to the sound crew. Often a film has a release date planned well in advance and that date sets the post-production schedule rather than the needs of the film itself. As a result, it's rare nowadays that a film is actually *locked* when it is turned over to the sound crew.

Locking a film means, simply, to finish cutting it. It doesn't mean that you're finished working on it, it just means that the picture edits are not going to change. I have only worked on one film, *Network*, that didn't have any picture re–editing during the sound editing phase.

So, as you may imagine, one of the things that you will have to be very aware of as you prepare to turn the film over to the sound department is how to transmit recuts to them as you make them.

Handing Over Materials

On most films, a black and white dupe print is made of the film for the sound department. You will not want to be giving up your color picture to them since there will be many things that you will have to do with the color print, as we shall shortly see. In fact, on films with a budget big enough to hire more than one sound editor, several black and white dupes are usually made and are divided between the different sound editing tasks. These divisions are sound effects editing, looping editing, dialogue editing and splitting, foley editing, and music editing. On most films these tasks overlap, so it might not be necessary to get a separate dupe for each category. On *Four Friends* we made five black and white dupes — one for the sound effects editor, two for the looping editor, one for the music editor, and one screening dupe. This screening dupe, which was kept by the picture department, was used as our master dupe. On *Heathers* we made four.

Before you even think of making the dupes there is one thing which is very important. Not only does the film have to be as close to locked as possible but the reels have to be balanced in their final form. Because of the mechanics of sound editing (where each reel will normally have at least fifty mix elements with matching cue sheets) it will be far more difficult and time consuming to make changes in the balancing *after* the reels have been sound edited than before.

Balancing for final release is very similar to balancing for your earlier screenings with one welcome exception — films are distributed on 2000-foot reels (often called *double reels*), not on the 1000-foot editorial reels you've been working on. So a reel change from an odd to an even reel (such as three to four) will actually not exist in the distributed version. This cuts down the number of problems by about one–half.

This does not mean that you should ignore those odd-to-even reel changeovers. Because your film will still be mixed in 1000-foot rolls it is more convenient to put reel changes at places where you will not have any kind of continuous sound, such as a police siren or music. The even-to-odd changeovers (such as from reel two to reel three), which *will* be projection changeovers in most theatres, should never come in places where you will want to have some continuous sound, particularly music. Because of the realities of film projection in theatres, there is no way that a reel change can be made without losing some of the end of the outgoing reel and the beginning of the incoming one. Though this is not usually noticeable in parts of the film where there is no dialogue, it is always noticeable (even to the layman) if it interrupts an active piece of music. Knowing this, composers who are forced to write music bridging reels either bring their music to a stop one second before the end of a reel (and don't begin it again for one second after it), or they bring it into a sustained hold for those lengths of time. From an aesthetic viewpoint, however, neither solution is perfectly satisfactory. So, if you know where music is going to be, it is advisable to balance your reels so that true projection change-overs will come where there will be no music.

Another factor to keep in mind as you create your final reel balance, is the lengths of the reels. While it may have been all right to include a few undersized or oversized reels as you were cutting, it is not good form to do so now. I try to keep each reel at about 950 feet. When this is not possible I make sure that the double reels run about 1900 feet. If it is necessary for one reel to run 1050 feet, for example, I make sure that the next one runs no more than 850 feet. The reason for this stems from the economics of lab work. Rolls of print film come in 2000 foot lots. If a double reel comes in at about that length there is no problem. If it is too large, however, the lab must attach another piece of film to the printing reel. That is not only an extra cost but may sometimes lead to problems in projection. If the double reel is too small, however, there will be an awful lot of print film wasted which the distributor will have to pay for anyway. In addition, reels much over 950 feet are difficult to work with on the editing table and on the mixing stage. Properly balanced reels take this, as well as the needs of the distributor, into account.

Once the reels have been properly balanced then you can send them out to a lab to be duped.

Sometimes, some reels of the film will be locked and others will not. In that case, if your schedule will allow it, you should only make dupes of the reels that are locked. However, this is not always possible. On *Rollover*, on which I was the music editor, the schedule was so tight that I needed all of the reels to give music timings to the composer, Michael Small, so that he would have enough time to write his music. He needed to know those timings even though there was a possibility that they might change. Often, looping editors will need to have all the reels as well. However you do it, you should give all the editors the same set of reels (either complete or partial), so that they will all be working from the same basic set of dupes.

Let's say that Adam and Wendy have finished all the reels except for one particularly troublesome scene in reel six (for some reason, every film has one or two problem scenes which either don't get solved until the very last minute or, more often than not, never get solved at all; they are always fiddled with until the end of the final film mix). You could leave reel six behind and dupe the remaining eleven reels or you could dupe everything and know that you are going to make changes on one scene in reel six. My preference would be the latter one, since the sound editors would at least be able to work with the rest of the reel. I would then let them know which scene it was that was liable to be changed.

At the same time that you are duping the picture you should be sending out the reels of track to be duped. Before you do so, replace any temp music or sound effects with work track, tone or fill. In this way the sound and music editors will be able to do their work against a clean work track, not one encumbered with sounds that won't end up in the final film mix. It will also be possible for the music to be recorded and cut in with a clean dialogue track as a reference.

In fact, all scratch mixes should be removed from the work track and replaced with the appropriate piece of work track (which should have been filed with the scratch mix elements). Your goal should be to hand over to the sound and music editors the following elements:

1. a black and white picture dupe
2. a dupe track of work track
3. the cut work track (to the dialogue editor)
4. all the elements used in scratch mixes
5. all appropriate paperwork

Though you will be removing the scratch mixes from your work track before it will be duped for the sound department, you will still want to have a mixed track, for any future screenings that you may be giving before the final mix is completed. Since you will be giving up your original soundtrack to the dialogue editors, you will need one soundtrack for your own use and this track should be the mixed track.

This is one big advantage to having scratch mixed the film in complete reels rather than in sections which were then cut into the work track. Your latest mixed reels should be fairly current. If not, you can easily construct one from them. If, however, you temp mixed sections of the reels, you should make one complete dupe of the film *before* you remove any of the mixes. This dupe should be marked up with codes as I've explained before in Chapter 9 in the section on "Complete Recuts." The dupes that you make for the sound editors need not be marked.

After you get the picture and track dupes back they should be coded. This will enable the editors to keep the picture and track in sync as well as making it easier to do conformations later on in the sound editing process. Though the picture dupe will have the printed-through key and code numbers, the sound track will not have any code numbers on it, so this coding is essential.

I code each dupe with its own special prefix. If you are working with a six-digit coding machine, music dupes for reel one would be coded beginning MX1000 at the start mark. Reel six would be coded MX6000 and reel 10 MX0000. Since *Silent Night*, as well as most movies, runs more than ten reels I would code reel 11 MY1000 and reel 12 MY2000. I'd code the screening dupe with the prefix codes SX and SY. The effects dupes would be coded FX and FY. The only variation on this system is for the looping department which will often have two dupes struck for it. I code them LX and LY for the first set and LV and LW for the second set. The exact letters you use are not important since they are really only for identification and sync. But I have found that this system easily identifies both the editorial category and the reel. If you are working with Acmade or Moy machines, which use more digits, you can code them differently. One handy Acmade system is to code the music dupe for reel one 001M0000. The screening dupe for reel seven would be 007S0000. The effects dupe for reel eleven would be 011F0000. This system has the added advantage of protecting you against duplicating code numbers at the ends of reels which run over 1000 feet.

You, as the assistant editor, will be the sound department's point of contact with the picture department. It is your responsibility to keep them informed of every change made in the film and in the schedule. I cannot stress enough that I consider this one of the assistant editor's most important jobs at this point in the film. It is all too easy for the sound department to be isolated from the picture-making process. But changes in schedule affect them at least as much as they will affect you. They should know about them and, in fact, be consulted about them before they are made. Sometimes your requirements will conflict with theirs. You, or Wendy, will have to make a decision as to which to change. Regularly sending them calendar revisions will be most helpful.

Because you will be the interface, you should set up some of the systems for that interaction (in consultation, of course, with the supervising sound editor). Code your dupes in an organized manner and let everyone know what your system is. When you splice the head and tail leader to the dupes you should do it uniformly. One workable system is as follows.

I assign each dupe/department a color for their dupe. The normal color assignment I use is green for effects, blue for music, red for the first looping dupe and orange for the second, white for the work track (you should already have done this, of course), silver or some other really classy color for the screening dupe and, finally, yellow if there is need for a *foley dupe* (don't worry about what the word "foley" means; you'll find out in the next chapter). On this tape I write the name of the film, the type of dupe (music/looping/etc.), the date of the dupe (VERY IMPORTANT!!), the reel number (I make this very big so it can be seen from a distance), the"pix" or "trk" designation, and the word, "HEADS." For the tail leader I put everything in the opposite order, and instead of writing "FX DUPE" I would write "DUPE FX." In this way there is just one extra clue as to whether a reel on a shelf is heads or tails out.

The black and white picture dupe will already have an Academy leader on it (duped from the color one on your work picture). Leave this on. Because of the relative thicknesses of color film versus black and white film a focus setting for one will not work on the other. If you were to cut a color Academy leader onto the head of a black and white reel, a projectionist would not be able to focus properly on the leader. So cut your picture head leader onto the black and white Academy a little before the start mark.

You should cut the tail leader onto the dupes at the last frame of action. In addition, mark a tail sync mark on the leader exactly one foot after the last frame of action. In addition, put a tail beep mark three feet after the LFOA (Last

Frame of Action). Some people actually use this beep as their tail sync mark.

When the dupes have been leadered and coded then you can give them to the sound department. At the same time that you do that, however, you should also hand over some other items as well. Every sound editor should get a complete crew list with home phone numbers. Sound editing often involves a lot of late night work and there will be questions that only you or another member of the picture editing crew can answer. They should know how to reach everyone. You should also submit a complete reel list to them either like the one you saw in Figure 8.4 or like the one in Figure 11.1. This list should contain the reel number, scene numbers contained on the reel, length of reel, and the tail sync. The total running time is also helpful though not necessary. As with any changeable list that you distribute, you should put a date on it so that any subsequent lists will not be confused with the earlier ones. I've seen some films where reel lengths changed so often that the assistant editor began writing the hour as well as the date on his LFOA lists.

Some sound editors prefer to use their own LFOA list in Figure 11.2 in addition to your LFOA list since it gives an easily readable list of all of the changes that have been made in the film since it was first handed over to them.

The sound department should also receive a copy of the lined script (with lined notes) and your logbook. They will need this information as they go back into original 1/4" tapes for sound retransfers and it will be inconvenient for everyone if they have to use yours.

As mentioned, you will give the sound editors your original work tracks. As they prepare the film's tracks for the final mix they will want to split the dialogue tracks to treat them for the best possible sound quality. This is nearly always done with the original tracks. More and more, however, sound editors replace every piece of original track with fresh track by reprinting every take used in the film and having the

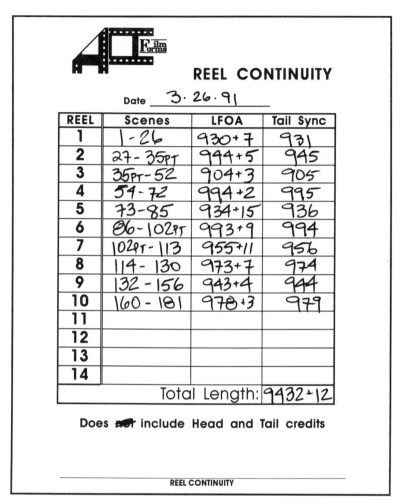

REEL CONTINUITY

Date 3·26·91

REEL	Scenes	LFOA	Tail Sync
1	1-26	930+7	931
2	27-35PT	944+5	945
3	35PT-52	904+3	905
4	54-72	994+2	995
5	73-85	934+15	936
6	86-102PT	993+9	994
7	102PT-113	955+11	956
8	114-130	973+7	974
9	132-156	943+4	944
10	160-181	978+3	979
11			
12			
13			
14			

Total Length: 9432+12

Does ~~not~~ include Head and Tail credits

REEL CONTINUITY

FIGURE 11.1 A reel breakdown for the sound department. Note that for reels with LFOAs on the fourteenth or fifteenth frame (reel five, in this case) the tail sync is not the next whole foot but the second whole foot. This is done to leave enough room for the tail sync tape marking to be placed on the tail leaders without overlapping into the picture area. Other ways of placing tail syncs are to have them one foot after the LFOA (905'03 for reel three) or at the same point as the tail pop — three feet after the LFOA (946'04 for reel nine).

LFOA CHANGES

1st Lock

REEL	LFOA Change #1	LFOA Change #2	LFOA Change #3	LFOA Change #4	LFOA Change #5	Final Combo Reels
1	930+7 (3.01)	965+6 (3.28)				
2	881+6 (3.01)	870+3 (3.07)				
3	890+7 (3.01)					
4	976+10 (3.01)					
5	936+3 (3.01)					
6	981+10 (3.01)	862+13 (3.18)	875+9 (3.26)			
7	947+12 (3.01)					
8	950+2 (3.01)					
9	976+13 (3.01)					
10	983+15 (3.01)	996+2 (3.28)				
11						
12						
13						
14						
Total Ftg						
Time						

LFOA CHANGES

FIGURE 11.2 An additional LFOA list which gives all of the LFOAs, from the first lock (on March 1, 1991), through each successive set of conformations. Note that the only reels which have been changed as of March 28 are reels one, two, six, and ten. When the film is finally locked and almost finished mixing, the sound editors will compute the footage for each double reel and list that in the final column. This information is helpful in the creation of optical tracks and 2000-foot printing masters. The listing for total footage and time is used only when one LFOA change column is used for each date's conformations.

dialogue editor cut these prints rather than the originals. The sound editors then use your original cut work track as reference during the cutting process.

Conformations

In case you go back to a scene for recutting after a dupe has been struck you will then have the unenviable task of telling the sound and music editors that you have made changes in the picture and that they must *conform* their dupes. Conformation is the process by which all dupes are brought into agreement with the color work picture. The process is never a particularly happy one but is made even more depressing when the sound elements for the mix have already been built. If there are seventy tracks for one reel (let us say), making a simple one foot addition or removal in the picture and work track requires making that change on seventy tracks. I've seen directors make changes in the film up until the end of a film mix, completely oblivious to the chaos they were causing. It is crazy, but it is done very, very often.

For that reason, some very clear and good systems for communicating these changes must be used. In all cases it is the assistant's job to make sure that the correct conformations are transmitted to the sound and music editors as rapidly as possible. You will be very busy in these final weeks making sure that the picture editing moves smoothly. There will be a temptation to regard the sound crew and their needs as a burden. But at this stage of the film editing process they are the major factor in terms of time, energy, money, and process. Without them the film would not be able to be projected in the theatres. Their schedule is difficult enough without you making it impossible.

Transmitting the conformations should be your first priority after they have been made. At the end of every day of cutting you should transmit to the supervising sound editor (as well as the music editor) exactly what portions of the film were recut that day, even if the cut has not yet been completed. In this way he or she can plan the disbursement of work for the sound crew.

As soon as a scene has been recut and approved you should take the new reel and put it up against your screening dupe in your synchronizer. By comparing the two you will be able to tell exactly what has been done to the film. By running the two together you will be able to get all the information on the film, since the color picture will tell you what Adam and Wendy want with the film, and the black and white dupe will tell you what everyone else thinks they want with the film. There should never be a discrepancy between the two.

The next step in processing conformations is a little tricky but essential. You are going to want to provide a black and white dupe of the changed sections of the film to all of the sound crew so that they will be able to have a completely current dupe of the film. There are two ways of doing this. The first is to recall all of the black and white dupes and recut them to match the color picture. The second is to provide the sound crew with all of the materials necessary to make the changes themselves.

The normal procedure followed is the second for two very good reasons. The flow of a sound editor's work is so defined that it may be very difficult for him/her to part with the black and white dupe for the time necessary for you to make the conformations. If, however, the editors are provided with the tools to make the changes themselves they can make them when it is convenient for them. This helps smooth out the sound editing process. The other reason is that many sound editors put odd marks all over their dupes that help them in various ways. Some of these marks may be important to transfer over from the old dupe to the new one, whereas other marks may be unnecessary. Only the sound editor will know this, and you could seriously disrupt the editor's process by making the conformations for him or her. So, the editors will make the changes themselves on *Silent Night*.

In order to correctly convey to them just what the

changes are, you will have to supply them with two, possibly three, things. The first is a precise list of all of the changes. The second is a black and white dupe of any material that they will have to add to their dupe. The possible third is your black and white screening dupe so that they may follow it if necessary.

Let's examine these in more detail. The first task that you will have is determining just which sections you will have to dupe. I usually use two guidelines. First, any new material (picture or track) which has been added and that the sound editors do not already have must be duped. Second, any material which has been recut or rearranged so drastically as to make it very complicated to explain and to conform should be duped. In this way, rather than recutting their black and white dupes, all they will have to do is remove one part of their dupes and replace it with the new piece. Make sure, however, that the changes are drastic enough to make this tactic worthwhile, as many sound editors prefer to keep as much of their already used dupes as possible.

When you have determined exactly which sections of the picture need to be duped, pull them out of the color work picture. Put short (one foot) slugs in between each one as well as leaders on the head and tail of the combined reel. Number each section with the reel number and the consecutive number of the change within the reel. Do the same for the track that needs to be duped.

When the dupes come back you should have them coded. Make no attempt to code each conformation separately or each reel of these conformations separately. Merely code each set of dupes with the proper prefix code for the department for which it is intended. Since the last codes you used for the music department were MY2000 (for reel 12, music dupe) code this conformation MY3000. Note in your conformation log, which you will begin keeping, that MY3000 are music conformations for such and such a date. Code all of the dupes with the proper prefix (FY, SY, etc.) and then the numbers 3000. In this way not only will all the dupes coded

CHANGE SHEET for
REEL 6
Date 3 · 26 · 91

#	At Footage	Add/Delete	Pix or Track	Information
1	121 7/8	– 21+5	P+T	
2	230 9/10	– 2+2	P	
3	231 4/5	– 2+2	T	
4	356 12/13	+ 34+7	P+T	
5	620 2/3	+ 1+12	P	
6	625 3/4	+ 1+12	T	Slug track

New LFOA 875+9

Old LFOA 862+13

CHANGE SHEET

FIGURE 11.3 *A change sheet (also called a conformation sheet). For changes four and five, black and white dupe picture should be supplied to the sound department with the numbers "4" and "5" written on them. The term slug track means that one foot and twelve frames of fill leadered should be added at 625+3/4.*

200

with a letter followed by 'Y3000' come from the same date's conformations but they will all line up with each other.

After the new dupes are coded, run them down together in the synchronizer and mark where the beginning and end of every conformation is on the track. Then cut them all apart so that you end up with one pin on your barrel for each department.

Now take your screening dupe and your color picture and line them up in the synchronizer. Run them down together until you get to where your first change will be (whether it be an addition or deletion). Note the footage and exactly what the change is. For instance, in Figure 11.3 we see that at 121'07/08 we need to remove 21'05 of both picture and track. This is conformation number one on this reel. The next conformation is the removal of 2'02 of picture only at 230'10. The next conformation is the removal of the matching amount of track at 231'05 to bring the picture and track back into sync. Conformation number four is an addition. At 356'13 the editors must add the 34'07 of picture and track that you are supplying them. And so on.

At each conformation point make the conformation yourself in your black and white screening dupe. Make sure that all your footages are correct. For this, it is helpful to have a second synchronizer to measure lengths added or removed. You should hang up all the pieces that you remove, putting all the conformations for any one reel on one pin. Mark, with grease pencil or on a piece of white tape attached to the top of the removals, exactly which conformation number it is and what its length is. Also, as you are making the changes in your own reels, keep one white box for each set of dupes open nearby. After you have made change number four, for instance, flange up the additional copies of the duped picture and track for that conformation, mark the reel number and the conformation number four on each copy. Put them into their proper boxes (FX dupes into the effects editor box, MX dupes into the music editor box). In this way, when you are done, each editor will have his or her own box of conformations plainly marked with the reel number and conformation number. This will make life much easier for you and for them.

When you are finished with all of the conformations for any one reel, run down to the end of the reel and get the new LFOA (Last Frame of Action). Make sure that it is the same on your black and white screening dupe as on your color work picture. Do the same for all of the reels that have conformations in them. The new LFOA must be listed on the conformation sheet so the sound editors making their own conformations will be able to check that they have made them all properly.

When you are finished, make copies of all your conformation sheets (use a different conformation sheet for each reel that has had conformations in it as different sound editors may be editing different reels)—one for each set of dupes. Then get the boxes of conformations and the conformation sheets to each editor immediately.

When this is done, and the inevitable questions are asked by the sound editors and answered by you, you will be ready to clean up after yourself. Have Philip box up all of the trims that you have deleted from your screening dupe. Have him flange up and cinetab each reel's conformations by themselves and then box up the conformations for that date together. Future conformations can be added to the same box as long as the box doesn't get too crowded and as long as a notation of which date's conformations are in the box is made on the outside of the box.

Then, correct your LFOA list and reel breakdown if you haven't already done so. Generally, I make new copies of this list only when there are drastic changes in the reel breakdown. Otherwise I tell the sound editing crew to make the LFOA corrections themselves from the LFOAs noted on the conformation sheets. Keep the conformation sheets in one place. I file them by date and then by reel number within that category. I can guarantee you that at some point during the sound editing, things will get just confused enough for you to want to find out what exactly it was that you did on such and such a date. It will be very handy for you to have these sheets filed safely away.

These are the primary tasks that will confront you as a picture assistant interfacing with the sound department. You will also have to answer many questions about where certain material came from, if there are alternates that were not used for picture but might be good for sound, exactly what things Adam liked in the scratch mixes, etc., etc., etc. You are the person who has been on the film for the longest time in an organizational capacity. You can answer all kinds of "where can I get...?" questions. If you are bright you will also be able to help them on the "why was it done like this?" questions. You will function as the focal point for their questions.

12
SOUND
EDITING

There are various facets to sound editing — dialogue splitting, sound effects editing, looping, and foleys. Dialogue splitting is the process that was described in Chapter 9 that places pieces of dialogue that need to be treated separately at the sound mix on separate tracks to allow the film mixer to mix from one to the other and create a seamless dialogue track. Sound effects editing is the process by which the sound editor adds the sound effects necessary to make a soundtrack sound real (traffic, backgrounds, and specific noises in a film's soundtrack are usually added by a sound effects editor). Looping (ADR or EPS) is the process of rerecording lines of dialogue which will replace or add to lines that are already in the film. Foley editing is the process of recording and adding specific sound effects which need to be done exactly in reference to the picture. Most body movement falls in this category, such as footsteps or various specific sounds of people's clothes. Many of these types of sound editing have similar systems though some of them do not.

Similarities To Picture Editing

To a large degree every sound editor and sound assistant must fit within the system that you, as the assistant picture editor, have devised for the picture editing. There are countless ways the two departments overlap. The first and most obvious one is your code numbers. The code numbers on both your color picture and the black and white dupes all refer to your logbook: in sound editing and, therefore, to your system. The sound department has to find the original 1/4" tapes from these codes and, unless you want to spend all of your time finding bits of information for them, your logbook and system had better be in a good enough order for them to find what they need.

In fact, any time that the sound department either takes material from you or creates new material they have to make sure that it fits into your system. You will want to make sure that material that they create but which you do not want confused with your material (this will usually happen when they make extra soundtrack prints) is coded so that it can't be confused with the original track.

This applies even more if you are doing your own sound editing, as often happens on low–budget jobs. You will want to make sure that you do not accidentally mix up two pieces of track that are not the same, such as a sound take and its reprint. When I was discussing reprints I made a big point of stressing that a track or picture reprint should completely replace the old take. In this way the old and new prints cannot get confused. Sound editing, however, often requires that the editor have two, three, or even more prints of the same take simultaneously. The editor should never get confused between any of them.

On any film where there will be more than one sound editor there will almost always be more than one assistant sound editor. Each editor often works with his or her own assistant as we shall soon see. In the case where there are multiple assistants, the assistant who is working directly with the supervising sound editor is normally assigned the job of supervising assistant. It will be this supervising assistant who will set up all of the sound editing systems to be used by the sound editors and assistants.

In addition, there should be at least one and usually two apprentice sound editors. Everyone will be generating vast numbers of trims and, since the assistants are busy at other tasks, the apprentice must do these trims as well as the hundreds of other minor tasks that an impending mix calls for. These apprentices will not be assigned to any particular editor or assistant but will be doing work for everyone in the sound department, directed by the supervising assistant.

Sound Effects Editing

In many editing situations an individual sound editor is assigned a reel in a film (or, more likely, four or five reels in each film). He or she will be responsible for all the sound work (except the looping) in that reel.

In other situations, there are editors hired for the dialogue editing, other editors hired for the sound effects editing, and still another editor (or two or three) hired for foleys. There are various pluses and minuses to doing the job in this way. It is certainly more efficient for one person to be doing only one job. Often, foleys take time away from sound effects editing that can hardly be spared in the rush to get to a mix. In addition, this enables an editor who is very good in one facet of sound editing to specialize in it.

However, there are also some problems with this way of doing things. Assembly-line sound editing leaves the editors feeling uninvolved, and the more people are involved with the film they are working on, the more they'll give that little extra effort. If an editor is doing all the sound work on any given reel then he or she will feel more of a sense of the sound on that reel (and, hopefully, on the film) as a whole. If would be lovely, of course, if one sound editor could do all the work on the entire film, but there is never enough time to do a top–notch professional job with a solitary sound editor, though this is often how a low-budget film works. As a result, more than one editor must be brought on to your film.

In some cases, a supervising sound editor is hired who selects all of the sound effects. In this case, his or her assistant will prepare boxes with all of the selected sound effects that will be given to each sound editor. This box is called a *kit*.

We will discuss each task individually as if different editors were performing each one, though ultimately it won't really matter to you if one or twenty sound editors are performing the tasks. You should be familiar with *all* the necessary skills.

When the supervising editor and assistant first come on the film they will be charged with many tasks, not the least of which will be developing a sound effects library for the film. But the first task that they have is to screen the film. They should try to get to know it as well as they can, for it is only then that they will be able to get the sense of the film necessary to do an effective and creative sound editing job.

They should first screen the film in a screening room so they can hear exactly what the tracks are like. Since every screening room has a different sound, it would be helpful to screen the film in a room that the sound editor knows fairly well so that he or she has a reference point while listening. After this, the editor and the assistant should begin to screen the film on a flatbed, Moviola or on a videotape machine so that they can analyze the film scene by scene. As they screen each reel, they should be taking notes on exactly what the needs of each scene are.

Figure 12.1 is a sample sound editor's note sheet. Some supervising sound editors use these to list every single thing that they will have to do with each scene. At the top is listed the *scene title* (this is taken from the reel breakdown or continuity which, of course, you will have already supplied to them) and scene number. Each scene gets its own page

SOUND NOTES—SC# 8

Scene Title Barroom Fight

General Comments ① Find alt for JAMES' "Cut!" (sync is noisy)
② Idea of fight is to show how unreal/stagey filmmaking
is. Make sound ~~after~~ the ~~fight~~ sound more real than the
fight itself.
③ Check all WTs. Wendy remembers good sound.

ADR/EPS
Wild lines - fighters
Grunting - fighters
A.D. whispering
Walla - crew members after fight

Foley
Entire fight
JAMES fts. after "Cut!"
Crew members

FX to record
Camera dolly squeaks

Pre-Recorded FX (Name/Source)
chair smash - fake sounding
Camera noise
Kleig lites on/off (WT1086).
Ass'td fx (WT 1087 - 89)

SOUND NOTES

FIGURE 12.1 A sound editor's note sheet. In this case, Charles has listed those items he will need for this scene as well as Adam's and Wendy's comments from the spotting session.

which is then inserted into a master book in the order that it appears in the film. Dividers can be placed between reels so that it is easy to find scenes on any given reel of the film. If the film is reedited so the scene continuity changes it will be a simple matter to rearrange the order of these sheets.

Underneath this header are five sections, each corresponding to a separate sound editing task. The first section is called "General Comments" and is for notes that can't be exactly translated into information for one of the other sections on the page. Adjectives, notes on sources for sound, and Adam's preferences should go here. Adam will say that he wants the scene to "feel festive." The sound editor should write this down. If Wendy says, "This scene will almost certainly be recut before next month," the editor should write this down along with the date.

In the section marked "ADR/EPS" the editor should list all possible candidates for looping. This list will, of course, not be definite at this time, but it will serve to remind the sound editor of any potential problems as well as help him or her provide the producers with a list of all of the characters who might have to be scheduled for looping.

Under "Foley," the editor will list all effects that need to be foleyed. The final two sections are for effects. Here, the editor will list the effects that he or she feels are needed for the scene. From experience he or she will know what effects exist in his or her own effects library, which will have to be purchased from a sound effects library, and which will need to be recorded especially for the film. In discussions with Wendy or you the sound editor should be told what effects were added to the scratch tracks by you and which effects need to be replaced or must be kept from those scratch mixes. All of this will be noted here. Effects which the sound editor knows will need to be recorded are listed in the first section. Effects which are already cut into the tracks and which Adam would like in the final film are listed in the last section ("Pre-Recorded FX") along with their original source, whether it be from an original production track (wild tracks, etc.), or from a sound effects library. In addition, any effects which the supervising sound editor knows he will purchase, rather than record, will go into this last section.

The notes on these sheets will grow as the sound editor gets more familiar with the film. Each time the editor looks at the film, he or she may get better ideas for the design of the soundtrack. This will mean changes or additions to these sheets.

As soon as the film is more or less locked (at the time the dupes have been struck), the sound editor should sit down with Adam and Wendy and go through the entire film on a flatbed or in a screening room asking detailed questions about what should go into every scene and what is definitely not necessary. This screening is called a *spotting session* since we will be spotting exactly where and what type of effects are going to go into the film. The sound assistant should be there taking plenty of notes. It is not uncommon for a director to know very little about sound. Sound editors learn, after a while, to know just which of the director's instructions to pay attention to and which to ignore. Sometimes a director will say that he or she won't need a certain effect which the editor knows damn well will be very helpful. If the editor is smart, he or she will do the effect even though the director has said it isn't necessary.

So let's say that you have hired Charles Lone and Liz Clear as supervising sound editor and assistant. They've just gone through the film with Adam, Wendy and you for special instructions. There is another spotting session which would be helpful at this stage and that is one for looping. This session is often combined with the sound editor's. The best way to do this is to have the screening at a mixing studio where it will be possible to hear what the tracks really sound like. Every reel is meticulously examined. Any lines which the sound or looping editor feels need to be looped should be discussed at this screening. Possible candidates are lines which are partially or completely obscured by some unwanted sound (backgrounds, another actor/actress talking, radio interference, etc.), lines on which the director wants to change the performance, lines that the sound editor feels may create problems in mixing once the tracks have been split, lines that must be added to help the story line (these lines are usually off–screen lines, that is, coming from a character while they are not seen on screen), or lines needed for a television version of the film. If it is not possible to have this spotting session in a screening room — or a dubbing stage — it is best to do them at a flatbed. Moviola uprights are not quiet enough; nor do they have a big enough screen for everyone to sit around them and talk.

At the end of all of these screenings, Charles and Liz will have accumulated enough notes to write a book and enough work to keep them occupied for some time. They can then begin to plan their sound editing tasks.

One of their biggest jobs will be building the effects library. Most editors, after working years on all kinds of movies, will have accumulated a large number of their own sound effects, encompassing everything from "Air Escaping From Balloon" to "Zoo Animals Going Wild." Those that are specific to *Silent Night* and that Charles does not have, can be purchased from any number of sound effects libraries, each of which will have tens of thousands of effects on tape or CD. Charles (but since we're working closely with him, we'll call him Chuck) will, after going through all of the notes that Liz and he have been accumulating since they first started working on the film, figure out just what effects they need to purchase for the film. He will then have Liz reserve a block of time at his favorite sound effects house for listening and transferring of those effects which he doesn't have in his own library. Six hours a day of screening sound effects is enough to drive any grown person insane, so many editors prefer to listen for no more than five or six hours, broken up by a lunch break, and then to work in the editing room for the remainder of their normally very long day.

At the same time, he will also be listening (normally on a Nagra which he probably owns and has brought into the editing room) to his library of effects as well as the original production 1/4" tapes, making notes of just what effects he thinks will be useful for the film and what can be used from the location recording.

Some sound editors, and most television shows, will have accumulated a large library of effects as well as a *cutting library*, which are complete transfers of those effects which have not already been used in other films or shows. Obviously, any effects which Chuck needs which are already in this cutting library will not need to be obtained from other sources.

At this time, Liz should begin to set up the library for the film. All of the effects which will be used will be transferred onto 35mm film (or 16mm film if that is the film gauge you are working in). She will buy a large quantity of stock and precode it before the sound effects house editing sessions come up and before she begins to transfer anything off Chuck's own tapes.

Every assistant has his or her own coding system. About the only real requirement is that none of the numbers duplicate any of the picture department's numbers. In fact, you (as the picture assistant) can work out with Liz just which codes she is free to use. A common set-up is to let her use all of the codes with the prefix 'F' (such as FA, FB, etc.). She would begin coding the first roll of stock for transfer FA1000, then FA2000, all the way up through FA0000. This would be followed by FB1000 and so on (or 001F1000, 001F2000, 001F3000 ... 002F0100, etc.).

In some cases, the production will not hire individual sound editors and assistants, but contract with a sound editorial house to do the entire sound job (less certain costs) for a fixed fee. This house will then hire all of the editors and assistants. In cases where a sound house has been hired, they will be probably be working at a different site from you and the chance of duplicating your codes is so small that they will code their track however they want, if they code it at all.

Whether Chuck is listening to effects at a sound house or from his own tapes, the procedure is more or less the same.

Let's say that one of categories that he will need is traffic. In one scene of the film there is a traffic jam. In another there is someone standing alone on the street at night with only one or two cars going by. In yet a third scene, Abby is in his apartment which is near a moderately busy street. Each slightly different sound will require a different effect (in fact, most of these sounds will require a combination of several different effects). On many television show there are certain standard sounds. A police car which appears in many episodes of a series will have one particular engine sound (along with one particular horn, one particular siren, and a set of car door slams) which will be used every time we see that car. In much the same way, Chuck will want to use similar sounds for traffic at similar locations at the same time of day and weather conditions (don't forget that a car driving by on a wet street sounds different than the same car driving by on a dry one), but he will try to use different sounds for other cases. It wouldn't do to have every bit of traffic sound the same.

If Chuck is sitting with a transfer person at a sound effects house, every time that he finds an effect that he likes, the transfer person will either make the transfer onto film stock right there or make up a list of the sound effects that are needed so that they can be transferred later. If Chuck is listening to the effects on his own Nagra from his own tapes, he will be making up a list of his selected effects himself.

Regardless of how the effects are transferred, when they come back to Liz there will be, at the head or the tail of every transferred effect, a piece of paper tape which the transfer person has attached to the mag which will list the identification number of the sound effect. Since every effects house has a different system, these numbers will look very

different from house to house but this number is very important. If Chuck ever needs additional transfers of one particular sound, Liz will be able to know just which effect it is by this
number.

At the end of the first day, the first page of Chuck's list
of sound effects for transfer might look like this:

C13-5   Medium day traffic, no horns
C11-2   Heavy traffic, many horns, type 1
C11-2   Heavy traffic, many horns, type 2
C23-5a Distant traffic, day—for Abby's room
C09-1   Light traffic, night, a few horns
C09-5   Light traffic, night, on wet street
C15-2   Single car by, 4x
C15-5   Car approaches and stops short, 2x
C15-6   Car slows down and goes by
C15-9   Revving engine—MG sports car
C16-23 Rolls-Royce engine idle

This is just a short sample of the kinds of effects that
Chuck might get for traffic. And, yes, they really do get that
specific.

After the transfers have been done, Liz will get several
rolls of 35mm mag which she will begin to break down. Each
sound effect should be separated out, just like the dailies'
wild track was. Each gets its own trim tab and its own line in
a sound effect logbook (*see* Figures 12.2 and 12.3.) The trim tab
will list, on its face, the code number and a short description
of the sound effect. In addition it is helpful to list, in the top
part, the category that the particular effect belongs in. In the
effects above, for instance, it might be wise to separate these
effects into two categories — cars and traffic. This is because
each effect will be used slightly differently. The traffic effects
will be used as general background while the car effects will
be used to match specific things that are happening on screen.
(Marvin M. Kerner's *The Art of the Sound Effects Editor* gives
one example of how to categorize a sound effects library.)
Somewhere on the trim tab Liz will list the source of the effect

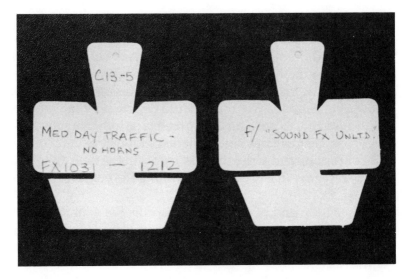

FIGURE 12.2 The front and back of a trim tab used for a sound effect transfer. This effect was purchased from a sound effects house called "Sound FX Unltd." This company gave it the number C13-5. This information will facilitate the reordering of this effect if more is needed.

—the sound effects library that the effect came from and its identification number.

On the effects log sheet much of the same type of information is listed. There is a column for "scene" which some sound editors find useful. Since some effects are used in many scenes it is not always helpful to list the scene number and, in fact, I rarely do. Instead, I list the set or location in the description ("Abby's house" or "Exterior sound stage", for instance). The *original source* is the place where the effect was gotten from. The transfer remarks are for special notes. In many cases, sound effects are "treated" in some special way. On one film I worked on we were trying to create a particularly eerie thunderstorm. Nothing that we were able to turn up seemed to work perfectly. Instead we took one of the better storms and slowed it down by 50 percent. This was then combined with the original thunder clap to provide the effect that we needed. The fact that one of our transfers was slowed down by 50 percent was noted in the 'transfer remarks' column and on the trim tab. In this way, the effect could be duplicated exactly, if we ever needed to reprint it.

As Liz breaks down each of these effects (or as one of the apprentices does so) they should be boxed by category. A good system is to put a piece of green tape (or whatever color the FX department has been assigned) down the center of one side of the box and write the film name on the tape, followed by the category in large letters spanning the height of the box (*see* Figure 12.4)

At the end of the effects sessions the sound department will have accumulated quite a number of shelves of effects. Some films have a room full of racks jammed solid with effects.

Pg 1

SOUND FX CODE BOOK

Code Numbers	Source	Category	#	Description	Comments
FX 1031- 1212	Sound FX Unltd	Traffic	C13-5	Med. day traffic. No horns	
1213- 1347	"	"	C11-2	Hvy traffic, many horns #1	
1348- 1452	"	"	"	" " " " #2	
1453- 1601	"	"	C23-9	Distant day traffic	For ABBY's room
1602- 1726	"	"	C9-1	Lt nite traffic - few horns	
1727- 1832	"	"	C9-5	Lt nite traffic - wet street	For Sc. 28
1833- 1872	"	Cars	C16-3	Single car-by	
1873- 1956	"	"	C15-5	Car approach - stop short	2 x
1957- 2036	"	"	C15-6	Car slows + passes	
2037- 2072	"	"	C15-9	Engine revs - M6	
2073- 2127	"	"	C4-5	Engine idle - Rolls	
2128- 2196	"	Chairs	F7-18	Single chair smashes	For Sc. 8
2197- 2256	"	"	F7-21	Many chairs smashing	For Sc. 8
2257- 2341	"	Camera	C2-3	Camera noise #1	For all on-set scs
2342- 2410	"	"	C2-4	" " #2	"
2411- 2472	"	"	C3-7	Camera mag on/off	"
2473- 2521	"	Lights	E17-3	Kleig light + hum	"
2522- 2567	"	"	E17-5	Kleig light - on/off	"
2568- 2598	"	"	E17-12	Brutes - on/off	"
2599- 2662	"	"	E17-19	Lites - hum. Inc. vol	"
2663- 2691	"	"	E6-2	Connecting spider box	"
2692- 2762	"	"	E8-1	Dragging cable	"
2763- 2830	"	"	E8-2	Dragging many cables	"
2831- 2901	"	"	E9-3	Light bulb - screw in/out	"
2902- 2960	"	"	E9-4	Light bulb bursts	10x "

CODE BOOK

FIGURE 12.3 A page from a sound effects logbook. Note the similarity of this information to that on the trim tab in Figure 12.2. The notation in the comments column—2X and 10X—denotes that the effect was transferred more than one time, in these cases twice and ten times.

FIGURE 12.4 A sound effects box. The category is written over green tape, which is used to signify the sound effects department.

Sometimes effects cannot be obtained from any sound effects house. These will have to be recorded specifically for the scene. On another film that I worked on we could not locate a specific sound effect for a modern elevator door closing. We took a Nagra, marched down to the end of the hall where we were cutting the effects, and recorded the sound of the building's elevator. Such occasions are not rare. Almost any film will have effects that need to be recorded specifically for it. Either a sound recordist or the sound editor takes a professional quality 1/4" portable tape machine and goes out and records them.

Let's say that, for *Silent Night*, Chuck cannot find various sound effects of movie making — a film crane rising and lowering, klieg lights coming on, fake-sounding gunshots, and many more. Liz would try and organize a recording session for these things. She might call people who were shooting a film and see if she could get permission to record a few effects one day. Or she might make arrangements with a film equipment rental house to do the same thing. Then, after ascertaining that the booked day was fine with Chuck, she would rent the sound equipment for Chuck or coordinate it with a sound recordist (they often supply their own re-corder). On the day of the recording she might go to the set with Chuck and take thorough notes of exactly what it is that he is recording. Before each effect is recorded Chuck would announce a voice slate into the microphone, such as "This is sound effect number fifteen, Chapman crane rising slowly." He would then record the effect.

After the day's session the tape would be given to your sound house for transfers. Liz should make sure that a proper *sound report* is included with the tape just as one was submitted with every roll from the dailies shooting. It will also save some time if Liz submits the required amount of precoded 35mm stock with the tape so that the transfers may be made onto it. In this way the track will not have to be coded when the transfers come back. Some editors like to leave the 1/4" tape with the sound house, others like to keep it in the editing room with them. If the job is being done at a sound editing house, it is likely that they will have their own transfer equipment. After the transfers have been made they will arrive back at the editing room. Liz or an apprentice will break them down just as was done for the library effects. The only difference is that in the logbook column for original source, and on the back of the trim tab, the 1/4" sound roll number and effect number should be written instead of the sound effects house. In this case, for instance, Liz would write "SR#1" (for sound roll number one), and "effect 15." She would also write "Chapman crane rising slowly" with the code numbers and category listed as usual.

Editing Sound Effects

Before any of these effects can be edited Chuck will need the proper equipment — a console Moviola (one with one picture head and two sound heads) along with a synchro-nizer having sound heads on all four gangs. He will also need a sound box (amplifier) that can accept and separately control at least four different sound inputs. As I've already mentioned, many sound editors bring their own sound equipment (such as amplifiers, mixers, headphones) with them onto a job.

Chuck will be editing these sound effects much as described in the section on scratch mixing in Chapter 9. He will run the black and white dupe and its track on the two outside gangs of the console Moviola. The middle gang is where he will try out all of the sound effects. He will be able to shift the position of the effect he is trying out against the picture to see where the most accurate and pleasing position for the effect should be. Then, when he has decided on the proper placement, he will do two things — the first will be to put a footage on the sound effect he wants cut in as well as noting which track it is to be put on. The second will be to enter it onto his cue sheets (*see* Figure 12.5). Chuck will then hang the effect on a pin reserved for all of the effects for that mix unit (or *element.*)

After Chuck has finished cutting the effects for a reel, he will give both the barrel with the effects, and the temp cue sheets, to Liz. Often, if the apprentices are experienced enough, they will end up *building the tracks.* Otherwise, Liz will do it.

Building the tracks means taking all the little pieces of track which Chuck has cut and putting them in their proper places in the units. The basic philosophy of mixing is quite simple. Every sound that has to be separately controlled should be on its own element so that it will come into the *mixing board* on a separate volume control knob. Its level (as well as its sound quality) can then be controlled without affecting any of the other sounds. The way that this is accomplished is to have a large number of reels (called *elements* or *units*) made up of fill. They will all have a start mark and can all be run together, just as you can gang up four tracks at one time in your synchronizer. Every time that you want to hear a sound effect you will cut the effect in at precisely the right place into one of these elements. Leading up to it will be fill; leading away from it will also be fill. But at the point where

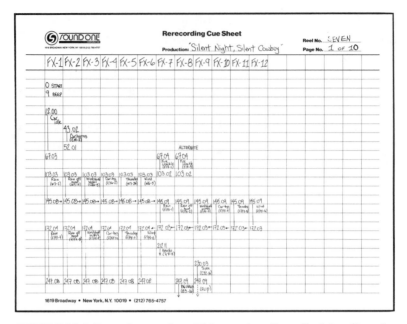

FIGURE 12.5 Part of a cue sheet. This cue sheet lists all of the effects for reel seven. Dialogue, looping, foley, music and any other types of effects which may be done separately, like background effects, would be listed on separate cue sheets. Note the splits at 145'08 and again at 172'03. We are cutting inside and outside of a car during a rainstorm and need to have separate control of the volume and equalization of the effects for the interior and exterior. Note also that all footages are given in 35mm feet, even if the film is shot in 16mm. This gives the mixers more precision in their numbers, so you will need to convert the 16mm footages.

the effect needs to be heard, it will be cut into the tracks so that it can be played back through the mixing board. If five effects need to be heard at the same time (in a thunderstorm, for instance, one might want to hear rain, thunder, wind, cars passing on a wet street, and dripping water) then each must be put on its own element. The more complicated the scene, the more elements will be used.

There are many subtleties that Chuck has to take into account in deciding how to apportion the effects on the elements, most of them too complicated to get into here. As an introduction, however, let us say that in the above mentioned rainstorm we cut from inside a car parked in the rain, to outside the car. Every time we cut from inside to outside all of the above mentioned effects would get louder. But if the characters inside the car were having a fight, that dialogue would get *softer* when we went outside. Also, the sound of the windshield wipers would change when we went outside the car. This gives us seven elements which must change at precisely the same time and on a single frame. This would be an impossible task if the mixer had to change seven sets of settings at the precise frame. To help the mixer out, the sound editor does something called *splitting for perspective*, which simply means that at the exact frame where we cut from the inside of the car to the outside, the seven effects that were running get cut and moved onto seven other (usually adjacent) tracks. In this way the mixer can set levels and tone controls separately for the inside–the–car elements (on one set of seven tracks) and the outside–the–car elements (on another set of seven tracks). When we cut back inside the car again the editor would move all of the sound effects back to the first set of tracks since the old set of levels and tone controls would still apply. Voila! You've saved everyone a lot of very expensive time at the mix (and, as this book is being written in 1989, mixing time is going for upwards of $700 an hour).

When Liz gets these pieces of sound and the temp cue sheet she will have to build the tracks that will eventually be used in the mix. Everything must be cut into these reels exactly right so that an effect which is supposed to come in at 145′08 does come in at exactly 145′08. Time lost at the mix looking for misplaced pieces of track wastes money and disrupts the creative flow of mixing.

All the mixing elements must have proper identification leaders on them since they will be leaving the editing rooms to go to the mixing studio where many other films are working. However, it is not necessary to make up scores of white leaders for every reel on the film. The elements can have head leaders made of fill. Commonly, only the dialogue units are leadered with white leader. In other systems, each sound category (dialogue, looping, effects, etc.) is leadered with a different color leader.

However they are made, the information on the leaders is usually written in red ink on the color of tape assigned to the particular category of track that it is. In this case, since this is an effects unit, Liz would leader it with green tape (or green leader, if that is the system Chuck wants to use.)

Looking at the cue sheet in Figure 12.5, we can see that the first effect that needs to be cut in is a car idle on element one at 12'00. Liz, or the apprentice, will put the black and white dupe for reel seven in the first gang of her synchronizer and then three rolls of fill in the next three gangs. She will label these rolls as FX–1, FX–2, and FX–3 (or FX–A, FX–B, FX–C, depending on what system you choose for identifying your elements; some editors use letters for stereo units and numbers for mono units) of reel seven. After about ten feet of blank leader, for the thread–up, she will put start marks on all three elements. Then she will zero out the counter and begin to roll down. She will then cut a frame of 1000-cycle tone in at exactly 9'00 on the first element of each category. In our case, this would be on FX–1 (or FX–A.)

At 12'00 on the first track (which will normally be in the second gang) she will make a cut and put in the car idle effect which Chuck should have hung on the FX–1 pin and put a footage on. She will do this by marking the 12'00 frame line (i.e. at 11'15/00) on the fill and then rolling it out to the left of the synchronizer (she will make *all* cuts to the left of the synchronizer since that is *before* it goes into the synchronizer and the footage counter). She will cut the fill there and then splice Chuck's already cut effect onto the piece of fill going through the synchronizer. This completes cutting the head of the effect in.

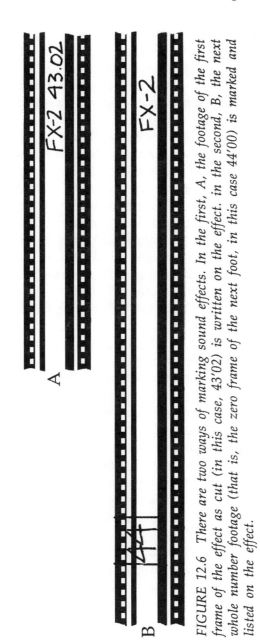

FIGURE 12.6 *There are two ways of marking sound effects. In the first, A, the footage of the first frame of the effect as cut (in this case, 43'02) is written on the effect. in the second, B, the next whole number footage (that is, the zero frame of the next foot, in this case 44'00) is marked and listed on the effect.*

While she is rolling down to the next location for an effect she will listen to the effect that she's just cut in. In this way she can verify that she has cut in the proper effect. Rolling down to about 43'00 she will stop and look for the car horn effect which should be hanging on the FX–2 pin. This effect, since it does not cut in at exactly 43'00, may be marked in either of two ways (*see* Figure 12.6). The exact footage (43'02) may be marked on it, or a box may be drawn at the spot where 44'00 will fall. In the first case all she would do is make a cut at 43'01/02 and cut in the effect, just as she did with the effect at 12'00 on the FX–l track. In the second case, however, she would roll down to 44'00, place the track on top of the fill in gang number two, aligning the track's sprocket holes with the sprockets of the gang, and then carefully roll back to the beginning of the effect while holding the track down against the fill and the gang. She will then mark the fill where the head of the effect is and, after rolling it back to the splicing block, cut the car horn effect into the fill where she has marked it.

Some sound editors like to mark their picture with the footage as well as the track. This means that, as Liz builds the tracks, she will have another visual check to make sure she is cutting the effect in at the proper place.

Additionally, some editors don't even bother to cut and mark general background tones (such as birds or ocean waves). They will simply indicate on the cue sheet what effect it is they want and what footages it should begin and end at. They might also mark up their picture at these footages. It will then be up to Liz to find and cut in the proper effect.

If you've been following this explanation so far you will have figured out that Liz will now be running the black and white dupe in the first gang of the synchronizer, two pieces of track through the next two gangs, and one complete roll of fill in the back gang. The two effects will not be attached to anything at their tail. The first two rolls of fill will be hanging loose from the left rewind.

As she approaches 52'01, Liz will slow down and stop. The end of the effect on FX–2 is coming up. She can then attach the end of this effect to the second roll of fill which is on the left rewind. At 67'03 she will do the same for the effect on FX–1. As she completes this she will also check off the two effects on Chuck's temp cue sheet so that she has a record that she has cut them in.

The next two effects (at 67'04 on FX–7 and FX–8) cannot be cut in just yet because Liz only has FX–1 through 3 up on the synchronizer now. The next effects that she can cut in are at 103'03 on all of her tracks.

In the case of these effects, which will be split off for perspective at 145'08/09 Chuck probably did not make the cuts at that point on the effects themselves. Instead he ran them long, for the *entire* length that they are needed on all tracks (which, in this case, runs from 103'03, through the perspective split at 145'08, through the next perspective split at 172'03, until the end of the scene at 247'08.) It will be up to Liz to make the splits at the proper places.

When Liz makes the cut she will refer to the footage count on the cue sheet as well as the black and white dupe running in gang number one. The fact that so many tracks begin and end at this point makes it almost certain that there is a change of location at this point. If the footage count does not come at the point in the picture where she can see a location change then this is a good time for Liz to ask Chuck if the footages are correct. In fact, every time she cuts in an effect she should look to see if it makes any sense in reference to the picture. Obviously there will be many things that she won't be able to judge by looking at the picture (and listening to the effect) in the synchronizer. But since she knows the film, there will be many that she can. The best assistants keep a lookout for any oddity and, if they can't figure out the solution to the oddity, ask their editors for an explanation.

After Liz makes the cuts in the long effects (which she will do at 145'08) she should mark the tail trim of the effect and hang it with the rest of the effects for FX–7, FX–8, and FX–9.

There are three little kinks in the cutting of the tracks listed on this temp cue sheet. The first will come when Liz gets down to 172'04 and is ready to cut in the continuation of the rain effects that are split off from FX–7 through FX–12. To do this she needs to find the proper frame in the middle of these effects. She would take the piece from FX–7 at 145'09 (which is, in this case, the piece that she cut from the earlier FX–1 piece), put it in another synchronizer at 145'09 and roll down to 172'04. She will mark the track there and cut it at this frame line (172'03/04). She should then mark the tail piece as FX–1 at 172'04. She can do this with the pieces she will need for FX–2 and FX–3 as well. Then, she can hang the head pieces back up in the barrel on their pins and cut the tail pieces into their proper tracks.

A second little kink occurs on FX–7 at 212'11 where the temp cue sheet lists 'Knocks'. You may notice that there is no end footage listed. Instead, there is a little 'X'. This is placed there to note that the effect is of very short duration.

The third little kink comes on FX–9 at 230'03 where the cue sheet calls for a siren to begin. Normally this siren would stop at the scene change at 247'08/09. However, Chuck was unsure whether it might not be a good idea to continue the effect for a little bit under the beginning of the next scene (where there is a *crowd walla* — which is simply a crowd in the background talking indistinctly). At the scene split, therefore, he wants Liz to keep the track running but to *flip the track*. The sound effect would be cut at the proper point but instead of attaching the tail of the effect to the fill it would be attached back to itself with the continuation of the effect flipped over. On playback the sound of this effect would disappear since the playback head would be riding over the back of the track (which has no sound on it). When the track runs out altogether then it would be spliced back onto the fill, making sure that the fill would continue to ride with its base side toward the mixer's playback head.

The advantage of flipping this piece of track is that if the director decides at the mix that he *does* want the siren to extend into the crowd walla it can be flipped back to its proper orientation with only a few minutes' lost time. If Adam does not like the idea, then nothing need be done at all, since a piece of flipped track acts just like a piece of fill —it has no sound on it. I should note that the only type of track which can be flipped is stripe. If you tried to flip full–coat stock the top track on the mag (e.g., the fourth track if the mag is four–track) would then come underneath the playback head. Even though the mag is flipped, the head would still be able to read the track and you would hear that fourth channel (it would sound muffled, but you would definitely hear it).

After all the effects for these three elements have been cut in and Liz is down at the tail of the reel she will make sure that all the LFOAs match the LFOAs listed in the reel breakdown. I also like to physically make a cut in the fill at the LFOA frame line and then resplice the pieces back together again. This makes the LFOA very easy to locate later.

After this, the tail syncs should be marked after the LFOA (the first unit of every set should also have a tail pop put on at this time) and then the reels wound down for an additional thirty feet beyond these tail syncs. In addition, about thirty feet of white leader should be added to the end of the black and white dupe (and the same amount of fill added onto the track dupe) so that it also extends out that far beyond the tail sync (try and make all the reels run out around the same time). This extra thirty feet is called the *run-out* and is there because the machines which play back these elements (often called *dummies*) at the film mix often take quite a bit of time to slow down to a stop. If the film mixer doesn't hit the stop button until ten feet or so after the LFOA (which is, after all, only about six seconds) then it would be likely that the reels would run out past their ends. This extra thirty feet at the end of every reel should be enough to ensure that this doesn't happen.

Tail leaders should then be taped on top of the fill at the end of the reels. The dupe can then be rewound and the process repeated with FX–4, FX–5, and FX–6. When those units are completed then the next three should be built and then the next three until all twelve elements have been built.

At some point it would be a wise idea to run these built reels on the Moviola or flatbed (obviously, you would not be able to do more than two or three at a time) against the picture to make sure that everything is cut together properly.

Often, there are adjustments to be made to the track after you have built them. There are two kinds of changes that are common. The first comes from the addition or deletion of effects. If you must delete an effect it is best just to flip it out, rather than to physically remove it from the tracks. This way, if Chuck changes his mind again and wants the effect back in, it is a simple matter to unflip it. If an effect is to be added Liz should roll down to that spot on the proper element (always rolling down against the black and white dupe) and mark the fill in the same way that she would for any piece of track to be cut in. However, Liz cannot just cut in the new effect (which is, say, three feet long) and splice it back into the fill since she would then be adding three feet in length to the entire unit from that point on. To compensate for the new footage, she must remove an equal amount of fill before the next sound effect occurs. The best place to remove it from is from the exact place where she is cutting in the new effect.

The second type of adjustment Liz will be making is the conformation. You, as the picture assistant, will provide detailed lists of all of the conformations as described in the last chapter. Liz should first conform the black and white dupe and put a piece of tape on the head leader of each conformed element and dupe listing the date of the conformation. Chuck will then go through all of these conformations and determine exactly which sound effects are affected by them. For instance, if the scene in the car was shortened (let us say by two feet at 120′03/04) then it will be necessary to delete two feet of all of the sounds going at that time. The sound changes will not always come at the same footage as the conformation so Liz and Chuck should determine exactly how he wants to approach each change. Then she should make them. On elements which have only fill running at the conformation point it will only be necessary to delete or add the proper amount of fill to make the conformation

If the conformation is an addition it might be necessary to obtain new sound for some of the areas of the film. Chuck will do this (or instruct Liz very thoroughly on how to do it) and Liz will end up with new pieces to add to the elements.

On the conformation sheet supplied to her she should list every element involved in the reel. As she makes the conformation in each element she should put a checkmark next to the element that the conformation has been done. Obviously, a simple conformation in the picture department turns into a much more time-consuming conformation in the sound department after reels are built.

There are two other types of sound effects which Liz may be dealing with. These are *goodies* and *loops*. Goodies are effects which Chuck has decided *not* to cut in, but which he wants available at the mix in case he does need to cut them in. Goodies are placed into their own white box, which is marked "GOODIES for Reel 7" (or whatever reel it is) on one side. On the top of the box, or on a sheet of paper inside the box, is a list of all the goodies in the box. This list should contain all of the effects, along with the footage where they would have to be cut in. If there is any conformation at all, these footages should be changed.

There might also be a separate box for loops. Loops are effects which are so general that it does not matter if they repeat after ten seconds or so. *Room tone* (the tone which the on-set recordist recorded of the background neutral sound of the location) is commonly treated as a loop since it doesn't really matter where it falls in the scene — it should all sound the same. These loops are filed by number and labeled on the top of the box or on a separate sheet of paper by scene and description. Often an editor will make an *analysis loop* which is a loop of a particular sound that needs to be treated. Some sounds, like hums or air conditioners, need to be filtered out of the soundtrack where they are buried amidst the dialogue or they would be too annoying for an audience. Since they appear only in the background of scenes, usually buried underneath dialogue, it is very difficult for the mixer to fool around with his equalizers over the few seconds that the sound is present by itself. In this case, Chuck would make a loop of just the sound that needs to be filtered out. This could be run continuously until the mixer discovers the proper settings to filter out the unwanted sound. This analysis loop is then filed away. It is not meant to be used in the final soundtrack. It is only a tool to get a better mix.

One other item which is often brought to the mix is an effects reel. These reels are full 1000 foot long reels onto which a loop of the effect or tone (ocean, cars, office sounds, etc.) have been transferred from the beginning to the end. These are then put up at the film mix and faded in and out as necessary, saving the editor the need to cut these tones individually and the assistant the job of building them in the tracks (as well as the expense of having the tone transferred to stripe). Often, these reels are full–coat, with four separate tracks of sound (usually four different, but related, tones).

Foley Editing

Often a scene which has been shot does not have the proper types of body movement. A scene in which a person walks across a creaky wooden floor or down a cavernous passageway may have been shot without any sound at all. If sound was taken with the shot, the footsteps might not have the proper spooky sound. In addition, scenes in which the dialogue is being replaced by looping will have absolutely no background sounds at all to them since all of the original background will be thrown out at the same time that the original dialogue is. The sound editor cuts in backgrounds and specific effects to help in all of these cases but there are many cases where a needed effect is too specific to be found in an effects library.

You have already seen that some effects may have to be recorded especially for the scene. In many cases this is done on location (on *Apocalypse Now*, for instance, a crew spent weeks recording the sounds of military aircraft) but what happens if you need to put in those footsteps down the cavernous hallway? How would you do that? One choice would be to actually go to a cavernous hallway and record someone walking down it. But this approach has two problems to it. The first is the uncontrollable nature of the resulting sound. It may be too echoey. While it is always possible to add echo to a sound during the mix it is almost impossible to take the echo out. So, if the sound you got by recording the footsteps in a big hallway had too much echo in it for Adam, you would be in a bad fix. The second problem is that, on location, you would have very little way to exactly mimic the pace of the actor's or actress' footsteps.

Fortunately, there is an easier way (you knew there would be, didn't you?). It's called *foleying*.

A foley is, basically, any kind of body movement effect recorded in a studio. A foley studio is a recording studio which has the ability to play back the picture and sound (either from film or videotape) while you watch them and mimic the action on the screen. In the case of our actor walking down the hallway, the scene would be projected and Chuck (or Liz) would mimic the way the actor walks on the screen. These footsteps would be recorded. Later on, they would be cut into perfect sync in the editing room (it is almost impossible to get these sounds 100 percent accurate on the foley stage).

In more and more cases, foley has become a way of

obtaining sync effects which might normally be bought from an effects library. In fact, the job of foley recording has gotten so complicated that the sound editor usually doesn't even create the foleys him or herself. Instead, the editor will hire a group of *foley walkers*. These people are specialists who know how to get every desired effect (they even come with a complete set of props and shoes) in the fastest way possible. A good group of foley walkers can save you thousands of dollars on the foley stage.

Foley stages are interesting places. They are usually large rooms with a number of surfaces to walk on. There may be a section of the floor which is dirt, another which is a polished wooden floor, another which is brick, another which is tile, a fifth which is hollow wood, and so on. The foley stage gives the sound editor most of the possibilities necessary to recreate footsteps in the studio.

There are tricks that foley walkers use to simulate some sounds. People walking in snow or sand are duplicated by having the walker walk his or her fingers through a bowl of soap flakes. Some sounds can be duplicated without actually recreating the action. For instance, it may be necessary to do the sound effect of someone taking off his pants. This sound is easily gotten by holding the sleeve of a jacket up to the microphone and pulling it inside out.

If the foleys are to be recorded to a film playback, Liz may have to prepare the film before it goes to the foley stage. First, she and Chuck should decide which things are to be foleyed. This is a decision which should not be taken lightly. Foleys are not only very time consuming to create (and expensive to record) but they are very time consuming to cut into the film. If elements in a scene do not really need foleying then by all means don't foley them. Many foleys are eventually not used in the film anyway. I've seen some editors foley practically everything in a film (including the "sound" of candles flickering in the back of a cave.) This seems wasteful to me. But if there is any doubt as to whether a scene should be foleyed, then it is wiser to take the time to foley it and cut it in than to show up at the mix without the proper sounds.

There is one additional proviso in determining what should and shouldn't be foleyed in a film. After you have finished doing the English language version of *Silent Night* the sound editors will have to create a foreign version of the film (*see* Chapter 15 on mixing). In this version, all of the English dialogue in the film will be stripped away so it can later be replaced with dialogue in the language of the country that is buying the film. However, if there is a particular sound effect which is married to the dialogue tracks (for instance, if the sound of someone pulling off his coat is married to his dialogue) then that sound will also be lost when the English dialogue is removed. You will have to foley all of the sounds which are married to the dialogue specifically for the foreign versions of the film.

After Liz has determined exactly what things need to be foleyed she should *streamer* the reel. Streamers are three foot long lines which, when projected, slowly cross the screen from left to right. They are used to warn a person making the foleys that a foley cue is coming up soon. If Liz is doing the foleys (and it is not uncommon to find an assistant editor doing it) she would watch for the streamer to appear. As soon as it hits the right side of the screen she would know to begin the foley.

These streamers are put on the film in the editing room before the foley session. On a Moviola a frame is chosen where the foley is to begin and marks are made there and three feet before that frame. The dupe is laid down on a table and a long three foot line is drawn with grease pencil (*see* Figure 12.7) from the top of the film at the three foot mark to the bottom of the film at the first frame of the foley. When projected this will appear as a two second line crossing from left to right on the screen. Some editors like to use architect's tape laid onto the film instead of grease pencil lines.

It is not necessary to streamer every single foley that

FIGURE 12.7 This streamer extends for one-half of a second to the frame with the X in it. Usually, streamers are three feet (two seconds) in length or longer.

is to be recorded. If there is a scene with five characters all dancing and each character needs to be foleyed, it is only really important to streamer the first character unless there is some difficult cue point for the beginning of another. Streamers are really needed so that the foley walker can find the beginning of his cue. If some other visual on the screen can do the same thing, it is not necessary to streamer it.

If there are several characters in a scene who need to be streamered then it is sometimes helpful to make the streamer lines in two different colors of grease pencil or to make them go in opposite directions on the screen (one going left to right, another going right to left).

In many cases today, the reels aren't streamered at all. Either the foley walkers are adept enough so that streamers aren't necessary (a great savings in Liz's time and, therefore, money) or the streamers can be added electronically during the projection at the stage. In some studios, they can be added whether you are projecting film or video.

Foleys are often recorded on four–track (or full–coat) 35mm track whether your film is in 35mm or 16mm. In that way you can do a foley up to four times if you are unsure of it. Or, if there is a scene with a lot of characters in it, one or two of them can be done together on one channel of the four–track, another one or two can be done on the B channel, and still more can be done on the C and D channels. In this way you can give the effect of an entire crowd using only a few people on the foley stage. Later on, each of the channels of the four–track will be transferred to its own coded 35mm (or 16mm) stripe track. It is these tracks that the editor will cut into perfect sync with the picture, not the four–track master. That will remain at the foley stage's transfer room until it is no longer needed.

More and more often, foley is not recorded onto 35mm magnetic film at all but is recorded on big 24–track two inch recording tape. This is interlocked with the picture using *SMPTE time code* (don't worry what that means, we'll get to it later). Recording onto 24-track tape means that all of the foley for any given scene can be recorded in sync and played back together.

It is helpful to have someone taking notes at these foley sessions. In that way when you get the transfers to cut in (and we will get to that very shortly) you will know exactly what to do (*see* Figure 12.8).

Let us say that we are going to do our foley ourselves and with a 35mm dupe. After preparing all of the needed reels, Liz brings them to the foley studio where either she or the walkers will actually do the foleys. Let us also say that for *Silent Night* Liz and a few others are doing the foleys, not a group of foley walkers. They begin a reel. Let's say the first foley is not until 125 feet. Rather than wasting 125 feet of full coat they will disengage the recording machine from the projector, roll down to about 100 feet and then lock the two of them up. When they roll forward together, Liz will be ready to record the foley.

It is possible that this foley may require more than four passes, if it is a large fight scene for instance. In this case, after making the first four passes (and filling up all the channels on the four–track) the film would be stopped and the recorder again disengaged from the projector. Then the projector would be rolled back to the beginning of the scene and locked in again. When they roll forward again they will be recording on a new area of the four-track and Liz will be able to get up to eight passes of the same area of the film.

It is helpful if someone voice slates these foleys so that it is easy to identify what set of footsteps goes with what

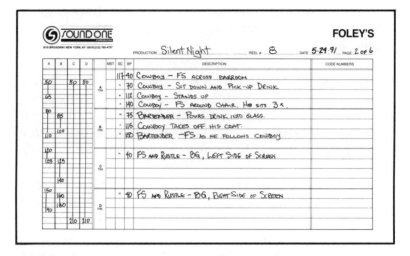

FIGURE 12.8 A page from a foley log. The four columns on the left represent the four channels on the full-coat mag that the foleys are being recorded onto. The footages marked show where foleys were recorded on those tracks. Each foley has a beep laid down before it in order to facilitate locating its proper sync against the picture. That footage is listed under the "BP" column. The description tells just what the foley is (you'd be surprised just how much one set of footsteps sounds like another). "FS" means footsteps. "BG" refers to background characters. Rather than taking the time to foley each background character separately, they are usually done four or five at a time.

picture later on in the editing room (you'd be surprised how much one set of footsteps sounds like another.) Liz, or the recording engineer, should call out "Reel 7, foley at 125 feet, take one" on the first pass and then increase the take number as each new channel is used.

So, let us say that Liz has done the foleys. Later, in the editing room, she will get (from the transfer house) four rolls of 35mm stripe soundtrack film for each roll of full–coat that she made. Every one will have some foleys on them and some blank space. After coding them she can, on a log sheet, write down the starting and ending code numbers for the foley along with the date recorded, the foley full–coat number, and the reel and footage it was designed for. In this way, reprints can be ordered very easily from the full–coat master. The reels do not have to be broken down into individual foleys unless Chuck requests it. Normally, the foleys can be cut off of the large 1000-foot rolls.

Then Chuck, or whoever is cutting the foleys (it is often the assistant editor), sits down with the dupe on his Moviola and begins fitting the foley to the picture much as he would any other effect. Foley cutting is an extremely tedious process, since every footstep must be cut in exactly right. Most foleys will require some sliding around from the position that they were recorded in. This involves either removing some track between two foleys or adding little bits of fill to lengthen the time between them.

After the foleys are cut Liz will end up with a number of long strands of track, with footages marked on them along with the element that they are assigned to. The foleys should then be built into reels in the same way that the effects are.

Preparing For The Mix

If *Silent Night* is like most other films, the tracks will be built no more than one day before they are to be mixed. After they are built it is a good idea to check them in the Moviola or on a flatbed against the picture dupe. Then someone with good handwriting should recopy the cue sheets so that they are neat and orderly. All footages within a half foot or so of each other are lined up on the cue sheets.

Sometimes, the film mix is done in the same building or on the same studio lot where the editing rooms are. In this case, it is a simple matter to ship everything over to the mix. But in many cases this is not so; the editing rooms are far removed from the film mix. In this case it is necessary to set up a little editing room at the mixing stage and to bring all essential trims and outs to the mix with the elements (production tracks as well as looping and effects trims).

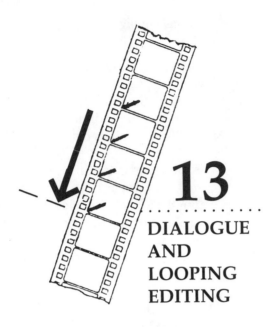

13

DIALOGUE AND LOOPING EDITING

There is, of course, a lot more to preparing for a mix than dealing with the sound effects. A major sound problem on most films is the condition of the dialogue tracks. Some tracks might have so much extraneous noise on them that they would be completely unusable, while other tracks have sporadic noises on them that make sections of the tracks unacceptable. And other tracks, while having no generally unacceptable portions on them, have backgrounds that sound slightly different from camera setup to camera setup, making cuts from one to the other noticeable. Each of these problems can be handled in the process of dialogue and looping editing.

In editing situations where one sound editor will handle multiple functions it is common for this person to do both the dialogue and effects editing but not the looping editing. However, since both dialogue and looping editing attack the same problems we will deal with them together here.

Let us take these three problems just mentioned in reverse order.

Dialogue Splitting

In Scene 11 (*see* Figure 4.5) there is a scene between Abby and his neighbor Bob in Abby's bedroom. Many different kinds of shots were done of the scene (as we discussed in Chapter Four, this is called *coverage*), including shots of Abby, shots of Bob, and shots of the two of them together. Because of the direction the camera was pointing during each shot the microphone had to be facing different portions of the set during each setup. This means that there will be subtle differences in the sound quality that might become evident when cut together. Correcting this is a fairly simple matter for . a mixer—he simply uses different *equalization* (the adjustment of the way the everything sounds, i.e. the relative amounts of high, middle and low frequencies), echo, and volume settings on each of the shots. To do this he needs to have each shot's sound on a separate track element (or unit.) In addition, to help make the point of the transition less apparent, he will want to *segue* from one to the other. A segue is a kind of audio dissolve in which one sound fades up through another sound, as that second sound is fading out. You hear musical segues all of the time on the radio when the d.j. fades from one song into another.

In order to accomplish this segue the mixer will need to have a short overlap of the two sounds. That is, he will need about ten to sixteen frames where both sounds are running simultaneously. This is accomplished by putting *extensions* on each of the tracks.

To understand what extensions are look at Figure 13.1. You can see that there are two pieces of track, one marked "Abby's Shot" and the other marked "Bob's Shot." These correspond to the two slightly different background sounds from the two different setups. If the mixer were to mix the tracks like this there would be a change in the sound at the point where one ends and the other begins. This change, called a *bump* would be slightly annoying to the audience.

239

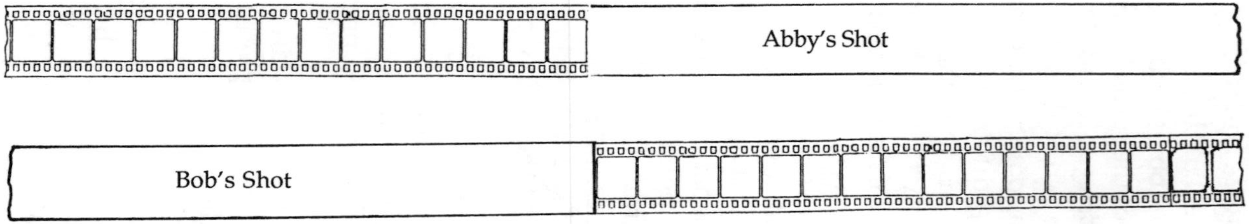

Abby's Shot

Bob's Shot

FIGURE 13.1 A pair of dialogue tracks split onto different tracks, before any extensions have been added (the film portion on the tracks is fill). If the sounds were to be mixed this way the mixer would no capability to ease from Abby's track into Bob's and the difference between the backgrounds would be quite noticeable.

Instead, Chuck or Liz would go through the entire take of Abby's shot and look for a short section where there was no dialogue or noise, only background sound (this means there would only be a general tone, no specific sounds at all). They would remove this small section and attach it to the end of Abby's shot. They would then try and find a section of tone from Bob's shot and attach it to the head of the dialogue piece on the second track. This would leave the tracks looking something like Figure 13.2. After the mixer had adjusted all his settings so that the two tracks matched as best as they could, he would then be able to run both together and one would automatically segue into the other.

Finding this tone is not as easy as it sounds. Often there are only six or seven frames that you can find where the actor or director isn't talking or where some crew person isn't moving some piece of equipment around. The best places to look for clean tone are either immediately after the slate hits and before the director calls "action", or at the end of a take after the actor or actress has finished but before the director calls "cut."

Often, if there isn't enough tone in one take, Chuck could try another take of the same setup. Another trick is to find some tone on one take, make it into a loop and then transfer twenty or thirty feet of it onto another piece of 35mm sound track. He would then use the tone from the loop transfer rather than the original track for his extensions. If he cannot find enough to make the loop, he might make several transfers of whatever piece he can find (he might have some transferred forward and some backward to help him cut them together) to make the length necessary.

Liz will most probably end up spending hours poring over takes and making loops, ending up with hundreds of tiny little trims in her barrel.

There are also digital machines now which can sample a tiny piece of sound (in this case it would be a very short piece of tone) and make an endless loop of it. As more sound houses

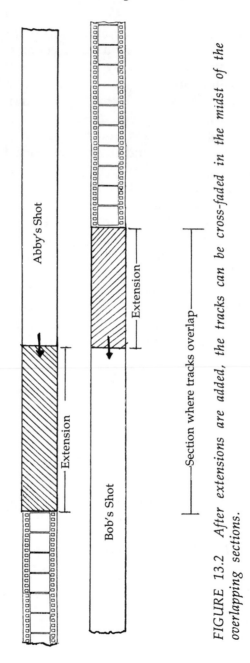

FIGURE 13.2 After extensions are added, the tracks can be cross-faded in the midst of the overlapping sections.

buy this equipment, as more films are mixed on tape, and as this equipment gets better, this practice will gain more favor, shortcutting the expensive and time consuming cutting of 35mm tone.

In the case where there is an isolated noise on a track that Chuck wants to get rid of, these sounds can be cut out of the track. This of course produces a *hole*, a section of the track where the sound drops out. This hole is filled by putting tone from the take either on another track (which the mixer will then fade into and out of to cover the hole) or cut directly into the track to replace the fill at the hole. Liz or Chuck must be very careful and listen to see if the tone inserted at the hole exactly matches the tone immediately before and after it. If not, they would cut the tone onto another track so that the mixer could treat it by equalization and seguing.

Looping

There are cases where these unwanted noises come directly on top of a line of dialogue. In this case there is no way to remove the noise without also removing part of the line of dialogue. This problem is treated very much like the third case of dialogue editing — where an entire scene is unusable because of lousy sound. The only way to cure these problems is with looping.

As I mentioned in the last chapter, looping is the process of re–recording words or lines that are unacceptable for some reason. The way in which this is done resembles the foley process because both are attempting to do the same thing — record some sound (either a foley or a looped line) directly in sync to a picture.

Looping got its name because lines used to be re-placed by cutting them into a loop in which the line of dialogue would be followed by a piece of fill of exactly the same length as the line. When this was made into a loop and played back, the actor or actress would hear his or her line followed by a space. Then the line would repeat, then the space. And on and on. This would enable the actor or actress to repeat the line immediately after hearing it. Each of the actor's repetitions would be recorded until the director was happy with the performance. There are some people who lament the passing of this system, but today, looping is no longer done with loops but in a process known either as *ADR* (Automatic Dialogue Replacement) or *EPS* (Electronic Post Sync.) Both terms mean exactly the same thing.

In ADR, the actor or actress faces the screen and hears, in a set of headphones, the dialogue immediately leading up to the line to be replaced. As the line approaches, they see a streamer and hear three beeps. At the moment the streamer hits the right side of the screen they begin speaking their line. Both the streamer and the beeps are clues to the actors or actresses as to when they should begin speaking their lines.

Looping requires a certain amount of preparation on the part of the looping editor and assistant. The first order of business is obviously to decide which things need to be looped. This is usually done at the spotting session (as described in Chapter 12) with Chuck, Wendy, and Adam. The kinds of things that determine whether a line should be looped are whether there are extraneous noises over it, whether it is audible, whether it is comprehensible, and whether it is a reading that the director is happy with. Sometimes the director will want to change the performance of a line or even its wording.

Another reason for looping a line is to obtain a television line. This is an alternate wording of a line which does not contain an objectionable word that was in the original. These television lines will be used in the "soft" or TV version of the film.

Often it is necessary to record lines for off–screen or background characters that were not gotten on the set. In a scene where a lead character is talking to someone at a party the sound recordist would never want to mike the scene so that the background characters could be heard and disturb the lead's dialogue. In fact, in many cases, the extras performing the parts of the background party–ers merely *mime* their conversation, without actually saying anything. This gives the cleanest track possible for the lead character's dialogue. Later on, of course, the background chatter must be added, probably by a library sound effect of party walla (a group of people murmuring). The same effect can be gotten by a group of actors in a looping session.

After it has been determined just what lines need to be looped then the actors and actresses involved should be booked for looping sessions. This should be done by the producer since it involves calling agents to determine the actors' and actresses' availability. The looping department should advise the producer's office of just how much time is needed with each actor or actress and give them the approximate dates when they would like to do all of the looping.

Then, the reels must be prepared for the looping session. This is done in one of two ways. Sometimes, the entire dupe of the film is brought to the looping stage and the reels are put up as they are needed for the session. However, if a character has one line to loop in each of five reels it would take a lot more time to thread up the reels and take them back down again then it would to record the individual lines. This is a phenomenal waste of everyone's time (as well as a needless cost of looping stage time). In cases like this, *character reels* are built.

To explain just what character reels are, let me briefly explain how a looping session works. An actor (Abby, for example) comes to the stage and records all of his lines. He is then followed by a second actor (let's say, Bob) who records all of his lines. Rarely do two actors or actresses loop at the same time, even if they are playing off each other in the same scene. Liz would, therefore, pull all the lines that Abby had to loop in the entire film and build them onto one or more reels which would be sent to the looping stage. These reels would be known as Abby's character reels. Similarly, Bob would have his own set of character reels.

In cases where both Abby and Bob must be looped for the same scene (and this happens all the time), either the character reels are unbuilt after Abby's looping session to be rebuilt for Bob's, or an extra dupe is made of the scenes with both characters in them. Normally, a quick dupe is made directly off of the first looping dupe. This obviates the need of going back to the color work picture to strike more dupes.

Once Liz has pulled all the scenes out of the looping dupe and has rebuilt them into character reels, the reels are given to the looping editor. The editor then proceeds to mark up exactly where he or she would want each loop to begin and end. This is not as self-evident as it all sounds. Most of the time you will want to loop a number of consecutive lines in a speech in one loop without stopping. But some actors and actresses get tired faster than others. It is often difficult to loop long lines and get acceptable sync. On the other hand, it is unwise to break down the lines too much since that would break up the actor's or actress' concentration and create a stiff, unnatural reading of each line. Some middle ground has to be found. A good looping editor will be able to make intelligent choices.

While the editor is marking up the character reels, he or she should also be making the looping cue sheet (*see* Figure 13.3) listing each loop by a loop number, footage on the character reel, and the wording of the line to be done. Loop numbers are assigned by character, reel number, and the sequential number of the loop. On the example given we see the looping for Abby's lines in Scene 10, which falls on Abby's character reel 1. The first line, "Evening Mister Hemingway", is given the number 1AB1 which stands for Abby's (AB) first loop line (the number one at the end of the number) on character reel number 1 (the number one before the letters "AB"). If this was the twentieth line on reel 3 for Abby, the number would be 3AB20. If this was the first line for reel 10 it would be 10AB1. Like anything else in editing, you should

Film Forms

ADR CUE SHEET

REEL 1 FILM Silent Night Page 1 of 16

CHARACTER ABBY

Line #	Footages	Channels 1	2	3	4	Dialogue
1AB1	46+12					"Evening, Mr. Hemingway"
	49+10					
1AB2	83+7					"Perfectly shitty"
	90+3					
1AB2-TV	83+7					"Perfectly shoddy"
	90+3					
1AB3	110+5					"Enough of that nonsense
	114+15					already"
1AB4	162+10					"Hey, did you see
	163+15					that?
1AB5	169+8					"Her!"
	170+1					

ADR CUE SHEET

FIGURE 13.3 A looping cue sheet. Each of the lines is given a unique number.

be aware that other numbering systems are also used. All that is important is to make sure that each line is uniquely numbered.

If the reels are not broken apart into character reels then each loop on a reel is given its own number (usually in the order they appear in the reel, though this is not crucial.) The fifth line in reel three could be 3005, the twelfth line in reel ten could be 10012 (looks like a Zip Code, doesn't it?) The crucial thing for any system, however, should be that it uniquely and quickly identifies each character and reel number.

The footage listed on the cue sheet is not normally the first modulation of sound of the line (this is simply the first frame at which there is any sound of the line). ADR equipment needs a few frames of time before the recorder completely kicks in. For that reason the studio will ask you to make all your footages a certain number of frames before the first modulation. The exact number will vary but they usually run from four to six frames.

After Chuck has finished with the character reels he'll give them back to Liz. She will then redo the looping cue sheets, if necessary and, at the same time, mark streamers on the dupe to that footage. These streamers are placed on the film in exactly the same manner as foley streamers are. On the redone sheets Liz will make sure that the line of dialogue to be looped is also listed completely and correctly.

Looping cue sheets generally come in one of two varieties. You have already seen one, where the characters' lines are grouped together on one page. Another form (*see* Figure 13.4) lists each line on its own page. The line is typed at the top of the form in very large letters so that it is easy for the actor or actress to read in the looping studio. At the bottom is a form to take notes on at the session. This is handier to take notes on, but creates much more paperwork.

Recently, computer systems have been handling the preparation of these cue sheets. After programming in the

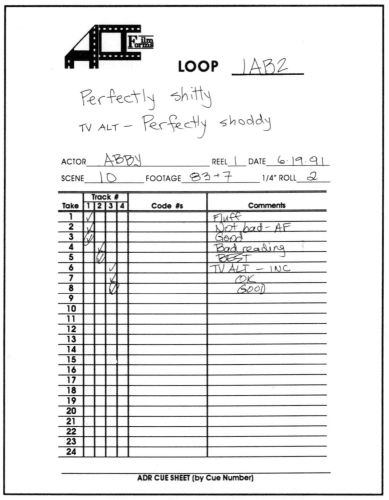

LOOP _1AB2_

Perfectly shitty

TV ALT — Perfectly shoddy

ACTOR _ABBY_ REEL _1_ DATE _6·19·91_

SCENE _10_ FOOTAGE _83 + 7_ 1/4" ROLL _2_

Take	Track # 1	2	3	4	Code #s	Comments
1	✓					Fluff
2	✓					Not bad – AF
3	✓					Good
4		✓				Bad reading
5		✓				BEST
6			✓			TV ALT – INC
7			✓			OK
8			✓			GOOD
9						
10						
11						
12						
13						
14						
15						
16						
17						
18						
19						
20						
21						
22						
23						
24						

ADR CUE SHEET (by Cue Number)

FIGURE 13.4 In this version of a finished looping cue sheet each looped line is given its own page. At the session, the information at the bottom of the sheet is filled in. In this case, Adam didn't like takes one and two enough to save them (even though he said that take two was "not bad"), so take three was the first saved take, on track one. Take five was the next saved take, on track two. In addition, the actor was also requested to give an alternate reading for a television version of the film. The third TV take (take eight on this cue sheet) was the best and was saved onto track three of the full–coat. All eight takes were saved onto 1/4" tape roll number two.

Line #	Footages	Channels				Dialogue
		1	2	3	4	
1AB1	46+12 49+10	2	4	5	–	"Evening, Mr. Hemingway"
1AB2	83+7 90+3	3	5		–	"Perfectly shitty"
1AB2 TV	83+7 90+3			8	–	"Perfectly shoddy"
1AB3	110+5 114+15	1	2	6	9	"Enough of that nonsense already"
1AB4	162+10 163+15	2	3	5	–	"Hey, did you see that?"
1AB5	169+8 170+1	1	2	–	–	"Her!"

ADR CUE SHEET

REEL __1__ FILM __Silent Night__ Page __1 of 16__

CHARACTER __ABBY__

ADR CUE SHEET

FIGURE 13.5 In this version of the finished looping cue sheet only the saved takes are noted. As a result, more takes fit on each page. Note that in this system the takes for each looped line are numbered beginning with one. In other systems, all of the takes for all looped lines are numbered sequentially. In this case, the preferred takes for line 1AB2 would have been Takes 8 and 10.

loop numbers, the line to be recorded, and the footages, the computer generates any kind of cue sheet requested — one with the line written big for the actor or actress, one with all of the character's loops listed, one with space for the looping editor's notes, etc.

Liz should call the looping studio and make sure that they have the proper amount of stock for the session. Just as in the foley session, the looped lines will be recorded either onto 35mm full–coat stock or onto 24-track two-inch tape. In addition, the lines will also be recorded onto 1/4" magnetic tape. Often they are simultaneously recorded onto 35mm stripe for the editor to cut. We will see why we need all these recordings in just a minute.

On the day of the session, Liz will show up a little early with the reels to be looped and give them to the projectionist and the recordist. Copies of the cue sheets should be given to the recordist, the looping editor, to the director, and to the actor or actress. The assistant should also retain a copy for his or her own notes.

The looping process works like this. The film is rolled and everyone listens to the dupe track. The engineer recording the lines announces a slate which will sound something like, "Loop 1AB7, Take 3." The actor, Abby in this case, watches the screen while listening to the track in his headphones. He sees the streamer and hears the three beeps. At the place where the fourth imaginary beep would be he begins speaking the line while watching the film, attempting to match his reading to the lip movements of the character on the screen, as well as trying to recreate the feeling of the scene (this is why the ADR/EPS system is nicer than the old looping system—he gets to see and hear the dialogue in the scene leading up to the line to be looped, since the assistant should have included it in the character reel). The first take of the loop gets placed on channel one of the full coat or two–inch multitrack tape. If it is unacceptable (either for sync, acting, or because of a mistake) then take two is made on the same

251

channel, wiping out the old one. However, the take is not erased on the quarter-inch tape. In this way, if a line doesn't work in the editing room or at the mix, there is always this backup to go to.

Once an acceptable take is done, Adam may want to do another one, either for safety or to get a different reading. The director may like the reading on the first track but the sync is not good (the looping editor should be very active in advising the director just what is acceptable, what is passable, and what is not good in terms of sync). In these cases, the take on channel one is saved and another take is made onto channel two.

At the bottom of the second type of looping cue sheet (*see* Figure 13.4) is a chart on which either the looping editor or assistant should be taking notes. In this example, Loop #1AB3 (Abby's third loop on reel 1) the first three takes went onto track one, of which the second reading was "not bad" according to Adam. He asked that it be saved but for another take to be done. The next two went onto channel two where the best take was Take 5. Track three was reserved for a television line of which Take 8 was the best. Note how this information is supplied on the other type of looping cue sheet in Figure 13.5.

In addition to these lines, the director may request certain lines from the actor without running the picture. These lines are called *wild lines*, much as track recorded on the set without picture is called wild track. The assistant should make a note as to exactly where these wild lines are. The best way to do this is to keep a separate wild line log which lists each take of each wild line recorded, along with the quarter-inch reel number it was recorded on, the date it was recorded, where on the tape it was recorded (e.g., "After 3AB21"), and any other information on it (the scene it is for, where it is supposed to go in the scene, comments, etc.)

Cutting In The Looped Lines

After the day's looping the 35mm full–coats should be transferred to four separate 35mm stripes. Each of the four should be lined up, using the beep which was transferred from your head leader (you did remember to put a head leader with a beep at the nine foot mark, didn't you?) They should then be coded in sync with each other. In the case of the first reel of Abby's looping, I would code the transfers from the A channel 1AB1000, the B channel transfers for the same reel would be coded 1AB2000 and the C channel transfers would get the codes beginning with 1AB3000 and so on. By a lucky coincidence, if you code the black and white dupe of Abby's first character reel 1AB0000, then (unless you did any moving around of the 35mm full–coat to accommodate lines which required saving more than four takes) all of the transfers will line up with the codes on the dupe. This will help the looping editor cut the loops into the film.

Some editors dispense with sync coding entirely since they feel that, so long as they have the loop line number, there is no need to sync code the track to the character reels. It is more important, they think, that they know where the line goes in the continuity of the film.

This illustrates one of the beauties of a flexible system. If you are working on a high budget film with a lot of systems and time (though there are increasingly fewer of those films around today) then you can take the time to code everything in the way you want it and to protect for every eventuality. But, you should know that you can organize a lot less thoroughly and still have a functioning system if you know what you can give up without compromising your editor.

In this case, it is important that Chuck be able to find out what line it is that he is listening to and where he should cut it into the finished film. If the voice slate is on the track, or if the transfer house has identified the take with a piece of tape at its head, then that (combined with the looping cue sheets) should be enough information for Chuck.

In some cases only the circled takes are printed off the full-coat at the time of the transfer. This saves stock and transfer time.

In case a 35mm stripe was recorded at the looping session, the only things which will need to be transferred will be additional takes that the looping editor or Adam wanted as options.

All the transferred lines should be broken down after they are coded and then flanged up with trim tabs. The lines should be logged in a logbook (there is also a column on the looping cue sheet for the code numbers). Then, when the looping editor is ready to cut in the looping, it will be a simple matter to give the editor all the loops for the reel that he or she needs.

The looping editor is concerned with much the same sort of thing that the foley editor is concerned with. Even though the loops were recorded directly to picture, there are always tiny adjustments which need to be made in order to make the line look *exactly* in sync. As Chuck cuts the loops he will mark the footage and the reel where the loop should be built into the elements directly onto the loops (the editor will be cutting to a second looping dupe, one which was never broken down at all and conforms exactly to the way the picture is cut, or it is possible that Liz may have broken apart the character reels and re–built them into looping dupe reels), hanging them in barrels and making scratch cue sheets, just as the foley and sound effects editors do. Later on Liz will build these loops into units and enter them onto the main dialogue cue sheets.

Any words or lines which are to be replaced by looped lines are physically removed from the dialogue tracks (where they are usually replaced by tone). They are shifted over to another set of tracks which are reserved exclusively for pieces removed from the production tracks. These units are generally called the *X and Y tracks*. There, the pieces are cleaned up and sit ready to be used if Adam decides at the mix that he does not want to use a looped line but prefers the original better (this happens all the time; it is difficult to know whether a line is really superior to the original until the sound editor and mixer have cleaned up the original). For this reason the X and Y tracks should be prepared just as if they were going to be used in the mix. This will involve inserting tone in between sections and removing unwanted noises that do not affect the dialogue.

Once all these things have been done, then the tracks can be built just as effects tracks are built. Dialogue tracks are never integrated with effects tracks but are kept separate, though they are sometimes listed on the same cue sheet.

14
MUSIC
EDITING

Eventually, as the film's editing is almost complete, Adam's thoughts will turn toward music — in particular, what kind of music would be exactly right for *Silent Night*.

Perhaps Adam will have decided that he wishes to work with the same composer that he's worked with on other films. Perhaps he will have decided that he wants no music, or to use pieces of already recorded music. Or perhaps he will have decided to take a chance on a new composer. But, if there is to be any type of music at all in the film there will have to be a music editor.

On many low budget films, if there is to be very little music in the film, the picture editor functions as a quasi–music editor, primarily assisting the composer in getting his *timings* and then *laying in the tracks* (don't worry, we'll learn about these terms in a short while). But even if this is the case, there will always be someone functioning as a music editor. That is what this chapter is all about.

There is already a good book for the music editor which lays out many of the music editor's tasks. *Music Editing For Motion Pictures,* by Milton Lustig, discusses many of the

256

tasks that a music editor must perform and some of the techniques for editing music. Though the book is hampered by being too out–of–date to deal with video, computers and the latest studio techniques, I would still recommend it for those with a further interest in the subject.

Before The Scoring Session

The music editor faces two major tasks. The first is to prepare the composer so that he or she can write the music, and the second is to edit the music to the film.

Let's say that you've hired Nate High to be your music editor and he has hired Betty Bound as his assistant. The first thing that they must do is to see the film as many times as they can. Then there must be a spotting session. A spotting session is usually held with the music editor and assistant, the film editor, and the director. You may or may not be able to attend. Spotting sessions can be held either in a projection room where the film can be run forward and backward, or (as is more common) on a flatbed in an editing room. Adam will go through the film reel by reel explaining where he wants the music, what kind of music he wants and where he wants accents in the music. The composer will ask for details so that he can better interpret just what it is the director wants musically. Meanwhile, Nate and Betty should be furiously taking notes.

Let's say that we are going to be spotting Scenes 8, 9, 10, and 11 (*see* Figure 4.5). You may remember that these are the scenes where Abby looks on during the shooting of a barroom fight. We then cut to the parking lot that evening as Abby, and the rest of the studio workers, leave work. Abby goes to his car, turns on his engine, and sits watching the cars leave. He then closes his car door and drives off. We cut to Abby as he walks into his apartment, looks around, goes to get a drink and then, hearing a typewriter from the other room, exits and goes to his bedroom. There, at a desk, sits Bob, a neighbor. They begin talking.

Adam's idea for scoring this scene is that the music should begin in the barroom set, continue through the parking lot and into the apartment scene where it should go out.

Nate wants to know where in the apartment it will go out.

The composer suggests that it cross–fade (segue) into the sounds of the typewriter as Abby notices them.

They will then begin to give adjectives to the cue. They will discuss whether the music should be wistful (underscoring Abby's sense of isolation from the filmmaking process) or happy (accenting his joy at the shooting of his film). This part of the discussion is very important to the composer since, more often than not, the director knows very little about the terminology of music. These adjectives are the best way of describing what he wants the music to sound like. This is why I sometimes refer to music spotting sessions as "adjective sessions." Everybody will also talk about at what points in the scene the music should change character to go with Abby's changing mood.

When the spotting session is over, Nate will have a list of where all the music cues will begin and end in the film. Copies of this list should be given to the sound editors as soon as it is typed up so that they know exactly where music is planned for the film (it will help them in the choice of sound effects and how they plan them.) A copy should also go to Adam and Wendy for their reference. It is then time to do the *music timing sheets* for the composer.

Nate will sit down with a dupe of the film as well as his and Betty's notes and go through the film, marking the exact point where the music is to begin at each musical cue. Each cue will be given a number much like the looping numbers. The fifth cue on reel two would be called 2M5 (some editors prefer to call it M205). Each cue will be given a title which is used for identification and copyright purposes.

Nate will go through the reels marking every potential accent point in every single musical cue. On a timing sheet (*see* Figure 14.1) he would list everything that the composer might ever want to accent musically. Normally, composers only use about 10 percent of this information but they rarely know ahead of time *which* 10 percent it will be, so the music editor must detail practically everything. The timing sheet also includes all of the characters' dialogue because it is very important that the composer's music not conflict with the dialogue.

You will also notice that the timing sheet lists the cue points in terms of sequential time from the beginning of each cue. This figure is the only number which the composer will find useful. But there is another figure, the footage in the reel which is important to the editor. Sometimes the editor will make a scratch, or preliminary, timing sheet which will include the footages, though they are not retyped onto the final timing sheet (I used to use a small Apple computer at home and asked it to print out sheets either with or without footages depending upon my need). Most often, these timings (in minutes and seconds) can be taken directly off a seconds counter on the Moviola or flatbed which is zeroed out at the start of every cue. Sometimes, if such a counter is not available, it may be necessary to convert these footages to timings.

In the last few years, computers have become more important in this process. There are several computer music programs which music editors use to make their timing sheets. The program which I like the best is called *CUE*™— *The Film Music System,* for the Macintosh. As the editor types in the footage or SMPTE Time Code number (we will get to a discussion of these numbers in just a few pages) of each cue point, the program will automatically create the timings which the composer can use to write his music. It will also generate cue sheets of varying types as well as create many other charts and notes that the composer can utilize. If the composer writes with a computer or synthesizer which uses *MIDI codes* (a standard for the synthetic electronic reproduc-

Production: **Silent Night, Silent Cowboy** Cue: **Abby Goes Back Home (1M4)**

Tempo: **16-4 (24 frm.)** Begins **123/5** from Start of Reel 1

----8 WARNING CLICKS BEGIN AT 115/1---

ABS FT / FRM (35)	REL TIME			CLICK #
			The DIRECTOR yells "Cut" and a cheer goes up from the set. ABBY is sitting, staring at the broken bottle on the floor. He looks up.	
			Adam: "He's like to join in, but he can't. He's an outsider. Not exactly melancholy, but sweetly sad somehow."	
			METER: 4 4	
123/5	0.00		BEGIN cue as ABBY lifts his head up.	1.00
126/4	1.96		He wakes up from his reverie.	3.85
133/6	6.71	CUT	to what he sees: a man is picking up the broken bottle	10.75
152/3	19.25	CUT	back to ABBY as he realizes that everyone is leaving the set.	29.00
162/4	25.96	CUT	to some GRIPS packing away cables.	38.75
166/12	28.96	CUT	to ACTORS shaking hands and leaving.	43.11
172/1	32.50	CUT	to the DEAD MAN getting up from the floor.	48.27
177/10	36.21	CUT	to ABBY as he shakes his head.	53.66
181/1	38.50	CUT	to the DEAD MAN getting shot (flashback) from before as ABBY saw it.	57.00
198/2	49.88	CUT	to ABBY.	73.54
200/0	51.13	CUT	to wider shot as he stands up.	75.37
210/1	57.83	CUT	to the parking lot, later. ABBY is entering the lot along with a number of other WORKERS on the film.	85.10
212/9	59.50		One of the crew waves goodbye to ABBY.	87.53
216/13	1:02.3 3		ABBY waves back.	91.65
219/15	1:04.4 2		... but realizes that the man wasn't waving at him.	94.69
221/8	1:05.4 6	CUT	to Abby's car.	96.21
222/14	1:06.3 8		ABBY enters the frame.	97.54
226/10	1:08.8 8		He begins to open the door to his car.	101.18
289/15	1:51.0 8		END of CUE.	162.56
			TOTAL TIME - 1:51.08	
			END CUE 1M4	

FIGURE 14.1. A timing sheet. The composer will use these timings to determine exactly where his musical accents should fall. Adam's notes at the top are important as they are a record of what he wanted the music to be like. (Courtesy OPCODE Systems.)

tion of music) he or she can take the numbers that the editor has typed in and use them directly to write his music, without needing the cue sheets.

Many composers still work in the old way and require typed timing notes, regardless of how they are generated. As soon as the first few are done they are given to the composer. He or she will then write the music for each cue based on the numbers Nate has given. As the composer writes each cue he or she will determine a tempo (speed) for the piece. Rhythms in film are given not in metronome settings common in music (120 beats of music per minutes, or 120 bpm) but in *clicks*. These are numbers that look something like this: 12/0 or 16/4. The click number represents the number of frames for each beat of music. Each frame is divided into eight parts, each corresponding to one-half of a sprocket. So a 12/0 click would mean that there were twelve and no eighths frames for each beat of music. This is the equivalent of two beats of music each 24 frames (one second) or, for the musicians reading this, 120 beats per minute. A 16/4 click means that there are sixteen and one-half frames per beat (four-eighths of a frame is one-half of a frame).

All of this is important because, after the composer determines the click of each cue, the assistant will have to set up each cue with streamers so that, during the recording session, the conductor will be able to look at the film and record the music to it.

Streamers are usually placed on the film at several places within each music cue. The beginning and end of each cue is streamered so the composer can know when to start and finish conducting the music. Any places *inside* the cue that the composer wants to accent may also be streamered. Finally, there will often be streamers *before* the cue, leading up to the first *warning click* before the piece begins.

When a cue is to be recorded to a click track (sometimes called an *electric metronome*) the conductor will need to hear some clicks before the cue begins so he can give the

261

rhythm to the musicians (this is called the *count–off*, which is the "and a-one..., and a-two..., and a-three..." that you may hear before pieces of music.) The tempo at which the conductor gives the musicians these counts will determine the tempo at which the song is played. In addition, many of the musicians are fed this *click track* while they are playing. The click track is a repetitive dull clicking sound that can be set to click at whatever tempo is needed.

The composer will tell Nate what tempo the piece is to be recorded at and how many clicks he would like before the beginning of the music. All that is needed then is to determine the length (in feet and frames) for the required number of warning clicks at that tempo (clicks/beat). When that is determined, a streamer can be placed on the film. When this is projected at the recording session this streamer will cue Nate to begin the click track generator.

Let me give an example. Let's say that cue 1M3 ("The Barroom Fight") is the musical cue to be streamered. The composer has written the piece in a 17/2 tempo and has requested eight free clicks. There is a book called Project Tempo (also known as the Click Track Book). This lists, for most tempi, the footages for every beat from the first beat to the six hundredth. For my own use, I have developed a computer program to do the same thing, a page of which is reproduced in Figure 14.2. This sample page lists the data for a 17/2 click. In addition, many computer programs, like CUE, have built-in click books.

To find the length of film needed for eight free clicks at 17/2, Betty needs to realize that if the first free click is the first beat then the first beat of the song would be on the ninth beat. She would then look for the length listed for beat number nine, which is eight feet, ten frames. She would then place the music dupe in the synchronizer so that the frame where the song is to begin (which Nate should have already marked) falls at 8'10. She would then roll back to 0'00. That will be the first frame of the warning clicks. She could then

The click is a 12/4   Metronome setting = 115.2

	0	1	2	3	4	5	6	7	8	9
0	0-00	0-0	0-12	1-9	2-5	3-2	3-14	4-11	5-7	6-4
	00:00.00	0:0	0:.52	0:1.04	0:1.56	0:2.08	0:2.6	0:3.12	0:3.64	0:4.16
10	7-0	7-13	8-9	9-6	10-2	10-15	11-11	12-8	13-4	14-1
	0:4.68	0:5.2	0:5.72	0:6.25	0:6.77	0:7.29	0:7.81	0:8.33	0:8.85	0:9.37
20	14-13	15-10	16-6	17-3	17-15	18-12	19-8	20-5	21-1	21-14
	0:9.89	0:10.41	0:10.93	0:11.45	0:11.97	0:12.5	0:13.02	0:13.54	0:14.06	0:14.58
30	22-10	23-7	24-3	25-0	25-12	26-9	27-5	28-2	28-14	29-11
	0:15.1	0:15.62	0:16.14	0:16.66	0:17.18	0:17.7	0:18.22	0:18.75	0:19.27	0:19.79
40	30-7	31-4	32-0	32-13	33-9	34-6	35-2	35-15	36-11	37-8
	0:20.31	0:20.83	0:21.35	0:21.87	0:22.39	0:22.91	0:23.43	0:23.95	0:24.47	0:25
50	38-4	39-1	39-13	40-10	41-6	42-3	42-15	43-12	44-8	45-5
	0:25.52	0:26.04	0:26.56	0:27.08	0:27.6	0:28.12	0:28.64	0:29.16	0:29.68	0:30.2
60	46-1	46-14	47-10	48-7	49-3	50-0	50-12	51-9	52-5	53-2
	0:30.72	0:31.25	0:31.77	0:32.29	0:32.81	0:33.33	0:33.85	0:34.37	0:34.89	0:35.41
70	53-14	54-11	55-7	56-4	57-0	57-13	58-9	59-6	60-2	60-15
	0:35.93	0:36.45	0:36.97	0:37.5	0:38.02	0:38.54	0:39.06	0:39.58	0:40.1	0:40.62
80	61-11	62-8	63-4	64-1	64-13	65-10	66-6	67-3	67-15	68-12
	0:41.14	0:41.66	0:42.18	0:42.7	0:43.22	0:43.75	0:44.27	0:44.79	0:45.31	0:45.83
90	69-8	70-5	71-1	71-14	72-10	73-7	74-3	75-0	75-12	76-9
	0:46.35	0:46.87	0:47.39	0:47.91	0:48.43	0:48.95	0:49.47	0:50	0:50.52	0:51.04
100	77-5	78-2	78-14	79-11	80-7	81-4	82-0	82-13	83-9	84-6
	0:51.56	0:52.08	0:52.6	0:53.12	0:53.64	0:54.16	0:54.68	0:55.2	0:55.72	0:56.25
110	85-2	85-15	86-11	87-8	88-4	89-1	89-13	90-10	91-6	92-3
	0:56.77	0:57.29	0:57.81	0:58.33	0:58.85	0:59.37	0:59.89	1:.41	1:.93	1:1.45
120	92-15	93-12	94-8	95-5	96-1	96-14	97-10	98-7	99-3	100-0
	1:1.97	1:2.5	1:3.02	1:3.54	1:4.06	1:4.58	1:5.1	1:5.62	1:6.14	1:6.66
130	100-12	101-9	102-5	103-2	103-14	104-11	105-7	106-4	107-0	107-13
	1:7.18	1:7.7	1:8.22	1:8.75	1:9.27	1:9.79	1:10.31	1:10.83	1:11.35	1:11.87
140	108-9	109-6	110-2	110-15	111-11	112-8	113-4	114-1	114-13	115-10
	1:12.39	1:12.91	1:13.43	1:13.95	1:14.47	1:15	1:15.52	1:16.04	1:16.56	1:17.08
150	116-6	117-3	117-15	118-12	119-8	120-5	121-1	121-14	122-10	123-7
	1:17.6	1:18.12	1:18.64	1:19.16	1:19.68	1:20.2	1:20.72	1:21.25	1:21.77	1:22.29
160	124-3	125-0	125-12	126-9	127-5	128-2	128-14	129-11	130-7	131-4
	1:22.81	1:23.33	1:23.85	1:24.37	1:24.89	1:25.41	1:25.93	1:26.45	1:26.97	1:27.5
170	132-0	132-13	133-9	134-6	135-2	135-15	136-11	137-8	138-4	139-1
	1:28.02	1:28.54	1:29.06	1:29.58	1:30.1	1:30.62	1:31.14	1:31.66	1:32.18	1:32.7
180	139-13	140-10	141-6	142-3	142-15	143-12	144-8	145-5	146-1	146-14
	1:33.22	1:33.75	1:34.27	1:34.79	1:35.31	1:35.83	1:36.35	1:36.87	1:37.39	1:37.91
190	147-10	148-7	149-3	150-0	150-12	151-9	152-5	153-2	153-14	154-11
	1:38.43	1:38.95	1:39.47	1:40	1:40.52	1:41.04	1:41.56	1:42.08	1:42.6	1:43.12
200	155-7	156-4	157-0	157-13	158-9	159-6	160-2	160-15	161-11	162-8
	1:43.64	1:44.16	1:44.68	1:45.2	1:45.72	1:46.25	1:46.77	1:47.29	1:47.81	1:48.33
210	163-4	164-1	164-13	165-10	166-6	167-3	167-15	168-12	169-8	170-5
	1:48.85	1:49.37	1:49.89	1:50.41	1:50.93	1:51.45	1:51.97	1:52.5	1:53.02	1:53.54
220	171-1	171-14	172-10	173-7	174-3	175-0	175-12	176-9	177-5	178-2
	1:54.06	1:54.58	1:55.1	1:55.62	1:56.14	1:56.66	1:57.18	1:57.7	1:58.22	1:58.75
230	178-14	179-11	180-7	181-4	182-0	182-13	183-9	184-6	185-2	185-15
	1:59.27	1:59.79	2:.31	2:.83	2:1.35	2:1.87	2:2.39	2:2.91	2:3.43	2:3.95
240	186-11	187-8	188-4	189-1	189-13	190-10	191-6	192-3	192-15	193-12
	2:4.47	2:5	2:5.52	2:6.04	2:6.56	2:7.08	2:7.6	2:8.12	2:8.64	2:9.16

FIGURE 14.2 A page from a click track book. This page is for a 12/4 click. Both the footage and the time from the first click can be found. The length from the first beat to any other beat, say the sixty-fifth, can be found by looking at the numbers at the intersection of the sixties row and the fives column. The top of the two numbers is the number of feet of frames from the first beat (in this case, 50 feet, zero frames). The numbers underneath it give the length in time (33.33 seconds).

make a streamer three feet long leading up to this 0'00 frame.

Going into a recording session with the complete dupe of the movie is a fantastically time consuming way of working. The music dupe should be broken apart so that only those sections that need to be scored go to the sessions. Because of the time needed to get the projectors up to proper speed and the time necessary for the recording engineer to announce the necessary slates, which we will discuss shortly, Betty should pull about thirty feet more of the picture and track dupes at the head of the cue than needs to be recorded. About twenty feet before the beginning of the free clicks she should mark a start mark on both the picture and track dupes. This mark will give the projectionist an easy way to thread up at the beginning of each cue every time there is another take or a playback of that particular piece of music (and, believe me, there will be plenty).

The reels that will be going to the scoring sessions should be leadered properly and contain the cues in the order that they are to be recorded (this is determined by the composer, the copyist, or the arranger).

At the end of every musical cue, I also like to leave twenty or so feet of the dupe so that the picture won't cut off so abruptly as the music ends. After that, I like to put a short (three–foot) length of white leader to clearly separate the cue from the next one.

When all the reels have been built then Betty should have a list of cues typed up (*see* Figure 14.3). This chart gives all the information that anyone at the recording sessions might need to set up the mechanics of the recording.

In many cases, nowadays, the music is not recorded to a black and white dupe of the film, but to a videotape copy of the film. This requires a few different tactics from the assistant.

First, it won't be necessary (or even practical) to break out, from the film, only those sections to be recorded. Fast forwarding and rewinding makes it much easier to find the

SCORING REEL SHEET

Film Silent Night   Date 7·10·91

Page 1 of 2

Cue #	Title	Start	Click	Free	Time	Comments
	Scoring Reel One					
1M1	Main Titles	30+00	Free	—	1:13.2	
1M3	Abby Meets Sean	171+10	16/2	4	1:12.3	Int. at 56.5
10M4	End Titles	312+06	Free	—	2:13.0	
3M1	Going Home	552+11	12/0	8	1:56.7	Don't use guide
3M2	Abby Returns	749+08	12/0	8	0:20.4	
4M4	The Baseball Game	793+05	10/6	8	1:51.6	
	Scoring Reel Two					
5M7	The Shoot Out	40+00	Free	—	0:32.2	2 Alternates.
5M7alt	The Shoot Out alt	40+00	12/6	6	0:32.2	
8M3	At The Beach	112+12	16/4	4	2:17.2	
6M2	Return to 'La Bar'	337+09	Free	—	1:52.3	Source
4M3	Backstage at 'La Bar'	560+03	Free	—	1:47.6	Source

SCORING REEL SHEET

FIGURE 14.3 A page from a scoring reel list. The footages are continuous footages within the scoring reels. Note the comment for an internal streamer at 56.5 seconds in cue 1M3. There is also a note that the music recording mixer should not play the guide track for cue 3M1; this is probably because there is a piece of temp music there already which would conflict with the recorded music. Note also that the cue titles are often the same as those on the detailed reel continuity (Figure 8.5).

needed spot on the videotape where a cue is to be recorded, so one or two 3/4" videotape copies of the complete film will work just fine.

In the early days of music recording to video, in order to get streamers onto the videotape it was necessary to actually streamer the music dupe and to transfer *that* to video. Nowadays, there are rather sophisticated computers which will actually take the numbers programmed into them and generate the streamers, meaning that it is possible to record to the original color videotape that is given to the music department, or at worst, a copy of that color video.

The numbers which are used in the video are not normally the film footages but are *SMPTE Code Numbers.* SMPTE (pronounced "simptee") numbers are electronic signals which have been standardized to include a lot of information which is used to identify the particular frame which the code number is associated with. In theory a SMPTE code number can be used very much like a film code number except, rather than calling a particular frame of the film CC2034, we can name a particular video frame 3:07:36:19. This number is the sequential hour, minute, second and frame from an assigned starting point. Thus, if we assign the start mark for reel number three the SMPTE code three hours (3:00:00:00), then the first frame of the picture (which would be at twelve feet, or eight seconds) would be called 3:00:08:00.

Video footages run a little different than film footages. For one thing, there are 30 frames to each second, rather than 24. Thus, a SMPTE number of 3:07:36:29 would be followed by 3:07:37:00. Also, because of the way that video works, each second of video time is not precisely one second of reel time. Thus, a reel which started at 3:00:00:00 and was nine minutes and 35 seconds long would not end at 3:09:35:00. This became confusing to people who needed to know real-time lengths. As a result, another type of SMPTE code standard was developed. In it, periodic frame numbers were dropped so that at the end of nine minutes and 35 seconds the SMPTE Code numbers would read, properly, 3:09:35:00. This type of SMPTE code became known as *drop frame* code. The original type of code was known as *non–drop frame*. Both types of code are still in use today and many recording studios and computer composing programs are able to use either type of code. The code of choice, however, seems to be non–drop frame.

In any case, if Nate's composer is going to be working on video, rather than film, he would get several copies of the film on video. The 3/4" video format is most common in studios because of its professional quality. Many composers use 1/2" tape to link up with their computers and synthesizers at home, though. On the videotape that the composer gets he would normally have the time code superimposed on the picture (sometimes known as *window code*) as well as put onto channel two of the audio channels, channel one being used for the production track of the film. Each reel of the film would be transferred with its own time code — the convention is usually to number each reel with its number in the hour position of the time code and to begin the reel at zero minutes, zero seconds, and zero frames at the picture start mark. Thus, reel five's start mark would be coded 5:00:00:00, and reel eleven's would be 11:00:00:00.

Sometimes film footages are also superimposed on the picture, in their own window. These can be helpful to the editor when he cuts the finished music on film.

Timing notes are then given to the composer using the time code instead of film footages and when everyone arrives at the recording session, the picture is projected onto television screens rather than a film screen.

But let us assume that we are going to record the music for *Silent Night* using the film method. Betty will be bringing the streamered music dupe to the recording session rather than video.

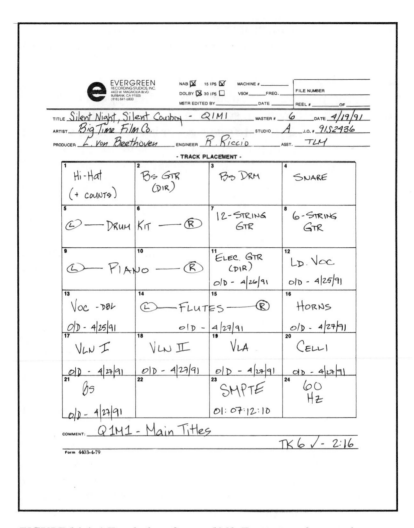

FIGURE 14.4 A Track sheet for cue 1M1. Two types of sync pulses were laid down—a 60-Hertz sync pulse (on track 24) and a track of SMPTE time code (on track 23). The number in the box for track 23 is the actual time code where the cue begins. The first ten tracks were all recorded at the same time during the original recording session on April 19. The other tracks were added later (overdubbed) on the dates shown. One track has been left open for technical reasons. (Courtesy Evergreen Recording Studios)

At The Recording Session

On the day of the scoring session (that is, the recording of the music) the assistant should get to the recording studio early. Copies of the scoring sheets should be given to all technical personnel.

Betty should have brought along with her the click track book, all the timing sheets, the continuity for the movie, a stop watch, plenty of note paper, and a few editing room supplies (a splicer, splicing tape, a ruler, grease pencils, etc.) in case changes need to be made in the scoring reels. All of these things might come in very handy in case the session does not go exactly as planned.

From the recording studio Betty can get some track sheets. These are preprinted sheets like the one shown in Figure 14.4 onto which are written exactly which instruments are being recorded onto which tracks of the recording tape.

Several recordings are made simultaneously. The first goes directly onto a 35mm piece of full–coat. The instruments are separated into three groups and each group is recorded onto a different channel. There may be some leakage of one group of instruments onto the channels of other groups because they are all playing at the same time into open microphones. But this separation will enable the music engineer to have more control over the sound.

A second copy of the music is made onto a piece of half-inch recording tape, which has four tracks on it, one for a *60–Hertz sync pulse* (or SMPTE code reference) and three for the three channels of music on the full–coat. The third recording is made onto twenty–four track tape. This is the same type of tape that we talked about in chapters 12 and 13 in the sections on recording foleys and looping. It is two inches wide and it has twenty–four different tracks on it so that the string section, for instance, can be split into violins, violas, celli, and basses if the recording engineer desires. This gives the engineer much more flexibility in the recording of the music since many things can be changed later if the original mix is not have to be precisely right.

On some films that I've worked on (*Hair, Fame, Rollover*) we made the original recordings solely on twenty–four track tape and mixed down to fewer tracks later. If this is the case, however, there will be certain other problems. First, since the music will not have been recorded onto sprocketed film there must be a way of making sure that the tape runs at exactly the right speed every time it is played, from recording all the way to the end of the mixing process. This is accomplished in one of two ways; either through the use of a 60–Hertz sync pulse or through the use of SMPTE Code. I prefer to put *both* on the tape, rather than run the risk (at some point during the recording process) of going to another music studio where they might not use that one particular type of sync. I generally put the two sync pulses on tracks 23 and 24 of the tape.

In some cases, the soundtrack is recorded digitally (much like the DAT machines now available for home use.) Because of the innate requirements of recording in this manner the tape must always be played back at precisely the same speed it was recorded at. As a result, you may dispense with recording a sync pulse on digital tapes.

Betty should list the assignment of instruments to individual tracks on the track layout sheet. Each cue should get its own track sheet even if they all have the same track layouts. You will eventually have to fill in other information about the selected takes and it helps to have each cue on its own sheet of paper.

When the first cue is ready to be recorded the picture is rolled either on film or video. The engineer or the music editor will slate the take ("Cue 1M3, Slate 1" — slate numbers run sequentially from the first take until the end of all of the recording sessions, they should not be restarted for new cues, new tape reels, or new recording sessions) and everyone will look for the warning streamer. The music editor will have his finger poised over the click track generator machine ready for the streamer to hit the right side of the screen. As soon as it does Nate will press the button, starting the clicks. The conductor will count out the free clicks and then begin conducting the piece while keeping one eye on the film being projected. Often the conductor will have a large clock with a sweep second hand in front of him during the recording session so that he or she can see how the piece is timing out compared to the timings that he has written on his score, which in turn came from Nate's notes.

During the cue, Nate and Betty should be keeping notes as to the positive and negative aspects of the take. There are often chair squeaks or misplayed notes that are difficult to hear from inside the recording studio but are quite noticeable in the control booth where they might be sitting (sometimes Nate might be out in the studio with the conductor). A take should not be approved until everyone is sure that there are no objectionable noises on the tape that cannot be mixed out later.

Either Betty or Nate should have also begun a stop-watch at the moment of the first note of music (most recording studios have their own digital stop watches that can be used). At the end of the take Betty should note in a sequential log the length of the piece along with any of the composer's or Nate's comments. The take will usually *not* be erased from the twenty–four track tape even though it may not be the pre-ferred take, and the conductor or composer (who are often the same person) may want to listen to it later at the music mixing session. In any case, if this was a take that the composer liked he will come into the control booth and listen to it played back and discuss its merits, technically and aesthetically, with the engineer and Nate, as well as Adam and Wendy.

At the end of the playback the composer will decide immediately whether to do another take or to go on to the next cue. If he or she decides to redo the cue Nate or Betty should immediately notify the projectionist who will then reload the dupes at the start marks for that cue. If the take is approved then the projectionist should be notified not to return to the top of the cue but to roll down to the next one.

As more and more takes are recorded, new reels of tape will be necessary. Betty should keep track of exactly what is on each reel of tape (there will be assistant engineers, sometimes called tape operators, to do this task but it is always very good to have your own notes to refer to).

Something else should be on the head of the first reel or at the tail of the last reel recorded on the first day — a set of *alignment tones*. These tones provide a standard for the relative recording levels on the tape. When the tape is subsequently played back the mixer can set his volume and equalization controls so that they make these tones conform to this accepted set of standards (usually the tones are standardized so that, when played back properly, they will hit the 0db level on the recording meters). In this way, the playback of the tape will sound exactly the same as it did when it was being recorded. In addition, since the tape operators or engineer will set their recording levels by these tones every day, each day's recording sessions will be done at the same standards. There should be a middle, a high, and a low frequency tone recorded (usually 1000–Hertz, 15,000–Hertz and 100–Hertz), about forty-five to sixty seconds of each is the norm. In addition, if the original tape was recorded in *Dolby®* (which it can be, regardless of whether the film is to be released in Dolby format), a *Dolby tone* (also called a *Dolby warble*) should be recorded. *Pink noise* is sometimes laid down in the case of Dolby films. See Chapter 17's discussion of Dolby films for more details on these tones.

On normal non-musical films it is necessary to come to the film mix with three, not twenty–four, tracks of music per cue. Nate will use the three–track that was recorded at the session (either simultaneously with the recording or at a later mix-down sessions) as his mix elements and use the half–inch tape as a backup for reprints.

About that mix-down session: after the recording is all over and the expensive musicians go home, the composer will often want to remix some of the cues. In some cases, as mentioned, no full-coat will have been running during the recording session at all and all the cues will have to be mixed down to three tracks. The normal manner in which this is done is to mix down to three channels of a four–track half–inch tape (the fourth channel will be used for the sync pulse; either SMPTE code or 60–Hertz). A normal mixdown arrangement is to separate the music into strings, rhythm section, and everything else. These three tracks are then transferred onto three–stripe 35mm track film.

Betty should, once again, keep accurate records of what is going onto each track of the mixdown and what mixes are on what half-inch tape reels. It is not uncommon to erase a mix which was no good and record over it. It is also not uncommon for a composer to want to mix down two re-corded takes and to have the two cut together to produce one take. Sometimes, this cutting together is done with the re-cording tape (either with the original two-inch tape or the mixdown half-inch) and then only one take needs to be mixed. At other times, two complete mixes are done and Nate will cut the 35mm mags of those mixes together.

Back In The Editing Room

After all of the recording and mixing is over with, Nate and Betty will end up back in their editing room with a lot of 35mm track and all the scoring reels. The scoring reels should be taken apart and returned to the music dupe reels from which they came. No marks should be removed from them since Nate will be able to use them to line the music up against the picture.

In addition, all the 35mm track should be coded. In cases of simple scoring jobs it is not necessary to code each cue and take individually. Instead, each reel of music can be coded (MA1000, MA2000, etc.; or 001M1000, 001M2000, etc.) After the reels have been coded they should be logged and given trim tabs which list the cue number, the name of the cue, and the codes.

The only time when a take must be coded specifically is in the case where there are several prints of the same recorded take (not different takes of the same cue). This can occur when three tracks proved to be too few for the mix, such as when a vocalist is singing with a band that's already on three tracks. In such cases both three–stripe mixes should be coded so that they line up together in the proper manner. This is done in one of two ways. At the mixdown a short beep would be put across all the tracks of the twenty–four track tape (except the sync pulse tracks) before the song began but after the sync pulse was engaged. This beep would, therefore, be on all of the mixdown tracks and could be used to line up the two mixdown three–stripes with each other.

Another way of lining up tracks is a bit more complicated. After the first mix has been done (that is, after most of the tracks have been mixed down to three tracks on the half–inch tape) then one of the elements that went into that mix is chosen and put onto an open track of the next half–inch mixdown tape during the next mix. For instance, if there was no room for a vocalist on the first three-track, when it came time to do the second three–track mix you would actually only need one of the three tracks. Transfer the vocal onto Track One and on Track Three put the drums. In this way, there would be drums on both the first and the second mixdowns. You would not use the drums from the second mix in the film mix but Betty could use them to line up the drums on the first mix. You would then code them in sync as we discussed in the section on coding musical dailies.

I like to have all music cues, whether they would fill up a three–track or single track mag, transferred onto full–coat since I have found it to be superior in quality to stripe. Music will show glitches easier than dialogue or effects because of its wide range of frequencies.

Nate will then cut the music tracks using the marks on

its wide range of frequencies.

Nate will then cut the music tracks using the marks on his dupe picture. He will mark the reel number and the footage on the cut piece of music, much as sound editors mark their cut effects. He will then give the cut pieces, the reel and the trims back to Betty. She is sure to end up with a lot of trims of music which are primarily head and tail pieces of the take, before and after the music. She will wrap everything up as trims.

After the music tracks have been built (and they will be built in the same way as sound effects tracks) and the cue sheets prepared (most mixers prefer their music tracks listed on separate cue sheets), all of the trims can be wrapped up and the tracks are ready to go to the mix.

At The Mix

Nate or Betty should bring with them to the mix all of their units, their cue sheets, their trims, their notes, as well as 35mm transfers of any Dolby tones or pink noise that were used in the recording or music mixdown process. The need for the loops is quite simple: the music recording engineers worked very hard to maintain consistency in the recording levels and equalizations of the music. It is important that the re-recording mixers play these tracks back at the proper levels and equalization in order to make sure that they re-record the music the way it was originally recorded.

They should also bring any alternate takes with them as well as the half–inch mixdown masters. Often a director will reject all or part of a music cue at the dub. Nate will then have to cut a replacement piece of music from cues elsewhere in the film and/or from additional prints of the acceptable parts of the rejected cue.

We will discuss more about the mixing process in the next chapter.

MUSIC REPORTING CUE SHEET

Film Silent Night, Silent Cowboy   Date 7/17/91

Cue #	Title	Footage	Timing	Voc	Instr.	Non-Vis	Visual	Composer	Publisher
	Reel One								
1M1	Main Titles	12 - 121½	1:13.2		X	X		L. Kumposeur	BTP Music
1M2	The Parking Lot	352 - 380	0:18.6		X	X		"	"
1M3	Abby Meets Sean	510½ - 619	1:12.3		X	X		"	"
1M4	Jimmy The Baby	625½ - 703	0:45.2	X			X	Mick Twiltone	Lotsa Music Inc
1M5	The Restaurant	736 - 900	1:22.7		X	x		L. Kumposeur	BTP Music
	Reel Two								
2M2	Can't Make A Nuisance?	716 - 769	0:35.3		X	X		L. Kumposeur	BTP Music
	Reel Three								
3M2	Abby Returns	422 - 483	0:40.6		X	X		L. Kumposeur	BTP Music
3M3	Birthday Party	483 - 560½	0:51.6		X	X		"	BTP Music
3M4	The Three Friends Party	794½ - 904	1:26.2		X	X		"	BTP Music
		(MORE)							

MUSIC REPORTING CUE SHEET

FIGURE 14.5 A page from a Music Reporting Cue Sheet which must be submitted by the music editor to the music or legal department after the mix is finished. The center columns tell whether the cue contained a vocal or whether it was entirely instrumental. When an actor or actress plays an instrument or sings part or all of the cue, the cue is considered visual (see 1M4, our bar song from Scene 19). Underscore is non-visual. Note that any cues which may have been recorded but not used in the final mix are not listed on this sheet (cues 2M1 or 3M1 for instance).

Paperwork And Other Sundries

The music editor has one responsibility that the sound editors do not and that is to provide something called a *music cue sheet* to the legal department of the company the film is being made for. As shown in Figure 14.5 this legal form describes exactly how much of each cue is in the film, who wrote the music, and who owns the copyright. This information is necessary for the musicians' performing rights organizations both in the United States and abroad.

Getting this information is relatively easy if the movie is all scored material. If it is not then there should be someone who is assigned the task of researching the rights of the music before it is used. All music must either be out of copyright protection (this is sometimes called "free and clear" or "in the public domain") or it must be purchased for the use of the film.

As a music editor it may not be your job to make sure that all the music in the film has been cleared before you go into the mix with it, but it is certainly in your interest to make sure that it is. On one film I worked on, we found out one week before our final mix that our music supervisor had not adequately cleared nine Motown songs that I had ready to mix. Five days before our mix, I found myself doing music timing notes so our composer could write all of the songs herself. We went back into the studio five or six days later and recorded nine acceptable but not as good alternatives to the songs that we were unable to buy.

In the cases where the film company is purchasing the rights to use an already recorded song, once the rights have been purchased then Nate and Betty must obtain from the record company that has the *master tape* (the original tape from which the album was pressed) a copy of the song so that they can make a transfer from it onto 35mm film for use in the mix. Nowadays, if a CD is available with the song on it, the quality of a transfer from the CD will be just as good (if not better). Because neither the CD nor the copy of the master tape will have a sync pulse, transfers from them will almost certainly not sync up in the same way as the copy of the song which is already being used in the movie as a piece of scratch music. In some cases this will not matter at all, but in other cases Nate will have to adjust the sync on the new tape (by transferring it to a tape while putting on a sync pulse and then varying the speed of a transfer off the new tape). When the proper sync has been established, 35mm full-coat copies can be made for the mix. These are coded and treated like any other piece of music.

In the case of musicals with playback material, the situation will be much more complicated. In musicals, certain instruments that are on screen may need to be heard above the other instruments on the soundtrack. In that case they should be on their own channels of the full–coat. This usually means that there will be many more than three tracks of music going into the mix on a musical film. In such cases, all of the music tracks should be coded so they line up with each other and they should all run simultaneously except when that particular instrument (or vocalist) is not playing or singing. Then Betty should cut out the track and replace it with fill. This will eliminate any unwanted noises from that portion of the song.

15

THE MIX

Finally, after many months of sound and music editing and way too many months of picture editing, *Silent Night, Silent Cowboy* will be ready to mix. Everybody will show up at the *dubbing stage* as it is called (or *mixing stage*, as it is called in New York). The picture, sound, and music editors, as well as other assorted editorial personnel will all be there with the mixers — everyone except Adam, who will show up later.

It will be the sound assistant's job to make sure that every piece of paperwork and every unit of track arrives at the dub before it is needed. The individual cue sheets are folded up, labelled on their reverse sides with their descriptions ("Reel 1, ADR" or "Reel 7, Background FX", depending upon how the sound editors have split up their tracks), and shoved into large manila envelopes which are labelled in the same way.

The units will be brought over, properly leadered, either on reels or cores and lined up in the *machine room* where the many playback machines are, and arranged on shelves so that the people who will be loading up these machines (these people are often called *dummy loaders* since the playback

machines are often called *dummies*) can easily find any specified unit.

And then, finally, the mix can begin.

In most mixing situations there are three mixers (or
re–recording mixers as they are also called) — one each for
dialogue, effects, and music. The dialogue mixer also functions as the supervisor of the team. In some situations one
mixer handles all three tasks. No matter how many mixers
you have, however, the procedure is pretty much the same.
You pre–mix, then you final mix.

Let me explain.

Often, the dialogue tracks will come spread across six
or seven elements (or units) with another two or three for
looping, the music might be on a total of eight channels, and
there might be as many as fifty effects elements as well as
eight or ten foley tracks. This gives a total of nearly eighty
separate channels of sound to be controlled individually. It
not only would be too confusing to do that many at one time,
but there are very few mixing boards in the world that could
handle that many tracks.

The solution to this problem is pre–mixing (or
pre–dubbing) the individual sections. The dialogue pre–mix
takes all of the original split dialogue tracks and combines
them into to one four-channel full–coat 35mm mag for each
reel, called the *dialogue pre–mix* or *pre–dub*. All necessary
volume and equalization changes needed to smooth out the
dialogue tracks are incorporated into this pre–mix. Looped
lines are either mixed onto a separate full–coat or onto two of
the channels of this pre–dub. Of course, combining seven
tracks into four isn't really combining all that many tracks,
but what the mixers are trying to do is save a lot of time at the
final dub.

At this stage in the mixing process the rerecording
mixers are going to want to accomplish as much of the minute
technical detail work as they can while still leaving themselves open to the possibility of changes when Adam starts to

sit in with them during the final mix (often the director will only come to the pre–mix to make choices of looped lines). For this reason, they won't mix down the dialogue to fewer than four or eight tracks (one or two full–coats), depending on how many they can fit into their mixing board. They are going to want to have the ability to change individual lines of dialogue as much as they can.

The sound effects are also combined into at least four or eight tracks, split in some intelligent way — general effects, specific effects for different characters, foleys, etc. Sometimes some effects will not be mixed into the pre–mixes at all but are held out and run as separate elements in the final mix.

Scored music is generally not pre–mixed at all, since it has been pre–mixed down to three tracks at the recording studio. Of course, on a musical film there would be plenty of need for a music pre–mix (on *Cotton Club* we pre–mixed music for several weeks), since music functions as importantly as dialogue in such a film (indeed, it often takes the place of dialogue). In cases like this, the music mixer at the dub will make all of the technical and volume adjustments as well as combining a few tracks. He will usually want to keep separate any instruments which appear on screen (the same goes for singers) which may need to have their volumes controlled separately.

During the pre–mixes, Liz, the sound assistant, should be taking thorough notes on exactly what is transpiring at the mix. Any track elements which were not put into the pre–mixes but will be needed in the final film mix should be kept on a list so they are not forgotten when the final mix for that reel is done. Effects which were in the built into the tracks but deleted during the pre–mixes should be plainly marked on the cue sheets (usually with heavy red slashes through them). After the final mix is over, these effects will need to be flipped out so it is helpful to have them plainly marked.

When all of the pre–mixes have been completed, the director joins the crew on the dubbing stage. Beginning with reel one, all the various sound elements will be combined into one soundtrack. Adam will be making decisions on the relative volumes of effects, music, and dialogue. He will be deciding if he likes the sound of someone's voice and, if he doesn't, how he wants to change it. He will be making decisions as to the texture of the film's sounds. The way that this is done is to play the various pre–mixes together. The mixer will struggle to get a pleasing sound and then everyone will begin discussing what they've just heard. Adam will ask for a little more door squeak at a certain point and a little less music. The film will be rolled backward until just before that point and the mix redone for that section. This method of repairing the mix at certain sections is called *punching in* and the process by which the sections to be mixed is called *rock and roll projection* (since you move backward and forward in the film finding the areas to correct).

The process is a long and tedious one, requiring a lot of concentration on minute details. Typically, a ten or twelve reel film might take as long as four to six weeks to pre–mix and mix.

When I said above that the sounds were being mixed down to one soundtrack I was actually simplifying the process a bit. In actuality, all the sounds are never totally combined. The mix is made onto a piece of four–track full–coat 35mm mag. All of the mixed dialogue goes onto the first track, the music goes onto the second, and the effects onto the third and fourth. This mixed full–coat is sometimes called the D–M–E as a result.

There are several reasons why this is done. The first is that it helps the rerecordist tremendously. If there is an effect which has to be redone they can just punch in the change on the effects channel of the mix, without touching the acceptable dialogue and music channels.

Another reason has to do with the creation of alternate versions of the film. After the completion of the domestic version of the film, the distributor will want to release the movie in foreign countries as well as the United States. In countries where English is not the native language they will be creating a foreign language version of the film in which that country's native language will be dubbed into the film, replacing the English language dialogue. Since the mix for our film was done in a way as to separate out all the English dialogue onto the first channel of the D–M–E it will be a simple matter to remix the film. The foreign country is supplied with a transfer of this mix full-coat. This transfer is called an *M&E*, or *foreign track*. The foreign distributors can then loop their dialogue and record over the English dialogue on the first channel.

There are, of course, certain complications to this approach. There will, naturally, be many sound effects which were part of the original dialogue track of the film (people moving, chair squeaks, etc). When the dialogue channel is omitted from the mix these effects will also be eliminated. Obviously, someone will have to put them back in, either by effecting them or by foleying them. This can either be done by the company in the foreign country or by the sound editors in the United States after the completion of the regular mix (the domestic version).

Most sound editors try to build their elements knowing that this foreign version will eventually be made. They split all these *production effects* off the dialogue track and put them onto the effects tracks (usually on units reserved for production effects, called "PFX"), filling in the resultant holes on the dialogue track with tone. Those effects that are married with the dialogue and, thus, cannot be split off, are foleyed and cut into reels which can later be used in the foreign version mix.

This M&E is part of the *delivery requirements*; those elements of the film that must be handed over to the film's distributor upon its completion (see the next chapter for a more thorough discussion of this). Some companies would rather not invest in making a new M&E for the foreign, preferring instead to send the foreign distributors a copy of the domestic M&E, letting the countries that they've sold the film to create their own versions. It is a rare case, however, where it is as easy for those in the foreign countries to make a good foreign M&E as cheaply as it can be done when the materials are all around — as they are when the original sound editors are still on the film. In any case, what kind of M&E the producer wants should be ascertained as early as possible.

When you have completed your final mix, it will be time to *marry* the soundtrack to the final picture answer print (about which we learn more in the next chapter). In order to do this, we will need to transfer the final mix full–coat (the D–M–E) onto a piece of film negative which will be printed together with the picture. This optical track is actually a piece of 35mm (or 16mm, if that is the gauge of the film you are working in) film with little squiggly lines on the left-hand side of the frame (*see* Figure 16.5). When light is pumped through a print of these lines it lands on a photo-electric cell in patterns that can be decoded to form the sounds that we recognize. This is how almost all films are projected in the-atres. This is why filmmakers have problems trying to sneak-preview a film with a *magnetic soundtrack*. Theatres are not used to anything other than an *optical soundtrack* (except in certain showcase situations; all 70mm films, for instance, have magnetic soundtracks).

This optical transfer is done on a special optical cam-era, which must be precisely set to the standards of the film laboratory that is doing the answer printing for the film. These standards are particular to each lab. In order to deter-mine exactly what they are, the transfer house which is making (or "shooting the optical", as it is also called) the optical track negative will make a *cross-modulation test* which is then developed by that lab and analyzed by the transfer person. Most of the time, your mixing facility will be able to shoot your track negative. In case they can't (some facilities cannot transfer Dolby track negatives, for instance) they can usually recommend a place that will do it.

Before the full-coat is transferred to optical negative there is one very important task that Chuck or Liz will have to do — they will have to prepare and cut the *pull-ups* for each reel. To explain just what pull-ups are I will have to back up a second and describe how soundtrack is married to and projected on a picture print.

You'll recall that film is projected one frame at time, each for 1/48 of a second. One frame is shown for that length of time then a shutter falls over the gate, blocking off the light, and in the 1/48 of a second when nothing is being projected, the next frame is pulled down in front of the gate. Then that frame is projected. The shutter is then dropped down again, and the next frame pulled down. And so on.

What we imagine is a continuously projected picture is actually a stop and go, stop and go, sort of process. The only reason why this works is because of something called the *persistence of vision*, which means that our eyes retain the image that we've just seen for a short time. If we project another image quickly enough (and 1/48 of a second *is* quick enough), the eye will never notice the difference between one frame and the next. We will see continuous motion. But the ear cannot be fooled in the same way that the eye is. It needs to hear one continuously moving soundtrack in order for it to hear continuous sound. None of this stop and go, stop and go stuff for our ears. So, when the soundtrack is married to the picture print, it wouldn't do to have it being jerked through the sound reader in the same way that the picture is dragged through the picture gate.

In order to get around this problem, the picture gate and the sound head are not located in exactly the same spot. The film goes through the picture gate (also called the "hot hole") and then is run through a series of rollers where its motion is smoothed back into a continuous one. Only then is it wound past the sound reader (in 16mm, the sound reader actually comes first and the process is reversed).

What this means is that the synchronous sound for any given 35mm picture frame is not sitting right next to it on the film, but comes earlier by a certain number of frames (20, to be exact). This type of sync is called "projector sync" as opposed to the sync that you have been used to where a picture frame and its synchronous track are exactly lined up. That type of sync is called "editorial sync" or "level sync."

Since the sound is ahead of the picture on the release prints (in "projector sync") there will be twenty picture frames at the end of each reel that have no track running next to them. There will also be twenty frames of track before the first frame of each reel. When the projection reels are spliced together at the theatres (as they are more and more), the projectionist will make the splice at the last frame of picture of the outgoing reel (let us say, Reel Two) and the first frame of picture of the incoming reel (let us hope, Reel Three). Since the track is ahead of picture, there will then be 20 frames at the end of Reel Two with no sound on them.

This would be a big problem.

Naturally there is a solution, and the solution is called "pull-ups" (we *finally* get back to them.)

Pull-ups, quite simply, are the additional twenty frames of the head of Reel Three's sound mix, which are spliced onto the end of Reel Two's. In this way, the track will run longer than the picture and when the track is pulled-up to get into projector sync, there will be enough sound to run all of the way to the end of the picture reel on Reel Two when it is spliced together with the release print of Reel Three.

In order to create these pull-ups the re-recording mixers will make an exact copy of the first several feet of the full-coat mix master of each reel. After the mix has been completed, Chuck (or Liz, often the assistant will cut the pull-ups) will take a picture dupe and the mix master full-coat of Reel Two into an editing room and put them up on the synchronizer. Then, very carefully (this is, after all, the sole copy of the very expensive mix), he will roll down to the last frame of action (LFOA) and mark that frame line (with a Sharpie pen or a pencil, not with grease pencil please, they are too oily) in the sprocket hole area of the track. Then, in another synchronizer, he will roll down the extra transfer of the head of Reel Three and find (using the pop on its head) the first frame of picture, the 12'00 frame. He will mark that.

Then, using a diagonal splicer, he will splice the short piece of Reel Three onto the end of Reel Two. He will only cut in about two feet (only 20 frames are necessary but there is no harm in adding a few more, so long as you leave a foot or so before the tail pop), making sure to remove the matching amount of Reel Two's mag.

He will then listen to each of the four channels of the full-coat separately on his sound head to make sure that there are no pops or funny sounds at the splice.

In some cases, the pull–ups are not actually cut by the editor but are created by the mixer during the mixing. This is preferable (though perhaps quite a bit more expensive) since it means that there are no physical splices in the full–coat.

When the pull–ups are done (and it is actually a hell of a lot easier to do than it is to describe) you will then be able to make an optical negative track from your four–track D–M–E. At the same time as this happens, it is wise to make a single stripe, *mixed mag* onto 35mm mag stock. This will be the soundtrack that you use for *interlock* screenings (that is screenings with separate picture and track), if you ever need to screen one of the silent answer prints.

In the case of television movies or shows (or when your feature is transferred to videotape for its videotape release), you will use either this mixed mag or the original full–coat D–M–E during the transfer to videotape. The reason for this is that mag film has a much better sound range than optical track (so much better that an entire industry—Dolby® — has grown up trying to get around optical sound's poor quality). The sound has a much better chance of being audible on television if it is transferred from the best quality masters. And, with the quality of home video sound systems improving every year, it is almost essential to have the best quality you can get on your videotape transfer. Mag film is the only way to get this caliber of sound.

There are a few other things that must be done after the mix has been completed. As I've mentioned, all the track elements should be conformed to accurately reflect what was really mixed into the film's soundtrack. Any effects which were not used in the final mix should be *flipped*, that is turned upside down so the underside of the track faces the sound head. Any new effects which were added should be cut into one of the units. Occasionally, new sound effects will be added at the mix from tape cartridges owned by the mixing company. Copies of this effect should be transferred onto 35mm film and cut into the effects elements so that if the film must ever be remixed the sound elements will truly reflect the movie's soundtrack.

In the end, all the sound effect trims and unused sound effects can be thrown away. All that really needs to be saved are the units, the original tapes from the looping sessions, the half–inch four–track music mixdown tapes, the original two-inch music recording tapes, and a set of proper cue sheets (as well as the other elements which you, as the picture assistant, have to supply; we will talk more about that in the next chapter.)

16

TO THE ANSWER PRINT—HO!

Much of what you will be doing to get the film ready for showing to Real People (translate that as "paying audiences") will overlap and be involved with what the sound and music editors are doing. Now that we have seen exactly what they will be doing during this period we can get back to what you will be struggling to do—get the entire film finished on time.

On The Way To The End

There's a toast that many picture editing crews I've worked on use whenever they are in the final throes of the editing of a picture. At this time we've probably been on the film for nine or ten months. We are preparing for the sound mix. The end of the film, while actually quite close, still seems to be very far away. At times like these, when we are clinking our glasses of wine (or whatever), I usually hear someone say something like, "To the answer print!" The answer print is what this chapter is all about.

The workprint that you have been cutting with for these many months is, in a sense, nothing more than a blueprint for the actual print of the film that audiences will see. With the amount of cutting and recutting that goes on during the editing of a film, it would be impossible to send that actual work picture out to the theatres. It would be so chopped up that it would be dangerous to run continuously through the projectors. And, of course, since the sound is on a separate roll from the picture very few theatres (other than screening rooms) would be able to handle that sort of arrangement. With all of this in mind, you can understand that you are going to have to come up with a way of making clean, spliceless prints to release to the theatres which are based on the print that you've been cutting for these many months.

The way this is done is quite simple in theory. The workprint that you have been working with was struck directly from the original negative that ran through the camera on the set (the *camera original* as it is sometimes called). In fact, this workprint is such a faithful copy of the original negative that it even includes the key numbers printed through from the negative. Any further prints from this negative will also be identical to your first prints from it.

When the film is locked someone goes back to the original negative and, using the key numbers, matches, cut for cut, everything that Wendy did on the workprint. At the end of this *negative cutting* you will end up with one reel of cut negative for every reel of cut workprint, and the two will have identical edits. When you then make a positive print from this cut negative you will end up with a clean, spliceless print of the reel that will exactly match your cut workprint.

The process by which you turn over your workprint to this *negative cutter* (as he or she is called) will be discussed in more detail shortly but the process by which he or she will cut your negative should be mentioned now. You have been splicing film together with pieces of tape during the editing. For negative cutting, however, the splices have to be made with cement if they are to be able to make it through the printing machines at the laboratory without being visible in the prints.

Actually there are three different ways of printing from cut negative in the lab. The first is with your one long strand of cut–together negative, sometimes called *single-strand printing* or *A roll printing*. This is the way that 35mm features are done. The second way is to make one long optical negative from the uncut camera original, incorporating all the cuts within this optical and printing with that. This is the way commercials are done. The third way is called the *zero-cut* method or *A and B rolling*. It involves printing the film from two (or, sometimes, three) parallel running rolls of film. We discussed this method in the chapter on opticals (Chapter 10). This kind of printing is used primarily for 16mm films.

The reason why A and B roll printing is used in 16mm films can be explained by describing the manner in which negative must be cut. In order to fasten one piece of negative to another, the pieces must be attached using cement. In order to do this, some of the emulsion is scraped off the top part of one frame and the piece of negative that it is getting attached to is laid on top of that. In actuality, the way this is done is to cut the outgoing shot a little long (by about one frame), scraping the first frame of the incoming shot, and overlapping these two frames. In 35mm the amount of frame needed to overlap in order to attain a firm splice is very small (less than one sprocket in length). But in 16mm, nearly one–half of the frame would have to be overlapped in order to make the splice hold. This would be visible when projected. It is for this reason that the zero-splice method is used.

One of the obvious problems with cutting the negative is that, unlike cutting the workprint, once the negative is cut (and that one–half frame is scraped off) you can never get back these frames to add to the head or the tail of the shot. Once that frame has been cut and scraped, it is gone for good. This is the main reason why commercials never cut the original negative but make an optical negative to print from. They very often have several different versions of the same commercial (ten seconds, twenty seconds, thirty seconds, sixty seconds) using differing lengths of the same shots. Though it is vastly more expensive to make an optical negative than it is to cut your original negative, it would be impossible for them to make all the necessary versions of the commercial without this expense, since by printing everything optically there is never any need to cut the negative. Features have neither the necessity for multiple versions, nor the budget to make an optical negative of the normally 11,000 feet of the released length of the film.

Of course, shots can be (and often are) shortened after the negative has been cut. That is not very difficult since the frame that was lost in the first negative cutting is not needed to shorten a cut. But this restriction on lengthening shots makes for something of a sense of finality when the negative is cut.

Previewing

Directors often have a sense of panic when the negative is about to be cut. One director I worked for almost refused to let the negative be cut until I explained to him that not only did every feature work that way but that no one was going to be able to see his film if he did not cut his negative. This panic is certainly understandable. Adam, Wendy, Philip, you, and everyone involved with the creation of *Silent Night, Silent Cowboy* will have been working on this film for

FIGURE 16.1 In the zero-splice method, cutting from shot A to shot B and then to shot C is accomplished by checkerboarding the negative so that the splices attach the picture to black leader which will not print up in the lab process.

three–quarters of a year or more. At this point everyone has certainly lost perspective on the film. What works and does not work is a subjective judgment in any case. It is complicated immensely by the fact that all of you know the film backwards and forwards, almost intimately. Things that are perfectly clear to you may not be at all clear to someone seeing the film for the first time.

For this reason, it is a common practice for the director to screen the film for an audience before cutting the negative. Some directors, like Arthur Penn on *Four Friends*, felt that open previews (that is, previews for the public as opposed to friends and advisors) were not useful. We screened *Four Friends* for several groups of friends and received feedback from them. Milos Forman, however, screened *Hair* many times for people who were given tickets on street corners. After each screening we handed out questionnaires and we re–edited the film based on any comments that seemed important.

Previews are virtually always done with the work print (since you haven't cut negative you couldn't possibly have an answer print yet), and are often at screening rooms that have double-system projection (separate track and picture). Some directors, however, will wait until the film is mixed (or scratch mixed) and then take it out to a neighborhood movie theatre to preview it. These sneak previews (or sneaks) are the final acid test of a film's acceptability to a normal audience before its release. These sneaks are generally not held in Hollywood or New York City, so that the reactions of a less movie-hip audience can be ascertained.

But screening in Denver, San Diego, Minneapolis, or such cities can create all kinds of other problems. For one thing, it is rare that you will be able to find a theatre that can screen double–system (in fact, it is rare to find such theatres in Los Angeles, though they do exist.) For another thing, the audiences are people who are used to seeing only finished films. Scratch mixes, bad prints, visible splice marks, and the like can upset them and taint their reaction to the film.

For these reasons, you try to create as professional a movie as possible at this early stage when you sneak a film. Films are only sneaked with a mixed track. If there are any shots in the workprint which are scratched, ripped, or missing frames, they must be replaced by reprints. If there are any shots in the film which have a distracting color balance, they are also reprinted. On *Network* we reprinted virtually the entire film in order to get the freshest, cleanest prints for the one preview that we ran.

The film itself must be treated with special care. If you are going to be screening a cut workprint (and you normally will be) you must have the film cleaned thoroughly before every screening. I like to have the film *sonic cleaned* before taking it out on the road. This cleaning, which is usually done at a lab or at a film treatment house, can remove all kinds of ingrained dirt which Ecco cannot. Sonic cleaning can often lighten your code numbers so it is not a good idea to do it more than once, but it does make the film look better than it could otherwise.

The problem of how to accommodate double–system projection is not an easy one to solve. There are two ways to handle this, neither of which is problem-free. The first is to rent a portable double–system projector (many of the big studios own their own), install it at the theatre, and use it instead of their normal projectors. There are many problems with this. The projectors are rarely as good as standard theatre projectors, they tend to break down more often and to be harder on the film. These are not good things to have happen during a sneak preview. Most of these problems can be ironed out if the people setting up the projectors get there early enough to locate all of the problems and repair them. Since this will often require flying in extra parts to the theatre, the first installation should be done several days before the actual sneak date. It is a rare case, however, when you will be given this much time. The screening, then, becomes an exercise in making do.

The second way of projecting double–system is to avoid projecting double-system. At this stage in the editing, however, you will rarely be able to provide the theatre with a final composite optical print. There is, however, another alternative if the theatre you are going into is properly equipped for it, and that is a composite magnetic track format. In this format (*see* Figure 16.2) a set of magnetic stripes is glued onto the edges of the film (this is called *striping*.) The sound is then transferred onto one of these stripes in a process called *sounding*. If the theatre has a magnetic head on its projector (and some of them still do, since it used to be a common format for "spectacle" films in the sixties; though I wouldn't expect to find it in any of the newer multiplex shopping mall theatres), and it is still hooked up, then the film can be run using the theatre's regular projectors.

The advantages of this approach are obvious, the disadvantages less so. Using the theatre's own equipment cuts down on the possibilities of equipment interfacing problems. It also makes for a better working relationship with the theatre owner and projectionist. Many people resent "those Hollywood types" coming in and completely taking over. It often seems to them that nothing that they have to begin with is good enough for "them Hollywood types," and that we want to change everything. In fact, this is usually the case. Most ordinary theatres have equipment which is so primitive and so badly kept up that it horrifies the average filmmaker. While we can do very little about how the released version of the film will be projected in Anytown, USA, we can control how it is projected during sneaks. And so we do. But this inevitably builds up a resentment. There is very little you can do about this except to be very diplomatic and polite while still fighting like the dickens to get what you want.

There are several problems due to the outmoded nature of 35mm magnetic single–system. First of all, since almost no film is released in the format anymore, it is quite

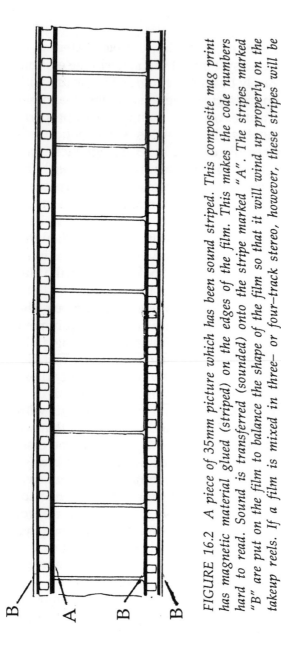

FIGURE 16.2 A piece of 35mm picture which has been sound striped. This composite mag print has magnetic material glued (striped) on the edges of the film. This makes the code numbers hard to read. Sound is transferred (sounded) onto the stripe marked "A". The stripes marked "B" are put on the film to balance the shape of the film so that it will wind up properly on the takeup reels. If a film is mixed in three– or four–track stereo, however, these stripes will be used for those extra channels of sound.

likely that the theatre projectors' sound heads are in a state of disrepair. One of the reasons that this method was abandoned in the first place (aside from the added cost of striping and sounding the film) is that theatre projectionists rarely kept the equipment in good shape. The sound heads got caked with the oxide particles from the track, making good sound impossible. Years later these particles are still sitting on the sound heads. Be prepared to clean the head very thoroughly and, possibly, replace the heads altogether.

Another problem with this form of projection is inherent in the medium itself. You will be striping a skinny little ribbon of oxide onto a spliced workprint. The oxide is placed on as a stream of liquid and allowed to dry on the film. At the splices it can often crack or peel off. This creates a sound dropout at the splice unless the striping, sounding, and projection are handled carefully.

The final and greatest problem with screening single–system like this is that most theatres across the country cannot run a magnetically striped print. If you are going to sneak your film in a number of different places, the chances of finding even a bad single–system projector in each of these cities is very low. You will have to screen double–system.

Most theatres nowadays don't even screen from two projectors anymore. They use what is called a *platter system* in which the film is spun head-in onto a very large plate, almost like a phonograph turntable. The film is then wound off this platter, over a system of wheels which guide the film into the projector, where it is projected and then sent over another system of wheels back onto another platter sitting either below or above the first one. There are no changeovers and all the projectionist or theatre manager has to do is rethread the film before each show, press a button and leave the room.

What this means to you, as the assistant readying for a preview, is that your film and your track will have to be set up so they can be *plattered* (as the process of putting your editing reels onto these large platters is called.) The first thing that you will probably have to do is put your movie onto 2000 foot reels, as opposed to the 1000 foot reels that you've been using in the editing room. The next (and perhaps the most important) thing you should do is to have both your film and the mixed track that you will be screening edge coded in sync with each other. If the film and track ever fall out of sync during a preview (either because of a breakage or a mechanical failure) you are not going to be able to put them quickly back into sync unless you have some new reference code numbers.

Taking the film "on the road" is not an easy thing. It is best to carry a mini-editing room with you. Try to bring a set of rewinds on a board, a splicer, tape, reels, cores, a script, a continuity and a box of supplies so you are prepared for any problem during the screening or any questions after the screening as to potential recutting.

There is no "normal" procedure for going out on these sneaks. There is only an "ideal" which is never reached. That ideal involves having several days before leaving for the sneak city to clean the film, make all reprints necessary (it could actually take a week to reprint, code and cut everything in), complete as many opticals —including titles—as feasible, stripe and sound the film if you are going single-system, and to run the film at least once with the film and track you will actually be using at the sneak. When you are certain that everything is fine, you would then fly out to the sneak city to meet the technician who has been installing your projectors in the theatre or checking out the projectors already there. Hopefully he or she will have cleared up any of the picture or sound problems that have been found. Then, preferably the day before the scheduled sneak, you will have a full run–through at the theatre with the projectionist who will actually be doing the projection work on the night of your sneak. In this way you can clear up any potential problems in the next day or so before the sneak.

An hour or two before the sneak you will go into the

theatre (which should be closed, rather than on its normal schedule) and run one or two reels of the film. I usually try to pick the reels with the widest range of sound so that I can set a good sound level. Check both projectors. You should then be ready to screen.

As I mentioned, however, this is the rarely attained ideal situation. Most often you will have to arrive at the sneak site the morning of the screening. If there are several sneaks planned in a row you will be lucky to get even that. You will platter your film and have a run–through the afternoon of your sneak. You will have very little time to correct any picture or sound problems. If you are lucky the theatre will not try and run their normal feature after your run–through and before your preview. If they do then you need thirty or forty minutes before your preview to run a reel of the film once more to check that the theatre's settings have not been changed. If you're plattering the film you should bring along an extra track print of one reel of the film (with the widest dynamic range) and run a sound-only test, since it is impossible to screen only *part* of a plattered print. In any case, most of the corrections that might have been tampered with are sound settings, so a track–only test will suffice.

Out-of-town screenings are a nerve-racking experience; everyone is tense. There is always a lot riding on the sneak, the director's (and the crew's) ego and the company's money, so everyone is incredibly nervous. For that reason you should try to get everything as perfect as you can and, if there are any egregious problems that cannot be resolved, to point them out to the director before the screening. That may not make Adam happy but at least he will know what to expect.

After the sneak there will usually be a hurried reading of the audience response cards and all sorts of hotel room meetings that you will not be invited to. This will be rather difficult but you have other work to perform. You should give the film a thorough cleaning on your portable rewinds, either at the theatre or in your hotel room. You should have everything packed up and ready to leave as soon after the screening as possible. If Wendy is going to any of the after-sneak talks you should try and provide her with whatever notes she may need (a continuity, script, etc.). Your primary job at this point is to expedite the movement of the film and the portable cutting room.

Negative Cutting

After all of the paranoia has passed, all of the screenings have been finished, and all of the recutting has been accomplished, you will find yourself at a point in the film that you probably never thought you would reach — the end of the editing.

When the film is finally locked you must begin to prepare for the negative cutting. This involves two things, marking up the film and preparing a negative continuity. Both tasks aim to do the same thing, provide enough information to the negative cutter so that he or she can cut the negative of your film quickly and completely correctly. After all, if there are any mistakes in the negative cutting they can't be corrected easily, if they can be corrected at all.

At this stage of the film you should have all pieces of the film cut into your workprint including all final opticals and titles. Make sure that every piece of film has key numbers on its edges. Occasionally the lab will forget to expose the blue edge of the film with the key numbers on it; if this happens have them reprint that piece properly. In addition, there are times when a shot that Wendy has cut in is so short that it has no key number on it. In this case, you will have to find the head or tail trim and scribe onto the blue edge where the key number would be the key number for the adjacent section. This will give the negative cutters the approximate frame they need. All that they need to do then is eye match the negative to the work print to find the exact frame.

All marks on the film should be erased so that the only markings there are the ones you are about to be putting on. The negative cutters should also have all of your negative — camera as well as optical negative.

The idea behind marking up the film is to mark every piece of film in the work picture in such a way that your negative cutters will be able to easily see how you want them to cut your negative to match. To do this you must mark where every cut in the film should be. You must also tell them where cuts will **not** be if there could be any confusion. You will write on the film any special notes that might help avoid chaos.

To help to understand why this is necessary let me briefly explain how a negative cutter works. The first thing that cutters do is determine exactly which takes they need to cut the negative of the film. Then they will separate out all these takes and keep them handy. They will then take your cut work print, put it in a synchronizer, and begin to run down on it. On a second gang they will be building the matched negative alongside the workprint. In this way they can check key numbers and visual action.

At this point all the cutters will do is cut (with a scissors) the negative on each side of the cut, cutting off the part of the next frame that they will need to make the cement join (as discussed earlier in this chapter). They will not actually cement the two takes together. Instead they put them together with a temporary wedge, which is actually a clip made of a cardboard-like material which holds the two pieces of negative together through their sprocket holes. This keeps the negative and the work print running in sync as well as postponing the messy cement work until later so that the negative cutter is not doing two things at one time. The actual splicing of the negative is done after this matching is all completed, often by another person. When the work is divided up like this the first stage is usually called *negative matching*, and the second *negative cutting*, though the two terms are often used interchangeably.

As you can probably guess, the process of matching the negative is very exacting. Once the scissors cut the negative there is no replacing it, so any help that you can give the matcher is that much more safety insurance for you. That is why you must be precise when you mark up your workprint for matching.

Figure 16.3 shows the various notations used in marking up the workprint for the negative cutter. There are notations for places where there are cuts, places where there are splices in the work picture but which are just extensions of shots, and places where a piece of leader was used to indicate where are shot has been extended (this last notation is rarely used except on lower budget films where a shot is damaged in cutting and there is not enough money to reprint it.)

There is also a second kind of negative cutting notation in which the run-through marks are smaller and appear only the track area of the film, and the cut marks are simply a vertical lines on the frame lines where the splices occur. The idea behind this style of marks is to keep the projected area of the film clear of all markings in case the picture needs to be screened again. Some negative cutters don't like this style of marking and you should check with your negative cutter first.

In many cases you will have to start marking up the work picture before all of your opticals have been completed (on *Meet The Applegates* we began cutting our negative while 18 opticals and the main and end titles were still incomplete). In this case you will want to make sure that your negative cutter knows that there is a piece of negative missing that will come later. The way to do this is to put a piece of paper tape on the head and tail of the shot that is to be replaced by the optical. You would then write "Do Not Cut!!! Optical To Come!!!" on the tape and draw an arrow pointing to the splice mark where the optical will be cut in. Sometimes you will need to move on with the answer printing and so you will ask

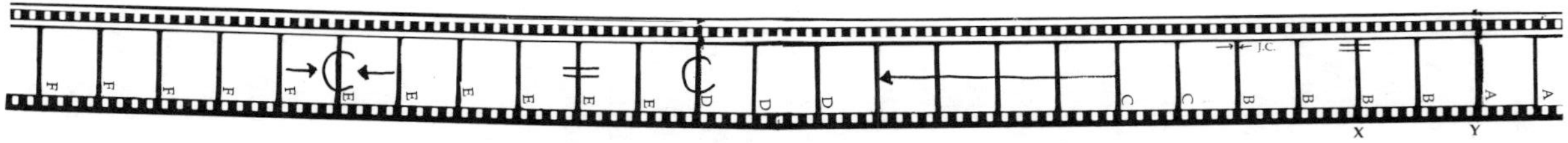

FIGURE 16.3 A piece of film marked for the negative cutter. Two types of markings are shown. The cut from shot A to shot B is shown with a thick line written in greased pencil. An alternate way of showing cuts is with the large letter "C" which comes between shots D and E. Run-through marks (at the letters X and Y) show where cuts were made in the work picture but are not to be made in the negative. The run-through mark at point X will not show up when the work picture is projected. When a jump cut (as between shots B and C) is made the notation "J.C." is written on the film. An extension of shot C up to the beginning of shot D is shown with the long arrow. Some negative cutters like to have cuts listed as shown between shots E and F.

the cutter to slug out the missing optical with an equivalent length of leader. This is called "papering."

In addition to marking up the workprint, some negative matchers request a *negative continuity*. This is, simply, a list of every cut in the film. See Figure 16.4 for an example of just how detailed this list must be. Many negative cutters do not want a negative continuity since they prefer to make their own lists. If so, it is a job that you can give up very gladly.

Answer Printing — At Last

After the negative has been cut, the reels are sent to the lab where a timer will look at them and decide what color balance each should have. Very often the timer will sit down first with the director of photography, the director, and the editor in a screening room and run the work picture once, usually without the work track. During this running, your director of photography (or d.p., as he or she is called) will discuss just how he wants the picture to be timed and Adam will pitch in with a few comments as well. Very often, the work picture has been processed with a *one–light timing* and no one will want the timer to match its timing exactly. In one-light timing, each day's dailies are timed at the same set of color balances and exposures, regardless of the individual needs of specific shots. Timing each shot, or even set–up, takes much more time and is therefore more expensive. But this means that many of the shots that are cut into the work picture will not be well timed. It is the timer's job, with the help of the d.p., Adam and Wendy, to correct the color of every single shot so that each looks perfectly balanced as well as perfectly matched to all of the other shots in the same scene.

Wendy's job at this point in time, aside from contributing a comment or two, will be to listen hard because it is more than likely that the d.p. will not be available to sit with the timer any more than this one time and she will have to supervise the timing of the remaining answer prints. By listening to what the d.p. and Adam want the film to look like

NEGATIVE CONTINUITY

FILM Silent Night, Silent Cowboy   REEL 3

DATE 6·21·   PAGE 1 of 7

Shot #	Footage	Key # In	Key # Out	Description
1	12 + 0	F32X63217 +10	228+5	MS - ROOM, MAN #1 in
2	22+11	F32X54098 +3	108 +2	MS - MAN #1
3	32+10	F32X54115 + 1	129+6	POV MAN #2 at desk
4	45+ 7	F32X54075+4	088 +1	CU - MAN
5	66+6	F32X63233+3	241 +6	MCU - MAN #2
6	74+11	F32X63262+4	261 +0	MCU - MAN #1
7	81+ 7	F48X21112+ 7	124 +3	MCU - MAN #2
8	93+10	F48X22124+5	129 +4	MCU - MAN #1
9	99+5	E23X26033+6	041 +6	MCU - MAN #2
10	107+6	E23X26052+2	060 +12	WS - 2 MEN
11	115+ 3	F32X63291+4	300 +15	MS - MAN #2
12	124+6	F32X66119+7	126 +11	CU - MAN #1
13	131+2	E17X14108+7	134 +11	CU - MAN #2
14	139+2	F32X66136+8	146 +10	CU - MAN #1
15	149+1	E17X14122+1	134 +13	CU - MAN #2
16	161+ 4	F32X66160+2	168 +3	CU - MAN #1
17	168+10	E17X14152+8	164 +15	CU - MAN #2
18	181+6	F32X66310+6	322 +14	CU - MAN #1
19	193+5	F32X63899+2	433+5	WS - ROOM w/ MEN
20	226+12	H16X11526+6	551+6	Dissolve to beach
21	251+12	F9X 76219 + 7	229+5	CU - MAN #1
22	261+10	E2X66606 +6	614 +3	his pov beach
23	269+ 7	F13X03219 +6	225 +2	MS - GIRL
24	275+6	F13X03620+1	623 +1	MCU - GIRL
25	278+6	F13X03811 +0	812 +2	CU - GIRL
26	280+ 1	F9X 76298 + 3	309 +10	CU - MAN #1
27	291+6	F13X03249 + 6	278 +0	MS- GIRL + MAN
28	320+0	F13X03416 + 1	422 +4	MCU - GIRL
29	326+ 3	F43X56219 + 6	200 +10	MCU - MAN
30	335+ 7	F13X03432 + 10	439 +3	MCU - GIRL
31	342+0	F43X56249 +6	255 +7	MCU - MAN
32	346+ 1	F13X03493+14	453 +15	MCU - GIRL
33	356+ 7	F43X56312 +10	318 +15	MCU - MAN
34	362+12	F13X03619 +6	624 + 6	MCU - GIRL

NEGATIVE CONTINUITY LIST

FIGURE 16.4 A sample section of a negative continuity list. Some assistants do not list the descriptions of the scenes. Some negative cutters do not even require a list, preferring to make their own.

at this first session she will be able to guide the timer through all of the subsequent answer prints.

Timing involves determining just what percentages of cyan (blue/green), magenta (red/purple), and yellow should make up each image. This is done by varying the amount of red, blue, or green light that passes through the film negative to the print film. These percentages are given as the number of *points* of each color, ranging from 0 points to 50. Most often the timer will go for what he or she assumes is the best skin tone color and attempt to match the rest of the shots to this.

In any case, after the run–through with the work picture, the timer will go away and, sitting at a color analyzer (called a Hazeltine), will determine exactly what balance he or she wants for every piece of cut negative in the film. When this task is completed this information is put into a machine (either computerized or on punched paper tape). During the laboratory printing process this machine senses when each cut is coming up (either by feeling for a metal tab pasted onto the edge of the film or by looking for a notch cut out of the side of the film). At each cut it adjusts the color balance according to the instructions given to it by the timer. For A&B roll printing, items such as fades and other optical effects are also programmed in.

When the first timed print comes out of the lab the most important thing for you to do is to make sure that the negative cutting was done properly. To do this you would take this *first answer print* (also called the *first trial print*) and line it up in the synchronizer with your cut work print at the start marks. Then roll down, stopping at every cut and making sure that the key numbers match on either side of the cut. Also make sure that no cuts were made when they were not supposed to be made. If there are no miscuts then you can approve the reel for screening.

Occasionally there are some miscuts. This has to be one of the worst kinds of mistakes for a film editor to deal with. At this stage, the film is either being mixed or has already been mixed. Depending upon how bad the error is, parts of the film may have to be recut and remixed.

The problem here obviously stems from the fact that all the sound editing and mixing was done to the dupes of the work print. If the negative for a shot of someone talking was cut in one foot later or earlier than it was supposed to be, the mixed dialogue will be out of sync by one foot. This is by far one of the worst kinds of errors to correct. It may be possible to find another take that can replace the ruined one, though it can never be as good (after all, Wendy originally chose the first take over the other one for a reason—correct?) Normally, some kind of fix in the mix has to be made to accommodate the correction, whether it is a new take or a correction to the already cut–in take.

The worst case that I've ever heard of regarding major laboratory screw–ups began when the lab storing the negative for a feature film accidentally destroyed a few takes of the film before negative cutting began. When the negative matchers went looking for the film they found nothing. As bad luck would have it there were no alternate takes that could be used and no possible way to correct the error with existing material. The editor had to make a duplicate negative directly off the cut workprint and use that negative instead of the camera original. The footage created was, necessarily, of a noticeably inferior quality than the surrounding material. It was the only solution to an impossible problem.

Horror stories like this are rare. Labs and negative cutters have to be extremely meticulous and careful when handling negative since their reputations and livelihoods depend on it. In the few cases where problems occur, they can usually be sorted out through the use of alternate takes. The splices in the negative are carefully pulled apart and the new negative is inserted exactly in place of the old one. If the editor is skillful the replacement will not be at all noticeable. On *Fame* there were a few problems with the negative cutting, all of which, though annoying, the editor Gerry Hambling was able to solve with a minimum of fuss.

When the first answer print is complete (or as complete as it can be; often there are a few reels which must be held back awaiting opticals), the editor, the timer, and the director of photography, if he or she is available, all get together and watch it (the director very often does not go to any answer print screenings). They will usually screen the film at the laboratory, making comments as each shot appears on screen (a side note here, lab personnel often use the word "scenes" when they are referring to individual "shots.") Changes are requested. The timer then makes new timing notes and the reel is reprinted. Several days later the second answer print comes out of the lab and is screened.

This screening process is repeated until all the reels are timed to everyone's satisfaction. As the process goes on, reels will be approved. Only the unapproved reels are then retimed and reprinted. It is probable that many reels of your film will be approved after the third answer print but it is also likely that at least one or two might have to be printed a fourth and fifth time. You will probably want to keep the printing to a minimum since the negative degrades each time it is used. But it is not uncommon to go through six or seven answer prints on some reels before approving them.

At this point a timed interpositive, (also called a *protection IP*, since it will allow the distributor to make prints of the film even if the original negative is damaged) is made of the film. From this IP, an internegative (IN) is made. Prints can then be struck from this dupe negative. The actual prints that get shown in most theatres are not struck from the original cut negative but from a copy of the negative made at the lab. For years, in order to get around the extra generations involved in printing an interpositive and then an internegative, these protection dupe negatives were made on another type of negative stock, called *CRI stock* (Color Reversal Intermediate). However, the interpositive process is now so good that it is rare that CRIs are struck.

But whether it is the IP/IN or the CRI process that is used, the theory is the same. All of the timer's color balancing instructions are incorporated into the striking of this dupe negative so that when prints are made they can all be made at the same setting, and no adjustment of the color controls will be necessary during the printing process. This considerably brings down the cost of making prints.

It is a good idea to screen at least one *check print* made from the dupe negative, since the timings will inevitably change slightly. It may be necessary to make some corrections in the IN in order to get a print that more closely approximates your original negative prints.

When the laboratory has a track negative in hand (as discussed in the last chapter) and has completely timed the film they will combine the track and the picture together. This answer print is called the *married answer print* (*see* Figure 16.5) and is hopefully the last answer print you will need. I never like to marry the picture and the track until I've got the picture timed properly, since that is the only protection you have that an earlier answer print will not get sent out for projection in some theatre somewhere.

As soon as the lab has struck the IP/IN for release printing (the number of IP/INs or CRIs struck will depend on the number of prints needed; distribution companies try and get at least 200 release prints out of each dupe negative, if they are cheaper they try to get more), they can begin striking the release prints. At the same time, you will also be able to get a few original negative prints (sometimes called *EK prints*). Since these prints are made directly from the cut negative they will be much better prints than the dupe negative prints since they will be at least one generation closer to the original (second generation as opposed to third or fourth). They will be less contrasty and sharper in focus than the IP/IN prints. For that reason a few EK prints are usually struck for the two or three big premiere cities. These are the prints that the big

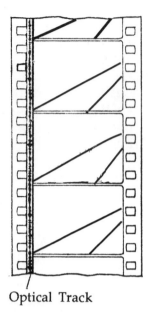

FIGURE 16.5 The optical track is the set of squiggly lines between the left edge of the picture and the sprocket holes.

Optical Track

critics usually see as well as the ones that open at the classy downtown theatres. EK prints, since they degrade the negative, are usually struck only for Los Angeles and New York openings, though sometimes they will be made for London, Chicago, or Boston. In such cases, it is common to make sure that two prints are available per theatre. On *Hair* we opened at the Ziegfeld Theatre in New York City and the Cinerama Dome Theatre in Los Angeles. Both theatres received two EK prints — one for projection and one for backup. Other major opening theatres, in Chicago, Washington, D.C., San Francisco, and Boston received two prints, though at least one of them was a dupe neg print.

Once the mix is over, therefore, you might be responsible for organizing the printing of the movie. You will be organizing the lab screenings for answer prints and making sure that the lab personnel have all of the materials they need to make a perfect release print. Once the answer printing of the movie has begun your tasks begin to get much simpler.

Special Requests

In the months before the release of a movie the distribution company is going to be gearing up for the release of *Silent Night, Silent Cowboy*. They are going to want to see the film as soon as possible so that they can begin to plan a marketing strategy and an advertising campaign for the film. Usually, their needs come almost at the same time as you are going through the worst crises in the editing room. You will probably be trying to lock the film as well as turning the picture over to the sound department. You will be involved in optical work and many other complicated items. Then the film company will call and ask if they can see the film.

The temptation at this point is to tell them all to go to hell in a handbasket and call back when you've got the time to talk to them — like in two months. Unfortunately, two months will be too late for them. I have seen directors so protective of their movies that they did not let the film companies have a look at the film until it was much too late. As a result, the advertising campaign was rushed and, usually, terrible.

Supplying the distribution company with its needs is part of your job as an assistant editor. Though you should never release anything to them without the prior knowledge and consent of Wendy and Adam, you must make it part of your job to do so. It can only help the film.

Early on, after they have already seen the film, the distribution company will want to get a black and white dupe of the entire film so that they can begin cutting a trailer. This is the "coming attraction" short you see in the theatres. The best time to give them this dupe is after the film has been turned over to sound. The reason for this is that you will then have already made an unmixed dupe track (which is what the trailer people should receive) to go with the picture dupe. It is possible that the company may need the film earlier, but in normal cases the sound editors begin to come on three months

311

or so before the mix and the mix is often six to eight weeks. At the absolute worst, this leaves five or six months between the first black and white dupe for sound and the release of the film, which is normally enough time for the trailer to be made, printed, and shown in theatres.

As post–production schedules become shorter and shorter, there are more and more cases where you will not have the luxury of this much time. On many recent pictures there have been as few as three months between the end of shooting and the release of the film. On many low–budget films this schedule might even be considered luxurious

But let's say that *Silent Night* is a normally scheduled film. You can then make an extra black and white dupe for the trailer department when you make the dupes for the sound department. In some cases it is necessary to give the company a dupe of the film earlier than that, even though the film will still be changing. When you find out who the trailer people are going to be (they are often an outside service that the distribution company contracts to do the job) ship them all of the material that they need. This will often be just the black and white dupe and the duped work track. If you have any music already recorded for the film they should receive that too. At the least they should be given the name and phone number of your music editor who can supply them with music materials as they become available.

After the trailer people have finished cutting the trailer they will do their own mix and make their own release prints of the trailer. In order to do that, however, they are going to need a negative. You, of course, cannot give up your own negative since you will need it for the film. Trailers, therefore, are made with dupe negatives. When the trailer company has finished cutting the trailer you will receive a list of all of the takes used in the film. Either you, or the assistant at the trailer house (from a copy of your logbook), will then order the necessary interpositives which will be used in the creation of the trailer struck from the original negative of the relevant scenes. The trailer house will tell you whether they need normal or registration IPs, (*see* Chapter 10 for more information on these). In no case is the negative to leave the lab or the optical house that is making the IPs.

If your film mix has already been done then it would be helpful to give them a copy of the mix in its D–M–E format. In this way they can do their mix from already mixed tracks. This will make for a better and faster trailer mix.

However, it is more often the case that you will not have even begun your film mix when the trailer people want their tracks. In that case they may want track reprints of some takes in order to do a reasonable mix. They are not going to be splitting tracks to quite the degree that your sound editors will be. However, they will need to split some of the tracks for overlapping dialogue as well as for some smoothing of backgrounds. You will have to get those reprints for them.

Throughout all of these tasks it is important to make sure that the bills for these orders are not charged directly to your production. This makes the accountants crazy. Even though all of the money will be coming from the same big pot, this pot has a lot of little categories in it. The making of the movie is considered a different thing from the selling of the movie and it is important that the bills for the trailer be separated from your own.

After the final answer print has been struck, the distribution company is going to start asking for prints of the film which they can screen for critics. It is a fact of life that a film which gets no publicity and no reviews is almost never going to make any money. Film companies, therefore, spend huge sums of money publicizing a film; more, in fact, than the film usually costs to make in the first place. Magazine critics must see a film months before it is released because their magazines have long lead times (this means that the time between when the writer writes the review and when it is published is often a month or more; often, as with *Life* magazine, it is over two months.) The publicity department will be anxious to get as many stories in as many magazines as they can. As soon as a print is available, then, and often before, they will begin demanding a print to screen for influential critics.

Often these requests can be accommodated quite easily. You will have a print or two at your disposal that can be shown (the first EK print that was fully approved should stay in the editing room for all your screenings). As soon as another print of the film is made it should go to the distribution company so they can set up their own screenings without continually bothering you. However, you should always make sure that you check the prints before sending them to the company. In their passion to sell the film the publicity people will often be willing to screen inferior prints simply to get the film seen. Make sure that no unacceptable prints go out for screening or, sure as the sun rises, they *will* be used.

Because of the increasingly short post–production schedules, however, you will probably end up breaking this rule more often than you would like. On *Heathers* we needed to start screening the film several months before a final, corrected mix was done. As a result we ended up showing a print with the incomplete mix just to have something to show. That was the only time that I ever knowingly allowed a bad print to get into the hands of the distribution company, and it was a decision which came back to haunt me when that print kept on showing up, long after we had the corrected prints to screen.

In many cases you will be finished with the film as soon as the final answer print is approved. In those cases, the distribution company will handle all the release printing and screenings.

Video Prints

There may be times when you, or Wendy, will be able to be involved in the transfer of the film to video. Because of the particularly contrasty nature of television, special prints need to be struck from the cut negative in order to provide a good looking videotape. This print is called a *lo-con print*, which is short for low contrast print.

This print is exactly what it sounds like it is. The timing lights that you determined for the EK prints are used with some adjustments (for instance, everything is normally made brighter by anywhere from three to eight points, as measured on a scale of fifty points) to strike a print onto a special stock which is very low in contrast. Then this print is put onto a *telecine*, a machine which projects a light through film and converts it into a television signal which can be manipulated and put onto a videotape. In fact, life being what it is, you will generally have to do several days worth of color manipulation to get the color balance that you put into the film answer prints out of the lo–con print and onto a 1″ videotape master. In some cases, you will never be able to get the exact colors again (reds, for instance, are particularly troublesome in a videotape transfer.) In some cases, you will be able to get better results on video than you were able to get on film. Shots which begin in light and move into darkness, for instance, are difficult to time on film since you can never get both ends of the shot perfect; you either get the beginning or the end, or compromise between the two. In videotape, on the other hand, you can program in a special effect called a *dynamic* as you are transferring the film. This will make the color balance gradually change in the middle of the scene.

As you transfer to video you will also have to be aware of another difference between film and videotape—*aspect ratio*, the ratio between the width and the height of the projected film image. The chances are that your film was shot to be projected in a 1.85:1 ratio. Television, on the other hand, is less rectangular and more square. As a result you will have to accommodate the difference somehow, since you will be showing more of the top and bottom of the frame than you did on film (another alternative is to show less of the two sides). Hopefully your camera operator framed most of his shots knowing that this video transfer would have to occur sooner or later. In that case, it is a simple matter to reframe those shots. In some cases, however, you will have to do some special contortions to get a visually pleasing frame.

Also be aware that, as you expose more of the top and bottom of the frame you might be exposing the boom microphone or parts of the set that shouldn't be seen.

Normally, the entire film is programmed into the color correction computer and then the original full–coat mix master (or a one-to-one copy of it) is put up in sync with it and the transfer is made. A 1" protection master tape is then made, just in case something were to happen to original tape.

After the transfer to the 1" master is completed a test print is made onto either 3/4" or 1/2" video (1/2" is what you are used to in the home—either on VHS or Beta) for the director to examine and approve, if he is involved in this process at all. Any additional changes that Adam requests are made and, after everything meets with his approval, several corrected 1" copies are made and the videotapes that you rent at home are copied from that.

Wrapping Out

Eventually, after all the screenings have been completed and all the prints delivered, it will be time to *wrap out* of the cutting room. That is, it will be time to pack up all of the footage for storage and close out the editing rooms. There are, of course, proper ways to do this.

At the time that the producer originally made the money deal for *Silent Night* he signed a contract with the distributor. That contract, called (oddly enough) the producer/distributor agreement, specified, among other items, exactly what things the producer had to hand over to the distributor at the end of the filmmaking process. A wording of the section of one such contract is shown below:

Delivery: Delivery of the Picture shall consist of making physical delivery, at the sole cost and expense of Producer, to the Distributor of the following items, it being agreed that Producer shall include in the Final Production Budget for the Picture, and pay for, as a production cost of the Picture, the cost of each of the items of delivery required hereunder:

1. One positive print,
2. One picture negative,
3. One set of separations (or an interpositive) and two soundtrack negatives,
4. One negative copy of the textless main and end titles,
5. One music and effects track,
6. A multitrack tape 15ips of the entire score of the Picture,
7. TV version of the Picture, as below
   - One positive print of each TV reel,
   - One 35mm CRI of each TV reel,
   - One 35mm soundtrack negative for each TV reel,
8. 125 copies of the Picture's dialogue continuity,
9. Twenty copies of the music cue sheets,
10. Such materials as Producer may have on hand at time of the completion of the Picture and also such material as Distributor may require for the making of trailers, TV spots, and teasers, and similar advertising and publicity devices to be used in connection with the distribution of the Picture. In this connection, Producer shall deliver the following:
    - 35mm black and white copy of cut picture,
    - 35mm copy of magnetic work sound 1track,
    - 35mm three-stripe magnetic sound track of Picture

10. cont'd.
- IP of sections of Picture used in trailer,
11. Three copies of the statement of credits,
12. Three copies of proposed main and end titles, and
13. One copy of the conductor's musical score.

We will now cover these delivery requirements in order:

One positive print—Simply, the final married EK print which comes from the lab.

One picture negative—This is the cut negative, with all opticals cut in, including main and end titles, that you used to make the EK prints.

One set of separations and two sound track negatives— 'Separations' is an old term which is now meant to refer to the IP/INs or CRIs used for release printing the film. This particular contract requires two soundtrack negatives. This is not uncommon.

Textless main and end titles—When a copy of the picture negative is delivered to the distributor it will, of course, have the main and end title credits in them. For certain forms of release (such as television or foreign releases) a different set of titles may be needed instead of the ones that you've put on. In that case, the distributor must have a copy of the background scenes used in the title sequences so that they can lay new titles on top of it. The easiest way to do this is to have the optical house, at the same time that they make your titles, also strike a copy of the title sequence *without* the titles. In the case of our main titles, where they begin in black and then fade into picture, that is exactly what we would see in the textless background negative. The length of the textless background should exactly match the length of the titles. The only exception to this delivery requirement is when the entire set of titles is over a non-pictorial background. There is usually no delivery requirement in this case. You will also have to deliver a textless background for any opticals in the film in which you superimposed any English words. On *Meet The Applegates* we had to generate textless backgrounds for all of the scenes in which the giant bugs talked with subtitles.

One music and effects track —This is the M&E track discussed in Chapter 15.

15ips tape of the music score —This is the half-inch four-track tape also discussed in Chapter 14.

TV version requirements—In the next chapter we will discuss the television version of your film. At this point, all that I will say about it is that any reel that contains dialogue or action which needs to be replaced for a television version must have new positive prints, CRIs (or IP/INs), and sound-track negative delivered.

Cutting continuity—Though this requirement is some-times handled by the distributor and then charged to the producer, it is often expedited by the editing room staff. For many reasons the distributor needs to have a detailed script of the film as it was actually cut (rather than as it was scripted). This rather tedious job is handled by a number of specialists who run the completed print of the film (often with a separate soundtrack) on a Moviola or flatbed and list every shot in the film and every piece of dialogue or special sound effect. This list is cued by footage so that the location of any shot in the release reels can be exactly pinpointed. There are a few cases where the editing room staff will hire the person to do this task. However, more often than not, the most involvement that you will have in this job is to supply whoever is doing the continuity with a separate mixed mag of the film. Please note that even though release reels are double reels (that is, made up of two of your editing reels) I have usually supplied a reel continuity with the reels as they were balanced in the editing room. This is to help the conti-nuity person know where the editing room reels have been joined to form the double release reels. This information will be listed on the cutting continuity because the original cut negative for the film is usually maintained on 1000-foot reels, not the double reels that the IP/IN consists of for the release printing. That is also why you will find that prints that are struck off the original negative usually come to you on single reels and all prints struck from the IP/IN come on double reels. In recent years some labs, notably Deluxe in Holly-wood, have been mounting their cut negative on 2000 foot reels for printing, as soon as the picture has been successfully timed (on the 1000 foot reels). In this case, the soundtrack negative must also be provided on 2000 foot reels. The advantage of printing in these large reels is that there will not be an annoying popping sound where the two 1000 foot reels of soundtrack negative are joined.

Music cue sheet—See Figure 14.5.

Trailer and other materials—This has already been cov-ered in this chapter except for the "other" item. What the contract means by, "Such material as the Producer may have on hand," is almost all of the material in the editing room. This is explained in more detail below under "Packing Up."

Credits lists—These lists should be supplied by the producer.

Conductor's score —Supplied either by the music edi-tor or the music copyist.

Packing Up

These delivery requirements should be delivered to the address supplied by the distributor. All of the special requirements, like the negative and release printing material, will probably already be in their hands (or at the lab that will be doing the release printing). In addition, certain of the materials may be sent to different addresses. For instance, if there is a music department at the distribution company, the scores, cue sheets, and 15ips tape may be sent to the music department. The various bits of paperwork will probably go to some office of the company. In the end, you will be left with several editing rooms full of material, much of which the distribution companies do not want.

They will, however, want a large part of that stuff. Among the things that they *will* request is all the original negative not used in the cut negative, all the original 1/4" tapes, all the work print and work track reels, all the trims and outs, all the mixing elements, the wild tracks, the lined script, and the logbooks. The reason for this is quite simple. Often, years after the completion of the editing of the film, changes will need to be made in it. This may be because of a possible re–release of the movie in a different version (such as was the case with *New York, New York, Lawrence of Arabia,* or *Heaven's Gate*) or a new television version (as was the case with the combined version of the two *Godfather* films on NBC-TV). All the material needed to recut the movie should be accessible.

It is therefore important that you pack the editing room material in as orderly a manner as possible. Thorough lists should be made of exactly what goes in every packing carton. Packing cartons are large cardboard boxes which are designed to hold a dozen of the two–piece, white trim boxes. The easiest way that I have found of packing is simply to begin at the AA (or the 001) trims and begin putting them into one box after another. On a packing list (such as shown in Figure 16.6) I list exactly what is going into each sequentially numbered packing carton. I also list the information on the outside of every box. I leave the boxes with the paperwork for last and, when everything is ready (and before packing the last box), make a dozen copies of the packing list. One copy goes into the last box, along with the logbooks and lined script. It is sealed and marked very plainly as "PAPERWORK — CONTAINS PACKING LIST." It will also have the highest sequential number (every box is marked with its number and the last number; e.g., "Box 45 of 103.") Copies of the list also go to the distributor and to the producer. I also find it helpful to keep one or two copies for myself.

Every box is then sent to wherever it is supposed to go. Most of these boxes are sent into storage, never to be seen

PACKING LIST

Silent Night, Silent Cowboy
(Name of Film)

Box#	Type	Contents
1	Trims/Outs	AA1000 - BB2000
2	Trims/Outs	BB3000 - CC4000
3	Trims/Outs	CC5000 - DD4000
4	Trims/Outs	DD5000 - EE4432
5	Trims/Outs	EE4433 - GG5000
6	Trims/Outs	GG6000 - HH6000
7	Trims/Outs	HH7000 - JJ6456
8	Trims/Outs	JJ6457 - KK6000
9	Trims/Outs	KK7000 - LL7000
10	Trims/Outs	LL8000 - MM7000
11	Trims/Outs	MM8000 - NN7630
12	Trims/Outs	NN7631 - RR7000
13	Trims/Outs +WT	RR8000 - 9000, WT - all
14	Trims - OPT	Optical Trims
15	Music	MX1000 - MY1000
16	Music/FX	MY2000 - 5000, FX1000 - 7000
17	FX	FX8000 - FY6000
18	Dupes	Reels 1-6 FINAL DUPE
19	Dupes	Reels 7-10 FINAL DUPE + DUPE TRIMS

PACKING LIST

FIGURE 16.6 A page from a packing list. Note that when trims with the same code prefix are packed in different boxes the last code number in the box (see box #4) is listed. Otherwise the code number refers to all trims with that prefix. For instance, Box Six would contain all of the HH6000 trims whether they are coded HH6236 or HH6999. Note also that because we have chosen to omit the code prefix letters II, OO (because they might be confused with 11 and 00), and PP (as it is reserved for musical playback) they do not appear on the packing list.

again. It is only the most important paperwork and the release and foreign release printing materials that are saved in a more accessible place.

While the boxes are being packed you should also be returning any equipment that you do not need (I usually hold onto one or two table setups and one Moviola until there is no more film left in the editing room since it is always necessary to check and repair things as you are packing them). Every piece of equipment should be accounted for and returned to the lessor. Any supplies that were bought and not used can often be sold back to the supplier or to another film which needs them. Sometimes the producer will want them if he or she has another film going into production.

After everything has been packed, shipped out, sold, or thrown out, the editing rooms should look pretty much as they did when you walked into them on the first day of your job — empty and somewhat depressing. I always feel a tinge of sadness at the end of a job, no matter how much I'm looking forward to a long time off. There is something a little naked about an editing room that has no editing being done it it.

I check around the room one last time, close the door behind me, making sure that it locks, march to the front office to turn the keys in, and then leave.

Usually for a long vacation.

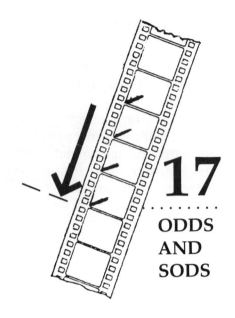

17

ODDS
AND
SODS

Now that you've been through the lengthy process of doing a film the "normal" way I should clue you in to a few of the kinks that you may occasionally meet along the way. These include 70mm films, Dolby® films, television versions of features and budgeting/accounting systems. This will only skim the surface of the various oddities that you will be encountering as you work in film editing, but it will be a start.

70mm Films

There are several reasons why a filmmaker might want to shoot and/or release a film in the 70mm format. The first is that the prevailing wisdom is that saying "in 70mm" on the marquee will bring in a larger audience. As a result some distributors will insist on a 70mm release for certain kinds of films. A second reason you might want to shoot in 70mm is for better picture quality. The picture area of the 70mm frame is about four times the area of a 35mm frame. This means that the film needs to be magnified less than a 35mm frame to fill a similar sized screen. In turn, this means that the picture quality of a film shot and released in 70mm will be better than

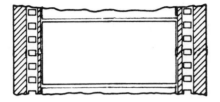

FIGURE 17.1 70mm film sound consists of six magnetic tracks which are pasted (striped) onto the film. Each of the wider bands on the outside of the film consists of two separate tracks of sound, and there are two thinner bands between the picture area and the sprockets.

that shot and released in 35mm. Certainly, some of the tricky optical work in the *Star Wars* series of films could not have been done as effectively in 35mm. In fact, whether the original negative was shot in 35mm or 70mm, all of the opticals in many of the recent special effects films were done in the larger format (usually in 65mm, for later integration into the final 70mm and 35mm prints). There is another plus that you can get with 70mm prints that you cannot get with 35mm, and that is good sound. All 70mm prints have a magnetic soundtrack placed on the film as shown in Figure 17.1. This leaves room for six separately running soundtracks. For this reason any film which wants to release in a six-track soundtrack format must release in 70mm. Because the sound is on magnetic stripe rather than on optical, as well as the fact that 70mm film moves one and a quarter times faster than 35mm, the sound quality will be better on 70mm than on 35mm. This is particularly desirable for musical films, which is why musicals are often have their initial release in a 70mm format.

A film need not be shot in 70mm in order to be released in 70mm, in fact very few films are still shot in the larger format. An *optical blowup* can be done to enlarge the 35mm frame to the 70mm size. However, there are two main problems with this. The first is that the quality degrades a little bit as a film goes through the optical process. A blow–up makes every little problem in the film's visuals stand out even more than most opticals since it will be enlarging the film's deficiencies right along with the image. Any shots which are right on the edge of sharpness will likely go out of focus. The picture will also become a little grainier. The second major problem with a blow–up is that 35mm frames are a different shape than 70mm ones as you can see in Figure 17.2. The common screen ratio, as I've mentioned, for 35mm film is 1.85 to 1, which is achieved in projection by chopping off the top and bottom of the full 35mm frame as shown. The normal 70mm aspect ratio is about 2.2 to 1.

Since the 70mm frame is far more elongated than the 35mm frame, the 35mm image will not fit properly onto the 70mm blowup negative without some adjustment. There are several ways in which this can be accomplished. The first, and most problematic, is to blow up each shot in the film in a slightly different manner, attempting to blow up the most important areas of action while losing the least important. In practice this means deciding how much of the top or bottom of your 35mm frame you can afford to lose. This way of blowing up is the worst when considered from all sides. It is extremely costly, since each shot must be blown up sepa-rately. It also destroys whatever composition the d.p. and

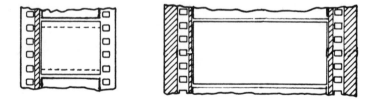

FIGURE 17.2 Note the difference between the 35mm picture size on the left, and the 70mm on the right. The 1.85 cut–off has been marked on the 35mm film and the 35mm optical track area is shown as a band with slashed lines. Note that the height of the 70mm frame is five sprockets, not four as in 35mm film.

camera operator chose for the frame; you are liable to end up with quite a few ugly frames.

The second solution is to do something that we did on *Fame*. That film was shot in 35mm but released in 70mm in its Los Angeles and New York premieres to take full advantage of the six–track Dolby soundtrack for the music. Rather than lose anything of the frame we decided to optically place a black matte on either side of the 70mm frame to reduce the screen ratio to more closely approximate 1.85 to 1. This was done as shown in Figure 17.3 and resulted in an image that was smaller than a normal 70mm image. As a result, we ended up with a 70mm print which looked very much like our 35mm prints but with a better soundtrack.

The third way to shoot in 35mm but release in 70mm is to shoot in what is called an *anamorphic* or *squeezed* format. In this format the image that is being shot is squeezed horizontally to fit onto a standard 35mm negative, much as the writing on a balloon appears to squeeze together as the balloon deflates. During projection the image is unsqueezed (or reinflated, if you will) by the exact amount that it was squeezed. This results in an image ratio of slightly under 2.2 to 1, the same as the 70mm print ratio. The 70mm prints are then made after unsqueezing the 35mm image. In this way no image is lost in the transfer to 70mm. This is definitely the preferred way to go if it is known that the film is going to be blown up to 70mm. The only problem with this method is that all of the 35mm prints made for the rest of the theatres in the world (and there will be far more 35mm prints made than 70mm prints) will be in this squeezed format. This will require a special lens to unsqueeze the image at the theatre. Most theatres are equipped to show anamorphic prints but since the alignment of the projector and the frame within the projector gate is much more critical than with regular 35mm film, anamorphic 35mm prints are rarely perfectly shown. The edges of the frame tend to be out of focus and frame lines at the top and bottom of the screen are often visible. For that

1.85 image

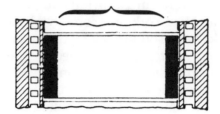

FIGURE 17.3 On Fame *we utilized a special 70mm blowup. We took the 1.85 image and placed it as large as we could get onto the 70mm frame. We then blacked out the remaining portion of the 70mm frame. In this way we took advantage of the superior sound of the 70mm format without ruining the picture image (which had been shot for projection in the 35mm 1.85 format).*

reason, the standard 35mm print is usually the best choice for projection.

Film which is shot in 70mm (actually the negative is 65mm, since no room needs to be left on the negative for the six magnetic soundtrack areas) is never edited in 70mm. 35mm reduction prints are made of the 70mm negative for dailies and cutting purposes. Opticals are, of course, done in the same manner. After the cutting is over, the negative cutter matches the 70mm negative to the 35mm workprint.

If the film is shot in 35mm squeezed format the work print will obviously also be in squeezed format. In that case, a large bulky lens must be mounted on the front of the Moviola to unsqueeze the image. This makes it a little more difficult to work with but otherwise it does not affect the cutting process. On a flatbed, the adjustment is much easier. There is a dial that you can turn to change from a normal lens to an anamorphic. In addition, on KEMs, you can get a special large wide-screen head so that you can see a very large image.

Dolby® Films

If you have been living anywhere but in Antarctica for the last ten or twelve years you have been aware of the Dolby phenomenon in motion pictures. The Dolby name seems to pop up on all of the biggest movies. As an assistant film editor you will have to be familiar with what Dolby is and what it can do because you are liable to be working on a Dolby film at some point.

Basically, Dolby does two things for movies. To describe just what they are let me take a short detour, to explain about normal film sound. As I briefly mentioned in the last chapter, sound is placed on the release print in the form of an optical track. The optical track system has been in use in the industry since the introduction of sound (magnetic soundtracks are a relatively recent development). As a result there are some standards that have been developed that are a bit outdated. The most important one of these standards is something called the *academy roll–off*. This roll–off is, simply, a standard way of softening the sound so that it will not harm most theatre sound systems. More specifically, it removes much of the high frequency sound from your soundtrack. This standard was much more practical in the old days of theatre sound when the equipment wasn't as good as it is now, but it remains a standard today and is something of an albatross in terms of cinema sound. It is just not possible to have very good soundtrack when there is no sound above 8000 Hertz, and decreasing amounts above 2000 Hertz.

The first advantage of using Dolby in films is that the Dolby noise reduction system (similar to that on a home cassette deck) puts much of that high frequency range back into the soundtrack. In essence, it sets its own standard, rather than adapting to the academy standard. Using this you can get sound up to 12,000 Hertz. Though this hardly touches the upper range of human hearing (the upper range of an organ scale is almost 20,000 Hertz, for instance), and is quite a bit less than good home stereos, it does add much to the fullness

329

of the sound that we can hear from a movie soundtrack. Dolby is, therefore, ideally suited to the soundtrack of a musically oriented film, or a movie in which there is a lot of higher frequency information.

The second use of the Dolby film system is the ability to get stereo sound in theatres. Prior to Dolby the only way to get stereo onto a film was to have separate tracks on magnetic stripes which had been pasted directly onto the film. This is the magnetic format that was described in the section on previewing films in the last chapter. However, it was never a very effective or cheap way of attaining stereo for the reasons discussed there. The Dolby system takes advantage of the fact that there are two squiggly lines on an optical track. It uses a special matrix to combine (in a process called *encoding*) four channels of sound into two. These two are then put onto the film on an optical track. At the theatre, during projection, these two are then *decoded* (through a similar matrix) back into the original four tracks. This method is often referred to as the 4-2-4 *method*, for obvious reasons. Since the Dolby four–track process is an optical process it costs no more to print (once the optical negative is made) than a normal optical soundtrack print. For this reason, stereo is now easier to accomplish than it used to be.

For the assistant editor, there is more work involved in the preparation of a Dolby release than for a monaural one. This comes primarily because the tolerances for a Dolby release are far stricter than for a normal film (you didn't expect there *not* to be a tradeoff, did you?) One of the most frustrating things about making a Dolby film is that the increase in sound quality that you hear in the theatres rarely comes close to what you heard in the mixing studio. In order to make sure that the best possible sound does reach the theatres it is necessary to keep strict controls on the sound during the mixing process and to do more policing of the prints and theatres.

During the mixing process it is important to make

sure that the *equalization curve* (the set of volume and equalization standards) that the film was mixed and transferred at is maintained throughout. The way you do this is through a series of alignment tones, much the same as I described in Chapter 14 in regards to recording the music. In this case, however, there are two different kinds of tones that are used to check alignment—*pink noise*, and *Dolby tone* (also called *Dolby warble* because it sounds like a regular 1000 cycle tone with a periodic hiccup in it). Pink noise is a combination of *all* frequencies of sound at very specifically set volume levels. It sounds to the ear like a sort of hiss (much like the sound you hear when you are tuned in between stations on the radio) When the pink noise is played back and read through a microphone by an oscilloscope, you can visually see how much volume level of each frequency exists in the sound. If it doesn't match the exact amounts that you expect in the Dolby standard (called the *Dolby curve*) then you have to adjust the playback system to compensate.

As a result, this pink noise and the Dolby tone are important references whenever you are going to play back a Dolby soundtrack (either married to a print or not). Liz or you should make sure that you always have a copy of the pink noise and Dolby tone (on loops, most often) when you are projecting your soundtrack, whether it be in a theatre or at the mix.

Once the soundtrack has been married to the print, however, it is important that you have these tones on optical loops instead of mags.

You will want to pay careful attention to the release prints of your film as well as the theatres in which they play in. On *Hair* three assistant editors sat screening release prints of the film almost around the clock in the weeks before the film's mass release. They were checking not only the quality of the picture print but whether the soundtrack was good. Because of the tighter tolerances of the Dolby soundtrack it is essential that better quality control exist at the lab. Many labs offer high–speed printing of release prints at a reduced cost. Most distributors take advantage of this savings. However, this increased speed usually results in reduced sound quality, especially if the lab allows their print bath to get dirty. It is important to check on these prints, as much as your budget will allow. Obviously, you can't check every print of a mass release; but you can try to check every print that you know is going to a major city or to an important theatre in a major city.

Another important check comes at the theatre showing the print. One of the biggest deficiencies of the Dolby process is that it is incumbent upon the theatres to upgrade and service their equipment so that they can play the improved soundtrack. Most theatres, being financially marginal operations, rarely invest the money needed to make sure that this better sound is played back properly. And, even if they do invest in new amplifiers, preamplifiers, and speakers, they rarely keep them in top–notch operating condition. Dolby has set up no policing policy for this and, as a result, many theatres which have the Dolby playback units still cannot play back proper Dolby sound. There is no point, after all, in having increased high frequencies if you are playing back your sound through a 30-watt amplifier that can't reproduce that better high end.

One of the features of George Lucas' THX system for theatre sound is that it forces the theatres to conform to certain requirements with the equipment that the theatres are using to playback the sound on films.

On many of the Dolby films I've worked on, I actually went into the theatres where we were going to open the film and tested the sound. To do so, we first played back the Dolby tone loop to determine the playback volume. Then we ran the optical pink noise loop (recorded at the Dolby standard), read the sound coming from the theatre's speakers with an oscilloscope, and finally adjusted the equalization of the theatre's sound system to get closer to the Dolby standard. We then ran a few reels of the film and adjusted the sound again, until I was hearing a sound as close to what I had heard on the dubbing stage as I could. It is axiomatic that no theatre's sound is going to equal the sound you get in a mixing studio. In fact, no two theatres are going to sound alike. Room acoustics are too different. I have even been in theatres where no two *parts* of the theatre sounded alike (this is especially true with domed theatres). It is most important to go for the best sound that the individual theatre can reproduce, even if it is not exactly what you mixed.

Dolby stereo prints on 35mm actually produce four–channel sound. There are three channels fed behind the screen—one each on the left, the center, and the right—and one channel is fed to the surround speakers which can be anywhere that the theatre chooses to put them. Common locations for surround speakers are on the rear wall or down the two side walls. I have been in theatres where they are placed in the ceiling, behind the screen, or all over the theatre. (I was also in one theatre where they placed the surround speakers in the floor, of all places, but that's another story.)

You can also get Dolby stereo on 70mm prints but it is of a slightly different type. First of all, it is a magnetic track, not an optical one. Second, there are six tracks of sound, not four. Dolby uses these two additional channels in a special way. They lead to speakers behind the screen in between the center speaker and the outside ones (for this reason the two additional channels are referred to as left-center and right-center). These channels, called *baby boom channels*, will only reproduce very low frequency information—rumbling sounds or low notes of the musical score. *Close Encounters of the Third Kind* used these channels extremely effectively during the landing of the spaceship. The low-frequency sound practically rattled the theatre seats.

Recently, a new kind of Dolby sound, Dolby SR, has come to the forefront. It is, simply, a way of getting even more high and low frequency sounds out of the theatre system. Films mixed in this format sound cleaner, fuller and more like really good home stereo systems. The biggest drawback to Dolby SR is that it is not compatible with earlier Dolby, called Dolby A. It thus requires theatres to upgrade their systems yet again, an expensive proposition, and means that a film has to be released in two Dolby formats. Though this situation in supposed to change soon it is anybody's guess just what a film mixed in the Dolby SR format will sound like when decoded in a theatre with a Dolby A box.

By and large, Dolby films are mixed in the same way as mono films though the effects and music need to be recorded on the tracks slightly differently. Effects will have to be planned to go either in the left or right channels (the surround channels are good for certain very specific effects—crowd sounds and the like—which come from all around rather than from a specific place).

The major difference between Dolby and mono film mixing comes in how the tracks are laid down on the mix master. The film is not mixed onto a single D–M–E full-coat. It must be mixed onto a four–track full–coat (or a six–track if it is a 70mm six–track Dolby stereo release). This four–track will not be split in the normal way (i.e., dialogue, music, and two effects channels), since it will be split for stereo—laying the tracks down in exactly the format as it will be heard in the theatre: left, center, right and surrounds. Therefore, music will always be mixed together with effects, and often dialogue (which almost always goes into the center channel) will be mixed with effects or anything else which also goes into the center channel. This would make it much more difficult to mix since, unlike a D–M–E system, everything would be mixed together.

The solution that has been adopted is a rather expensive one, but it is exactly analogous to creating a D–M–E mix. Instead of mixing on a three-track full–coat, you will mix a Dolby film onto three *separate* full–coats, one each for dialogue, music and effects. The music full–coat, for instance, will have the music laid down on it in the same stereo perspective as you mixed it, so instruments which come out of the left channel are on one position on the full–coat and instruments intended for the surround channel would be on yet another position. Each of the full-coats is called a *stem*. For instance, the stem which the sound effects are being recorded onto is called the effects stem.

You thus end up with the equivalent of a D–M–E, spread between three full–coats. This makes mixing the film as well as creating a foreign Dolby version much easier.

Another way in which the Dolby process is different from the monaural is in the creation of the optical track. Because the Dolby stereo format works by collapsing the four tracks into two in a special way, it must be treated differently. The last day of the mix is set aside to create the Dolby two–track *print master*, which is made from the four-track mix master. Then this two–track goes to a transfer house (not every optical transfer facility can do Dolby transfers) where a Dolby optical track negative is made. This is what then goes to the lab. Care should be taken to listen to the first print from this optical track since Dolby sound is more sensitive than monaural to dirt and printing errors and may not be correct on the first try.

There is much else to be learned about Dolby sound, enough to fill a small book of its own, but armed with these facts, and a knowledgeable helper, you can control the quality of the picture and sound of your film.

Television Versions

It is no secret to the millions of viewers of television that movies that have played in the theatres and are later broadcast on TV are "edited for television." This is usually because of excessive sex or offensive language in the original version which the television censors will not allow on network television. Six or seven years ago it was not uncommon for the network to reedit the film for their needs and, in the process, completely butcher the film. Recently, however, distributors have taken to insisting that directors shoot alternate versions of potentially objectionable scenes. In *Fame*, for instance, there was a scene where some boys in a school bathroom were looking through a hole in the wall into the girls' room where a number of girls were walking around bare–breasted. The director, Alan Parker, shot an alternate version of the boys' point of view in which none of the girls was fully uncovered. This type of *television coverage*, as it is called, is now more the rule than the exception in shooting films. No one is particularly proud of knowingly creating a bowdlerized version of their own film but the prevailing wisdom is that it is better to do it yourself than let the networks do it.

After the completion of the feature version of the movie it is the responsibility of the editor to create a television version of the potentially objectionable dialogue and action in the film. On *Fame* one of the M–G–M vice–presidential types came down to the editing room and, for a few days, went through the entire film compiling a list of everything that he thought would have to go. The list was actually quite amusing, being topped with a tally sheet counting the number of occurrences of each "dirty" word.

Someone, either the editor or a vice–presidential type, must make up such a such a list. Then the director and the editor should decide just how to deal with each incident. Some of the objectionable words will be easily replaced by looping them — words like "shit" can be replaced by "shoot", for instance. It is the responsibility of the looping editor to get these replacement lines when he or she is doing the original looping sessions. If some were missed then the actors or actresses must be called back to do these lines.

Items which can't be replaced by looping (either dialogue or action) must be replaced by recutting. In some cases, a shot of someone saying an objectionable word can be replaced with a shot of another person. The offending word/ sentence is either removed or looped. Always remember when making these reedits that any time a picture cut is made one frame is lost in the already existing material for the negative cutter's splicing.

This recutting is done with a black and white dupe and dupe track of the feature version of the film. New shots are cut into this dupe (using the color work picture and original dailies track).

After all the reediting is done you will have a black and white dupe of the film with the color print changes cut into it, and a dupe soundtrack with additions and deletions made in it. For all the reels that have had changes made in them, then, a mix and a new cut negative must be made. Obviously, you won't want to recut the actual negative made for the theatrical version of the film. You will, instead, want to make an alternate cut with a dupe negative. You will make a dupe negative of the reels that need to be changed. The negative cutter receives your television recut of those reels (if you've been a good assistant, these TV recuts should be plainly leadered as such) and will match to this new cut. It is also very helpful if you submit a television conformation list — that is, a list of all of the conformations made for the television version (the sound department will get a copy of this conformation list as well so they can create a television soundtrack). The negative cutter can then match the new negative to this print, cutting the new negative into the reel's dupe negative.

In actuality, however, if the negative cutter were to cut the new negative into the dupe negative, any resultant print would look very odd since the difference in quality between a print from the duped portion of the reel and a print from the new portions of the reels with original negative in them would be quite extreme. This happens because of the difference in generations; when prints from different generations are cut together it is usually noticeable.

The way to solve this problem is to make a dupe negative (usually an internegative) of the new material and cut *it* into the reel, not the original negative. When a print is made from this new cut there will be no difference in genera- tion between the two versions of material —the IP/IN of the original film and the IP/IN of the new footage.

You will also have to have a new mix made for the reels where sound changes occurred. You will often find that many more sound changes will be necessary than picture changes. It is your responsibility to make sure that all such changes are communicated to the sound department. When they have had a chance to make the adjustments in all of their reels then they will remix those reels and end up with new mix full-coat for the television reels.

The television version of the film is often the version that is transferred to videotape for distribution to airlines for showing on their flights. For that reason, it is a bit of a misnomer to call this version the television version. It is usually referred to as the *soft version*.

Money, Money, Money

One of the awesome things about working in films is the incredible amounts of money that are spent every day. Some recent films have cost almost as much to make as the yearly budget of many small countries. It is all a little obscene.

Though no editing room can ever spend anywhere near the amount of money spent every day during the shoot- ing, you will spending tens of thousands of dollars every week during the editing. About the only comforting fact of all of this is that it isn't your money you are spending. But the producers, who are responsible for seeing that the money that is spent is spent wisely, will be very interested in just how you are spending your money. You will be expected, profession- ally, to treat it as if it *were* your money.

During the shooting of a movie there are usually at least two or three accountants working for the film who are responsible for paying the bills and keeping track of how the money is spent everyday. Every week they must file reports to the money people which, in essence, track how much money has been spent that preceding week and estimating if the film is running on budget or not. As part of that process, an elaborate method of payment has been worked out.

Though that system will change slightly from film to film, the basics always stay the same. Every time you commit the production to spending some money you will either have to pay it in cash (and get a receipt for the expense) or write a *purchase order* for the order, listing just what it is that you are ordering and approximately how much it will cost. Each purchase order, or p.o. as it is abbreviated, is given a unique number and filed in (at least) triplicate. You will keep one of the copies, one will go to the vendor who is renting or selling you something, the other copy (or copies) go to the production accounting office.

Later, when the bills come from the vendor, you will get them so you can approve them. You must check the bill against your purchase order (the vendor will, hopefully, write the p.o. number on the bill) to make sure that the work was properly performed and that the quantities and prices are correct. That is why it is helpful to be very specific when you write out these p.o.s. If you've written a p.o. for one and one–half hours of interlock screening time, you will know that there is a potential problem if you are billed for three hours.

A month or so after the film has finished shooting, the production accountant will probably move on to another film. At this point, either a *post-production supervisor* will come on to the film to keep control of the costs, or Wendy and you will have to keep rein yourselves.

Film budgets are rather complex affairs, dividing every conceivable expense into strictly defined categories. Before the film is approved for shooting, numbers are plugged into all of the necessary categories. Salaries are multiplied by the number of weeks everyone will be working (this is figured out by the producers, the studio, and the production

Acct #	Description	Amount	Units	X	Rate	Subtotal	Total
855-00	**SOUND (POST PRODUCTION)**						
855-01	SOUND EFFECTS EDITORS						
	Supervising Sound Editor	14	Weeks		2,500	35,000	
	Effects Editor	12	Weeks		1,800	21,600	
	2nd Effects Editor	8	Weeks		1,500	12,000	
	Dialogue Editor	10	Weeks		1,800	18,000	
	Foley Editor	10	Weeks		1,800	18,000	
	1st Assistant	14	Weeks		1,200	16,800	
	Additional Assistants	12	Weeks	2	900	21,600	
	Apprentice Editor	12	Weeks		600	7,200	150,200
855-02	ADR EDITOR						
	ADR Editor	8	Weeks		1,800	14,400	14,400
855-03	LOOPING/ADR						
	Stage	56	Hours		300	16,800	
	Full-Coat	40,000	Feet		0.07	2,800	
	Single-Stripe	40,000	Feet		0.04	1,600	
	1/4" Tape	4	Rolls		15	60	
	Loop Group	1	Day	10	400	4,000	25,260
855-04	FOLEY						
	Stage	90	Hours		300	27,000	
	Stock Costs	40,000	Feet		0.07	2,800	
	Stringoffs - Stock	100,000	Feet		0.04	4,000	
	Stringoffs - Labor	100,000	Feet		0.04	4,000	
	Walkers	10	Days	2	350	7,000	44,800
855-05	MUSIC EDITOR						
	Music Editor	12	Weeks		1,600	19,200	
	Assistant Music Editor	8	Weeks		900	7,200	26,400
855-10	SOUND EFFECTS TRANSFERS						
	Stereo Effects - Labor	100,000	Feet		0.03	3,000	
	Mono Effects - Labor	125,000	Feet		0.025	3,125	
	Dialogue - Labor	80,000	Feet		0.025	2,000	
	Full-Coat Stock	100,000	Feet		0.04	4,000	
	Single-Stripe Stock	205,000	Feet		0.03	6,150	18,275
855-11	SUPPLIES & EXPENDIBLES		Allow		2,500	2,500	2,500
855-12	MUSIC TRANSFERS						
	Transfer - Labor	20,000	Feet		0.04	800	
	Full-Coat Stock	20,000	Feet		0.07	1,400	2,200
855-30	TEMP DUB						
	Stage	18	Hours		500	9,000	
	Stock	10,000	Feet		0.07	700	9,700

FIGURE 17.4 A section of a post-production budget, in this case created on the computer program "Movie Magic." The account numbers on the left hand side of the page can be broken down even further. When you receive and okay a bill, the production accountant can give it a very specific number. In this way the costs of a film can be tracked and, hopefully, controlled. (Courtesy Screenplay Systems Inc.)

manager). A total for the entire film's production cost is arrived at and that amount of money is approved. Actually, the process is much more complicated than that since a studio might want to spend less money on the film than it is budgeted at. Then the production manager will have to figure out where to cut costs — in the number of weeks the crew will work, in the number of crew members, or in salaries, for instance.

In any case, every bill which the production accountants receive has to be coded into the particular category that the cost is to be charged against. Music transfers should be charged to the music budget, picture reprints should be charged against the reprint category but B–negative prints ordered during the shoot should be charged against the production's laboratory expenses. A portion of one particular budget's post–production section is shown in Figure 17.4. You can see the complexity of the budget's various details.

Almost all budgets and accountant work is now done on computers. Programs, like 'Movie Magic', from Screenplay Systems in Burbank, California, 'MacToolkit Budget', available from Max3, Inc. in Santa Monica, California and the DISC System are in wide use. Some of the programs are only budget programs, others track all expenses as they are incurred, write checks, and can project how over or under budget the film is.

It is not necessary that you be aware of exactly how the accountants on your film do their job. But the more you know what it is they do, the better you can interface with them. At lease you will understand why they are asking you for the complicated purchase orders and bill approvals.

18

VIDEO
IN THE
EDITING
ROOM

Over the last few years there has been an increasing awareness of video technology by film directors, producers and editors. Video was first used on the set, where a simultaneous video recording of the scene being shot on film could give everyone an instantaneous playback of every take (almost like an immediate dailies session). Many directors liked this ability, called *video assist*.

Then, on *Apocalypse Now*, Francis Coppola began doing some of his editing on a small videotape editing system. Using this system he was able to experiment with opticals in a way that would have been extremely costly and time consuming on film. Though all the optical and editing work was ultimately done on film, the time that video editing saved him obviously intrigued Coppola enough to try and edit his next film, *One From the Heart*, completely on video.

Though there are still problems associated with it, video/digital editing (more on that in a minute) is plainly the wave of the future. As more and more filmmakers begin to turn to video in the editing process the technology will improve. And as the technology improves, more and more films will be edited in that way. Virtually all television news is now edited on videotape. Many episodic television shows are being shot on film but edited on video. Some independent filmmakers are also turning to video to help speed up their schedules and to save them money. Can big budget feature filmmaking hold out forever?

Obviously no one really knows the answer to that question. But my instinctive feeling is that the editor of the future who knows nothing about video/digital editing will be in an anachronistic minority.

At the very least, many feature editors today will transfer their dailies to a set of videotapes so that they can go back and look at complete takes even after they have been cut into the work picture. Many will even transfer a finished workprint so that they have a visual reference for different versions.

On *Meet The Applegates* we went one step further. We first cut the title sequence, a long sequence of dissolves from one jungle scene into another, on videotape. We did this both to save money (actually testing each of those opticals on film would have been ferociously expensive) and to help us determine exactly how much of the stock footage we needed to order. After we had a cut on video that we were happy with, we ordered the IP and prints from the stock footage house and matched our film cut to the video cut. In another case, we tried a new arrangement of scenes out on video rather than cutting it all on film, saving ourselves a bit of time and wasted energy.

These examples, however, just scratch the surface of what video can do in a cutting room.

Recently, several computer video editing systems have been developed which promise to lead the way towards the day when film can be more practically edited using video technology. Eventually, when digital video and sound (in which all picture images and sound can be encoded in a computer) become a practical and financial reality, computer editing systems will be able to shuck their dependence on cumbersome videotape or videodiscs. When that happens, computer editing will become a fact of life in feature editing rooms.

How A Cut Is Made

The basics of the videotape editing process rest on the SMPTE code number described in Chapter 14 (Music Editing). The editor tells a computer on what frame he or she wants to cut out of a particular take. The editor will also tell the computer what frame he or she wants to cut *to* on another take. The computer reads the SMPTE numbers from the videotape (or videodisc) of these two takes, adjusts the video electronically so that the images will line up perfectly and then, on another piece of tape, makes the edit for you. The editor never actually cuts the videotapes of the takes; instead he or she creates an entirely different tape which has the cut on it (the "edit.")

On the newer systems, the computer doesn't actually transfer the cut to another piece of tape at all, but instead stores the edit information in a computer's memory. It then controls a large number of video playback machines to recreate the edit each time you make it.

These systems, such as the Montage, the Editroid, Touchvision, and Ediflex, are called *non-linear* because they do not need to create an actual video copy of the cut until the editor wishes to make one for screening elsewhere. To see the *assembled edit* (which is like the *cut* in film) these systems, using a computer and multiple video copies of the footage, move very quickly from one edit point to another on many different video machines, playing back the cut for you each time. In effect, it recreates the cut for you, rather than physically making it. At present, these editing systems use videotape or videodisc to store and retrieve the images that the editor is cutting. Eventually these images and sounds will be able to be digitally stored inside the computer's memory. At that point, video editing will cease to exist and these systems will become true computer or *digital* editing systems. Cutting will be faster and less cumbersome, since you won't need to transfer the picture and sound dailies to a dozen videotapes in order to work. Soon, the term "video editing" will become a misnomer. "Computer editing" or "digital editing" will be the terms of the future.

Each of these video editing system has its own rules and tricks, many of which take weeks to learn and months to master. In fact, before you start work on a film using any of these systems you will take a short course to learn the details about how each works. What I am going to take you on is a cursory tour of how you might set up *Silent Night, Silent Cowboy* on one of the systems, in this case, the Ediflex.

General Overview

The processes of editing electronically has both similarities and differences to what you are used to by now in a film–based editing room.

One similarity is that the film will still be shot on 35mm film and the sound recorded on 1/4" tape. The negative will still go to the laboratory to be processed. No one on the set need do anything differently (though they might put SMPTE code on the sound and picture).

It is only at this stage that the process begins to look different, and the degree of difference depends on how much work on film will be done. On many television shows and all rock videos, nothing further is done with the film. No work prints are made, no soundtrack is transferred. Everything is done electronically. After the negative has been processed it (and the 1/4" sound) will go to a video transfer house where they will be sunk up for you while they are transferred to a videotape which we will call a *video master roll* (or a *CMX roll*, since that is the prevailing standard machine in most video-tape houses). You will receive a copy of this video master roll in the editing room. You will then have the responsibility of letting the computer know what take is on each roll of videotape, the SMPTE code numbers for each take, and exactly what lines of the script are contained in each take.

Since non–linear systems work by shuttling around a large number of videotaped copies of the film's footage under the command of a computer, you will have to prepare all of these copies for Wendy. She will then take these tapes and the information that you put into the computer and proceed to cut the film. When she (and Adam) are all finished cutting, the computer will spit out a list of where all of the edits have been made which your negative cutter can work from as he or she matches the negative.

Some directors, producers, editors and directors of photography need to screen dailies on film, even if that is the last time that they will see anything that way. Optimally though, the producer of a big budget film will want to take full advantage of both media, viewing dailies on film, establishing a cut on tape and then conforming the printed dailies into a workprint for each screening. This method is more labor intensive since film dailies will have to be sunk, and film edits conformed to the electronic edit in addition to performing all of the video tasks. But this enables the crew of a feature film to see the film the way the audience will — on 35mm, though this also may change in the future (see the section on High Definition Television at the end of this chapter). Though many movies skip the synching and conforming of film in order to save time and money, that is how we will approach *Silent Night, Silent Cowboy*.

To see how the film and electronic editing process differ take a look at Figure 18.1 and 18.2.

Before You Receive The Dailies

One of the advantages of the Ediflex system (*see* Figure 18.3) is that it is very script and image oriented, much like a film cutting room system. There is no keyboard to type numbers, instead you will work with one computer screen, a pair of television monitors where you will see your film, and

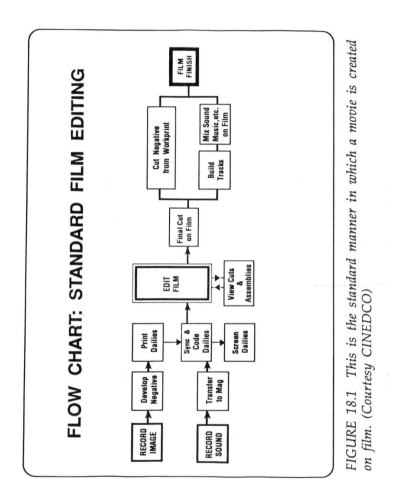

FIGURE 18.1 *This is the standard manner in which a movie is created on film. (Courtesy CINEDCO)*

347

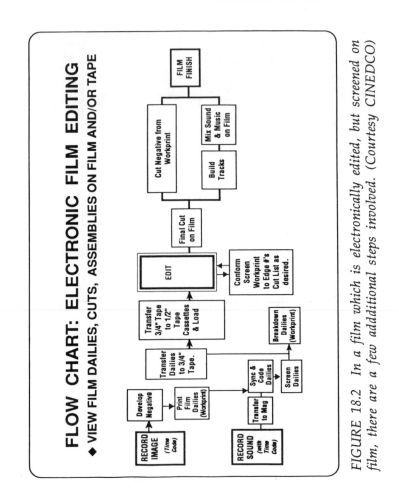

FIGURE 18.2 *In a film which is electronically edited, but screened on film, there are a few addditional steps involved. (Courtesy CINEDCO)*

a little light pen (which will act as your pointing finger and splicer all rolled into one). You, as the assistant, will have to prepare the many 1/2" videocassette tapes that are used in the editing process, as well as tell the Ediflex system just what code numbers line up with what lines of dialogue or action.

To do this, you will need to *line the script*. This is a two step process. First, you will divide the script into *files*. A file is simply a chunk of the script which is small enough for the computer system to handle. In television, it is handy to divide up each scripted act into two or three files (each containing about seven to ten minutes of screen time). In feature films it is more common to divide up the script into sequences, with each file containing three or four scenes.

Take your script (you can do this even before the first day of shooting) and draw big thick lines in between scenes that you are placing in different files. For example, if you are making file number one go from scene one through four you would draw a big line (I like to do mine in red or some color that is different from the black that the script is typed in) in between scene four (the end of File #1) and scene five (the beginning of File #2).

After determining which scenes each file will contain you should then divide the script up into *lines*. A line is, simply, a further subdivision of the file. It can be a single line of dialog, a section of a longer speech, or a short description of action. In the Ediflex system each line can be no more than about one minute in length (or less than one–third of a second), but you will probably find it more helpful to break long speeches into more manageable chunks of about 15 to 20 seconds. Try to anticipate how long action sequences will be: obviously the one line "He crosses to the door" will need less time to execute than "There is a submarine fight off the English coast." A good rule of thumb is to break each action sequence into short sections, with each line referring to a separate action or element (*see* Figure 18.4). It is a good idea

FIGURE 18.3 The Ediflex system, one form of non-linear computer editing. The system works by shuttling a large number of video machines (in this case, twelve 1/2" VHS machines) back and forth, finding and projecting edit points on the two television monitors on top of the desk where the editor sits. In the desk is a computer which controls the VHS machines, as well as the 3/4" master machine on the right. The editor controls the computer by pointing a little light pen at the computer screen in the desk. (Courtesy CINEDCO)

to keep the number of lines in any one file limited to around 60.

You will then give each line a sequential number within the file. Write this number down in your script next to the line on the left–hand side of the page. This will make it easy to see. In this way, when the first day's dailies come in you will already know just what file and line numbers apply to the footage.

In addition to lining the script you will need to make labels for the videotapes and computer disks you will be using over the course of the show. Each file will have its own set of 60 minute videotapes (in most feature situations you will be making 12 videotape copies of each file's footage) and computer disks (you will make three disks for each file). The video labels should list the name of the show, the file number, the scenes contained in the file and a number from one to twelve corresponding to the VCR machine that the tape will be copied and later played back in (*see* Figure 18.5). The disk label will show the film's title, the file number, the scene numbers contained in the file and the disk's type. In the Ediflex system there are three types of disks: Main Data Disk, Backup Data Disk, and Script Mimic Disk. You will need to have one of each type of disk for each file. (*see* Figure 18.6)

You will also need to keep your normal set of logs, as well as filing all of the paperwork you receive: camera, sound, lab and sound transfer reports, script supervisor's notes, etc. etc. The paperwork you receive from the set will be the same as you are used to on a film-based show.

As soon as you receive this paperwork you can transfer your lined notes onto the script supervisor's script pages. You should make note, of course, of any changes in the script that might affect your line numbering system and adapt to those changes.

The Dailies Arrive

While you've been doing this, the film has been making its way around town, stopping at various facilities along the way. As soon as the print has been struck at the lab and the sound transferred at the sound house the dailies will be sent to you for synching. After viewing the footage in the screening room, code the dailies and then send them off to the transfer house. The transfer house will then telecine the sunk dailies onto a 3/4" videotape in a letter-box matte format (this is where the full 1.85 image on the film is surrounded on its top and bottom by dark black bars). Burned into these black bars will be a visual indication of the SMPTE time code as well as the edge code numbers in footage and frames. Typically, these numbers are burned into the image only between the camera flash and the slate for each take.

351

8   INT   BARROOM SET   DAY

On the right we can see JAMES sitting next to the
cameraman as COWBOY and PETE are fighting. They aren't
really hitting each other, of course, and the absence
of the smacking sounds is highlighted by the absence
of most of the other sounds normally associated with a
bar brawl: cheering people, smashing chairs, etc. etc.
There is a complete silence, broken occasionally by
the grunts of the actors and a command or two from
JAMES./COWBOY falls to the ground and is immediately
set upon by the four other EXTRAS. He has his money
bag and gun taken from him./All of the extras back off
the set, guns drawn, until they are out of camera
range, where they break character and sometimes watch
the remainder of the take. Finally, James stands up
from his director's chair.

               JAMES
   Cut!

There is an immediate roar of noise.

               JAMES
         (to the cameraman)
   Did the zoom look okay?

             CAMERMAN
   Fine, James, fine.

ABBY enters and leans on part of the set in the right
of the frame.

                      CUT TO:

9   EXT   LOT   TWILIGHT

It is twilight as a number of people exit the studio.
Several technicians who we recognize are walking to
the parking lot./In the back of the crowd is ABBY,
walking slowly, in a bit of a fog. He crosses the
parking lot as several cars whiz by him. By the time
he has rached his car and gotten inside the car,
almost all of the other cars have left the lot. ABBY
starts his engine and watches as all the cars leave,
their noise dying out, only their taillights visible.
He revs the engine once and then slams the door shut.

                      CUT TO:

10   INT   ABBY'S APARTMENT   NIGHT

ABBY's apartment is a fairly modest one with a few
extravagances and concessions to life in a world of
fads and fashions. He enters and crosses over to a
large plastic rocking chair, sitting on a huge white

FIGURE 18.4   The lined script that you saw back in Figure 4.5, this time after it's been lined for the Ediflex system. Notice that each line of dialogue is marked as a separate line and the action is broken up into manageable sections. If there had been longer speeches, then they would also have been divided up.

shag rug. Throwing his script down on a glass coffee
table, he reaches for a small metal filing cabinet. He
touches it and receives an electric shock.

> ABBY
> Damn!

He reaches inside the file for a bottle of whiskey,
and is pouring himself a drink when he hears a
typewriter start up in the next room. He follows the
sound around the corner and into his bedroom.

11   INT ABBY'S BEDROOM   NIGHT

As ABBY enters he sees a man sitting at a small desk
by the window. He is hunched over a typewriter making
yet another correction. As soon as Abby sees him his
face relaxes a bit — he knows this man. It is BOB, his
next-door neighbor.

> ABBY
> Evening Mister Hemingway.

Bob, startled, turns around.

> BOB
> Why don't you move into the twentieth
> century and get a word processor already?

> ABBY
> How'd you get into my apartment?

> BOB
> I told the landlady I needed some
> typewriter ribbon. How'd the filming go Mr.
> DeMille?

> ABBY
> Perfectly shitty. I don't even recognize
> what he's filming.

> BOB
> He didn't switch movies on you, did he?

> ABBY
> No, I still recognize some of the plot

He stops, at a loss for words.

> ABBY
> How's the Great American Novel coming?

> BOB
> Fine, except for the part where I have to
> pay the rent. Speaking of which … your
> agent called.

FIGURE 18.4 - cont'd.

353

*FIGURE 18.5 A videotape cassette label for an Ediflex show. This 1/2"
tape goes in machine number one, corresponds to file number two and
contains all of the transferred footage for scenes 10 through 15. You could
also handwrite or type this label.*

So, finally, at about noon the day after the shoot, the 3/
4" copy of the Video Master Roll of that day's dailies should
arrive at your cutting room. By this time you should have
finished lining the script (as well as checking all of the reports
just as you would on a film-based system) and you should
have all of your disks, tapes and paperwork ready to begin the
transferring of the footage to the 1/2" VHS video-tapes that
the Ediflex system requires.

To repeat myself for a second, the Ediflex works by
lining up a number of videotape machines (in this case, VHS),
under the control of a computer, all of which have the identical footage. When Wendy tells the computer that she wants to
cut from shot one to shot two, the computer lines up the
outgoing frame from the copy of shot one in machine number
one, and the incoming frame from the copy of shot two in
machine two. It then plays the two tapes at the same time,
switching between the image on tape one to the one on tape
two at the exact moment that Wendy has called for.

As a result of this method, it is necessary to have a
large number of videotape machines so that the computer can
be telling machines three, four, five and six to get lined up and
ready for cuts number two, three, four and five. In fact, the
minimum number of machines to accommodate most simple
shows is eight. In almost any feature situation, you are going
to need the twelve that Ediflex has as its maximum. Even so,

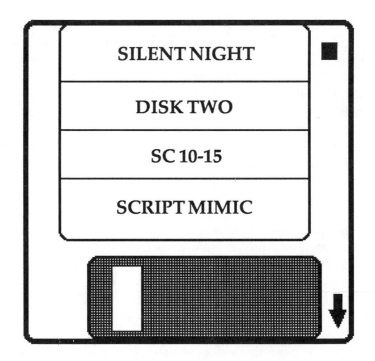

FIGURE 18.6 The matching disk label for the videocassette label shown in Figure 18.5. Note that this computer disk is the Script Mimic disk. There would be two other disks for this file: the Main Data Disk and the Backup Data Disk. You could also handwrite or type this label.

there will be times when Wendy has cut a sequence with a lot of quick cuts and the twelve machines will not be able to keep pace. There are ways of getting around this problem, but they aren't very elegant. Eventually, the technology should catch up to the needs of editors, but for now we must sit and wait.

In any case, Wendy is going to need twelve VHS videocassette copies of the material which you have just received on 3/4" cassette. You are going to be the one who will do the transfer, and along the way you will be programming the material into the computer so that Wendy can work with it later.

The actual procedure that each electronic editing system uses to create these tapes is slightly different and they all require a little schooling to master, so I will avoid a detailed discussion here. I am, however, going to give a general outline of what you need to do and what paperwork you will need to keep.

The Ediflex system boils down to two main preparatory tasks: making the videocassettes and logs, and making the *script mimic*, which is essentially an electronic version of the lined script.

With the 3/4" videocassette you should receive a *Video Master Log* that looks something like the one in Figure 18.7. Depending on what type of film you are working on and what arrangements you have made with your transfer house, the columns for descriptions and file numbers will probably be empty. In some cases (most notably in episodic television) the post-production supervisor of the series will add the description during the video transfer operation. If no one has yet done that, you should do it during this Ediflex transfer.

To make the videocassettes you will put the 3/4" video master in the 3/4" playback machine and find the beginning of each set of takes that you want to copy. Your eventual goal is to have all of the takes from any one file on their own set of VHS tapes. Normally a day's dailies will include takes from scenes which are from different files. In that case, you will transfer these takes onto other sets of VHS tapes. It is simpler to transfer all of the material from one file first, then return to the top of the 3/4" videotape and transfer everything for the second file, and so on.

By pointing your light pen at various places on the Ediflex's screen (*see* Figure 18.8) you can play, stop, freeze, fast forward, fast rewind and perform a number of other functions which you are used to doing on your home videotape machine. You will insert the twelve videocassettes you have already prepared for the first file you are transferring into the proper machines (copy #1 into machine #1, copy #2 into machine #2, etc.) and then fast forward down on the 3/4" master until you reach the first take that belongs in this file. You will press your light pen on a few more points on the computer screen and, after a few seconds, the 3/4" master will begin playing and the 12 VHS machines will begin recording.

Continue recording without stopping until you reach a take that you do not want on the VHS tapes for this file. Stop all of the tapes (you can do this easily from the computer console) and speed down on the 3/4" machine until you get to the next take that belongs in this file. Begin recording this take onto the 12 VHS machines.

Continue in this manner until you have recorded all of the takes that you want in this file. You can then rewind all of the tapes back to their heads and remove the 12 VHS tapes. Insert the 12 tapes for the next file that you want to transfer takes for and repeat the above process for all of *these* takes.

Often, you will receive takes for scenes in a file that you have already started a set of tapes for. In this case, you will add the new takes to the end of the previously recorded takes. It makes no difference in what order the takes are laid down on the 1/2" tapes. It is only important that they all be on the tape.

When you have completely transferred all of the day's dailies onto their appropriate file tapes, you need to create the electronic lined script, which Ediflex calls the *script mimic*.

To do this you will call up a computer screen which, in essence, is a computerized version of a page of a script (*see* Figure 18.9). Each of the numbers down the left side of the screen corresponds to the line numbers which you have given to each piece of dialog and action in the script. What you will be doing is telling the computer exactly where every take on the videocassettes begins and ends in reference to these numbers. This is exactly analogous to having the script supervisor draw a line down a script page showing where the take begins and ends, drawing over all of the dialogue lines

VIDEO TRANSFER LOG

Film _Silent Night_ Page _1_ of _2_ Date Shot _9·10·90_
Video Master Roll# _1_ Date Transferred _9·11·90_

File #	Scene #	SMPTE #s	LR	SR	Description
2	10-5	01:00:00:00	1	1	Master
1	6	0:47	1		''
	10A-2	1:32		MOS	POV- Empty room
	10B-2	1:56		1	MWS- ABBY to cab
	10C-1	2:28		1	CU- ABBY at cab
	10D-2	3:03			MS- ABBY at desk
	3	3:33			
	10E-2	4:13			MS-ABBY exits room
2	11-6	4:36			Master
	B	9:06		1	''
	All pu-3	10:55	1	2	'' pick up
	11A-4	11:26	2	1	MS- BOB, ABBY enters
	11B-3	12:52		1	CU- BOB
	A11B-1	13:52			'' pick up
	11C-2	14:29			MS-ABBY
	11D-3	17:16			CU-ABBY
	5	18:46	1		''
	11E-3	19:58	3		CU-ABBY exits
	11F-1	20:15	1		CU-BOB exits
	2	20:32			''
7	46-3	20:52			MASTER
	4	27:10			''
	7	25:19			''
	46A-1	27:41		3	MWS- ABBY enters
	46B-3	28:15		1	MCU- ABBY to desk
	4	29:36			''
	46C-1	31:16	4		MCU- ABBY o/s CLAIRE
	2	32:45			''
	46D-4	34:15			MS- CLAIRE
	5	36:14			''
	6	38:26			''

DAILY VIDEO TRANSFER LOG

FIGURE 18.7 A video transfer log made at the video transfer house. The file numbers are added by the assistant. Often the descriptions must be added by the assistant as well unless there is someone at the video transfer who knows the film well enough to make up these descriptions. Some video transfer logs also list the camera roll.

```
                    LOAD RECORD
RETURN
                   PHASE: 13
  RESET          OFFSET:        ***MANUAL PLAYBACK CONTROL
    SOURCE: 1        * *        ***MANUAL LOAD OPERATION
    RECORD ON: 23                ***START PLAYBACK
    MODE:                        ***START LEADER
    >*<COPY                      ***START RECORD
     * START NEW CASSETTES
     * EXTEND CASSETTES          *** AUTO START
                                 *** AUTO EXTEND
                       ** RW FF  *** END SEGMENT
   SOURCE REEL NO.-    FR ◄◄►►   *** END CASSETTES
          HEAD         ** X 10
  MARK PB ***    STP      ◄◄►►
  MARK REC ***
                  BLK  ** X 2
  ░01234567      PL ◄◄►►         ABORT
  ◄◄89ABCDEF↓    ** X 1/5        PHASE    REWIND
                     ◄◄►►
```

FIGURE 18.8 The Ediflex screen used for transfers. Note the lower center section of the screen. It has notations for rewind and fast forwarding of the VHS tapes. "X 10" means ten times speed, "X 2" means double speed and "X 1/5" means one–fifth speed. Many other functions of the videotape machines can be controlled from this screen. (Courtesy CINEDCO)

contained in the take (as shown in Figure 4.5).

To do this on the Ediflex, you take one VHS cassette, put it in its appropriate machine, and call up the script mimic screen. You would then play the tape until you got to the slate for the first take. There is often a punch at the slate, put on by the video transfer house. You would press your light pen on the script mimic screen to show where, horizontally, you want the script line for this take to appear on screen (this is equivalent to the script supervisor deciding where, horizontally, on the typewritten script page he or she wants to draw the script line). You would then tell the computer what take you are working with (using a three digit label, as shown in Figure 18.11), at which numbered line the take begins, and then tell the computer that you are at the slate for that take. This will cause the computer to automatically read in the

SMPTE Time Code (as well as the 3/4" video master roll number) at the point at which you have stopped the tape.

Either at this point or at the end of the script mimic session, you will also type in the key or edge code number, which should be printed somewhere on the screen. Enter this number in your log (*see* Figure 18.10). With the advent of Kodak's Keykode (in which SMPTE code numbers are recorded directly on the **film** negative), the entering of key numbers may well become fully automated.

You will then play forward until you get to the beginning of the action (usually just after the director has called "Action!") and mark that with your light pen. Continue to play forward until you get to the end of the first line as you numbered it in your script. You will mark that with your light pen as well. You will proceed in this fashion, letting the

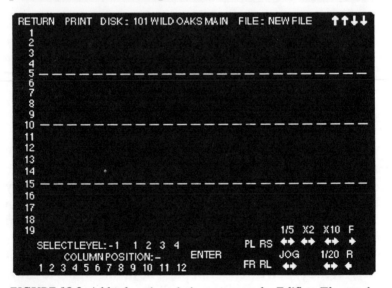

FIGURE 18.9 A blank script mimic screen on the Ediflex. The numbers down the left hand side of the screen refer to the line numbers which you entered into the lined script. Each dashed line is the location where another set–up will be lined. Note the videotape movement controls in the lower right. (Courtesy CINEDCO)

computer know exactly where each numbered line ends, until the end of the take. When you have finished with the take, the computer screen will show you exactly which lines are covered by the take. After you have completed entering all of the takes your screen will look something like the one in Figure 18.11. In this example (which does not come from *Silent Night* but from an actual film) take four of the master (if this were scene ten, this would be called take 10-4) runs from line 15 through line 24. Take 10A-2 runs from line 16 through 22, take 10B-5 runs from line 15 through 19, take 10B-6 from line 15 through 22, and so on. This screen shows that only six takes were shot for this scene; the maximum number allowed is about 48, though there are some tricks to extending this limitation a bit. Obviously, you will exceed this number of takes in many cases on complicated features. Eventually, with more computer memory and faster computers, this number will increase.

At the same time, you should also program in any of the wild tracks which have been transferred over from the 3/4" master.

Once you have programmed in all of the lines for all of the takes from this VHS tape, you can save all of the information onto the Script Mimic disk. Then, when Wendy begins to cut the scenes in this file, all she has to do in put the 12 VHS tapes into their proper machines, put the Script Mimic disk for the file into the Ediflex, and she will be able to begin editing.

One of the major problems with most computer based editing systems (other than Touchvision) is that they require the assistant to work on the same computer as the editor. This is the same as if both the assistant and the editor were working on the same KEM or editing bench. Obviously, they both can't be doing their work at the same time. As a result, you will find yourself doing the transfers either during lunch hour or after Wendy has gone home for the day. In some cases, assistants come into the editing room early so they can

File Number: **2**

FILM/VIDEO LOG

Date **9·10·90**

Sc & Tk	CR	SR	Slate Key Number	Slate SMPTE Code Number	File	Disk	X
10-5	1	1	F13X63839	1:00·00	2	2	
-6	1	1	63911	0:47	1	1	
10A-2	1	Mos	63997	1:32			
10B-2	1	1	64070	1:56			
10C-1			64128	2:28			
10D-2			64219	3:03			
-3			64256	3:33			
10E-2			64336	4:13			
11-6	2		E3X 21019	4:26			
8			21306	9:06			
A11pu-3	1	2	22156	10:55			
11A-4	3	1	F23X17136	11:26			
11B-3			17349	12:58			
A11B-1pu			17745	13:52			
11C-2			179	14:29			
11D-3			18065	17:16			
5	4		18246	18:46			
11E-3			18419	19:58			
11F-1			18972	20:15			
2			18520	20:32			

FILM/VIDEO LOG

FIGURE 18.10 A log book page. As each take is entered into the script mimic screen it is checked off in the final column. Note that this assistant has chosen to group takes by file numbers, with each file number on its own log page. Other scenes which were shot on the same day would be entered onto other log pages. Scenes which are from the same file number but shot later on in the shooting schedule can be entered below scene 11's takes, on this same page.

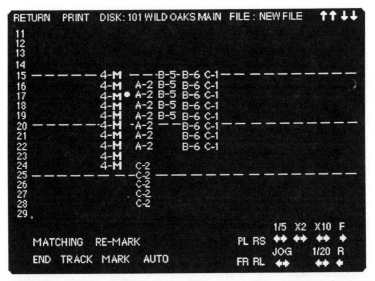

FIGURE 18.11 The Ediflex script mimic screen after entering information. If this were scene 10, you can see that take four of the master would cover lines 15 through 24, take 10A-2 covers lines 16 through 22, and so on. Note that each of the takes is given a three digit label. (Courtesy CINEDCO)

complete the transfer and script mimic processes before the editor arrives for the day. You will often end up working a completely different shift than Wendy. This will require you to develop a very different set of relationships with your suppliers and the outside work since you will not be around during a part of the day when a lot of the interaction outside the cutting room will be happening. Often, this means that you will work quite a bit longer than the editor. Ediflex offers a smaller set-up which is used by the assistant for the script mimicking process. It is, obviously, an extra rental cost, but it will pay for itself by allowing the assistant and the editor to do much of their work simultaneously.

Cutting

Once all of the shooting has been finished and Wendy is cutting away the assistant editor has much less to do. However, in much the same way as on a filmed show, there are countless tasks which will occupy your time: finding temp music and sound effects (you will transfer these to 1/2" VHS tapes, exactly as you transferred the dailies), making continuities, dealing with labs and stock and optical houses, etc.

As Wendy is cutting, she will be saving all of her edits (that is, the computer instructions on where to cut from one 1/2" tape machine to another) onto the Main Data Disks you prepared for her. To save this information, she will take the Main Data Disk for the file that she has been working on and use the 'save' portion of the Ediflex program. She should also save the same list on the Backup Data Disk.

After Wendy's first cut of the entire film has been completed, two things will have to occur. First, the cut (which, until now, has only existed in computer memory, across many files) will have to be *assembled* onto one 3/4" tape for viewing, and the film will have to be *conformed* on film for viewing in a screening room. Once again, many films skip this conforming process, but we are going to go through it for our film.

Since the Ediflex works with only one file at a time, Wendy has up until now only been able to see how the scenes within any given file look when they are cut together. In order to view the entire film (or a section of the film which spans more than one file) you will have to transfer the film from the 1/2" tapes onto one cut–together 3/4" tape.

To do this, you should write down, on a *Video Assembly List* (*see* Figure 18.12), all of the files in the order of the film from start to finish. Often many different versions of each file exist. The editor may have multiple versions of her cut, the director will certainly have alternatives to that, and the producers and distributors will also have their versions of the film. Rather than going to the time and trouble of black and white duping each version of the film (assuming you've even got all of them conformed on film) you can have the computer keep each and every version available to you in its memory.

In order to keep the video assembly moving as smoothly as possible you should list which version of each file you need. The best way of doing this is to supply Wendy with an assembly list with the scene and file numbers already listed on it. She can then write down in the version column, the version number (or combination of versions, if she desires) she would like assembled for every file.

You should then *pre-black* a 3/4" tape. To do this you simply record a *control track* signal (this is a signal which is used to control synchronization during the playback of the tape; every videotape needs one and it is generally placed on the tape during the record process) onto the tape. Blacking a tape is a simple process —all you have to do is record a tape with no audio or video signal being fed to it. This process takes place in real time. That is, if a tape is 90 minutes long, the blacking will take 90 minutes, so it would be smart to have a number of pre–blacked tapes of various lengths handy in the editing room. After you've blackened each tape, you should rewind it back to its head.

You will then load the twelve 1/2" VHS tapes for the first file you need to assemble into their correct machines. You then load the 3/4" pre–blacked tape into the 3/4" machine. You will get the information on the first file from its Main Data Disk, find the proper versions of the cuts for all of the scenes included in the file (they will be listed on the data disk), and let the computer play back the cut scenes for you while you are simultaneously recording them on the 3/4" machine.

It is a good idea to watch the cut as it is being assembled. You should do this for two reasons. First, it is a check to make sure that everything is being recorded onto the 3/4" properly and in order. Second, since you will probably be working much more separately from the editor than you would on a film show, this is one of the few times when you will get a chance to actually see the film that you are working on.

When the file has been completely recorded you will

Date *1·8·91*

ASSEMBLY LIST

Page *1* of *2*

Cut: *2ND SCREENING*

X	File #	Vers. #	Scene #s	Time	Comments
✓	1	1	2-9	4:16	
✓	2	1	10-15	3:26	
✓	3	1	17-20	4:38	
	4	2	22-26	:	
	5	1	27-30	:	
	6	1	31-34	:	
	7	1	35-37	:	
	8	3	39-44	:	
	9	1	45-48	:	
	10	1	A49-54	:	
	11	1	55-59	:	
	12	1	60-65	:	
	13	1	66-72	:	
	14	1	73-78	:	
	15	2	79-83	:	Watch f.o at end
	16	1	84-87	:	
			Total:	:	

VIDEO ASSEMBLY LIST

FIGURE 18.12 In this Video Assembly List the assistant has marked up all of the file and version numbers to be assembled from the script mimic disks, along with their scene numbers. He or she has already completed assembling the first three files of the picture. There is a notation from the editor on file number fifteen to be careful to include the entire fade out at the end of the file.

hit the "Shutdown" button on the screen with your light pen and, when the machines have stopped whirring and whining, you can take out all of the twelve 1/2" tapes for this already–recorded file.

At this time, it is a good idea to note on the Assembly List that you have completed assembling the first file. A check or an "x" can be put into the first column so you don't lose track of exactly what you have already assembled.

Now you can load the set of 1/2" tapes for the next file you wish to record into their proper VHS machines. When that is done you will load the computer data disk for this file and, after selecting the proper versions, once again have the Ediflex play back the cut scenes while recording them on the 3/4" tape. There is a special command on the Ediflex to let you automatically pick up the recording on this tape from where you left off without leaving any ugly gaps or glitches.

When you are done with the second file, you will hit "Shutdown," remove the VHS tapes and begin the process over again with the third file. You will continue doing this until you either run out of tape on the 3/4" machine or you are finished with the transfer process. This process generally takes up to two times the length of the finished show. A two hour film can take anywhere from three to four hours to assemble, for instance.

As you assemble the entire show you can also figure out a total running time by adding together all of the cumulative times for each file as listed on the screen. Write this number down on the Assembly List and, when you are done assembling the film, you can total everything up. The computer will also automatically add up all of the time for each 3/4" assembled tape.

Putting the cut together on videotape is fine if Adam or Wendy wants to take the cut home and look at it, but it does not replace the experience of watching the film on a big screen. In order to be able to do this you will need to match the printed 35mm film and soundtrack to the cuts that Wendy has made in the video, creating a cut work picture and track which will exactly match her cuts. To do this you will need to have the Ediflex create a list of all of the edits, both picture and track, with some numbers that make sense to you. This is where the fact that you've programmed in the key numbers or the edge codes will help you out.

The process of conforming a film cut to the video one is somewhat analogous to the process that a negative matcher goes through in conforming the negative to your cut work picture. First, you will get a *Film Conversion List* from the computer. This list (*see* Figure 18.13) will catalog all of the edits (called *events*) in the film in the order in which they occur. You can tell the computer whether you want a list of track cuts as well as the picture cuts.

You would then go through the list, cutting the picture and track at the specified frames. Before conforming a scene it is helpful to pull all of the film for the takes involved in the cut from their trim boxes and line them up on your bench's back rack. The Ediflex can supply you with a pull list, which lists all of the takes used in each file. You should then surround yourself with a few trim barrels — you'll need them. Then, find the first frame of the first take (picture and track) and cut it onto the end of the head leaders (which you or Philip will have already prepared, right?). After hanging the head trim of the take in the barrel, roll down in the synchronizer until you get to the place where you will be cutting out of this take into another one. Make your cut there, on the left side of synchronizer, so the cut piece stays in the gangs. Hang up the tail trim in the barrel, or leave it on its hand roll if it is a large tail trim. Then, on a second synchronizer or by hand, find the incoming frame on the next take. Cut it at this point and splice it onto the tail of the piece already in the synchronizer. Hang the head trim up in the barrel. You have now cut your first two takes together.

In essence, you are duplicating what Wendy's actions would be if she were cutting the show on film (*see* Chapter 6,

"The Editor Edits,") except that you have a list of code numbers to tell you where to make the cuts, rather than hunting through the footage and finding the best frames yourself. Of course, that "hunting through the footage" is what creative editing is all about, so you miss the fun stuff as well — but that's part of the job of an assistant.

To conform a full feature could take one person up to a week. So it's a good idea to let Philip handle as much of the work as possible, even conforming some scenes himself.

With each subsequent recut, there will probably be less work for you to do in terms of conforming picture to video. You will need to check that the edits are still valid at places where no changes were made, and make the changes that were done in video. Hopefully, you will have been involved in the discussion and executions of the changes, so you will have a good idea where in the continuity the recuts were made.

Locking The Film and Beyond

Once the film is locked, and you have made the final conformations in the cut work picture and track, you hand the film over to the sound and music departments in pretty much the same way as you would on a film–based show. In many cases nowadays, the composer and sound editor will want to have a copy of the film on videotape with time code. In fact, many of the phases of both processes are now done on video—foley, ADR, music recording, sometimes even the sound effects creation and the final dub. Obviously, creating these videotapes will be very easy for you. You don't even have to send the film footage out to a video transfer house; you've got the 3/4" already made.

Another distinct advantage to doing the editing process electronically is that you will be able to generate a film conversion list of all your track cuts for the sound and dialog editors. Often they will end up creating a list like this anyway (they call it a "continuity") so this can save them quite a bit

```
INITIAL OFFSET= -2
DISK: HSE PTY ON/LINE MAIN    SECTION 1 -- FILE: 002-006
                                                 VERSION 3/B
          FROM           THRU     LENGTH      CUM.

  1   >>>> BLANK FILL >>>>         3+02        3+02    5A3

      ==== DISSOLVE  48 FRAMES <<<< END A --------
                                   START B    0+02
  2   F33X 38350+01    -357+07     7+07        7+09    m-3

  3   F33X 38835+08    -851+07    16+00       23+09    B-3

  4   F33X 38367+13    -372+04     4+08       28+01    m-3

  5   F33X 38586+14    -591+04     4+07       32+08    A-6

  6   F33X 38870+08    -880+07    10+00       42+08    B-3

      ==== DISSOLVE  48 FRAMES <<<< END B --------
                                   START A   39+08
  7   F33X 38599+15    -607+10     7+12       47+04    A-6

  8   F33X 38885+06    -902+03    16+14       64+02    B-3

      ==== DISSOLVE   8 FRAMES <<<< END A --------
                                   START B   63+10
  9   F8X  24239+06    -259+11    20+06       84+00    A-2

 10   F33X 38936+07    -939+10     3+04       87+04     4m

 11   F33X 38996+12    -034+04    37+09      124+13    A-2

 12   F8X  24101+09    -109+01     7+09      132+06    m-5

 13   F8X  23459+08    -462+11     3+04      135+10    6m2

 14   F8X  24113+02    -115+03     2+02      137+12    m-5

 15   F8X  23464+03    -469+07     5+05      143+01    6m2

      ==== DISSOLVE  48 FRAMES <<<< END B --------
                                   START A  140+01
 16   F8X  23853+03    -862+07     9+05      149+06    C-4

      ==== DISSOLVE  24 FRAMES <<<< END A --------
                                   START B  147+14
 17   F8X  23606+01    -609+04     3+04      151+02    A-3

 18   F8X  23955+03    -957+08     2+06      153+08    E-1

 19   F8X  23865+14    -868+05     2+08      156+00    C-4

 20   F6X  23630+02    -634+10     4+09      160+09    A-3

 21   F8X  23923+04    -933+03    10+00      170+09    D-1

 22   F8X  23667+02    -671+06     4+05      174+14    B-1
```

FIGURE 18.13 A page from a film conversion list. Each cut shows the beginning and ending key numbers, total length of the cut, the total length from the beginning of the reel, and the take number that the shot comes from. Cut number four, for instance, begins at F33X38367^{+13} and runs through F33X38372^{+04}. It runs for 4' 08 and ends 28' 01 from the beginning of the reel. If this were scene 10 then its take number would be 10M-3. Note that opticals are listed in their proper place. More detailed information about these opticals can also be generated on a separate list for the optical house (see Figure 18.14). Note that no numbers for the soundtrack are supplied on this list; you can ask the computer to give you that information as well. (Courtesy CINEDCO)

of time.

At the completion of the editing process you will make one final Film Conversion list and conform the picture for, hopefully, the last time. You can then submit that list and the cut work picture, with any necessary opticals cut into it, to the negative cutter as well as make any black and white dupes that the sound or music departments.

The computer is also able to generate an optical count sheet (*see* Figure 18.14) which, after you check it, can be sent to your optical house along with your interpositives to begin the optical process.

In the case of television shows, there is often no need to complete on film. In this case, you might never have had filmed dailies at all; your dailies would only be on tape. After the editing is done, you would create an *Edit Decision List*. This is a printout, much like the Film Cut List, which lists every cut made in the show, along with all of the pertinent information needed to match the cuts on a professional *on-line* editing system. This is a video editing system, found at expensive video editing houses, which uses the 1" master reels that were originally made from the shot negative and 1/4" production tapes, to create edits and optical effects that are of professional enough quality for airing on a television network. The Edit Decision List is also put onto a computer disk which can be brought into the on-line session and used by the computer there.

Wendy would then go into an on–line editing bay and supervise the matching of the cuts (as well as color correction) of the show, and any other opticals which she needed. On an episodic television show, the editor rarely goes to these sessions. Instead, an associate producer or the post-production supervisor goes instead.

Wrapping Up

The actual process of editing and assistant editing on digital/computer systems is a constantly changing one. Not only does it differ from one system to the next, but it often differs from one version of the system to the version in operation only a month or two later. Progress in computer hardware as well as the rewriting of the computer software used to control these machines is continually refining and (hopefully) improving the process.

Both the Los Angeles and New York editing locals offer introductory courses in electronic editing. In addition, many of the companies that market these machines offer their own (sometimes free) classes attempting to help to drag the film editing world into the computer age.

Just because learning these systems is like trying to hit a moving target is no reason for you not to attempt it. Though the specifics of each system are different, the experience of working with one is normally translatable to some degree to another one. In any case, the more familiarity you have with computers and computer assisted video editing, the better off you'll be in the coming years.

High-Definition Video

In addition to the difficulties inherent in editing video-tape that are only now being addressed, one of the major disadvantages of the video format as compared to the film medium is that the images look very different. When filmed images are cut together with shots originally made on video the difference in contrast and sharpness is immediately apparent. And any attempt to project a video image onto a large screen has always ended up looking vastly inferior to that of a projected film image.

There are several reasons for these differences. The first is that film has a much higher *contrast ratio* than video does. Contrast ratio is, simply, the ratio of the brightest area of the image to the darkest area. Because of the properties of the way video is recorded and played back it simply cannot handle the intense light and dark as satisfactorily as a well–lit film can.

```
EDIFLEX OPTICAL COUNT SHEET
INITIAL OFFSET= -2
DISK: HSE PTY ON/LINE MAIN    SECTION 1 -- FILE: 002-006    VERSION 3/B

        START PRINTING     START OUT      FULL IN         STOP PR. LENGTH   TYPE

    1
    2                                   F33X 38353+00        -361   3+00   FAD IN

    6   F33X 38867        -877+08
    7                                   F33X 38602+14        -611   3+00   DISOLV

    8   F33X 38882        -901+12
    9                                   F8X 24239+13         -263   0+08   DISOLV

   15    F8X 23461        -466+08
   16                                   F8X 23856+02        >>>>    3+00   DISOLV

   16   >>>>>>>>>>>>>>>    -861+00
   17                                   F8X 23607+08         -613   1+08   DISOLV

FINAL OFFSET= +1
```

FIGURE 18.14 An electronic editing optical count sheet. This sheet lists five different effects, rather than the one per page that you would normally do on an optical count sheet. Note the key numbers listed for both sides of the dissolves. Note also that the last two dissolves are actually one optical with two dissolves in it. The little arrows at the out point of cut number 16 indicate that it continues at the beginning of the next optical. (Courtesy CINEDCO)

The other reason film looks so much better than video has to do with the mechanics of how a video image is projected. A television set is nothing more than a blank screen of phosphors with a big light gun sitting at its back. The light gun shoots a continuous stream of signals at the back of the screen, causing the phosphors to glow at various colors and intensities. This stream of signals is precisely controlled so that each frame of video is created by activating the phosphors from the upper left hand corner of the frame, more or less horizontally to the right side of the screen. The gun then moves back to the left side of the screen, down a tiny bit and begins shooting another line of signals from left to right. Each of these lines of signals is called a *scan line* and in the United States, it takes 525 if them to make one full image (or *video frame*). In Europe, the standard is 625 lines per frame. Unlike film, there are 30 frames in each second.

In point of fact, because of the technical limitations and demands of television, each video frame is scanned twice before moving on to the next frame. The first time, only the odd numbered scan lines are projected; the second time, only the even numbered ones are. Each one of these scannings is called a *field*. Thus, there are two fields in each video frame, and 60 fields in a second.

This is the reason why the images on large screen televisions tend to look fuzzier and worse than film images: you can actually see the boundaries of the scan lines. So long as video images are made up of no more than 625 scan lines per frame, large images will always be impractical. So someone came up with the bright idea of increasing the number of scan lines in each video frame and thus HDTV (High Definition Television) was born.

HDTV is a system of recording images on video and projecting them onto a special television set with many more scan lines than normal. Recently, the Eastman Kodak Co. has developed a digital HDTV system which has 2,160 lines per frame. Though I have yet to see a demonstration of this system, at that many scan lines per frame the visual image is bound to be improved tremendously. In fact, the company claims that this HDTV video image can be blended imperceptibly with 35mm film images.

If this is true, it promises exciting changes for the film and video industries. For once the barrier to producing excellent quality video images has been broken, and after all of the kinks have been ironed out in the manner in which those images can be shot and edited together, then the day when movies will be shot, edited and projected solely on video cannot be far away.

19

THE HARDEST JOB OF ALL— FINDING A JOB

Anyone who has ever tried to find a job in the film industry, or any other industry in the known world, has heard of something called the Catch-22 of job seeking. Put simply it goes like this —you can't get a job without experience and you can't get experience without a job. It is a revolving door of missed opportunities. You can't get a job without first having a job. Yet somehow, people still get that first job. It is not impossible, merely absurdly difficult. This chapter will try to give you some hints to help you get that first job.

The Resume

When people come to me looking for work I always ask them for a resume. I don't do this only so that I can see all of the experience that a job applicant has, but for two other reasons as well. First, it gives me an association between a name and a face (often I can use one of the jobs listed on the resume as a mnemonic key). Second, it gives me an address and phone number in case I do decide to hire that person.

This illustrates something about the problems in looking for work. There are so many people who would like to work in film editing that it is all too easy to forget just who everyone is. Anything that can differentiate you from the next job applicant is helpful.

This is advice that I give everyone who asks me how to look for work. Find out what makes you more valuable than the next person — if you speak a foreign language, if you used to work in journalism, if you can read music, etc. List *that* on your resume. Your differences will be what gets you, as opposed to the next person, hired.

Your resume need not be an elaborate one. Most people get by with a simple typed list of their jobs, including short descriptions of the tasks they performed on each. The resume should, however, be neat and well organized. Editing situations require both characteristics and if a person's resume is lacking in either, I would think twice about hiring them. There are so many people looking for work that anything that gives an indication that you would be unsuitable for the job should be avoided on your resume.

A sample resume is given in Figure 19.1. Betty has worked in features for the last several jobs. Since she is looking for feature work, that is what she is listing on her resume. She mentions who she has already worked with and that she is in the editors' union. This is the type of resume that she can give to almost any editor and be guaranteed consideration for an open job.

Most jobs at the level that Betty is at are given to people with whom editors have already worked. A look at Betty's rise in the editing room will show you this. She began as an apprentice sound editor on a film that Charles Simpson cut. She apparently impressed him enough that when it came time to hire an apprentice editor on his next film he asked her. On the basis of this experience she was asked to be Nate High's assistant music editor on a film. She continued in that

---

BETTY BOUND
123 Alphabet Street
New York, NY 10000
212/123-4567

May-June 1989	**Silent Night, Silent Cowboy** — Assistant Music Editor. Feature film directed by Adam Free. Edited by Wendy Libre. Music Editor — Nate High.
January-March 1989	**Bootleg, Bootleg** — Assistant Music Editor. Feature film directed by Cecil B. DuhMille. Edited by A. Beeg Editor. Music Editor — Nate High.
January-October 1988	**The Escape Of The Monsters From Outer Space With Flashy Cars** — Apprentice Picture Editor. Feature film directed by Eric von Stroheim. Edited by Charles Simpson.
August-November 1987	**Daddy Weirdest** — Apprentice Sound Editor. Feature film directed by Eric von Stroheim. Edited by Charles Simpson. Supervising Sound Editor — Wallace Foley.

Member, Local 771, IATSE
References Available On Request.

FIGURE 19.1 Resume for an experienced person.

function on *Silent Night, Silent Cowboy*. Though Betty's rise is a bit more meteoric than most (many sound apprentices work three or four jobs before being able to move up — either to apprentice picture editor for four or five jobs, or to assistant sound editor) it is illustrative of the way in which most people move up in the field — through impressing the people with whom they've worked enough to be asked onto other jobs with them.

Unless your father happens to own a film studio, when you are first beginning to look for work, you won't have this kind of proximity to those who do the hiring. In this case, the only kind of association that you can get with them is to constantly go out on job interviews. A sample of the kind of resume a newcomer might take around is given in Figure 19.2. Edward Zee, being someone with no contacts in the film industry, has had to stretch his credits a bit. The truth of his career, as opposed to his resume, is as follows. The trailer company that he worked for was a small company run by a friend of his. They had one job in the entire month that he was there and Ed really didn't do much more than order IPs from the lab. But he did learn how to do that. The film *The Apple of Your Eye* was a low budget short that a friend of his directed after he graduated from UCLA. The short, paid for through family money, never went anywhere but Ed's friend does have a print lying around his house somewhere. Ed, though he did not get paid a cent for working on the film, did learn a lot about editing from the woman who cut the film (who was working as an assistant editor on a feature during the day while cutting this film at night with Ed.)

You can see how to subtly stretch the truth in a resume. The idea is never to misrepresent what you know but to give your experience in the best possible light. What the editor who needs an apprentice is really looking for, is someone who seems enthusiastic about working long and hard hours, someone who knows enough about filmmaking and film editing that it won't be necessary to explain what a

EDWARD ZEE
987 Sixth Street
Santa Monica, CA 90000
213/765-4321

Objective
To work as an Apprentice Editor or anything that will lead to a job in the
    editing room.

Work Experience

1989 — *Sample Trailer Company* — Worked in this trailer editing house in
    many facets of the editing process. Ordered IPs from labs, assisted trailer
    editors in the editing, prepared tracks for dub, etc.

1988 — *The Apple of Your Eye* — Worked as an assistant editor helping with
    dailies and trims on this low-budget short. Sunk dailies, filed trims,
    helped prepare for the dub. Phyllis Murphy, Editor.

1988 — Edited the following films at UCLA Film School:
        "Cheaper By The Baker's Dozen"
        "Smoked Out"
        "Enough Is Too Much"

1984 - 1988 — UCLA Film School, graduated BFA

Have edited several films of my own.

References
B. I. Hertz — Editor, Sample Trailer Company — 213/555-1212
Phyllis Murphy — Editor — 213/936-1212

FIGURE 19.2 Resume for an inexperienced person.

frame line is, and someone who gives the impression that they will be easy to work and live with for a long duration of time in a confined area.

Hitting The Pavement

Instead of the connections made by working with other editors, most beginners have only their own personalities to sell themselves. The only way that they can be seen is to go out and knock on doors. They should try to visit every editing company or editing room that they can find so that they may introduce themselves, drop off a resume, and make their needs known.

How does one find these editing rooms? Sometimes you can call the phone numbers of production companies listed for movies being shot in the Thursday and Friday editions of *Daily Variety* or the very thorough Tuesday edition of *The Hollywood Reporter* and ask them where the movies are being edited. Sometimes they might even tell you. There are several books which are published which list, among other things, editorial services. Motion Picture Enterprises Publications, Inc. (Tarrytown, New York 10591) publishes a book called *Motion Picture, TV, and Theatre Directory* which is a yellow-covered book listing services for film and television. Called the "yellow book," it is a good place to begin looking for locations of editing rooms either under the "Editing Services," "Cutting Rooms," or "Editing Equipment—Rental" categories. This book is primarily useful for the East Coast, however. On the West Coast there are similar guides published. Two are the *Pacific Coast Studio Directory* and *411*.

The best way to reach people is to go to their cutting rooms. This is a minor annoyance to the editors but it is impossible to effectively sell yourself otherwise. And, make no mistake about it, you *will* be selling yourself. You will be in competition with at least twenty or twenty-five other people for each job that is available. On an average six-month job an editor will accumulate about fifty resumes.

Once again, the best things to try and sell are your differences. There will be plenty of people looking for work who will have worked more than you. They can sell themselves on the basis of their experience; you cannot. You must sell yourself on the basis of your energy, and your willingness to work hard and learn.

Often it is necessary to work for free while you are looking for a toehold in the industry. Everyone that I know in the motion picture business has worked for nothing or next to nothing at the beginning of their careers. It is one way of getting experience; it is also one way of getting to meet people. In the introduction to this book I talked of my first week on the movie *Lenny*, my first paying editorial job. Let me briefly describe what went before that for you.

I went to a public university in New York State, a school which is much better known for its science students than for its film students. There were about forty of us altogether in the Theatre Arts department (the division I eventually ended up in; they didn't have a film department). There were, at the time, four film courses, all taught by one professor. One day in my junior year Karl, a Columbia University graduate film student who was doing a project near the college, called and asked if there was anybody who would be interested in working on the set of his film for two weeks for no money. My film professor announced it in his class and several people expressed interest. I, however, was the first one to the phone after the class (I remember dashing into the department office so fast that I lost several papers I had been writing; but that is another story.)

I got the job and ended up working fourteen hours a day for two straight weeks on a rather charming fiction film about a boy who was an outcast at his school. I ended up working in a crew composed of the director, a cameraman, an assistant camerawoman (who later edited the film), and a soundman. I was the "assistant everything." I learned more in those two weeks than I could have learned in two years in my film classes.

The next year, when Karl was shooting another film, he called me directly and asked if I would like to work on the new film. I did. The summer after I graduated Karl began directing public service announcements for a small production company. He had been given enough of a budget to hire someone to help out on the set as a production assistant (also known as a "gofer" since they "gofer coffee" and "gofer sandwiches," etc., etc.). Karl hired me. But after having made a few of my own films at college (in lieu of term papers) I had discovered that I liked editing more than any other part of the filmmaking process. I asked to be able to assist him in the editing room. I would do it for free. Karl agreed.

These little jobs did not occur very often. In order to support myself in between these jobs, I worked as a temporary secretary, typing at accounting firms and law offices. In the meantime, I would work for a day or two on the set and several days for free in the editing room with Karl, who was editing his films himself.

Finally, a job came where Karl had enough money to hire an editor — a woman named Kathy. We worked together and liked each other a lot. While we were working together she was hired to be the supervising sound editor on *Lenny*. She asked me if I would like to work on it as the apprentice sound editor. I thought about it for about two nanoseconds and said "yes."

I tell you this story not to bore you, but to show you the difference between being lucky and making your own luck. It was luck that Karl called my college to ask for help, but it was *my* doing that I raced to the phone as soon as I found out about the job. It was Karl's talent that got him paying work at about the time I was graduating from college, but it was my work on the earlier films that got him to call me when those paying jobs became available. And while it may have been luck that Kathy was hired to work on the little public service announcement at about the same time that she was hired onto

Lenny, it was I who volunteered to work for nothing in the editing room on these films and it was my work that Kathy liked enough to prompt her to ask me to work on *Lenny*.

There is no such thing as pure, unadulterated "luck." There is only the ability to put yourself in the position where luck can work on you, and that requires the proper aggressive attitude and need to work in the field. Sometimes, that aggressiveness will mean that you work for free. I don't think that it is a bad idea to accept those kinds of jobs, if you can afford it. People get paid in many ways besides money — experience is more valuable in the long run than money in this field.

When you go around looking for jobs the best thing that you have to sell is yourself, your desire to give the person who will hire you a lot of effort and energy. Everyone starts with no experience. Most editors remember that when it comes time for them to hire someone.

Unions

One of the first stops in looking for work should be the editors' unions in whatever city you are looking for work. In Hollywood and San Francisco it is Local 776 IATSE (the International Alliance of Theatrical and Stage Employees — whew!) In New York, it is Local 771 IATSE. There are other editors' locals in Canada and Chicago. There are also other unions, most notably NABET. Though their editors rarely do feature films, they are fairly active in commercials and other low budget ventures.

The main job of a union is to serve its membership and, for many, that means trying to keep the number of people looking for work low so that their own members will have more of a chance at the available work. This makes it very difficult to get into the union. There is a federal law which says that any person working on a job for 30 days must not be denied the right to continue working. On a union film, this means that you must be allowed to join the union after 30 days. What this law does, however, is introduce another Catch-22 into the work equation — you cannot work on a union job without being in the union and you cannot get into the union without working on a union job. Like all Catch-22s, it is not an easy catch to break through. Like all Catch-22s, however, it is constantly broken by people who have the right combination of luck and the ability to generate opportunities for luck.

The Los Angeles working situation is also complicated by something called the *Producers' Experience Roster*, called the "Roster." Basically, this is a list of people who have worked on union films. It is divided into three categories, called Groups One, Two and Three. When you first get onto the roster, you are placed in Group Three. Two years later you rise to Group Two and three years after that you move up to Group One. Producers and editors who are looking to hire people are obligated to fill those positions first with anyone who is available from Group One. If there is no one suitable available in that group, then they can look in Group Two. If there is no one there, then they can look in Group Three. It is only when all of the qualified members are busy in all three groups that producers and editors are allowed to hire from outside the Roster. Needless to say, this almost never happens. This leaves virtually no chance for the unknown job seeker to break into a union film.

Yet people do it all the time. How? Some people do it because their parents or their friends are already on the Roster and are willing to hire them, despite the rules. Thirty days later they can join both the union and the Roster. What these people have going for them is their connection into the industry. *That* is what makes them different from other job seekers, however unfair it may be to those of us who have no one in the business to give us our first step.

So how does a normal person break into film and the union? The easiest way is to acknowledge to yourself that this is really two separate tasks, not just one. Your first step should be to try and get into film. *Then* you can try to break into the unions and the Roster. Once you have worked enough in non–union film work (and there is a lot of it around in Los Angeles and some in New York, though New York non-union filmmaking is rarely in features) then you can begin to accumulate the contacts and knowledge to make a break into union work.

In recent years it has become a bit easier to break into the union and the Roster in Los Angeles. People with enough work experience can usually get accepted into both if they have the proper proof. In addition, there is an increasing amount of non–union work, adding to the possibilities that young filmmakers can, at the low salaries they are usually willing to work at, get their foot in the door of filmmaking. In addition, new technologies such as Ediflex, Montage, CMX et al, are being developed faster than established editors can keep up with them. If a newcomer is able to work on these systems, he or she will be much in demand.

In the end, looking for the first job boils down to being able to be at the right place and being able to do the right job when you are at that place.

I have always found that good work does not go un-rewarded. If you work hard enough and learn well enough you will be able to move in whatever direction you want. First you must hit the pavements and meet a lot of people; then you will get work (if you are persistent enough without being obnoxious). Then you must be good enough at that work to impress people. Once that happens, you will be able to move toward whatever kind of filmmaking you want to do — whether it be in features, television, documentaries, or any-thing else. There are too many people in this industry for it to be easy. But it is never impossible.

. . . .
APPENDICES

Appendix I

To convert the length of your film, in feet, into time, you can use either a calculator or the following chart.

If you use a calculator it is helpful to have the following conversion chart, which lists the percentage of a second for each number frames in one foot.

FRAME-TO-SECONDS CONVERSION CHART			
Frames	1/100s of Seconds	Frames	1/100s of Seconds
1	.04	21	.88
2	.08	22	.92
3	.13	23	.96
4	.17	24	1.00
5	.21	25	1.04
6	.25	26	1.08
7	.29	27	1.13
8	.33	28	1.17
9	.38	29	1.21
10	.42	30	1.25
11	.46	31	1.29
12	.50	32	1.33
13	.54	33	1.38
14	.58	34	1.42
15	.62	35	1.46
16	.67	36	1.50
17	.71	37	1.54
18	.75	38	1.58
19	.79	39	1.62
20	.83	40	1.67

Let's find out how long *Silent Night, Silent Cowboy* runs in terms of time. Our film's total footage is 9432'12 (9432 feet and 12 frames)

To convert using this chart and a calculator, first multiply the number of feet in your film (in this case 9432) times 2/3, which is the ratio of seconds to 35mm film feet. This gives you 6288, which is the number of seconds in your film. Dividing by 60 to get the number of minutes gives you 104.8. This is 104 and eight tenths minutes. Eight tenths of a minute is equal to 48 seconds (60 seconds times .8). And, according to the above chart, twelve frames is .50 seconds. The length of *Silent Night, Silent Cowboy* is therefore 104 minutes, 48 and one-half seconds. Put in terms of hours, the film is one hour, 44 minutes, 48.5 seconds.

This may seem a little overwhelming to those of you who are terrible at math and at calculators. For these people I give you my footage-to-time conversion chart. Here's how to use it.

Find your film's length, in feet, in the column marked "feet" in the first chart (forget about the number of frames for now). The time will be directly across from it, in the proper column for you film gauge (each film format runs at a different number of feet per minute). Then use the second chart to find the number of seconds corresponding to the number of frames. Add this to the time obtained from the first chart and you've got it!

Let's figure out our film's length using the chart:

9000 feet	is	1:40:00.0	(1 hour 40 minutes)
400 feet	is	0:04:27.0	
32 feet	is	0:00:21.0	
12 frames	is	0:00:00.5	
TOTAL	**is**	**1:44:48.5**	

FOOTAGE-TO-TIME CONVERSION TABLE			
FEET	**16mm** (Hour: Min:Sec)	**35mm** (Hour: Min:Sec)	**70mm** (Hour: Min:Sec)
1	0:00:02	0:00:01	0:00:01
2	0:00:03	0:00:01	0:00:01
3	0:00:05	0:00:02	0:00:02
4	0:00:07	0:00:03	0:00:02
5	0:00:08	0:00:03	0:00:03
6	0:00:10	0:00:04	0:00:03
7	0:00:12	0:00:05	0:00:04
8	0:00:13	0:00:05	0:00:04
9	0:00:15	0:00:06	0:00:05
10	0:00:17	0:00:07	0:00:05
11	0:00:18	0:00:07	0:00:06
12	0:00:20	0:00:08	0:00:06
13	0:00:22	0:00:09	0:00:07
14	0:00:23	0:00:09	0:00:07
15	0:00:25	0:00:10	0:00:08
16	0:00:27	0:00:11	0:00:09
17	0:00:28	0:00:11	0:00:09
18	0:00:30	0:00:12	0:00:10
19	0:00:32	0:00:13	0:00:10
20	0:00:33	0:00:13	0:00:11
21	0:00:35	0:00:14	0:00:11
22	0:00:37	0:00:15	0:00:12
23	0:00:38	0:00:15	0:00:12
24	0:00:40	0:00:16	0:00:13
25	0:00:42	0:00:17	0:00:13
26	0:00:43	0:00:17	0:00:14
27	0:00:45	0:00:18	0:00:14
28	0:00:47	0:00:19	0:00:15
29	0:00:48	0:00:19	0:00:16
30	0:00:50	0:00:20	0:00:16

FOOTAGE-TO-TIME CONVERSION TABLE			
FEET	16mm (Hour: Min:Sec)	35mm (Hour: Min:Sec)	70mm (Hour: Min:Sec)
31	0:00:52	0:00:21	0:00:17
32	0:00:53	0:00:21	0:00:17
33	0:00:55	0:00:22	0:00:18
34	0:00:57	0:00:23	0:00:18
35	0:00:58	0:00:23	0:00:19
36	0:01:00	0:00:24	0:00:19
37	0:01:02	0:00:25	0:00:20
38	0:01:03	0:00:25	0:00:20
39	0:01:05	0:00:26	0:00:21
40	0:01:07	0:00:27	0:00:21
41	0:01:08	0:00:27	0:00:22
42	0:01:10	0:00:28	0:00:22
43	0:01:12	0:00:29	0:00:23
44	0:01:13	0:00:29	0:00:24
45	0:01:15	0:00:30	0:00:24
46	0:01:17	0:00:31	0:00:25
47	0:01:18	0:00:31	0:00:25
48	0:01:20	0:00:32	0:00:26
49	0:01:22	0:00:33	0:00:26
50	0:01:23	0:00:33	0:00:27
51	0:01:25	0:00:34	0:00:27
52	0:01:27	0:00:35	0:00:28
53	0:01:28	0:00:35	0:00:28
54	0:01:30	0:00:36	0:00:29
55	0:01:32	0:00:37	0:00:29
56	0:01:33	0:00:37	0:00:30
57	0:01:35	0:00:38	0:00:30
58	0:01:37	0:00:39	0:00:31
59	0:01:38	0:00:39	0:00:32
60	0:01:40	0:00:40	0:00:32

	FOOTAGE-TO-TIME CONVERSION TABLE		
FEET	**16mm** (Hour: Min:Sec)	**35mm** (Hour: Min:Sec)	**70mm** (Hour: Min:Sec)
61	0:01:42	0:00:41	0:00:33
62	0:01:43	0:00:41	0:00:33
63	0:01:45	0:00:42	0:00:34
64	0:01:47	0:00:43	0:00:34
65	0:01:48	0:00:43	0:00:35
66	0:01:50	0:00:44	0:00:35
67	0:01:52	0:00:45	0:00:36
68	0:01:53	0:00:45	0:00:36
69	0:01:55	0:00:46	0:00:37
70	0:01:57	0:00:47	0:00:37
71	0:01:58	0:00:47	0:00:38
72	0:02:00	0:00:48	0:00:39
73	0:02:02	0:00:49	0:00:39
74	0:02:03	0:00:49	0:00:40
75	0:02:05	0:00:50	0:00:40
76	0:02:07	0:00:51	0:00:41
77	0:02:08	0:00:51	0:00:41
78	0:02:10	0:00:52	0:00:42
79	0:02:12	0:00:53	0:00:42
80	0:02:13	0:00:53	0:00:43
81	0:02:15	0:00:54	0:00:43
82	0:02:17	0:00:55	0:00:44
83	0:02:18	0:00:55	0:00:44
84	0:02:20	0:00:56	0:00:45
85	0:02:22	0:00:57	0:00:45
86	0:02:23	0:00:57	0:00:46
87	0:02:25	0:00:58	0:00:47
88	0:02:27	0:00:59	0:00:47
89	0:02:28	0:00:59	0:00:48
90	0:02:30	0:01:00	0:00:48

FOOTAGE-TO-TIME CONVERSION TABLE			
FEET	16mm (Hour: Min:Sec)	35mm (Hour: Min:Sec)	70mm (Hour: Min:Sec)
91	0:02:32	0:01:01	0:00:49
92	0:02:33	0:01:01	0:00:49
93	0:02:35	0:01:02	0:00:50
94	0:02:37	0:01:03	0:00:50
95	0:02:38	0:01:03	0:00:51
96	0:02:40	0:01:04	0:00:51
97	0:02:42	0:01:05	0:00:52
98	0:02:43	0:01:05	0:00:52
99	0:02:45	0:01:06	0:00:53
100	0:02:47	0:01:07	0:00:53
200	0:05:33	0:02:13	0:01:47
300	0:08:20	0:03:20	0:02:40
400	0:11:07	0:04:27	0:03:33
500	0:13:53	0:05:33	0:04:27
600	0:16:40	0:06:40	0:05:20
700	0:19:27	0:07:47	0:06:13
800	0:22:13	0:08:53	0:07:07
900	0:25:00	0:10:00	0:08:08
1,000	0:27:47	0:11:07	0:08:53
2,000	0:53:33	0:22:13	0:17:47
3,000	1:23:20	0:33:20	0:26:40
4,000	1:51:07	0:44:27	0:35:33
5,000	2:18:53	0:55:33	0:44:27
6,000	2:46:40	1:06:40	0:53:20
7,000	3:14:27	1:17:47	1:02:13
8,000	3:42:13	1:28:53	1:11:07
9,000	4:10:00	1:40:00	1:20:00
10,000	4:37:47	1:51:07	1:28:53

FOOTAGE-TO-TIME CONVERSION TABLE			
FEET	**16mm** (Hour: Min:Sec)	**35mm** (Hour: Min:Sec)	**70mm** (Hour: Min:Sec)
11,000	5:04:33	2:02:13	1:37:47
12,000	5:32:20	2:13:20	1:46:40
13,000	6:00:47	2:24:57	1:55:33
14,000	6:27:53	2:35:33	2:04:27
15,000	6:55:40	2:46:40	2:13:20

Appendix II

To find the length, in feet and frames, for a piece of film of a given length of time, locate the amount of time you want to convert in the "seconds" or "minutes" column (there are two charts: one for "seconds" and one for "minutes.") The length, in feet and frames, will be directly across from it in the proper column for your film gauge.

For example, a 16mm film that lasts 21 minutes and 11 seconds is 762'24.

TIME-TO-FOOTAGE CONVERSION CHART			
	16mm	35mm	70mm
Secs	Ft'Fr	Ft'Fr	Ft'Fr
1	0'24	1'08	1'11
2	1'08	3'00	3'09
3	1'32	4'08	5'08
4	2'16	6'00	7'06
5	3'00	7'08	9'05
6	3'24	9'00	11'03
7	4'08	10'08	13'02
8	4'32	12'00	15'00
9	5'16	13'08	13'11
10	6'00	15'00	18'09
11	6'24	16'08	20'08
12	7'08	18'00	22'06
13	7'32	19'08	24'05
14	8'16	21'00	26'03
15	9'00	22'08	28'02
16	9'24	24'00	30'00
17	10'08	25'08	31'11
18	10'32	27'00	33'10
19	11'16	28'08	35'08
20	12'00	30'00	37'06

TIME-TO-FOOTAGE CONVERSION CHART			
	16mm	35mm	70mm
Secs	Ft'Fr	Ft'Fr	Ft'Fr
21	12'24	31'08	39'05
22	13'08	33'00	41'03
23	13'32	34'08	43'02
24	14'16	36'00	45'00
25	15'00	37'08	46'11
26	15'24	39'00	48'10
27	16'08	40'08	50'08
28	16'32	42'00	52'06
29	17'16	43'08	54'05
30	18'00	45'00	56'03
31	18'24	46'08	58'02
32	19'08	48'00	60'00
33	19'32	49'08	61'11
34	20'16	51'00	63'10
35	21'00	52'08	65'08
36	21'24	54'00	67'06
37	22'08	55'08	69'05
38	22'32	57'00	71'03
39	23'16	58'08	73'02
40	24'00	60'00	75'00
41	24'24	61'08	76'11
42	25'08	63'00	78'10
43	25'32	64'08	80'08
44	26'16	66'00	82'06
45	27'00	67'08	84'05
46	27'24	69'00	86'03
47	28'08	70'08	88'02
48	28'32	72'00	90'00
49	29'16	73'08	91'11
50	30'00	75'00	93'10

TIME-TO-FOOTAGE CONVERSION CHART			
	16mm	35mm	70mm
Secs	Ft'Fr	Ft'Fr	Ft'Fr
51	30'24	76'08	95'08
52	31'08	78'00	97'06
53	31'32	79'08	99'05
54	32'16	81'00	101'03
55	33'00	82'08	103'02
56	33'24	84'00	105'00
57	34'08	85'08	106'11
58	34'32	87'00	108'10
59	35'16	88'08	110'08
60	36'00	90'00	112'06

The chart below gives the footages for time in minutes:

TIME-TO-FOOTAGE CONVERSION CHART			
	16mm	35mm	70mm
Mins	Feet	Feet	Ft'Fr
1	36	90	112'06
2	72	180	225'00
3	108	270	337'06
4	144	360	450'00
5	180	450	562'06
6	216	540	675'00
7	252	630	787'06
8	288	720	900'00
9	324	810	1,012'06
10	360	900	1,125'00

TIME-TO-FOOTAGE CONVERSION CHART

Mins	16mm Feet	35mm Feet	70mm Ft'Fr
11	396	990	1,237'06
12	432	1,080	1,350'00
13	468	1,170	1,462'06
14	504	1,260	1,575'00
15	540	1,350	1,687'06
16	576	1,440	1,800'00
17	612	1,530	1,912'06
18	648	1,620	2,025'00
19	684	1,710	2,137'06
20	720	1,800	2,250'00
21	756	1,890	2,362'06
22	792	1,980	2,475'00
23	828	2,070	2,587'06
24	864	2,160	2,700'00
25	900	2,250	2,812'06
26	936	2,340	2,925'00
27	972	2,430	3,037'06
28	1,008	2,520	3,150'00
29	1,044	2,610	3,262'06
30	1,080	2,700	3,375'00
31	1,116	2,790	3,487'00
32	1,152	2,880	3,600'00
33	1,188	2,970	3,712'06
34	1,224	3,060	3,825'00
35	1,260	3,150	3,937'06
36	1,296	3,240	4,050'00
37	1,332	3,330	4,162'06
38	1,368	3,420	4,275'00
39	1,404	3,510	4,387'06
40	1,440	3,600	4,500'00

TIME-TO-FOOTAGE CONVERSION CHART			
	16mm	35mm	70mm
Mins	Feet	Feet	Ft'Fr
41	1,476	3,690	4,612'06
42	1,512	3,780	4,725'00
43	1,548	3,870	4,837'06
44	1,584	3,960	4,950'00
45	1,620	4,050	5,062'06
46	1,656	4,140	5,175'00
47	1,692	4,230	5,287'06
48	1,728	4,320	5,400'00
49	1,764	4,410	5,512'06
50	1,800	4,500	5,625'00
51	1,836	4,590	5,737'06
52	1,872	4,680	5,850'00
53	1,908	4,570	5,962'06
54	1,944	4,860	6,075'00
55	1,980	4,950	6,187'06
56	2,016	5,040	6,300'00
57	2,052	5,130	6,412'06
58	2,088	5,220	6,525'00
59	2,124	5,310	6,637'06
60	2,160	5,400	6,750'00

....
....

GLOSSARY

A

A & B Roll Printing The process of cutting negative, and then printing from it, so that alternating shots are placed on two strands of cut-together negative running parallel to each other. All the odd cuts are placed on one strand (cuts one, three, five, seven, etc.) and the even cuts on the other (two, four, six, eight, etc.). Black opaque leader is cut in between these shots. Thus, when the negative is printed, both strands are run at the same time, printing all of the shots together onto one piece of print film. This method is more expensive than regular *single strand printing* (also called *zero cutting*, or *A-roll printing* since all cuts are placed on one single strand) but is used on some films to create fades and dissolves without going to a second generation optical. It is also used in 16mm films.

A-Wind Used in 16mm films to describe the position of the emulsion relative to the center of the wound–up film. A-wind film has its emulsion facing down to the center. A-wind film is common to projected film (work picture, release prints, etc.). See also *B-wind*.

Academy Leader Leader which conforms to the standards set up by the Academy of Motion Picture Arts and Sciences. From the projection start mark on this leader, it is exactly eight seconds (12 feet in 35mm, four feet and 32 frames in 16mm) until the beginning of the picture.

Academy Roll–Off A standard, established by the Academy of Motion Picture Arts and Sciences, for movie theatre sound. It involves decreasing quite a bit of high–frequency sound. This roll–off is what Dolby® film sound tries to avoid.

A.C.E. The Association of Cinema Editors, an honorary society of editors.

Acmade® Coding Machine A coding machine which uses a heating element to emboss eight–digit code numbers onto the film from a roll of colored tape.

Act Break In television, that time in the running of the film where the action is stopped to make room for a commercial. The best act breaks come at natural points in the story. The television networks also put time constraints on the placement of act breaks so the commercials do not come too close together.

Add-A-Plate See *Console*.

ADR Automatic Dialogue Replacement. See *Looping*.

Alignment Tones A set of tones which conforms to industry-established standards for recording sound. They are of specific frequencies and are laid down at a specific volume so that whenever the tape that they are recorded onto is played back aligned to these tones it will have the same volume and equalization properties as it did when it was originally recorded.

Anamorphic A method of getting wide-screen images from normal 35mm film. In the shooting, a special lens is used which squeezes the image. A matching lens reverses the process during projection. If you were to look at a frame of anamorphic film without "unsqueezing" it (such images would be called "squeezed") it would look like an image on a balloon after the air has been let out of it.

Answer Print A timed (color-corrected) print of a film. It may or may not have a soundtrack married to it.

Aspect Ratio The ratio of a projected image's screen width to its screen height. Most movies today are shot at a ratio of 1.85:1. A second, less-used feature ratio is the slightly taller 1.66:1. Widescreen anamorphic films have a 2.35:1 ratio. Television is shot at a 1.33:1 ratio.

Assembly A rough piecing-together of the cut, sometimes called a "rough cut". The assembly consists of all of the scenes shot, and usually runs quite a bit longer than the finished film.

B

B-Negative Takes which were shot and developed but not printed.

B-Wind Used in 16mm films to describe the position of the emulsion relative to the center of the wound–up film. B-wind film has its emulsion facing away from the center (an easy mnemonic is to say that it has its *base* wound down). B-wind film is common to camera original and film which is used as a printing element. See also *A-wind*.

Balance Stripe See *Stripe*.

Balancing See *Reel Balancing*.

Base The bottom side of 35mm film. It is shiny, as opposed to the top part of the film — the emulsion — which is dull. Actually, the base is a plastic material onto which the three layers of color film stock (or the one layer of black and white) are glued. 16mm reversal film projects properly when its base is on top. Also called the *cel* side of the film. See also *Emulsion*.

Beep A brief tone which can be used to mark a specific location on a soundtrack. It is commonly used at the beginning of a reel (where it is called a "head beep"), two seconds before the first frame of the picture (nine feet after the start mark in 35mm, three feet and 24 frames in 16mm). It is also used in the tail leader, two seconds after the last frame of picture (where it is called a "tail beep.") Also called a *pop*.

Betamax Also called "Beta". A videotape format which uses 1/2" tapes. This is the less common of the two video formats used in the home; the more common one is *VHS*.

Blacking The process of recording nothing more than the *control track* onto a videotape. When tapes are used which have already been blacked, they are called *pre-blacked tapes*.

Blow-Up An optical in which a portion of the frame has been enlarged to fill the whole frame. Often used when some unwanted object (such as a microphone) appears in the frame. The image is then blown up so that the object is pushed outside of the frame and disappears. When a film is shot in 35mm but released in 70mm (or shot in 16mm and released in 35mm) the entire film is optically blown-up. This larger format print is called the "blow-up print."

Broadcast Quality A video show which is of professional enough quality (in terms of technical standards) to be able to be aired by a television station.

Bump When two sounds are cut together it is possible that the background sounds will not match exactly. The effect of the different sounds cutting together is called a bump. The tasks of "dialogue splitting" and "mixing" are designed to smooth out these bumps and end up with one seamless soundtrack.

Burn-in Superimposing something (usually titles or some other wording) over already shot action.

Butt Splicer A splicer which joins picture or track with a vertical splice. See also *Diagonal Splicer*.

C

Camera Original The actual film that went through the camera during shooting. See *Negative,* and *Reversal*.

Camera Report The form filled out by the camera department which lists all of the takes shot on any particular roll of negative and their cumulative footage. Takes which the director liked are circled for printing. All other takes are processed but not printed (see *B-negative*).

Card A credit which stays stationary on screen, usually fading in and out. A credit with only one name is called a *Single Card*.

Cel See *Base*.

Change Notes See *Conformation Notes*.

Changeover Cue The second projectionist cue. When the projectionist sees it, he or she is supposed to switch the projection from one projector to another.

Changeovers The marks placed in the upper right hand corner of the frame to cue the projectionist to change from one reel to another. The first set of marks is called the *Motor Cue* and the second is called the *Changeover Cue*.

Changeover Tails The amount of footage added to the end

of reel (usually 24 frames, but sometimes less) which guarantees that the projectionist will not make the changeover too early in the action.

Character Reel A reel for an ADR session which is set up for the recording of one character's lines only.

Cheated Track A piece of track which is cut into the work track purposely out of sync with the picture.

China Girl A standardized image of a white woman's face which is used by labs and optical houses as a reference to determine skin tone colors.

Cinetabs Small tabs which are slid into rolled-up film and used for the identification of rolls of picture and track. Also called *Trim Tabs*.

Cinex A test strip of film in which the same frame is sequentially printed at precisely varying colors and densities. This cinex is used to test color and density timing at an optical house. When a preferred color balance and density is selected (by marking the frame that looks the way the director, editor and d.p. want), the optical is shot at that set of *timing lights*. Also called a *wedge*.

Circled Takes Takes of picture or sound which are selected for printing or transferring. Also called *kept takes*.

Clapper See *Slate*.

Click Track A musical rhythm. Each click represents the length of film for one musical beat. A click of 12/0 denotes that one beat of music comes every 12 frames.

Code Number A number which is physically printed onto the edge of the film, in ink. It is used to identify pieces of film and track in the editing room and to keep the picture and track in sync. These numbers usually run one every 16 frames (one 35mm foot). Also called an *Edge Number*. Not to be confused with a *Latent Edge Number*.

Color Bars A standardized set of graduated colors recorded to a precise standard onto a videotape. On playback, the monitors can be set to match this standard.

Color Card A standardized card which contains a scale of colors. When these are photographed, it is easy to tell just how far the printed colors deviate from the actual colors. Such cards facilitate the color correction (or *timing*) of the dailies at the lab.

Color Correction See *Timing.*

Conformation (1) A change made to a reel after it has been locked. (2) Also used to describe the process of negative matching, i.e. *negative conforming.* (3) In video editing, the process of matching the edits made in video to the 35mm film so that there is a complete 35mm cut work picture and track, which matches the video cut in every way.

Conformation Notes A list which minutely and accurately documents any conformations made to a reel. Also called *Change Notes.*

Console A Moviola with one picture head and two sound heads. Often a second sound head is attached onto a regular Moviola. This attachment is called an *add–a–plate.*

Contrast Ratio The ratio of the brightest area in a film or video image to the darkest area. Film has, inherently, a larger contrast ratio than video.

Control Track A signal on a videotape which is used to control synchronization during playback.

Core A two– or three–inch diameter plastic disk, which is exactly the width of the film you are using. The film, or track, is wound onto the cores for editing or projection, instead of winding it onto take–up reels.

Coverage The various angles that a director shoots for a scene.

Crawl A particular kind of credit optical in which the names move up (or, in rare cases, down) the screen. Also called a "roll–up."

CRI Color Reversal Intermediate. A kind of film which can be struck directly from the negative, resulting in another piece of negative, without going through an interpositive stage. CRIs were used more when interpositive stock was inferior to that used today. Then it was preferable to avoid the extra generation that going to an interpositive and then an internegative would necessitate.

CRI Print A release print from a CRI, rather than from an internegative (*IN*) or original (*EK*) print.

Cut (1) The cut-together work picture and work track. The term is used either for picture and track together or singly. (2) The place where the editor goes from one take to another.

Cut Picture See *Work Picture.*

Cutter (Moviola) A type of upright Moviola which has no takeup arms. It is easier to thread and is gentler on the film than a regular take-up Moviola, all of which makes it better for its use as a cutting machine. Some editors work with two cutters, others use one cutter and one take-up.

Cutting Copy The work picture.

D

Dailies Every day during the shooting of a film, the director and some members of the cast and crew view the footage shot the preceding day to verify that everything is satisfactory. If it is not, some of the footage may have to be reshot. These screenings are called "dailies screenings" or *rushes.* Also used to refer the material that was screened at the rushes.

Degaussing The process of erasing all sound from a piece of magnetic stock or tape. "Degaussers" are also used to make sure that all of the editing equipment which comes into contact with the soundtrack is demagnetized.

Density The degree of darkness in an image. An image which is dark is denser than one which is light. Changes in density are achieved by changing all three *timing lights.*

Diagonal Splicer A splicer which will join two pieces of track diagonally instead of vertically. Used in sound and music editing since diagonal splices often smooth out the differences between the sounds at the cut. See also *butt splicer.*

Dialogue Splitting The process of separating work track pieces which *bump* when played together, onto separate *units* or *elements* so that each may be treated separately at the mix.

Dirty Dupe See *Dupe.*

Dissolve An *optical* in which one image slowly changes into another.

D-M-E Track An *M & E* (music and effects) full-coat track which also includes, usually on channel one, the mixed dialogue, to be used a reference for foreign looping.

DNU Abbreviation for "Do Not Use."

Domestic Version The major release of a film, in the United States and English speaking countries.

Double Print An *optical* in which frames are printed more than once. This is usually done to slow down the action. An optical in which each frame of the original shot was printed twice would appear to move twice as slow.

Double Reel When the film is ready to be distributed, the 1000 foot editing reels are combined into 2000 foot reels for theatres. This is accomplished by combining reels one and two into Double Reel One, editing reels three and four into Double Reel Two, and so on. The original single reels are then referred to as Reel 1A and 1B, Reel 2A and 2B, etc.

Drop Shadow A design for titles in which the letters in the titles have a dark shadow superimposed, slightly askew of them. This makes the letters more readable.

Double System Projection The process of screening a film which has separate picture and sound reels. You will almost always be screening your film in this manner until the final *answer print*.

Dub See *Mix*.

Dubbing 1) Mixing the film. 2) Looping.

Dummy A machine which can play back 35mm or 16mm magnetic track at the film mix interlocked with the picture and other dummies.

Dupe A copy. Picture is often duped onto a piece of black-and-white film. Such dupes are called *slop dupes* or *slop prints*. When track is duped, it is normal to ask for a *one-to-one* dupe, which is a copy made at the same volume and equalization as the original.

Dupe Negative A piece of negative which has been created from another piece of negative. Most opticals are dupe negatives.

E

Edge Number See *Code Number*.

Edit Decision List A list generated by the computer on which a video edit has been made which lists all of the cuts (called *events*), the type of cut (e.g. picture only, track only, both) and all of the pertinent time code information from the footage. A list which gives the matching cuts in terms of the original film footage is called a *Film Cut List.*

Editing Bench A wide table on which most of the editorial equipment sits. As a result, most of the physical cutting of the film, as well as a bulk of the assistant's work, is done on the bench. Both the *rewinds* and the *synchronizer* are on this table, as well as the splicers and a host of other equipment. Editors who cut their films on *flatbeds* do not generally use editing benches as much as editors who cut on an upright since the flatbed itself functions as the bench for most of their work. Sometimes referred to as the "Editing Table."

Effect (1) In picture editing, an optical or special photographic manipulation of the film. (2) In sound editing, a specific sound, such as a tire squeal or water dripping. (3) Also used to mean a special manipulation of elements during the shooting of the film, such as the creation of rain or snow.

EK Print A release print from the *camera original* (so-called because, until recently, most feature films were shot on original negative made by Eastman Kodak) as opposed to an *IP Print* or a *CRI Print.*

Element An individual sound track at the mix. Also called a *unit.*

Emulsion The light-sensitive top side of 35mm film. It is dull, as opposed to the bottom part of the film — the *base* — which is shiny. Your lips will leave a mark when pressed to the emulsion side of the film. In 16mm reversal film, the emulsion side is the down side of the film.

EOR End of Reel. See *LFOA.*

EPS Electronic Post-Sync. The same thing as *ADR.* See *Looping.*

Equalization The process of adjusting the volume level of individual frequencies of a sound so as to change its tone.

Event In video editing, some visual or sound change which needs to be programmed into the editing computer. The most common examples of events are picture or sound cuts or optical effects.

Extension In sound or picture editing, a trim which is added to a piece already used in the film.

Eye Sync The process of synching up the picture and track when slates do not exist. It involves finding points in the sound which can also be easily located on the picture, such as door slams. Certain letters of the alphabet also provide good sync points. Words beginning with the letters *b, d, k, p,* or *t,* are likely to be easier to locate pictorially and sound-wise than others.

F

Fades *Opticals* in which an image gradually goes to black (fade–out) or emerges from black (fade–in). It is also possible to have images fade in from other colors besides black. Sound can also be said to fade–in or fade–out.

Field In video, one-half of a full video frame. A video frame is created when the electronic gun at the back of your television set shoots a beam of electrons in a continuous stream onto the back of your television screen, activating the phosphors on the screen. The stream is shot in a series of horizontal lines, called *scan lines,* from left to right across the screen. First, the odd-numbered lines are scanned, then the even-numbered lines. Each of these two scanning passes is called a field. Thus, there are two fields in each video frame. In the United States there are 525 scan lines per video frame. In Europe there are 625. In high definition television (HDTV) there are quite a bit more, though the exact number varies with each competing system.

File In computer editing, one complete section of the film, all of whose footage and editing information is stored on one computer disk. Normally, a film will contain many files. This is actually a computer term, used to denote a block of information on a computer disk, accessed by one name.

Fill (1) In picture editing, waste film. It is used to space out soundtracks within a reel to preserve synchronization with the picture. It is also called *slug film* or *spacing.* (2) In sound editing, background ambience or tone which is used to replace any unwanted sounds on the soundtrack. Also called *room tone.*

Film Cut List A list generated by the computer on which an edit has been made which lists all of the cuts (called *events*), the type of cut (e.g. picture only, track only, both), all of the pertinent time code information from the footage, as well as information needed to help *conform* the printed dailies or cut work print and track to the video edits.

Flange A large platter with a small core at its center. It is used to wind film up.

Flash Frames As the camera is slowing down at the end of a take it lets more light in. This shows up as a frame or two on the film where the image is very bright. Flash frames, as they are called, are handy for identifying the ends of takes.

Flatbed A kind of editing machine. The separate film and soundtrack are run horizontally across this table-like device in sync with each other.

Flipped Track Track which has been turned upside-down, so that it will not be read by the sound head. Track is flipped so that it will be in sync and ready to be used in case it is needed. All that has to be done is to unflip the track. Because this places the backside of the *balance stripe* under the sound head, no sound should be recorded on that stripe. This is also why it is not a good idea to flip *full-coat* track.

Flop An *optical* in which the frame is turned around so that what was the left side of the frame becomes the right and vice versa.

Foleys Effects, usually body movement of some sort, such as footsteps or clothes rustle, which is recorded in sync with picture.

Foreigns Another name for the *M&E tracks*, so called because these are the tracks which are supplied to the foreign countries for dubbing.

Four–Stripe See *Full–Coat*.

Four–Track See *Full–Coat*.

4-2-4 The method of recording and playing back Dolby® Stereo sound for film. The tracks are mixed down from their four-track format to a two-track form (called a *Print Master*.) It is this two-track version which is transferred to *optical track* and married to the picture. At the theatres, the Dolby equipment expands the two tracks back into four.

Frame (1) In film, an individual picture recorded onto the film. Each frame is exposed for 1/48th of a second. The camera shutter is then closed for another 1/48th of a second while the film is pulled down to the next film frame, where is then exposed for 1/48th of a second. It is the rapid projection of these succeeding still picture frames, in which the position of the elements within the picture changes slightly from frame to frame, that gives the audience the illusion of motion. There are 24 frames in each second of film. See also *Persistence of Vision*. (2) In video, one frame is composed of a series of *scan lines* projected rapidly onto the television screen. Each video frame is made up of two *fields* of scan lines which interlace. There are 30 video frames per second.

Frame Line The thin horizontal line between two consecutive frames of film.

Freeze Frame An *optical* in which a single frame is held for any desired length.

Full Coat 35mm track which is completely covered with oxide. As many as six tracks of sound can be recorded onto its surface. Other configurations are four and three tracks. For that reason, full coat is also known as *three–track, three–stripe* (though this, more accurately, should refer to a strip of film with three separate stripes of oxide), *four–track*, or *six–track*..

G

Gang One of the wheels of a synchronizer through which film or track is run. Most synchronizers have four gangs.

Generation A stage in the duplication of film or track. A copy of a first-generation recording will be second-generation. Thus, an interpositive is a second generation piece of film, as is the work print struck from the original negative. In film, sound and video, each time a new generation of material is made, the quality of the image or sound degrades from the original material.

Goodies Sound effects which have been cut but not built into the units. They are brought to the mix boxed and ready for insertion into a unit if they are needed.

Grading An English term for *timing*.

Gray Card A standardized card which works exactly like a color card except that it shows graduated black-to-white rather than colors. Also called a "gray scale."

Guillotine Splicer A type of splicer, commonly used in Europe and in 16mm films, which uses an unperforated roll of clear splicing tape, and which has the cutting blade to the right side of the block rather than in the center.

H

Handle An extra number of frames attached to the head and tail of an optical, added as a safety precaution. The exact number varies from one optical house to another.

Hand Over To give all of the necessary footage and paperwork to the sound and music departments for the beginning of their work. When you hand over your film, you are (in essence) beginning the sound job.

Hazeltine The machine that the color timer at the lab (or at the optical house) uses to determine how to time the negative. The footage is run through the machine by hand (on a set of rewinds) and the timer adjusts the amount of red, blue and green light that the film will be printed at. While he is doing that, he is looking at a television monitor which shows him what the projected film should look like at those values. Also called a color video analyzer. See also *Timing*.

HDTV High Definition Telvision. A television format which uses many more scan lines per screen image than the normal. This enables video to have much sharper images as well as getting a look and feel much closer to that of a 35mm filmed image.

Head Pop See *Beep*.

Head Trim See *Trim*.

Hi-Con Short for "high contrast." A black and white optical stock often used for credits or special effects. It reduces all elements to black and white, thus giving you the maximum contrast between the light and dark elements in the frame.

Hole A portion of a soundtrack which has no sound in it. Holes should be filled in with *room tone* before screening.

I

IN Print See *IP Print*.

Inching Knob A knob on a flatbed or other editing machine which moves the film one frame at a time.

Insert Shot A close shot of a particular object (such as a newspaper headline) or an action (such as a person turning a key in a lock).

Interlock Screening A screening in which the picture and track are on separate elements and are run locked together in sync. Also called *double system projection*.

Internegative A duplicate negative, also called an IN, struck from an interpositive, by contact printing.

Interpositive A piece of negative film stock , also called an IP, which has a positive image printed on it (having been struck by contact printing directly from a piece of negative).

IP/IN The process of making a new negative of a film by striking an interpositive and then, from that, striking a new negative — the internegative. A few years ago this two-step process was replaced by the *CRI* process, which eliminated one extra generation of duplication. But advances in the IP/IN stocks now make this the preferable method for release printing and preparing new negatives for opticals.

IP Print A release print from an IP, as opposed to an *EK Print*. In actuality, the release print is struck from the internegative, which is why the print is also called an *IN Print*.

K

KEM A brand name for a common *flatbed* editing machine.

Kept Takes Takes of picture or sound which are selected for printing or transferring. Also called *circled takes*.

Key Number A number which is imprinted into the edge of the film negative. This number is then exposed onto the print film, giving a permanent record of every piece of film used in the movie. Also called a *latent edge number*.

L

Lab Report The report sent from the laboratory with the picture dailies which lists all of the takes which were printed, along with their timing lights.

Latent Edge Number See *Key Number*.

Leader Film with no image on it, generally a solid color (white, black, green, red and yellow are common colors) which is used for a myriad of purposes. Most commonly, it is used at the head and tails of reels to protect the film when it is being wound and rewound since *it* is wound on the outside of the reels rather than the valuable picture. It also provides the thread-up necessary for projection. Since it can be easily written on, it is also used for identification purposes.

LFOA Last Frame of Action. The last frame on a reel of film or track before the leader begins. Also called LFOP (Last Frame of Picture) and EOR (End of Reel).

Lift A piece of cut picture and/or track which is removed from the film and stored intact, rather than being broken apart and stored as trims.

Line The Script (1) During the shooting, the process that the script supervisor goes through to create the *lined script*. (2) In computer editing, breaking the script down into manageable sections for the computer to handle.

Lined Script The shooting script of the film onto which the script supervisor has noted all of the set–ups which were shot and what lines of dialogue and action each of the set–ups covered.

Lock That point in the editing of the film when the picture editing is completed. The cut is then "locked". This rarely happens until the very end of the film, so it is common parlance in my editing room to say that a film is "latched" instead (locked, but liable to be opened again).

Loop (1) An individual lined to be looped. (2) A short piece of track (usually of a sound) which has been joined at its ends to form a continuous band. When played, it will go around in a circle, providing a smooth, continuous sound.

Looping Dialogue replacement. Sometimes called dubbing, ADR or EPS. The actor watches the film and hears the dialogue to be replaced in a set of headphones, while speaking the line into a microphone.

M

M&E Track A mixed *full-coat* which has the music on one channel (usually channel two), the mixed effects on another channel (usually track three or tracks three and four), and no dialogue. This track is sent to foreign countries for versions of the film in their language. There, they lay their own dialogue onto the already mixed music and effects channels (thus, M&E). Actually, the English dialogue is generally put onto channel one as a reference for them, creating a *D–M–E* track.

Mag Soundtrack stock. If the track is wound so that the oxide part of the track is facing up the reel is said to be wound *mag up* or *mag out*. If the track is wound so that the oxide is facing into the reel, the reel is said to be wound *mag down*.

Main Titles All of the titles which appear at or near the beginning of a film. The card which has the name of the film is sometimes called the Main Title.

Married Print At no time during the shooting or editing of a film are the sound and picture on the same piece of film. It is not until the film is ready to go into the theatres that the two are combined, or "married" to each other. The resultant print is called the married print or married *answer print*. See also *Optical Track*.

Matte Shot An *optical* in which part of one shot is combined with part of another to create a new shot which did not exist to begin with. An example would be taking a shot of an astronaut shot in a studio, combining it with a shot of a lunar landscape, to give a final shot in which the astronaut appears to be on the moon.

MIDI A standard for the electronic reproduction of sound and music as played back on one or more synthesizers.

Mix Also called a *dub*. The combination of many sound elements—dialogue, music, and sound effects—into one cohesive and balanced soundtrack.

Mixed Mag A single mono stripe of the mix of a film.

Mixing Board An electronic console which has separate volume and equalization controls for each of a large number of sounds. The mixer or "recordist" adjusts each of the sounds and then is able to combine them into the final soundtrack.

Monitor   A television screen designed solely to accept signals from a video playback machine, such as a videotape player. The best monitors do not pick up standard television signals from the air.

MOS   A picture take for which no sound was shot. The rumor is that this term comes from the old German filmmakers who used to say that a shot was done "mit out sound." (I'm not kidding here.)

Motor Cue   The first *changeover* cue. When the projectionist sees it, he or she is supposed to start up the motor on the next projector without turning on its picture or sound.

MOW   A Movie Of the Week. A feature length film shot specifically for television. Typically, MOWs will have longer editing schedules than episodic television shows but far shorter schedules than features.

Moviola®   A brand name for a common upright editing machine. The separate film and soundtrack are run vertically from the feeding reels below onto the takeup reels above in sync with each other. Also called an "upright Moviola" to differentiate it from a *flatbed*, which the company also makes.

N

Negative   Original film exposed in the camera, in which the polarity of the image is reversed — black becomes white, white becomes black. Original camera film which records an image without reversing the polarity is called, paradoxically, *reversal* original.

Negative Cutter   The editor who takes the camera original and cuts it to exactly match the cuts which the editor has made on his or her work picture. Also called a negative matcher.

NG Takes   Takes which were *No Good.*

Numbering Machine   A machine which inks *code numbers* onto the edge of the film and track. Also called a *numbering block.*

O

Off–Line Editing System A video editing system which usually creates cuts only and is not capable of color correction. The edits are not of a high enough technical quality for broadcast by a television station (called *broadcast quality*.)

One–Light Dailies Dailies which are not individually timed at the lab, but are all printed at one set of *timing lights*.

One–to–One Copy A sound transfer which is at exactly the same level and equalization as the original sound.

On–Line Editing System An expensive video editing system which generates cuts and opticals, as well as color balancing the image, that are of professional enough quality to be aired by a television station (called *broadcast quality*).

Optical A piece of film which has been manipulated in some way, after it has already been shot, to create some special effect. See also *blow-up, dissolve, double print, fades, flop, freeze frame, matte shot, reposition, reverse, skip prit, superimposition, split screen* and *wipe*.

Optical Track The soundtrack on a *married print*. It appears as a set of squiggly lines at the left side of the picture. When light is projected through the optical track (which is a piece of *film*, not a piece of oxide layered track), the light coming through it is read by a photocell behind the film. This photocell decodes the patterns of light into sounds — providing us with the dialogue, music and sound effects that we hear on a film's soundtrack.

O/S Over the Shoulder. Used to denote a shot in which one character is visible over the shoulder of another. As an example, a shot in which Abby is visible over Bob's shoulder would be described as ABBY — o/s BOB.

Out A take, no part of which has been used in the film.

Overcranked Shot A shot which is made at a faster than normal (24 frames per second) camera speed. When projected, the action will appear to be moving slower than normal.

P

Perfs The sprocket holes in the film.

Persistence of Vision The human eye can only differentiate movement down to as short a time span as approximately 1/20th of a second. The very foundation of filmmaking is based on this, since it tricks the eye into thinking that still frames, projected 1/48th of a second apart, are actually one continuously running image. Though each frame is slightly different from the preceding one, the eye merges them, retaining each image until it is superseded by the next one. See also *Frame*.

Phasing The hollow sound that occurs when two identical tracks are run in near-perfect sync.

Pick–Up Shot After a shot has been made on the set, the director sometimes wishes to re-do part of the take. This re–do is called a pick–up shot since the director "picks up" the filming part way into the previous set–up. Some script supervisors slate it with a new set–up letter, others use the same letter as the original shot and add the letters "p.u." after the shot number. For instance, a pick–up to shot 11A could be called 11B or 11Apu.

Platter System The most common form of projection in movie theatres today. The entire film, shipped to the theatres on 2000 foot reels, is rolled heads-in onto a huge horizontal metal platter, much like a large record turntable. All of the release print reels are joined together, after removing their head and tail leaders. The film is then threaded over a series of guides, into the projector, out of the projector and over another series of guides where it winds back (heads-in) onto another huge platter. In this way, the film can be projected without changeovers. All that is necessary is for someone to rethread the film before each show. As a result, in multiple cinema operations, one projectionist can take the place of four or five. As another result, a scratch or other problem which begins to occur in reel two (let us say) will go all the way through the film until the end.

Playback A musical recording which is played back to the actors and actresses on the set to maintain the same performance and sync from take to take.

Pop See *Beep*.

Pre–Blacked Tape A tape which has already had a *control track* recorded onto it, but no picture or sound.

Pre–Dub When many units are involved in a dub it is difficult, if not impossible, to play them all at one time. In this case, similar elements are mixed together onto four channels of a *full-coat* (all of the dialogue, all of the looping, all of the foley, all of the effects, for instance) and this new dub (also called a *pre-mix*) will replace those many elements at the mix.

Print Master See 4–2–4.

Protection IP An *interpositive* copy of the cut negative (though sometimes protection IPs are struck of individual takes) struck for the purpose of providing a useable negative of the film in case should anything happen to the original negative. Protection IPs are often ordered when you are going to be shipping the negative to another place by air, or when you have finished cutting the negative and are going to be striking many prints of the film.

Pull–Up An additional amount of track added onto the end of each mixed reel which is the same track as begins the next incoming reel. Used to prevent a sound drop–out when successive reels of married release print are cut together in movie theatres.

Q

1/4″ Tape The standard width magnetic tape used in recording original production sound. As a result, the original tapes (recorded on the set) are often called "the quarter-inch."

R

Rank Properly called a "Rank-Cintel Flying Spot Scanner." This is a name for a machine which takes a film image and transfers it to signals which can be recorded onto videotape.

Reconstitution The act of taking the KEM rolls after the editor has removed the footage needed in the cut and adding leader to the picture or track to bring the rolls back into sync.

Reel Balancing The act of apportioning the footage between all the reels so that no reel has too little or too much film on it, and so that *changeovers* can be made in the theatres without disturbing the sound or music in a way that would be disconcerting to an audience.

Registration IP A special type of *interpositive* in which a special stock and printing process is used so that the image on the IP will be as rock–steady as possible. This type of IP is often made for the backgrounds behind titles because superimposing the two things would cause any slight jiggle in the backgrounds to be very visible.

Release Print The *married print* which is sent to theatres for showing. Normally it is not made directly from the original camera negative but is struck from a *dupe negative*, usually an *internegative*.

Reposition An *optical* in which the image has been reframed or moved in some way, usually up or down.

Resolution Line See *Scan Line*.

Reverse (1) A piece of *coverage* which shows the reverse of the scene from another set–up. For example, if Scene 18A is a shot of John over George's shoulder, then the reverse shot (sometimes known as the "complementary angle") would be a shot of George over John's shoulder. (2) An *optical* in which the action is reversed. For example, if Paul was shown giving a dollar bill to Ringo, the reverse action optical would show Paul taking the money from Ringo.

Reversal An original film stock which results in a positive image rather than a negative one, as on a piece of *negative*.

Rewinds Two high posts which stand up on the edge of the editing table. Shafts, which stick out of the rewinds, are used to hold the reels of film. These reels are fed off the left rewind onto the right one.

Room Tone Background sound, usually just general ambience, made at the scene when the footage was originally shot. The general idea of room tone is that it is the sound behind all of the dialogue and other sounds recorded in that location.

Rough Cut The first assemblage of all the cut footage.

Rough Mix See *Scratch Mix*.

Run-out The 30 or more feet of excess leader or fill put onto the ends of the picture dupes and mix units so they will not run out of the projector or dummies during the mix.

Running Another term for the screening of a film.

Rushes See *Dailies*.

S

Scan Line In video, one complete horizontal line of electrons made across a television picture tube. Depending upon the system used, it takes either 525 or 625 scan lines to make up one normal television frame. High definition television uses more scan lines per frame to create a sharper image. Scan lines are also called *resolution lines*. See also *field*, and *HDTV*.

Scoring Session The music recording session.

Scratch (1) An abrasive mark on the film, which actually removes one or more of the layers of *emulsion*. Scratches which are on the negative generally appear as white on the print, scratches which are on the print usually appear as colored or black. Some negative scratches can be removed, others cannot. (2) A term for something which is only to be used temporarily, such as "scratch music" or a "scratch mix."

Screening Viewing the film in a projection room.

Scribe An instrument with a sharp metal point which is used to write on the *emulsion* of the film. It is normally used to etch code or key numbers onto the edge of the film when a piece of film in the cut is too short to have either.

Script Notes The notes that the script supervisor provides the editing room. Typically, they contain a list of every take shot on the film, whether it was printed, what lens sizes were used in the shot, the camera and sound roll numbers, the date shot, as well as a short description of each shot.

Segue To dissolve from one piece of sound gradually into another.

Set–Up (1) An individual camera position. A given scene will usually be covered with several different camera angles and lens sizes. Each of these is a different set-up. In American notation, each set-up for a given scene (say, Scene 11) will be given a different set-up letter: 11, for the master, and 11A, 11B, 11C, etc. for each succeeding angle shot. In English notation each set-up, from the first day of shooting until the last, regardless of what scene it is meant for, is given a sequential set-up number, beginning with Scene 1, Take 1 on the first day. (2) Can also refer to the editing room table equipment — synchronizer, rewinds, splicing block, et al.

Single Card A credit in which only one name appears on the card.

Single Strand Printing See *A & B Roll Printing*.

Single Stripe See *Stripe*.

Single System Projection The process of screening a film which has its sound and picture married onto one piece of film. Unless you mag stripe your work picture for previews, you will never screen single system until you have your *married print*.

Skip Print An *optical* in which frames of the original shot are eliminated. Normally this is used to speed up a shot. If every other frame were skipped then the action would appear to move twice as fast. Also called a "skip frame" optical.

Slate (1) The black-and-white board which is struck together at the beginning of every take. It is used to provide a visible and audible sync point for synching, as well as providing a visual record of the set-up and take numbers that is captured on the negative as well as on the print. Also called a "clapper." (2) Can also be used to refer to the scene number of a particular take (e.g. "This is Slate 11A.")

Slop Dupe See *Dupe*.

Slop Mix See *Scratch Mix*.

Slop Print See *Dupe*.

Slug See *Fill*.

SMPTE Code A method of sync which is used for tape media, such as music recording tape or videotape.

Sneak A preview of a film, at which audience response is gauged for the purpose of re-editing the film or determining an advertising campaign for the film.

Soft Version A version of the final film, recut to eliminate offensive material. This version is usually played on airlines and television. Also called *Television version*.

Sound Reader An amplifier. Sound from the soundtrack film is picked up from the sound heads on the synchronizer and fed into this reader, where it is translated into sound that we can understand and amplified so that we may hear. It is also called a *squawk box*.

Sound Report The list submitted by the sound department on the set which lists all of the takes recorded on each 1/4" sound roll and which takes have been selected to be transferred.

Sounding The process of transferring sound from the mix *full-coat* onto the already *striped* magnetic tracks of a 70mm or, more rarely, a 35mm release print of a film.

Spacing See *Fill*.

Split Reel A *take-up reel* which can be unscrewed into two sides. A *core* is placed inside and, after the sides have been screwed back together again, it can be used as a regular take-up reel. Since *flatbed* editing machines use film wound onto cores, rather than on reels, being able to put these cores into split reels enables the film to be used in places that would normally take film only on take-ups (like projectors).

Split Screen An *optical* in which the entire screen is divided into sections, into which different images are placed.

Spotting Session (1) A meeting in which the director, composer, editor and music editor determine exactly what the music for the film will be and where it will fall. Called a "music spotting session." (2) A similar meeting to determine all of the sound elements (effects, looping, etc.) held with the director, film editor, supervising sound editor, and looping editor. Called an "effects spotting session," a "looping spotting session," or, more generally, a "sound spotting session."

Sprockets The teeth on the film-driving mechanisms. These teeth link up with *sprocket holes* on the edge of the film, and transport the film forward at the standard rate. Standard 35mm film has four sprocket holes for each frame, 16mm has only one, standard 70mm has five.

Sprocket Holes The holes in the side of the film which fit over the sprockets, allowing the film or track to be moved. Also called *perfs*.

Squawk Box See *Sound Reader*.

Squeezed Image See *Anamorphic*.

Start Mark A particular frame of picture or track which has been marked near the head of the reel to give an easily seen reference point for threading up in an editing machine, projector, coding machine, or similar machine.

Stock Shot Often, a production will need a shot that they cannot shoot themselves, an establishing shot of a city on another continent or an airplane flying, for instance. These shots are called stock shots and are usually obtained from a library which specializes in hard-to-obtain shots. Other libraries specialize in historical or nature footage.

Steenbeck A brand name for a common *flatbed* editing machine.

Streamer A long line, usually three feet in length, drawn on the film, which is used to cue someone — either an actor or actress to let them know that a line to be looped is coming up, or a conductor to let him or her know that a musical cue is upcoming.

Stripe A piece of clear 35mm film that has one strip of oxide glued onto it for the recording of sound. In order for the track to take up correctly on reels, another, thinner stripe is also glued to the top of the film. It is called the *balance stripe* and is usually not recorded onto.

Striping The act of gluing a thin layer of oxide onto a 70mm (or, occasionally, a 35mm) release print. Later on, sound will be transferred onto it in a process called *sounding*.

Superimposition Also called a "super." An *optical* in which one image is seen on top of another.

Sync The exact alignment of picture and track so they are lined up in the manner in which the events actually occurred during the shooting. Actors' words seem to be properly coming from their lips, door slams are heard at the exact moment when we see the door shut, etc.

Synchronizer A machine which has several rotating wheels with *sprockets* on them. By placing pieces of film or soundtrack on these wheels these pieces can be run in perfect sync with each other. Also called a "sync block."

Sync Point Any visual or aural place in the film which can facilitate the finding of the proper sync between the picture and sound. A common sync point is the *slate*.

Sync Pop A beep which is usually placed at a point exactly three feet before the first frame of action and three feet after the last frame of action on each reel. Since there is no sound for a distance before and after these pops, they will be quite visible on the optical soundtrack and are quite useful for correctly lining up the optical track negative with the picture negative for printing *married prints*.

T

Tab   Short for *Cinetab* or *Trim Tab*.

Tail Pop   See *Beep*.

Tail Trim   See *Trim*.

Take   When the director shoots a particular set-up he or she will shoot it as many times as necessary to get the exact combination of acting, camera and sound performance desired. Each time the scene is shot, from the clapping of the slate through the director's scream of "Cut!", we call it a take. If take one is not satisfactory, the director will do take two, then take three, until he or she is happy. The next set-up will start with take one again.

Take-Up Reel   A metal or plastic reel on which film is stored.

Television Version   See *Soft Version*.

Three-Stripe   See *Full–Coat*.

Three-Track   See *Full–Coat*.

Time Code   See *SMPTE Code*.

Timing   The act of correcting the color balance from the negative so that prints made from it look the way the director of photography wants them. After the negative has been cut, each shot has to be timed individually so that they match each other, and the naturally occurring slight differences between them can be evened out. Also called "color correction," "color balancing" or "grading."

Timing Lights   The amounts of red, green and blue (or yellow, cyan and magenta) put into the timing of a shot. The amounts are represented by a number on a scale from one to 50 points. Timing lights are generally listed like this: 32-47-36. See also *Y–C–M numbers*.

Tracking   (1) Cutting music not recorded specifically for the film. This is normally the way music is prepared for a temp dub. (2) The movement of the camera during the shooting of a take.

Trailer   The "coming attractions" that we see for films soon to arrive in theatres.

Transfer A sound copy. The sound recorded on the set has been laid on 1/4" inch tape. It is transferred onto mag stock for use in editing. Also refers to a videotape copy.

Trim A piece of a take which is left over after a portion of that take has been cut out and used in the film. A piece which comes *before* the section used in the film is called a *head trim,* a piece *after* the section used is called a *tail trim.*

Trim Bin A large barrel into which takes of film are hung. They are usually rectangular and lined with a felt-like material to prevent the film from scratching as it hangs down into the bin, from a bar of pins above it. Also called a "trim barrel."

Trim Boxes Cardboard boxes, usually about one foot square, which are used to store the trims and outs.

Trim Tabs See *Cinetabs.*

TV Safe The portion of the filmed image which is generally considered safe for projection on a normal, home television set. In most cases this involves losing a bit of the top and bottom of the frame. Actually, nearly the full 35mm frame is used on television, but many home television sets have a tendency to show less image than is received by them.

U

Ultrasonic Cleaner A device, usually found in film labs, to clean film. You can often use this method to remove dirt that will not come off in any other way, though it does tend to remove inked code numbers as well.

Undercranked Shot A shot which was made at a slower than normal (24 frames per second) camera speed. When projected, the action will appear to move faster than normal.

Unit See *Element.*

V

VCR A Video Cassette Recorder and playback machine.

VHS A videotape format which uses 1/2" tapes. This is the more common of the two video formats used in the home; the less common one is *Betamax*.

Video Assist The process of simultaneously shooting a (usually black and white) videotape of each take through the lens of the camera. In this way, performance, framing, camera moves and a host of other factors can be evaluated right on the set, as soon as a take is completed, rather than waiting until the next day at *dailies*.

Videocassette A form of video recording, which uses a magnetic recording device to record, and later play back, images on a long, thin tape. This tape may have any one of a number of widths: 1/2" (as is common to the *VHS* and *Beta* home formats), 8mm (a more recent home format), 3/4" or 1" (used for *broadcast quality*). Years ago, broadcast quality tapes needed to be recorded on 2" tape, in the near future 3/4" may be the standard.

Videodisc A form of video recording, which uses a laser to imprint and, later, play back images on a shiny, flat disc.

Virgin Stock Magnetic soundtrack (or videotape) stock onto which no sound has yet been recorded.

Visual Time Code See *Window Code*.

W

Walla A background sound effect of a crowd murmuring. In England, walla is often called "rhubarb" since a small crowd murmuring "rhubarb, rhubarb, rhubarb" sounds indistinct enough (i.e. no individual voices can be heard) for a murmuring crowd effect.

Wedge See *Cinex*.

Wet Gate Printing A laboratory printing process in which the film is run through a solution of wet tetrachlorthylene before printing. This chemical fills in many kinds of surface scratches and is therefore used to clean up negative defects before release printing.

The process of wet gating takes much longer than a normal printing bath.

Wild Line A line of dialogue which was recorded, either on the set or on a looping stage, without any picture running.

Wild Sound See *Wild Track*.

Wild Track Sound recorded on the set with no accompanying picture.

Window Code *SMPTE Time Code* which is laid onto the picture area of a videotape so it is visible. It is normally placed in a little rectangular black box somewhere near the bottom of the screen. Also called *Visual Time Code*.

Wipe (1) A particular kind of *optical* in which one image is replaced in some graphic form by another image. There are many different styles of wipes; some common ones are those in which the new image is wiped across the frame horizontally, vertically, from one corner to another, or from a circle starting in the center of the frame. (2) To completely erase a magnetic sound or video tape.

Work Picture The cut-together film. Also called the *cut picture*. Together with the work track, the pair is called the *cut*.

Work Track The cut-together soundtrack. Also called the "cut track." Together with the work picture, the pair is called the *cut*.

Y

Y-C-M Numbers The *timing lights* that the negative is printed at, representing the amounts of red, green and blue lights. These colors are also referred to by their complements: yellow, cyan and magenta, and are given on a scale of one to 50.

Z

Zero Cutting See *A & B Roll Printing*.

Zeroing Out Setting the synchronizer, moviola, or flatbed footage counter to zero (0000'00).

....
BIBLIOGRAPHY

Anderson, Gary H. *Video Editing*. Knowledge Industry Publications, 1988. A very detailed textbook about videotape editing. Though it doesn't go into the various film-oriented video editing systems like the Ediflex, Montage, et al, it does give a very good description of what on-line tape editing systems are like.

Arijon, Daniel. *Grammar Of the Film Language*. New York: Hastings House, 1976. A discussion of the most basic of editing concepts — the shot, especially in regard to how one shot will cut with another. Extremely thorough though undeniably dull. Useful for directors, editors, and script supervisors who want to have an encyclopedia (in the smallest detail) of how scenes should be staged so they will cut together.

Baker, Fred, and Firestone, Ross. *Movie People*. New York: Douglas Book Corporation, 1972. Has a wonderful interview with the late editor Aram Avakian in it, in which he discusses some of the thought processes behind cutting.

Bazin, Andre. *What Is Cinema, Vols. I and II*. Berkeley and Los Angeles: University of California Press, 1971. Not really a book on editing, though parts of it discuss the theoretical aspects of montage.

Burder, John. *The Technique of Editing 16mm Films*. Boston: Focal Press, 1988. A reissue of an older text on the nuts and bolts of cutting 16mm films. It has a lot of detailed information, though some of it is still woefully out of date.

Case, Dominic. *Motion Picture Film Processing*. Boston: Focal Press, 1985. A very good, often technical, discussion of what exactly a lab does to film. It spends a lot of time discussing the properties of light and how film stock reacts to light, but the last half of the book works as a companion volume to the Happé book listed below.

Chambers, Everett. *Producing TV Movies*. Los Angeles: E.C. Productions, Inc. 1986. Discusses the role of the editor within the television movie process. Useful for the light that it throws on the shortening of the editorial process in the interests of time and money.

Chase, Donald. *Filmmaking: The Collaborative Art*. Boston: Little, Brown, 1975. The very short section on editing has fragmented interviews with several established editors, a few of which occasionally go beyond the anecdotal into the practical.

Chell, David. *Moviemakers At Work*. Redmond, Washington: Microsoft Press, 1987. An entertaining book which contains interviews with cinematographers, editors, sound recordists and mixers, production and costume designers, makeup artists, animators, computer graphics specialists and special effects designers. The interviews with editors Carol Littleton and Thom Noble both give some personal stories and advice on how to get started in the editing profession.

Crittenden, Roger. *Film Editing*. London: Thames and Hudson, 1981. A very basic, dryly written description of the film editing process.

Dmytryk, Edward. *On Film Editing*. Boston: Focal Press, 1984. A rather entertaining, and sometimes enlightening, look at the process of film editing as told by an accomplished director. Also valuable from the same author are *On Screen Writing*, *On Screen Directing*, and *On Screen Acting*.

Eisenstein, Sergei. *Film Forum* and *Film Sense*. New York: Harcourt, Brace, 1949. Both of these works show the initial stages of an editing philosophy. Eisenstein, perhaps justifiably, is considered the titular father of montage. These works are a careful combination of theory, experiment, and inspired conjecture on the nature of editing.

Happé, Bernard. *Your Film and the Lab*. Boston: Focal Press, 1983. A very easy-to-read and informative book on what happens to your film in the lab, discussing different printing stocks and processes. A bit out of date but very useful.

Kerner, Marvin M. *The Art of the Sound Effects Editor*. Boston: Focal Press, 1989. A very succinct (sometimes, too much so) and nicely written book focusing on the job of the sound editor. Kerner gives a lot of information on the organization of the sound editing room, as well as a general overview of the entire sound editing process.

Lipton, Lenny. *Independent Film Making*. San Francisco: Random House, 1972. This is one of the many how-to books for the independent or college filmmaker who knows very little to start with. It is also one of the best of the lot. It caters largely to the 8mm and 16mm filmmaker, but discusses much terminology and procedure that all filmmakers need.

Lustig, Milton. *Music Editing for Motion Pictures*. New York: Hastings House, 1972. A little reference work on the details of preparing a motion picture for scoring, and dealing with other musical problems in films. Though not particularly thorough or detailed it does compile many facts for the first time, all in one place. It has not been updated since its original release, which makes it woefully behind the times in regard to the music editor's new friends—videotape and computers.

McBride, Joseph. *Filmmakers On Filmmaking, Volumes One and Two*. Los Angeles: J.P. Tarcher, Inc., 1983. Two books which collect many of the American Film Institute's interviews with working filmmakers. Some of the directors discuss the editing process and one editor, the late Verna Fields, is interviewed. Among other things, she discusses the flow of work in the editing room from the editor's point of view.

Nizhny, Vladimir. *Lessons with Eisenstein*. New York: Da Capo, 1979. Notes from Eisenstein's teachings. Largely concerned with the purposeful choice of camera angles and blocking. There is much to be learned from all of this as it applies to editing.

Oakey, Virginia. *Dictionary of Film and Television Terms*. New York: Barnes & Noble Books, 1983. A very thorough dictionary of most of the technical terms involved in filmmaking.

Pudovkin, V. I. *Film Technique and Film Acting*. London: Vision Press Ltd. Possibly the seminal work on film editing. Though a bit dated by developments in other branches of film (notably writing, sound, and acting) his theories stand up today as among the most basic and important.

Reisz, Karel, and Millar, Gavin. *The Technique of Film Editing*. New York: Hastings House, 1968. A down–to–earth discussion of editing principles which never gets too theoretical and nearly always has a valid point to make with pertinent examples.

Rosenblum, Ralph, and Karen, Robert. *When The Shooting Stops....* New York: Viking, 1979. Basically an anecdotal look at the editing process. Some amusing incidents are recounted.

Rowlands, Avril. *Script Continuity and the Production Secretary in Film & TV*. New York: Hastings House, 1977. A short book describing many of the duties of the script supervisor. Much of the discussion is valuable in regards to the paper-work as well as the aspects of continuity.

Sarris, Andrew. *Interviews With Film Directors*. New York: Bobbs-Merrill, 1967. Some of these directors mention their editing theories. Some of them even make sense.

Schneider, Arthur. *Electronic Post-Production and Videotape Editing*. Boston: Focal Press, 1989. A good, thorough discussion of the methods of various forms of video editing.

Sherman, Eric. *Directing The Film: Film Directors On Their Art*. Los Angeles: Acrobat Books, 1976. More interviews with directors who have spoken at the American Film Institute, this time grouped by subject matter. The chapter on editing is fun to read, though not particularly illuminating for an assistant editor. There is a lot of discussion of the director/editor relationship.

Spottiswoode, Raymond. *A Grammar of the Film*. Berkeley and Los Angeles: University of California Press, 1950. Though the book is rather turgid and pretentious, for some unknown reason, friends of mine have found some wisdom in the theoretical discussion of editing.

Walter, Ernest. *The Technique Of the Film Cutting Room*. New York Hastings House, 1973. An excellent and thorough work on the editing process from the technical point of view. It primarily covers the English system and is, at present, quite a bit out of date. But it remains a readable and reliable guide to the editing room.

....

INDEX

A

A & B rolls 167, 179, 291
Academy Leader 18, 50, 67, 135, 193
Academy roll–off 329
Accountant, production 338-340
ADR (Automatic Dialogue Replacement) (*see* Looping)
Alignment tones 272, 275
  Dolby 331
Analysis loop 230
Anamorphic 327-328
  Moviola 328
Answer print 289-292, 304-308
  Dolby 331
  first 306, 308
  married 4, 284, 309, 318
  screening 308
  second 308
Apprentice editor
  coding dailies 78, 127
  duties of
    dailies, during 86-87
    flatbed films, for 120
  filing trims 96

hiring the 36
  sound 206
Aspect ratio 326
Assistant editor
  chain of command xvii
  checking prints 331
  duties of xiv-xv, xvii, 24, 25
  requirements of xii
  sound 205

B

B-negative 41, 73
Backsplicing 140
Base 49
Beep tone 23, 147, 253, 274
    elements, on 163
    popping tracks, in 60
Blacking a videotape 365
Blow-up 325-328
Blurred slates 56-58, 65
Breaking down dailies 82-84
Budgeting 338-341
Building tracks (*see* Sound editing, building tracks)
Bump, sound 158, 239

C

. . . .
ABOUT
THE
AUTHOR

Norman Hollyn has worked in motion picture editing since the mid-Seventies. He began as an apprentice/assistant editor on such films as *Lenny* (United Artists), *Network* (MGM), *You Light Up My Life* (Paramount), and *Hair* (United Artists).

He then began to work as a music editor on films such as *Fame* (MGM), *Four Friends* (Filmways), *Sophie's Choice* (ITC Films), and *The Cotton Club* (Orion).

He has also worked as a film editor on the television series *The Equalizer*, a number of television films for Walt Disney and other companies, and on several rock videos. He has edited such feature films as *Heathers* and *Meet The Applegates*.

Norman is a member of the Academy of Motion Picture Arts and Sciences (AMPAS), the Independent Feature Project/West (IFP/West), and the National Academy of Television Arts and Sciences (NATAS).